P9-DXO-112

Praise for JESUS: A PILGRIMAGE

"Do we *really* need yet another book about Jesus? If the book is this one, the answer is yes. James Martin's approach is unique and original, and it will net the reader a glimpse into the Nazarene not available elsewhere. He combines three 'sources': the biblical accounts, his own Ignatian-trained prayer life, and highly perceptive visits to the places where Jesus lived and taught and died. The result is a fully contoured picture of Jesus not to be found elsewhere. No matter how much or how little one knows already about Jesus, this book is invaluable."
— Harvey Cox, Hollis Research Professor of Divinity at Harvard Divinity School

"During the past decades, many books have focused on Jesus from the vantage point of either the quest for the historical Jesus, or systematic Christology, or personal spirituality. Rarely has any one book attempted a synthesis of all three. The engaging Father James Martin has not only attempted but also achieved such a synthesis. Every reader will enjoy the journey—nay, the pilgrimage—through this triple territory with such an insightful companion."
— Rev. John Meier, author of *A Marginal Jew: Rethinking the Historical Jesus*

"*Jesus: A Pilgrimage* is part travel guide, part spiritual reflection, and part Scripture study—and an altogether delightful read. Father Jim Martin, SJ, ably blends these elements to help seekers encounter the Jesus of history through the eyes of a modern pilgrim. Whether you've visited the Holy Land a dozen times, or simply have a pilgrimage at the top of your wish list, his reflections will bring you fresh insight."
— Cardinal Timothy M. Dolan, archbishop of New York

"There are no dull moments in this book. What a joy to take this fascinating pilgrimage with James Martin, a journey from a theological and historical perspective, and one that leads to a refreshing awareness and understanding of the beloved carpenter from Nazareth. As I read *Jesus,* I yearned for a more deeply committed relationship with him."
— Joyce Rupp, OSM, author of *Praying Our Goodbyes*

"*Jesus: A Pilgrimage* is a delight to read and a work of substance for the committed Christian. Vividly written and rich in historical detail and analysis, it's also a movingly personal journey of faith, a diary of the author's pilgrimage to the land where God and human destiny intersect, the land Jesus called home."
> —Charles J. Chaput, OFM Cap., archbishop of
> Philadelphia

"This is not a dry theological manual, nor is it merely a commentary on the Gospels; it is a sensitive, heartfelt inquiry into the person of Jesus. In James Martin's book the great texts of the Gospels come to life and are transformed for the reader into an encounter with Jesus as he really was."
> —Rev. Gerhard Lohfink, author of *Jesus of Nazareth*

"This is an invaluable book for anyone desiring to know more about Jesus and how his life can illumine our own spiritual pilgrimage."
> —Kathleen Norris, author of *The Cloister Walk*

"Want a pilgrimage to the Holy Land with a reliable guide? Travel with Jim Martin, who is at his best here, opening the Gospels with a light touch. Serious scholar, yes, but mainly a pilgrim, trying to make his way, just like us."
> —Helen Prejean, CSJ, author of *Dead Man Walking*

"*Jesus* is a must read for those who want the Bible brought to life with accuracy, sincerity, and sparkle."
> —Candida Moss, professor of New Testament and early
> Christianity at the University of Notre Dame

"What can be said about Jesus that's never been said before? James Martin answers that question with an insightful, balanced, intelligent, widely embracing, and faith-filled account of his journey in search of Jesus. This is a book for everyone, regardless of creed or background. This is James Martin at his best!"
> —Ronald Rolheiser, OMI, author of *The Holy Longing*

"The ancient practice of pilgrimage, Ignatian spirituality, delightful wit, and astute observation of the complex contemporary reality of Israel and Palestine meet in this account by James Martin, SJ. He offers a personal meditative memoir, but informed by critical biblical and archaeological scholarship and graced with his accustomed narrative skill. His entertaining, thoughtful, and inspiring account will delight both seasoned pilgrims and those who want to be."
    —Harold W. Attridge, Sterling Professor of Divinity at
        Yale Divinity School

"It takes a 'human one' to write well about the consummate 'Human One,' Jesus. James Martin does that very well! Come to see, and be seen by, the One who has loved so many of us into life."
    —Richard Rohr, OFM, author of *Everything Belongs*

"This delightful book combines personal reflections and spiritual nuggets along with insights from top biblical scholars, theologians, and archaeologists in an engaging style. Martin makes Jesus and his land and times come alive, inviting others to meet Jesus and embark on their own pilgrimage."
    —Barbara E. Reid, OP, professor of New Testament at
        Catholic Theological Union, Chicago

"Father James Martin's book on Jesus is a gem. Learned yet highly accessible, he weaves together insights gleaned from the Gospels, a pilgrimage to the Holy Land, Ignatian spirituality, and his personal and pastoral experience. This is a Jesus book I highly recommend."
    —Thomas D. Stegman, SJ, associate professor of New
        Testament at Boston College

"It isn't often that a book invites you to make a journey through the Holy Land in the company of an inspiring, well-informed, and entertaining guide like James Martin. Discover things you never knew about Jesus's homeland. Enter into the Gospel narratives firsthand. Enjoy the journey, but don't be surprised if it changes you."
    —Margaret Silf, author of *Inner Compass*

"This engaging book is solidly based in contemporary Jesus studies but its charm lies in the insight a fellow Christian has gleaned into the God-man of the Gospels through his personal and deepening relationship with Jesus. Accompanying Martin on his journey will stir the sensitive reader to explore her or his own."
—Sandra M. Schneiders, IHM, author of *Written That You May Believe: Encountering Jesus in the Fourth Gospel*

"Father James Martin does something remarkable in this book. He invites you to accompany him on a pilgrimage through the Holy Land but, at the same time, you begin to see the world through the lens of Jesus and his disciples. As the world of first-century Galilee and Judea comes to life, you find yourself a disciple, walking alongside Jesus in the Gospels. Even more remarkable, Father Martin brings to life the ancient world in which Jesus lived. In Father Martin's hands, New Testament scholarship opens up the life of Jesus so the Gospels can speak to each of us today and transform us as they did their first hearers."
—John W. Martens, associate professor of theology at the University of St. Thomas

"Whether encountering Jesus for the first time, or wanting to know him better, you will find a wonderful guide in Father James Martin. Not only does he walk us through the Gospels, sharing his own reflections and the fruit of the best modern scholarship, but he takes us along on his own tour of the Holy Land, treading in the virtual footsteps of Jesus and his disciples, dipping his hand in the same waters, experiencing the same sights, sounds, and heat. More than a travelogue or a commentary on Scripture—it is a moving and life-transforming pilgrimage."
—Robert Ellsberg, editor of *The Duty of Delight: The Diaries of Dorothy Day*

JESUS

ALSO BY JAMES MARTIN, SJ

*Between Heaven and Mirth: Why Joy, Humor, and Laughter
Are at the Heart of the Spiritual Life*

The Jesuit Guide to (Almost) Everything: A Spirituality for Real Life

*A Jesuit Off-Broadway: Behind the Scenes with Faith, Doubt,
Forgiveness, and More*

*Becoming Who You Are: Insights on the True Self from
Thomas Merton and Other Saints*

Lourdes Diary: Seven Days at the Grotto of Massabieille

My Life with the Saints

Searching for God at Ground Zero

This Our Exile: A Spiritual Journey with the Refugees of East Africa

*In Good Company: The Fast Track from the Corporate
World to Poverty, Chastity, and Obedience*

Together on Retreat: Meeting Jesus in Prayer (e-book)

JESUS

A Pilgrimage

JAMES MARTIN, SJ

HarperOne
An Imprint of HarperCollins*Publishers*

HarperOne

Scripture quotations are from the New Revised Standard Version Bible, copyright © 1989 National Council of the Churches of Christ in the United States of America. Used by permission. All rights reserved.

Imprimi potest: Very Rev. Myles N. Sheehan, SJ, Provincial, New England Province of the Society of Jesus

JESUS: *A Pilgrimage*. Copyright © 2014 by James Martin, SJ. All rights reserved. Printed in the United States of America. No part of this book may be used or reproduced in any manner whatsoever without written permission except in the case of brief quotations embodied in critical articles and reviews. For information, address HarperCollins Publishers, 195 Broadway, New York, NY 10007.

HarperCollins books may be purchased for educational, business, or sales promotional use. For information, please e-mail the Special Markets Department at SPsales@harpercollins.com.

HarperCollins website: http://www.harpercollins.com

HarperCollins®, ■®, and HarperOne™ are trademarks of HarperCollins Publishers.

Maps by Beehive Mapping

Library of Congress Cataloging-in-Publication Data

Martin, James.
Jesus : a pilgrimage / James Martin.
  pages cm
ISBN 978-0-06-202423-7
1. Jesus Christ—Biography. 2. Jesus Christ—Person and offices.
3. Israel—Description and travel. I. Title.
BT301.3.M35   2014
232—dc23   2013036031

14 15 16 17 18   RRD(H)   10 9 8

For Daniel J. Harrington, SJ,
who teaches Jesus
in his classes,
through his books,
and with his life

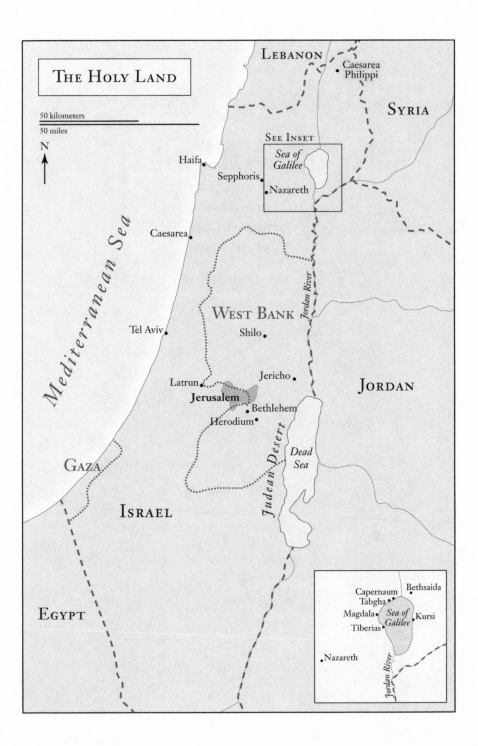

THE HOLY LAND

50 kilometers
50 miles

N

LEBANON

Caesarea
Philippi

SYRIA

Haifa

SEE INSET

Sea of
Galilee

Sepphoris

Nazareth

Mediterranean Sea

Caesarea

Jordan River

WEST BANK

Tel Aviv

Shilo

Latrun

Jericho

JORDAN

Jerusalem

Bethlehem

Herodium

Judean Desert

Dead
Sea

GAZA

ISRAEL

EGYPT

Capernaum

Bethsaida

Tabgha

Magdala

Sea of
Galilee

Kursi

Tiberias

Nazareth

Jordan River

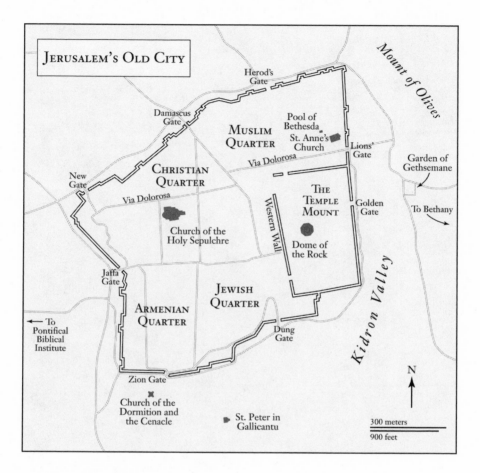

JERUSALEM'S OLD CITY

Mount of Olives

Herod's
Gate

Damascus
Gate

Pool of
Bethesda

MUSLIM
QUARTER

St. Anne's
Church

Lions'
Gate

CHRISTIAN
QUARTER

Via Dolorosa

Garden of
Gethsemane

New
Gate

Via Dolorosa

THE
TEMPLE
MOUNT

Golden
Gate

To Bethany

Western Wall

Church of the
Holy Sepulchre

Dome of
the Rock

Jaffa
Gate

JEWISH
QUARTER

Kidron Valley

To
Pontifical
Biblical
Institute

ARMENIAN
QUARTER

Dung
Gate

N

Zion Gate

Church of the
Dormition and
the Cenacle

St. Peter in
Gallicantu

300 meters

900 feet

Contents

Introduction

Who Is Jesus?

JESUS IS WALKING WITH his friends to Caesarea Philippi, a town roughly twenty-five miles north of the Sea of Galilee. The story comes midway through the Gospel of Mark. Out of the blue Jesus asks, "Who do people say that I am?"

His friends seem caught off guard. Perhaps they are embarrassed, as when someone mentions a taboo topic. Perhaps they have been discussing that very question furtively, wondering who would be forthright enough to ask Jesus about his identity. Maybe Jesus had even overheard them arguing over who he was.

The disciples offer halting responses: "John the Baptist; and others, Elijah," they say, "and still others, one of the prophets." That's probably a fair summary of popular opinion at the time. Herod, the first-century ruler of Galilee, thought that Jesus might be John the Baptist come back to life. A number of Jews believed that Elijah's return would herald the reign of God, which some in the region expected to come soon. And the comparison to a prophet like, say, Jeremiah seemed sensible because of similarities between the prophet and Jesus. But the disciples are careful to avoid saying what *they* believe.

So Jesus asks them directly, "But who do you say that I am?"¹

Who is he? Why another book on this first-century Jewish man? Why have I spent years studying the life of an itinerant preacher from a backwater town? Why did I spend two weeks traipsing around Israel under the broiling sun to see places where a former carpenter lived and sites that he may (or may not) have visited? Moreover, why have I committed my life to Jesus? The answers turn on the question of who I believe Jesus is, so it's fair to tell you before we begin our pilgrimage.

My starting point is a classic theological statement: Jesus Christ is fully human and fully divine. This is one of the first things that Christians learn about their faith. But what does it mean?

To begin with, Jesus of Nazareth, the person who walked the landscape of first-century Palestine, wasn't God pretending to be human.[2] He was a flesh-and-blood, real-life, honest-to-God man who experienced everything that human beings do.

Jesus was born and lived and died, like any human being. The child called Yeshua entered the world as helpless as any newborn and just as dependent on his parents. He needed to be nursed, held, burped, and changed. As a boy growing up in the minuscule town of Nazareth, Jesus skinned his knees on the rocky ground, bumped his head on doorways, and pricked his fingers on thorns. He watched the sun rise and set over the Galilean countryside, wondered how far away the moon was, and asked why the stars twinkled.

Jesus had a body like yours and mine, which means that he ate, drank, and slept. He experienced sexual longings and urges. The adult Jesus felt joy and sadness, laughing at things that struck him as funny and weeping during times of loss. As a fully human being with fully human emotions, he felt both frustration and enthusiasm. He grew weary at the end of a long day and fell ill from time to time. He pulled muscles, felt sick to his stomach, and maybe sprained an ankle or two. Like all of us, he sweated and sneezed and scratched.

Everything proper to the human being—except sin—Jesus experienced.

Jesus's humanity is a stumbling block for many people, including a few Christians. Incidents in the Gospels that show Jesus displaying intense and even unattractive human emotions can unsettle those who prefer to focus on his divinity. At one point in the Gospel of

Mark, he speaks sharply to a woman who asks him to heal her daughter.[3] The woman is not Jewish and, as a result, Jesus seems to dismiss her with a callous comment: "It is not fair to take the children's food and throw it to the dogs."

That is a stinging rebuke no matter what the context. When the woman responds that even the dogs get crumbs from the table, Jesus softens. And he heals her daughter.

Why did Jesus speak so sharply? Was it because he was visiting what Mark calls "the region of Tyre," a non-Jewish area, where he was presumably not expected to perform any miracles? If so, why didn't he respond to the woman more gently, rather than using a term that was seen in his day as "highly insulting"?[4] Was Jesus testing her faith, challenging her to believe? If so, it's a harsh way of doing so, at odds with the compassionate Jesus whom many of us expect to meet in the Gospels.

Perhaps, however, Jesus needed to learn something from the woman's persistence: his ministry extended to everyone, not just Jews. Or maybe he was just tired. A few lines earlier in the Gospel, Mark tells us, "He entered a house and did not want anyone to know he was there." Perhaps his curt remark indicates physical weariness. Whatever the case (and we'll never know for sure) both possibilities—he is learning, he is tired—show Jesus's humanity on full display.

But there is another part of the story: a healing. Jesus says to the woman, "For saying that, you may go—the demon has left your daughter." She returns home, says Mark, and finds her child lying on the bed, "the demon gone."

"Fully human and fully divine" means that Jesus of Nazareth wasn't just a great guy, an inspiring teacher, and a holy man. Moreover, the charismatic carpenter wasn't merely a clever storyteller, a compassionate healer, or a courageous prophet.

In response to Jesus's question "Who do you say that I am?" Peter finally answers, "You are the Messiah." But Jesus is divine—far more than Peter could comprehend even while identifying him as the Messiah.

Jesus performed astonishing deeds, which the Gospel writers call either "works of power" or "signs." Today we call them miracles—healing the sick, calming storms, raising people from the dead. Time and again the Gospels report that Jesus's followers, no matter how long they have been with him, are "amazed" and "astonished" by what he does. "We have never seen anything like this!" says the crowd after Jesus heals a paralyzed man in Mark's Gospel.[5] After he stills a storm on the Sea of Galilee, Matthew writes, "They were amazed, saying, 'What sort of man is this, that even the winds and the sea obey him?'"[6] Even his *detractors* take note of his miracles, as when they castigate him for healing a man on the Sabbath.[7] The miracles are an essential part of the story of Jesus, as are other signs of his divinity. So is the Resurrection.

If Jesus's humanity is a stumbling block for many, his divinity is even more so. For a rational, modern mind, talk of the supernatural can be disturbing—an embarrassment. Many contemporary men and women admire Jesus, but stop short of believing him to be divine. Despite the proportion of the Gospels that focuses on his "works of power," many want to confine his identity to that of a wise teacher.

Thomas Jefferson went so far as to create his own Gospel by focusing on Jesus's ethical teachings and (literally) scissoring out the miracles and other indications of his divinity. Jefferson preferred his own version of Jesus, not the one he found in the Gospels. Like many of us, he felt uncomfortable with certain parts of the man's life. He wanted a Jesus who didn't threaten or discomfort, a Jesus he could tame. After studying Jefferson's edited version of the New Testament, the New Testament scholar E. P. Sanders concluded that the Sage of Monticello created a Jesus who was, in the end, "very much like Jefferson."[8]

But humanity and divinity are both part of Jesus's story. Omit one or the other, scissor out the uncomfortable parts, and it's not Jesus we're talking about any longer. It's our own creation.

THE TRADITIONAL BELIEF ABOUT Jesus's simultaneous humanity and divinity may raise as many questions as it answers. "Fully human and fully divine" is, to use a loaded word, a mystery. Something not to be solved, but to be pondered.

This book will explore that question, but it will not set forth any new theological propositions. For one thing, I believe in the traditional Christian understanding of Jesus Christ. For another, I'm not a theology professor. If you want a lengthy theological discussion, for example, about how the Son is "consubstantial" or "one in being" with God the Father or how to begin to understand the Trinity, there are many books that can handle those topics much better than I can. I'll point you to some of them as we progress through these chapters.

Neither is this book a Bible commentary, a scholarly work providing a detailed analysis of each verse of the Bible, in this case the Gospels. Bible commentaries concentrate on the historical, political, and sociological context behind the books of the Bible, including authorship, date, and place; the way that the texts were edited; the meaning of the original Hebrew or Greek words; the likely implications of the texts to the readers of the time; the religious underpinnings of the texts; parallels between the verse in question and other parts of the Bible; and the theological interpretations of the text throughout history. Throughout this book, I'll draw on commentaries written by the best scholars. But this is not a reference manual.

So what *is* this book?

It is a look at Jesus, as he appears in the Gospels, through the lens of my education, experience, prayer, and most recently a pilgrimage to the Holy Land. And through the lens of faith.

Much of my understanding of Jesus comes from studies, both formal and informal. Like any Catholic priest, I studied theology for several years in graduate school. During that period, my classmates and I spent a great deal of time poring over the New Testament. Through careful study of the narrative, often a line-by-line and word-for-word analysis of the texts, we tried to plumb the meaning of Jesus's words and deeds.

But even before theology studies, I studied the New Testament. A few years earlier, during my philosophy studies as a Jesuit, I even learned some Greek in order to read the Gospel texts in their original language. In fact, learning New Testament Greek was the most satisfying educational experience of my life. One spring afternoon, the professor called on me to translate the first lines of John's Gospel, and when I read aloud, "In . . . the . . . beginning . . . was . . . the Word," I thought my heart would burst with elation.

Knowing a little Greek helps you notice things that even the best translations miss. It's one thing to read an English translation of the Gospels that says that when Jesus saw a sick person he was "moved with compassion." It's another to read the Greek *splagchnizomai*, which means that Jesus was moved in his inmost parts—literally, in his bowels. In other words, Jesus felt compassion *in his guts*. I'll use some Greek whenever it can help us better understand what the Gospel writers may have meant by a particular word or phrase.

Besides academic courses, I've also done a good deal of informal study about Jesus. Since entering the Jesuits I've become an admirer of books on what is called the "historical Jesus." In historical Jesus studies, scholars try to explain as much as we can know about the life and times of Jesus of Nazareth. Books and articles about the historical Jesus focus on topics like religious customs in first-century Jewish culture in Palestine, the socioeconomic realities of living under Roman rule, and the ways that a carpenter would sustain his family in a small village in Galilee.

Such research helps us better understand Jesus within the context of his time. One quick example: In one of his parables Jesus spins the compelling tale of a steward who is given care of his master's "talents."⁹ If you know that a "talent" was a huge sum of money, equivalent to fifteen years of wages for a day laborer, you'll have a better understanding of Jesus's reason for using that term in his story. You'll understand the parable—and therefore Jesus—better.

Historical Jesus scholars use every tool available—our understanding of first-century cultures, our knowledge of the local languages, even archaeological finds in the region—to understand his life and times. Such studies are closely aligned with what is called a "Christology from below," an attempt to understand Jesus by beginning with his humanity. The starting point is Jesus as a human being, the "Jesus of history."

But I've read just as many books and articles about Jesus that focus less on the details of his time on earth and more about his place in the Christian faith. These writings consider topics such as the Resurrection, how Christ "saves" us, and the nature of his relationship to the Father and the Holy Spirit. They focus on the "Christ of faith" and begin with the divinity of Jesus Christ. This is called a "Christology from above." Here the starting point is Jesus as the Son of God.

The difference between these two approaches can be shown with a brief example, which we will revisit in more detail later: the dramatic story of the raising of Lazarus. Midway through the Gospel of John, the brother of Jesus's friends Mary and Martha dies in the town of Bethany, just outside Jerusalem. Jesus hears the news, waits two days, meets with the two sisters, and finally visits the man's grave. Jesus asks for the stone to be rolled away and calls out, "Lazarus, come out!" And the dead man emerges from the tomb.¹⁰

The historical Jesus scholar, doing theology "from below," might ask questions like: What were Jewish burial practices at the time? Is there a religious significance to the two-day period? Did any customs prevent Jesus from going immediately to the tomb? What was the role of women in Jewish burial rites? Did any Jewish traditions of the time incorporate the idea of resurrection? Answers to these questions help us to understand the story more fully, and they shed light on what Jesus said and did in Bethany on that day.

Someone starting from the vantage point of the Christ of faith, and doing a theology "from above," might pose slightly different questions: What does the raising of Lazarus tell us about how divine power is at work in Jesus? How do Jesus's actions at the tomb underline his words? How does the idea of Jesus as "life" show itself in this story? In what ways does the raising of Lazarus foreshadow Jesus's own resurrection? And what does the story of Lazarus say about our response to God's voice in our lives today?

Both sets of questions are important, and if we lose sight of either perspective, we risk turning Jesus into either God pretending to be a man or a man pretending to be God. The two approaches are complementary, not contradictory. To fully meet Jesus Christ, believers need both to understand the Jesus of history, the man who walked the earth, *and* to encounter the Christ of faith, the one who rose from the dead. Both approaches seek to answer the question that the disciples grappled with on their way to Caesarea Philippi: Who is Jesus? Both approaches are essential, and both will be used in this book, though the emphasis may shift depending on the story.

Moreover, Jesus is always fully human and fully divine. That is, Jesus is not human during one event and divine in another, no matter how it might seem in any particular episode of his life. He is divine when he is sawing a plank of wood, and he is human when he is raising Lazarus from the dead. In our reading of various Gospel passages we may feel we are seeing his humanity more in some, his divinity more in others. And in this book, some chapters highlight parts of Jesus's life that readers may associate with his human nature (for example, his work as a carpenter); others focus on events some may associate with his divine nature (his healing a paralyzed man). But even speaking in those terms is misleading, for Jesus is always human and divine, whether he is building a table or healing the sick. His two natures are inseparable, united in one person at all times.

There are also questions about the fully human, fully divine person that we cannot answer. What went on inside Jesus's mind? How does his humanity "cooperate" (to use a dull word) with his divinity and vice versa? To what extent was the human person conscious of his divinity? These questions, like so much about Jesus, must remain a mystery.

But although Jesus's identity as the fully human Son of God remains a mystery, it is a beautiful mystery, the most beautiful one I know, and well worth pondering.

BEYOND ACADEMIC STUDIES, I have come to know Jesus in three other ways: prayer, experience, and pilgrimage.

Twenty-five years ago, I entered the Society of Jesus, the Roman Catholic religious order better known as the Jesuits. Shortly after I entered the Jesuit novitiate (the first stage of training), I was introduced to a marvelous way of praying popularized by St. Ignatius Loyola, the sixteenth-century founder of the Jesuits. This method of prayer goes by many names: Ignatian contemplation, imaginative prayer, and composition of place.

Ignatian contemplation encourages you to place yourself imaginatively in a scene from the Bible. For example, if you're praying about Jesus and his disciples caught in a boat during a storm on the Sea of Galilee, you would try to imagine yourself on board with the disciples, and ask yourself several questions as a way of trying to place yourself in the scene.

You might ask: *What do you see?* How many disciples are in the boat? What is the expression on their faces? How rough is the sea? *What do you hear?* The howling wind? The fishing tackle shifting about in the boat? *What do you smell?* You're in a fishing boat, so you might smell residues from the day's catch. *What do you feel?* Homespun clothes were probably heavy when soaked by storm-driven water. *And what do you taste?* Maybe the spray on your lips. With such imaginative techniques you let the Gospel passage play out in your mind's eye, and then you notice your reactions.

Ignatian contemplation doesn't require any special spiritual talents. Nor does it require you to believe that every single detail of the narrative is accurate. (As we will see, some Gospel accounts of the same events disagree.) It merely asks you to enter into Bible stories imaginatively and to accept that God can work through your imagination to help you see things in fresh ways. Jesus himself asked people to use their imaginations when he offered them his parables. When someone asked, "Who is my neighbor?" Jesus responded not with a definition, but with the story of the Good Samaritan, in effect saying to his listeners, "Imagine something like this happening."

Some parts of Jesus's life easily lend themselves to Ignatian contemplation—the vivid stories of his healing the sick almost cry out for this kind of prayer. Another example is the period of Jesus's life in Nazareth between the ages of twelve and thirty. Because only a single line is written about that long stretch of time, those years are called his "Hidden Life."[11] It's important to ponder what his daily life might have been like, and here the results of historical Jesus scholarship can fill in some of the gaps and help us to imagine his life in first-century Nazareth.

Parts of this book, then, came from my prayer; and in preparation for writing I reread my spiritual journals. But here's an important point: When discussing the life of Jesus, I'll be clear about what comes from the Gospels, the Christian tradition, and historical research—and what comes from scholarly speculation and my own personal prayer. I'll be clear about what is speculative and what is not.

My insights into Jesus's life also come from experiences. Christ lives, truly risen, not only at the "right hand of the Father," as the Nicene Creed has it, but in the lives of people around us. One beautiful image, from St. Paul, is that the community of believers is the "body of Christ" on earth. So in the ministries in which I have worked, I've met Christ. In Kingston, Jamaica, alongside Mother Teresa's sisters. In

Nairobi, Kenya, with East African refugees. In Chicago with street-gang members. In Boston, with incarcerated men and women. And in a parish in an affluent neighborhood in New York City.

Mother Teresa often spoke of encountering Christ "in distressing disguise" when working among the poor. And often I have found Christ among the poor. But you can find Christ in anyone. As the Jesuit poet Gerard Manley Hopkins wrote:

> *for Christ plays in ten thousand places,*
> *Lovely in limbs, and lovely in eyes not his*
> *To the Father through the features of men's faces.*

Put less poetically, we can encounter Christ in the people around us. Every person's life can tell us something about God. So I will share stories of encountering God in and through others.

Many New Testament passages have also taken on greater meaning thanks to particular events in my life. When you encounter Scripture at a critical moment it often feels as if you've never seen that passage before. You notice something new, and the passage takes on an unmistakable urgency. Reading about Jesus's stilling a storm at sea is one thing when your life is calm, but when things are stormy, it is quite another. In connecting some of these biblical passages to my own experiences, I hope to help you connect them to your own.

Finally, much of the book will be informed by, and structured around, the idea of pilgrimage. Two years ago, I traveled with a Jesuit friend to the place that Christians call the Holy Land, the region in and around Israel where many events of the Old and New Testaments took place.

MY PILGRIMAGE TO THE Holy Land was overwhelming. It was almost unbelievable to visit the places where Jesus had lived. When I first caught sight of the Sea of Galilee, its shimmering blue-green waters surrounded by pinkish sandy hills under a blazing sun, it was like a dream. A few days earlier, during our time in Jerusalem, my friend George and I stumbled upon the Pool of Bethesda, which the Gospel of John names as the place where Jesus healed a paralyzed man.¹² John describes it as a pool with "five porticoes." For centuries, some scholars doubted that the pool ever existed. But archaeological excavations in the nineteenth century uncovered almost the entire complex—including the five porticoes, just as John had described. Seeing not only the site at which Jesus had performed a miracle, but also one confirmation of the Gospels' accuracy was deeply moving. There were the five porticoes: one, two, three, four, five. There they were. And here he had been.

Over two weeks, George and I visited almost every spot Jesus had visited: Jerusalem, Bethlehem, and Nazareth, of course, but also the locales traditionally connected to his ministry around the Sea of Galilee: the Mount of Beatitudes, where he preached the Sermon on the Mount; the rocky beach where he called the first disciples; the bay from which he preached the parables while sitting in a disciple's boat. Seeing what Jesus saw and standing where he stood (or at least near there) deepened my appreciation of the Gospels, and deepened my faith.

The pilgrimage also taught me things that I had not learned from books. For one thing, how *close* the places were in which many of the miracles occurred around the Sea of Galilee. In just a few hours, you can walk along the coastline and visit the sites of many of what the Gospels call *dynameis,* dynamic "works of power." For another, how *far apart* some of the towns were. It's one thing to read that Jesus and his disciples walked from Jerusalem to Jericho; it's another to traverse that distance by car (about an hour) and picture how punishing the trip must have been on foot in first-century Palestine.

Small details leapt up at every moment. One hot day, standing in the place where Jesus most likely preached the parables, on the shoreline of the Sea of Galilee, I looked around and noticed that the surrounding landscape included rocky ground, fertile ground, and thorny plants. Immediately I thought of Jesus's parable of the sower, in which a farmer spreads his seed on just those kinds of terrains.[13] For the first time I realized that when Jesus was preaching, he may not have been describing abstract plots of land (as in "Try to imagine rocky ground"), but what his listeners were standing on. I could envision him pointing and saying, "Look at *that* ground over there."

That experience reminded me of something a friend told me before I left. Traveling through the Holy Land is like visiting the family home of a good friend. No matter how well you know the person, you'll understand your friend better afterward. Overall, the pilgrimage made the Gospels more vivid, deepened my understanding of specific stories, and afforded me an enormous amount of fascinating information about the life and times of Jesus of Nazareth. This is why the Holy Land is often called the Fifth Gospel.

All of this will be brought to bear on the life of Jesus: study, prayer, experience, pilgrimage—and faith. All of this will be brought to bear on the question first posed to the disciples on the way to Caesarea Philippi: Who is Jesus?

AS FOR THE BOOK'S structure, I will present the life of Jesus sequentially—starting from the announcement of his birth, moving through his childhood, adolescence, and young adulthood, continuing through his baptism by John, concentrating especially on his public ministry, and ending with his last days, his death, and his resurrection. The four Gospels don't always agree on the sequence of events (often they don't include the same events), but they progress in a more or less logical order. So it is possible to use all four in tandem. My guide will be the various "Gospel parallel" books that match passages from Matthew, Mark, and Luke according to chronology. John is somewhat harder to match up, but not impossible; it too follows the progress of Jesus's life.

As we arrive at significant "places" in Jesus's life, I'll share stories of what I saw at those sites during my pilgrimage. In this way I hope to bring you into that trip as I experienced it. Also, I'll offer reflections on what particular episodes in Jesus's life might have to say to us today.

Each chapter, then, will include some travel narrative, some study of the text, and some spiritual reflection. At the end of the chapters I will include the corresponding Gospel passages, to encourage you to experience these parts of the Bible for yourself.

Needless to say, I won't cover every event in Jesus's life as recorded in the Gospels. As I said, this is not a Bible commentary. Nor does anyone care to read a four-thousand-page book. Instead, I'll focus on the specific events in Jesus's life that have held the most meaning for me and about which I think I might have something new to say. Nor will I treat each passage with the same level of detail. Some stories require more analysis, and there's no need to stretch things out. For example, I won't discuss passages about Mary and Joseph in as much detail as I will those in which the adult Jesus appears. Finally, I won't tell you about every place George and I visited. You can do without my description of buying toothpaste in a drug store in Jerusalem or soap in Tiberias.

This book is designed to be accessible to anyone—from those just starting to think about Jesus to those who feel that they may know the topic well. It is designed for people of deep faith or no faith who want to know about Jesus. But my own approach is that of a Christian. So I won't be shy about talking about my faith. Finally, I won't assume too much previous knowledge about the Gospels, or about the life and times of Jesus, but I will assume that you can quickly come up to speed and, as Jesus said, follow me.

WHENEVER I TOLD FRIENDS that I was writing a book about Jesus, they inevitably laughed. The scale of the project seemed impossible.

But after I explained that the book would focus only on specific Gospel passages, one friend asked sensibly, "What can you say that hasn't been said?"

"Well," I said, "I'll write about the Jesus whom I've met in my life. This is a Jesus who hasn't been written about before." It may be similar to hearing a friend tell you something unexpected about a mutual friend. "I never knew that about him," you might say wonderingly. Seeing a friend through another pair of eyes can help you appreciate a person more. You may end up understanding your friend in an entirely new way.

So I would like to invite you to meet the Jesus you already may know, but in a new way. Or, if you don't know much about Jesus, I would like to introduce him to you. Overall, I would like to introduce you to the Jesus I know, and love, the person at the center of my life.

Getting to know Jesus, like getting to know anyone, has been a pilgrimage. Part of that pilgrimage was a trip to Israel, one that changed my life.

CHAPTER I

Pilgrims

"YOU SHOULD GO TO the Holy Land," said the editor in chief of *America*. We were sitting in my boss's office in the magazine's headquarters in New York City. "If you're planning to write a book about Jesus, it will be of great help."

While I appreciated his advice, I was doubtful. Thanks to years of experience in the field of Jewish-Christian relations and multiple trips to Israel, Drew, a Jesuit priest like me, had a natural affinity for the loose geographic region known as the Holy Land. So I thought he was speaking more out of personal interest, much as a baseball fan might say, "You've got to visit the Hall of Fame in Cooperstown!"

As Drew prodded, my objections came to mind. For one thing, I had read the Gospels every day since entering the Jesuit novitiate. And I had pored over dozens of books about Jesus and prayed hundreds—maybe thousands—of times over the Gospel stories. What more could a trip teach me?

Another friend voiced similar sentiments. We had read (and heard) these stories so often, and had prayed about them so frequently, that we had formed our own mental images of the places mentioned in the Gospels. I already "knew" what Bethlehem, Nazareth, Jerusalem, and the Sea of Galilee looked like, because I had imagined those locales so often. We feared that laying eyes on locales overrun with tourists would sully our pristine mental pictures. Would seeing the ornate Church of the Holy Sepulchre in Jerusalem, one of history's original tourist destinations, supplant my own image of Jesus's tomb in first-century Palestine? "I like my own Gospel," said my friend. Me too.

"No," I responded to Drew's encouragement. "I don't think so."

But gradually, I started to doubt my doubts.

"Are you *crazy?*" said a friend who had visited the Holy Land several times. "How could you pass up a chance like that?" Then he added, "Don't you usually do your annual retreat in August? Why not go then, and think of the pilgrimage as a retreat?" Finally, he said, to clinch the argument, "You'll *love* it!"

My objections began to seem insignificant compared to the opportunity to see the land in which Jesus lived.

Little by little, a plan took shape. The end of August would be a convenient time to go (though, as Drew pointed out, the weather would be "brutally hot"). Phone calls and e-mails to knowledgeable friends helped me map out a tentative agenda.

My enthusiasm grew as I listed places to visit: the Sea of Galilee, Nazareth, Jerusalem, Bethlehem, Bethany. Just thinking about seeing these places, which I had long prayed about, filled me with joy. Of course I wanted to go! When I first entered the Jesuits, I told an older priest that the first thing that I would ask God when (or if) I made it to heaven would be to show me exactly what Jesus's life was like. Please show me what the landscape looked like. Please show me what Jesus saw. Now I had an opportunity to realize something of that dream, on this side of heaven.

Then a friend reminded me that the Jesuits run a house in Jerusalem. The Pontifical Biblical Institute was founded in 1927 to house Jesuit biblical scholars studying in Jerusalem and archaeologists working on digs. Today the institute hosts Jesuits from around the world, students of all stripes who study at various universities in Jerusalem, and many pilgrims. And by happenstance (or Providence) a Jesuit who had overseen the "PBI" for many years was spending a few weeks in my Jesuit community in New York.

"The PBI would be perfect!" he said, pointing out that it was lo-

cated only a few blocks from the "Old City." I had no clue what the
Old City was, but it sounded reasonably important. He put me in
touch with David, a Jesuit living there. A few e-mails later, I had a
place to stay in Jerusalem.

Another friend, a Jesuit studying in Rome who had visited the
Holy Land several times, helped me with another dilemma: Should
I sign up with a tour group? As a first-time traveler I was worried
about missing certain sites, not finding others, and overlooking the
significance of some. I could imagine returning home and someone
expostulating about a particular locale, "You *missed* that? How could
you overlook the most moving site in Galilee?"

You'll do fine without a tour company, my Roman friend wrote
in an e-mail. All you need is a reliable guidebook. Plus, you'll be able
to spend as much time as you would like in each place. You can pray
as long as you would like, which you might not be able to do as easily
with a group.

He had another piece of advice: rent a car for your excursion to
Galilee.

Galilee? Wasn't that just outside Jerusalem?

"No," Drew explained patiently, "it's several hours away." A
quick glance at a map proved that, despite my love of the Gospels, I
knew almost nothing about the topography of the region. Another
Jesuit had a more specific recommendation for a sojourn in Galilee:
a retreat house run by some Franciscan sisters right on the Mount
of Beatitudes. "It's a perfect spot," he said, wistfully recalling a retreat he made there decades ago. From Jerusalem, David sent me an
e-mail address for the sisters.

I rolled my eyes (at least inwardly); I doubted that I would be able
to make reservations from the States. I imagined a sleepy Franciscan
monastery that owned a single ancient computer stored in a dusty
anteroom, which was checked once a week by an elderly nun with
poor eyesight and worse computer skills. Reluctantly I e-mailed.
To make things easier I wrote in both French and English, politely
asking for a room.

Within a few hours I received a reply, from a Sister Télesfora: *"Avec plaisir je vous informe . . ."* With pleasure she informed me that their hostel would be delighted to host me, at ninety dollars a night. It looked as if the trip might happen after all.

That's what I told my friend George around that time, over the phone. George was one of my closest friends; we had known each other since the Jesuit novitiate. A longtime prison chaplain, George had accepted a new assignment just a few months before: Catholic chaplain at San Quentin State Prison in California. And a few years prior, he had stayed at the PBI as part of a month-long seminar on interfaith relations.

"Would you like some company?" he asked.

"You're kidding," I said. The prospect of a travel partner, and a good friend to boot, was something I hadn't considered, especially on such short notice.

"No," he said. "I have some time at the end of August, and I'd love to go."

George would be the ideal traveling companion: prayerful, easygoing, and knowledgeable. Another benefit: he volunteered to drive the rental car. "And we can go wherever you want," he said, "since I've already been there." A final benefit: George has a terrific sense of humor. Besides some moments of prayer, I knew we'd have fun.

We decided to aim for a pilgrimage as close as possible to a spiritual retreat, praying every morning before we began our travels, ensuring that Mass was part of our daily routine even if things were hectic, not dashing from place to place but lingering at sites that invited meditation, and bringing along not just our guidebooks, but our Bibles.

By June the trip was nearly planned. Several Jesuits offered their lists of can't-miss places, and I ordered a superb guidebook called *The Holy Land,* written by one of the world's leading biblical scholars, Jerome Murphy-O'Connor, a Catholic priest and a member of the Dominican order. Finally I booked a flight to Tel Aviv.

A pilgrimage to the Holy Land, which I hadn't wanted to do and which seemed impossible to arrange, ended up being the trip that I couldn't wait to do and that seemed to have arranged itself.

THE FLIGHT TO ISRAEL would be long; I knew that. What I didn't know was how unusual it would be. Naturally I expected tight security, but I was still surprised at Newark Airport to see that passengers flying to Tel Aviv were cordoned off in a special section, demarcated with barriers that prevented us from leaving, once passing through customs. Before boarding we would be searched again, extensively, patted down as an additional safety measure.

Milling around in the terminal were, not surprisingly, many Orthodox Jewish men and women. That upped my excitement—I really *was* going to Israel! What made me less excited was seeing how many rambunctious children there were on our flight—dozens of them. Boarding the plane I discovered that I was seated directly in front of a row populated by four children, each of them screaming. Their harried mother, her head covered modestly in a scarf, was gamely trying to calm them, but to no avail. Discreetly, I asked the flight attendant if any other seats were available. Shaking her head dolefully, she leaned in close to explain. "This flight is always filled with kids; it's the one preferred by families who fly from New York to Israel."

Fortunately, my doctor had given me a prescription for sleeping pills in case I needed them. As soon as the plane took off, I popped one in my mouth, eagerly awaiting the pleasantly drowsy feeling that would signal eight uninterrupted hours of blissful sleep. But after an hour, nothing. I was as wide awake as ever. Oh well. I pulled out Jerome Murphy-O'Connor's *The Holy Land* and tried to ignore a child regularly kicking my seat and shouting, "I *hate* you, Mommy!" I wondered if George, who was flying from San Francisco, was having a similar experience.

Murphy-O'Connor's book was precisely the kind of guide I was looking for. For one thing, his reputation was sterling.[1] A scholar at the École Biblique in Jerusalem and the author of numerous books on the New Testament, Murphy-O'Connor was eminently trustworthy.[2] He deployed words like "unlikely," "possible," and "very probably," as he carefully sifted through the entirely authentic and the obviously legendary places in the Holy Land. Every few pages his wit would shine through. Writing about the Church of the Holy Sepulchre, he said, "In subsequent centuries the church suffered desecration and destruction more than once. Inept repairs were no less damaging." His book helped me pass ten hours in relative peace.

BEN GURION INTERNATIONAL AIRPORT, in Tel Aviv, was stunningly modern, with a high-tech fountain that poured water from a circular opening in the ceiling into a pool on the floor. My friend David had told to me to locate a *sherut* to Jerusalem.

I had no idea what a *sherut* was. So I followed all the other tourists, had my passport stamped by a friendly Israel official ("*Shalom!*"), exchanged dollars for shekels, and eventually spied a row of vans outside, idling under the broiling Middle Eastern sun. Immediately I felt that frisson of embarrassment you experience in a foreign country when you realize that you are about to sound like a fool for not knowing the most basic words.

"Is this a cheroot?" I shouted over the din of the motors. The driver laughed and said, "*Sherut!*" (It's the Hebrew word for "service.")

"Are you going to Jerusalem?" I asked.

Laughing, he jerked his thumb to a sign on the bus that said "Jerusalem."

Aboard was a mix of Israeli citizens, Orthodox Jews (from my flight), and an American student, all of whom chatted merrily as the *sherut* bounced down the streets. We wended our way through the sandy countryside dotted with olive trees and scrub, and passed by the high metal fence that delineated the Palestinian territories.

America magazine had published many articles about the wall, but it was still a shock to see: tall, gray, metal, forbidding.

We entered a small town. This was an Israeli settlement, a city for Jewish "settlers" within otherwise Palestinian territory, a deeply controversial political issue. I asked our driver the name of the town, but he declined to give it, instead outlining the various forms of governance: A, B, and C. A: Complete Palestinian autonomy. B: Shared control between the Israeli military and the Palestinians. C: Full Israeli control. The other passengers fell silent as he spoke.

Our *sherut* dropped off several people at their tidy yellow sandstone houses. After we pulled back onto the highway, I saw signs for Jerusalem.

Soon we were in Jerusalem's bustling center, threading our way through its narrow streets. Many buildings—from skyscrapers to more modest dwellings—were creamy white, built from what is called Jerusalem stone, the pale limestone used to construct everything from a corner drugstore to the Western Wall. Often highly polished, it gleams almost pure white in the sun. Enchanted, I thought of the Bible verses about pilgrims "going up" to Jerusalem and what a glorious sight it must have been in ancient times.[3]

"Three Paul Émile Botta Street, please," I said to the driver. When we entered the heart of the city, I was the only passenger. My heart leapt when I saw the walls of the Old City. Among the most ancient structures in Jerusalem, the walls, or at least their outlines, date back to biblical times; they were improved on by rulers from around the time of Christ, and by Suleiman the Magnificent in the sixteenth century.

"Here!" said the driver, as he parked beside a high metal gate. I offered what I calculated to be the correct number of shekels and helped him unload my bags.

"Heavy!" he said, laughing. "How long are you staying?"

Prior to departure I had read the Gospel passages in which Jesus counsels his disciples to "take nothing for your journey" and felt a pang of guilt.[4] My practice is to take *everything* with me on the journey, having endured too many trips when I've been forced to spend money for a sweater that I should have brought along. Traveling heavy saves money, even if it makes me appear extravagant. Still, I wondered if Jesus would have approved.

Next to a small sign that said "Pontifical Biblical Institute" was a bell. A cheerful workman opened the door, and I was shocked by what I had predicted would prove to be a poky Jesuit residence. Instead, a three-story, sand-colored edifice that looked like a Crusader castle (complete with crenellated towers) was fronted by a gravel courtyard that boasted three tall palm trees. At the main building I rang another doorbell.

A smiling, dark-haired Indian Jesuit opened the door. Brother Tony introduced himself. "You are *very* welcome!" he said. "Would you like something to drink?" He led me through a high-ceilinged foyer paved with terrazzo stone. On the right was a spacious, airy chapel with simple chairs and an impressive crucifixion scene on the wall. On the left, behind glass doors, was a small archaeological museum featuring long vitrines that housed antiquities: statues, pieces of pottery, scrolls. And a mummy—not the most common addition to a Jesuit community. Tucked under the main staircase was a miniature elevator; to the right was a dining room and a living room, both lit by copious sunshine that poured through the frosted windows.

But our destination was the large metal container outside the dining room. "This is *very good*," Tony said, as he poured a cup of pale yellow liquid from a plastic spigot on the front. "You can fill your bottles when you go around town." I took a sip: lemonade! During the next two weeks, the lemonade machine would be as eagerly sought a destination as any holy site.

As Tony prepared a plate of lunch, Joseph Doan Công Nguyên entered the room. Father Doan, the head of the Jesuit community at the PBI, was a Vietnamese Jesuit who had spent several years working in the Jesuit headquarters in Rome. He had also spent eleven years in a Vietnamese prison after the Communist takeover there. Father Doan offered to help me plan my itinerary for the next few days, a service he offered frequently to pilgrims.

After lunch Tony said, "You look tired, James. Why don't you have a lie down?"

Though I wanted to start touring immediately (even sans George), I couldn't resist the invitation. Tony accompanied me in the elevator to the second floor and escorted me to a large, spotless room with two immense desks, a narrow bed, a sink, and a tall window looking out onto the spacious courtyard.

"Rest now, and see Father Doan later."

But once I lay down, the sleeping pill kicked in. Four hours later, I awoke with a start and peered out my window—I was in Jerusalem! Groggily, I found my way to Doan's neatly organized office. In the hallway, I ran into George, who had just arrived. "*Shalom!*" he said.

A taciturn, scholarly man, Doan asked which sites we most hoped to see. After we ran through our lists, he went over to his bookcase and pulled out a large, creased map of Israel, which he carefully spread out on his desk. For the next hour, we planned the next two weeks. He suggested we start in Jerusalem and visit the most important sites; next, rent a car for the trip to Galilee; and then, upon our return, see whatever we had missed in Jerusalem. His use of so many names that I had heard only in Scripture classes delighted me: Jericho, Gethsemane, Bethpage, Bethany, the Mount of Olives.

A stone's throw from our residence, said Doan, was Gehenna, the section of Jerusalem where residents in antiquity burned garbage; this was the vivid image Jesus often used to illustrate hell. A few days later over dinner, one of the Jesuits was speaking about some improvements made in the city and said something I never thought I'd hear: "Gehenna is lovely these days."

George inquired about the possibility of making a retreat nearby. Doan said that in the Garden of Gethsemane the Franciscan friars ran a cluster of about fifteen small buildings, hermitages, that were available for prayer, though reserving them was difficult, so high was the demand.

As Doan described more places on his worn map, sleep almost overcame me. Thrilled and exhausted, I promised myself to review his notes later. Thanking him, we gathered up our notes and left behind his map.

"Oh no," he said, "that's yours for the week. Also, we have our big meal in the afternoon and a smaller meal for supper, after Mass, at seven o'clock. And you are most welcome to celebrate Mass if you wish, Fathers."

As we walked from Doan's office, George smiled. "Ready?" he said.

CHAPTER 2

Yes

"How can this be?"

IN A PERFECT WORLD George and I would have visited the important places in the life of Christ in sequence: we would have started in
Bethlehem, moved to Nazareth, continued on to the Sea of Galilee,
and ended up in Jerusalem. But since that would have meant flying
from the States into the so-far-nonexistent Bethlehem Airport,
we couldn't arrange it. So Nazareth, where the story of Jesus truly
began, came in the middle of our pilgrimage.

After a few days of touring around Jerusalem, as Doan suggested
(more about Jerusalem later), George and I took ourselves to the Avis
car rental around the corner from the Pontifical Biblical Institute.
The details of the transaction were marginally less complicated than
applying for a mortgage, but early one morning we rented a little gray
car for a reasonable sum, found a GPS for a few thousand shekels,
and picked up a road map for free. The GPS was, oddly, rented not
from Avis but from a suspicious-looking gas station across the street.
The helpful woman at the car-rental desk estimated that Galilee,
northeast of Jerusalem, was a four- to five-hour drive.

The GPS seemed largely uninterested in taking us in the right
direction. Though George is an excellent driver (i.e., better than
me) and we expertly navigated our way out of Jerusalem, we quickly
found ourselves lost. At first it had seemed a straightforward journey. All we had to do was find Highway 90, which snaked north,

alongside the west bank of the Jordan River, and follow it to the Sea of Galilee. But it soon became clear that we were far from any highway, stuck in the middle of an arid countryside of rolling hills dotted with small gray-green bushes.

George's patience dwindled as the roads narrowed. Who could blame him? At one point, the GPS said, "Turn right," and we pulled onto a deeply rutted dirt road.

"Uh!" he said. "Where *are* we?"

I examined the map. "Shilo," I said.

"Yeah, right!" said George, evidently doubtful that we were near one of the great cities of the Old Testament where the Ark of the Covenant rested for many years.

"Where do we want to go?" he said. "I'll plug it into the GPS."

We wanted to go north to Galilee and along the River Jordan, so I searched the map for a location on the way. "Gilgal," I said.

"Oh, come on!" said George. Another famous Old Testament town, one that figures prominently in the life of Saul—he was made king there, among other things.

But it was true. I was constantly surprised how the storied names of biblical locales popped up in the most familiar of circumstances: on a simple map, on a graffitied street sign, or in everyday conversations. "The traffic to Bethlehem was *terrible* last night!" said a Jesuit over dinner one night. Which still didn't beat "Gehenna is lovely."

As our GPS kept insisting on right turns, I examined the map. George slowly steered the car down the faux road. Presently an Israeli guard station appeared. A young, dark-haired man with a thin beard and a rifle slung over his shoulder walked menacingly toward our car. (Later I discovered that Shilo is a Jewish settlement, which explained the rifle.)

"Okay, Navigator," said George. "Ask the guy with the gun."

The guy with the gun spoke zero English, and my Hebrew consisted of five phrases: *Thank you, You're welcome, Hello, Good-bye,* and *Peace*—the last three of which are the same. So I said, "Jordan River?"

He squinted his eyes, unslung his rifle, and jabbed the point of the barrel into his left forearm. "Dead! Dead! Dead!" he said. *Uh oh.*

"Then . . . left!" he said and grinned. It dawned on me what he meant. Follow the road to where it dead-ends. Then turn left. His apparent death threat was instead a helpful driving instruction.

"Toda!" I said.

He saluted, and I returned to the car.

"Good job," said George. "I'm glad he didn't shoot us."

In a few minutes we were zipping up Highway 90 through the Jordan Valley. In another hour we reached the Sea of Galilee.

We spied it first through the trees, as we drove through the city of Tiberias. The cornflower-blue waters and the pink rocks on the opposite shore seemed the most beautiful thing my eyes had ever seen. And I thought, *Jesus saw this!* Not through the window of a rented car, but he had seen it. From years of reading Bibles illustrated with crummy black-and-white photographs of the Sea of Galilee, I immediately recognized the surrounding hills, which in the hazy summer light looked like folded pink cloth.

We continued up the west side of the sea, heading north toward the Franciscan hostel on the Mount of Beatitudes. As the number of buildings between the highway and the water lessened, the view became clearer. I couldn't take my eyes off of it.

"Jesus saw this," I said.

"Yeah," said George. "Pretty great, huh?"

When I saw the sign that said "Capernaum," I almost laughed for joy. The town where Jesus made his home during his ministry in Galilee. The town where Peter lived. The site of many of the miracle stories. The place that I had *most* wanted to see. But we weren't going straightaway to Capernaum (or, as the sign read, *Kfar Nahum,* which, translated into English, would be "village of Nahum" or perhaps "Nahumsville"). First we needed to find the Mount of Beatitudes hostel.

"Well," I said, pointing up a gently sloping hillside, "that must be it."

We both peered up a hill blanketed with dried grass and capped with an impressive gray church. After a few unsuccessful tries, we made it up the side of the mountain and spied a small sign pointing to the monastery.

Having stayed in countless religious houses and monasteries, I expected an unlovely building with closet-size rooms furnished with the following items: a narrow metal bed with a lumpy mattress, a rickety wooden chair, a tiny desk, and, if we were lucky, a small sink with a leaky faucet. We were lodging in a Franciscan hostel, run by an order known for their love of simplicity, so the poverty was bound to be extreme.

We pulled into the driveway, and a handsome four-story sand-stone building loomed on our right. To our left was a white marble building, by all appearances brand-new, with a large fountain in front. I wondered what it was. Clearly that building was too elegant to be part of the Franciscan holdings. Stretching out before us, at the far end of the property, the Sea of Galilee sparkled.

When we emerged from the car, the heat hit me like an anvil. A very humid anvil. It must have been five thousand degrees. A sprightly woman in a white habit bounded down the stairs of the sandstone building.

"*Bienvenue, mes pères!*" she said with a smile. "I am Sister Téles-fora," the kind sister with whom I had corresponded. After a merci-fully brief conversation in the stunning heat, we started to drag our bags toward the sandstone building.

"Oh no, Fathers," she said. "You aren't in *this* building."

That's the worst thing you can hear when visiting a religious community. The translation is: we don't have room for you in the main house, so we're going to put you somewhere far worse. As a novice working in Kingston, Jamaica, I had heard those words and was escorted to a room with a (functioning) wasps' nest on the ceiling. During my time in East Africa I had heard those words on a visit to a religious community in northern Uganda and was led to a mud hut where fat bugs crashed angrily against my mosquito netting throughout the night. As a Jesuit who has taken a vow of poverty, one makes do, but one is also occasionally disappointed.

Sister Télesfora pointed across the driveway. "You're staying *there*." I peered at the glorious white edifice gleaming in the blinding sunlight.

"Really?" I said. "What is it?"

"Our new hotel," she said with a smile. George looked at me, goggle-eyed. We lugged our suitcases past the fountain and into an air-conditioned lobby furnished with overstuffed white leather couches. From behind a *luxe* wooden desk, a woman purred, "Welcome. Your names?"

Surely this was a mistake. Weren't we staying in a simple Franciscan hostel? But in a few seconds she handed us our card keys. As George and I wheeled our bags down the carpeted hallway, I almost laughed. When I saw my room I *did* laugh: two comfortable beds, a pristine bathroom, a TV, and, through the huge windows, a panoramic view of the Sea of Galilee.

After George and I compared rooms we met up with our host. "Sister," I said. "These rooms are . . . *incredible*."

"What did you expect?" she asked.

"Well, you're Franciscans," I said, "so I expected something . . . simpler."

"Father, *we* are Franciscans," she said. "Our *guests* are not!"

Later that afternoon, overwhelmed with emotion, I instinctively opened up the Gospels to the passage in Mark where Jesus had first called the fishermen along the shores of Galilee. "Follow me," he said, and he said it right here. At that moment the Gospels felt more grounded, more tangible, more real than ever before. I looked out at the pale blue sea, barely able to believe what I was seeing.

A tiny red cupola in the distance looked familiar. Then I remembered it from the back cover of Jerome Murphy-O'Connor's *The Holy Land*. What was it? I fished my book out of my luggage. The caption read: "The Greek Orthodox Church at Capernahum, on the Sea of Galilee, with the Golan heights in the background."

Capernaum! I'm not embarrassed to say that I wept upon realizing that I was looking at Jesus's hometown, perhaps from one of the vantage points from which he once saw it. There it was, right on the water. Of course it would be by the shoreline—that's why Peter the fisherman made his home there. Or rather, here.

Jesus was here, I kept thinking. *Jesus was here.*

THE DAILY BREAKFASTS AT the Franciscan hostel deserve comment. They were gargantuan. Each morning George and I walked from our hotel to the modest monastery building where the sisters and their staff covered two long tables with local delicacies: dates, figs, olives, fruits of all sorts, cereals for the Americans, yogurts, cheeses, toast, croissants, pastries, cookies, biscuits, coffees, teas, and juices, as well as meats, including a mysterious ham. Since there was no lunch, George and I consumed breakfasts meant to last us until dinner.

One day, we journeyed to Kursi, the traditional site of the healing of the Gerasene demoniac. In that story, Jesus drives a "legion" of demons from a possessed man into a nearby herd of pigs, which immediately rush into the sea and drown.[1] Over breakfast the next day George said, "This ham is delicious. Do you think it's from one of the Gerasene pigs?"

Today our destination, however, was Nazareth. Fortified with enough food for the rest of the day (if not the rest of the week), we took our supplies to the car: several bottles of water, our Avis map, the Murphy-O'Connor guidebook, smartphones, cameras, and a Bible. Back in the States, George and I had promised ourselves that we would begin each day with a prayer and a reading from Scripture that corresponded with our destination. Today we read the story of the Annunciation, Mary's dramatic encounter with the Angel Gabriel, in our car, its air conditioner humming.

We had an easy time reaching Nazareth—just an hour or so from Capernaum. En route we passed a small sign for the town of Nain, where Jesus raised from the dead the only son of a widow from that town.² It was harder to find our way to the center of Nazareth, as the signs dwindled inside the city limits. Also, any directional signs bearing pictograms of a church (a black triangle topped with a cross) were usually defaced with black spray paint.

In Jesus's day Nazareth was a backwater town, with perhaps only two to four hundred residents, what one scholar called an "insignificant hamlet."³ Its less than impressive status gave rise to the Apostle Nathanael's sarcastic retort when he learned where the Messiah was from: "Can anything good come out of Nazareth?"⁴

But though the town is not mentioned in the Old Testament, it may have enjoyed something of a religious reputation in Jesus's day. Some residents in Nazareth were "Nazoreans," a clan who claimed to be descendants of King David. Some scholars surmise that both words come from the Hebrew *netzer,* meaning "shoot of." Thus, the townsfolk may have considered themselves "offshoots of Jesse," David's father. Nazareth itself means "village of the shoot."⁵ So it was an insignificant, even laughable, place to outsiders, but perhaps to those living there, a holy place, associated with the coming of the Messiah.

Today Nazareth is a bustling, hilly city. Homes and shops and churches and mosques are jammed next to one another, and small cars buzz through the narrow streets at alarming speeds.

Now populated by a mix of Muslims and Christians, the town is dominated by the gray cupola of the Basilica of the Annunciation, which stands atop a steep hill. Completed in 1969, the basilica is vast. Inside the upper church, a high ceiling is supported by crisscrossing concrete pillars; on the walls are colorful depictions of Mary donated by some two dozen nations, a testimony to the widespread appeal of Jesus's mother. The current church is built on the ruins of several older churches, the most ancient dating from around the fourth century.

Today the lower church is centered on a small limestone grotto that was crowded with tourists on the day we visited. This is the Grotto of the Annunciation, the limestone cave where the Angel Gabriel is said to have appeared to Mary, to announce the birth of Jesus.

On a small altar in the grotto is a unique inscription to which Father Doan had alerted us before we left Jerusalem. It's hard to see unless you look carefully, for the altar is behind an iron grille. Many artistic representations of the Annunciation include one of two phrases: either *Ave Maria,* "Hail, Mary," from the angel's first words to Mary in the Gospel of Luke, or *Verbum caro factum est,* "The Word was made flesh," from John's Gospel. Here at the site, however, the inscription reads: *Verbum caro hic factum est,* "The Word was made flesh *here.*"

I gripped the cold iron grille and prayed, wondering if the words to Mary, so familiar to Christians, were first uttered here. Or somewhere very near here.

Despite the important fact that Jesus lived for some thirty years in Nazareth and is frequently referred to as "Jesus of Nazareth," what is celebrated in the main church in Nazareth is not his young adulthood, or his career as a carpenter here, or even his later preaching in the town synagogue (something that would get him kicked out of town), but something else: his mother, and how she discovers that she will give birth.

Perhaps the people behind the naming of the basilica understood that as important as these other incidents in Jesus's life were, something else was equally important: the strange circumstances of his birth. Our pilgrimage into the life of Jesus, then, begins with a look at his mother. And with the story of her encounter with the divine.

THE GOSPEL OF LUKE moves swiftly to introduce the protagonist of the story: Jesus of Nazareth. After a short prelude telling his readers that he plans to set forth an "orderly account" of the "events that have been fulfilled among us," Luke begins his Gospel with the announcement of the birth of John the Baptist.

Zechariah is fulfilling his priestly duties in the Temple in Jerusalem when the Angel Gabriel appears to announce that his wife, Elizabeth, an elderly woman thought incapable of conceiving, will bear a son. The couple, says Gabriel, are to name the baby John.

Not surprisingly, Zechariah doubts. "How will I know that this is so?" For his doubting, he is struck dumb until the child is born. Elizabeth then remains "in seclusion" for five months.[6]

About a half a year later, something even more extraordinary happens. "In the sixth month," Luke says, "the angel Gabriel was sent by God to a town in Galilee called Nazareth."

With that dramatic sentence Luke tells us not only that the angel (the Greek word is *angelos,* meaning "messenger") was sent by God, but also that he was sent to a particular place. Luke is greatly concerned with history; his Gospel will pinpoint towns and cities and months and Jewish festivals and which rulers were in charge, to ground his account in time and place. For anyone who imagines God as far above something as banal as human history, here is God choosing a particular time (the sixth month), a particular location (Nazareth), and a particular person (Mary). Theologians call this the "scandal of particularity."

The angel comes to a woman named Mary, who is betrothed to Joseph. Betrothal was a formal agreement to marry that lasted for a year. The woman involved was usually quite young, sometimes in her late teens.[7] But it was a binding contract. Thus, Mary would have been seen for all practical purposes as Joseph's wife.[8] This is why, later on, when Joseph discovers that Mary is pregnant, he would be well within his rights to divorce her. Luke also tells us that Joseph was of the line of David.

The angel's words to the young woman may be the most famous greeting in the New Testament. *Chaire, kecharitōmenē* is the Greek,[9] usually rendered "Hail, full of grace" or, in an unfortunate translation, "Greetings, favored one," which sounds like the first words of an alien newly landed on earth. It may be impossible to replicate the beautiful alliteration of the Greek, but one reference book provides a lovely series of possible explanations of how the angel addresses Mary: "endowed with grace, dearly loved, endued with divine grace."[10] The tense used indicates that Mary has *already* been gifted. It is not the angel's visit that confers grace; God has done this. Though Mary holds no great position like Zechariah, and though she is most likely poor, and though as an unmarried woman she occupies a lowly state in society, God loves her—lavishly.

Mary is the forerunner of all those in the Christian life who will be judged by human standards as unworthy of God's grace. But God has other ideas.

"The Lord is with you," the angel continues.

It is not surprising that Mary is surprised, utterly confused, or, in some translations, terrified. Encounters with the divine often engender fear. Sensing her reaction, the angel says, "Do not be afraid, Mary."

The angel explains that she will bear a son. The boy will be called Jesus (*Iēsous* in Greek). The Hebrew name—Yeshua—was common at the time, a shortened form of Joshua (Yehoshua), the successor to Moses. The name means "God helps" or "God saves."

In *A Marginal Jew,* his magisterial study of the historical Jesus, the Reverend John P. Meier, professor of New Testament at Notre Dame, notes that for most of the period covered by the Old Testament, Israelites were *not* named after the great patriarchs and matriarchs. But a century or two before Jesus, there came an upsurge in "native-religious" feeling in Palestine. That Jesus's mother and her husband bear names from the Old Testament (Miriam and Joseph) may indicate that he was born into a family who participated in the desire for a reawakening, or reaffirmation, of Jewish identity under Roman rule.[11]

Mary's child will be "Son of the Most High," says the angel. (Later in Luke's Gospel, a ranting demoniac will identify him with a similar title.[12]) He will inherit the throne of his ancestor David and will rule over the house of Jacob. "Of his kingdom," Mary is told, "there will be no end."

But the young woman is less concerned with what her son will do than with something more immediate: the pregnancy. So she asks the angel plainly, "How can this be, since I am a virgin?"

When Zechariah questions how the birth of his son would be accomplished, the angel offers an explanation but also strikes him dumb, as if punishing him for doubting. The angel treats Mary more gently, offering a mysterious explanation: the Holy Spirit will "over-shadow" her. The angel again emphasizes the significance of her child: "He will be called Son of God."

Then the angel further reassures her. If Mary questions, she can look to Zechariah's wife, Elizabeth, who is Mary's cousin. "This is the sixth month for her who was said to be barren," says the angel. (The reader already knows this.) Finally comes one of the clearest biblical affirmations of God's power: "For nothing will be impossible with God."

Mary decides. "Here am I, the servant of the Lord," she says. The Greek word is *doulē,* or slave. "Let it be with me according to your word." With that the angel leaves her.

THE STORY OF THE Annunciation never fails to move me. And for many years I wondered what drew me to this particular Gospel story. Is it the irruption of the extraordinary into an ordinary woman's daily life? Is it how a single decision—Mary's yes—changes history? Is it how God chooses the unlikeliest people to accomplish God's desires for the world?

All of those things speak to me, as well as something more personal. For the more I reflect on this passage, the more the story appears to encapsulate the progress of a person's relationship with God. What happens to Mary happens to us.

First of all, the initiative lies entirely with God. God begins the conversation with Mary, as God does with us, breaking into our lives in unexpected ways. We find ourselves touched by a Scripture reading, moved to tears by a friend's comforting words during a confusing time, or befuddled by joy at a glimpse of autumn leaves shining in the late afternoon sun. And we think, *Why am I feeling these feelings of longing, gratitude, wonder?*

This is God beginning a conversation. And when we realize that this might be God's voice, what happens? Sometimes we're grateful. But just as often we're fearful—like Mary.

Fear is a common reaction to the divine. When one realizes that it is *God* who might be drawing near, we instinctively withdraw. Thinking about the Creator of the Universe entering into the "particularity" of our lives can be terrifying. Sometimes on retreat, when I feel that I've suddenly received an answer to a long-standing problem or been given an insight that seems to have originated from outside me (as in "There's no way I could have come up with that on my own"), I grow frightened or, as one translation describes Mary, "greatly disturbed." God is paying attention to us. How could that not frighten?

We may also struggle with the notion of God's paying attention to us in our littleness, in other words, "Who, *me?*" It may be hard for modern-day believers to appreciate this aspect of Mary's life, particularly when conditioned by the kinds of images of Mary that decorate the Basilica of the Annunciation—ten-foot-high mosaics of a strong, proud woman—but we must remember who Miriam of Nazareth was. First, she was a woman. Second, she was young. Third, she was most likely poor and living in an insignificant town. Finally, she was a Jew living in a land ultimately ruled by the Roman Empire. Taken together, Mary can be seen as a figure with little power. For a more contemporary image, think of God's appearing to a young girl in a small village in Africa.

The angel gently counsels her to set this aside: "Do not be afraid, Mary." Among the first words Mary hears are ones that her son will frequently use in his ministry, as when he walks on water in full view of the terrified disciples. Perhaps Mary shared her own experiences with Jesus. Why wouldn't she? Who knows if Mary repeated the angel's calming words to a frightened boy, a confused adolescent, or a worried adult: "Do not be afraid, Jesus."

The angel then explains things for her. Again, as in our own lives. Take the example of a young person from an affluent background who hears a call to a different way of life. Naturally, it's not as dramatic as Mary's encounter, but it is an encounter with grace all the same. Imagine a college professor inviting you to consider working among the poor in the developing world. You're initially stunned— "*Me?*"—but you also intuit a sense of God's voice in the invitation. After the initial shock wears off, the professor describes what life overseas will be like. You'll be living in a remote village; you'll have to learn a new language; you'll be separated from your friends and family; but your encounters with those living in poverty, she says, will transform you. This is what the angel does for Mary once she surmounts her alarm: he helps her discern.

At this point, along with Mary, you would probably ask, "How can this be?" This may be the facet of Mary's life that intersects most with our own. We feel inadequate to what God seems to be asking—even if we are sure that it is God who is asking. This happens not only with an invitation to something wonderfully new and exciting, but also with a sudden turn of events that darkens life. An illness. The loss of a job. A ruptured friendship. Who hasn't said, "How can this be?"

A few years ago, my father was diagnosed with lung cancer. When I heard the news from my mother over the phone, I was seized with fear. By then in my forties, I knew friends who had accompanied their parents during a terminal illness and I could see the future: sorrowful hospital visits, painful conversations, monumental feelings of fear and loss. And finally the terrible reality of seeing my father suffer and die. I knew that God was asking me to accept this, but I wanted to say, "How can this be? How can I do this?" Mary asks the same questions.

In response the angel is considerate. Gabriel doesn't threaten her for the insolence of asking a question or burden her with a physical malady for speaking up, as he did with Zechariah.[13]

Instead, the angel simply asks her to look around. "And now, your relative Elizabeth in her old age has also conceived a son; and this is the sixth month for her who was said to be barren." Sometimes this verse is interpreted as the angel's revealing something unknown to Mary: "Here's a secret—Elizabeth is pregnant." But it's just as likely that Mary, Elizabeth's cousin, would already have heard the astonishing news of the elderly woman's pregnancy. To my mind, the angel is saying: "You have doubts about what God will do? Then just look at what God has already done." Looking backward helps Mary to look forward. Awareness leads to trust.

Frequently I meet with people struggling with devastating news. During those times even the most devout can begin to doubt God's presence. But often what helps them to regain trust is a simple question: "Has God been with you in difficult times in the past?"

In the same way that the angel reorients Mary by pointing to what has already happened, a friend can invite us to remember. "Were there times in the past," a friend might ask, "when you felt like things were confusing, but where you can now see God's hand?" And often we will pause and say, "Now that you mention it, when I thought I couldn't possibly go on, I found that something or someone helped me to face my difficulties. God was with me." Memories of God's activity in the past enable us to embrace the future.

Newly confident, Mary says yes. Notice that she does so in absolute freedom. No one coerces her. And she was free to say no. Mary also makes her decision without appealing to a man. She doesn't ask Joseph for permission. Nor does she tell the angel that she must consult with her father. The young woman living in a patriarchal time makes a decision about the coming king. Someone with little power agrees to bring the powerful one into the world: "Let it be with me according to your word."

A close friend recently told me how important this passage has been to her as a mother. She prays with Denise Levertov's poem "The Annunciation" every week, she said. The poem reads, in part:

> *But we are told of meek obedience. No one mentions*
> *courage.*
> > *The engendering Spirit*
> *did not enter her without consent.*
> > > *God waited.*

My friend told me, "Both the Gospel passage and the poem remind me to consent with grace and courage in a *physical* way to the presence of God in my life." This reality was made clearer to her after giving birth to her two children. "I can't emphasize how important this freedom to respond to God is in my life, and to do so bodily only heightened this."

With God's help the world is poised for something new, something that even Mary may not be able to understand fully, perhaps until the Resurrection. Remember that Mary was told that her son would be the Son of God, not that he would be tortured, put to death on a cross, and then rise from the dead. Mary says yes to a future that she does not know. She is an example of letting God do God's work, without trying to figure it out.

When we say yes to God, we are usually surprised by the results. We say "I do" during a wedding and receive blessings far beyond what we could have imagined. We accept a position as a teacher and our lives are changed by our students. More simply, we say yes to God and are completely transformed.

THE FIRST MIRACULOUS STORY in this book is a good place to ask a question that will arise frequently during our pilgrimage into the life of Jesus: Did this really happen? To begin to answer that, let's look at how the Gospels were composed.

There were several distinct stages to the writing of the Gospels.[14] First was Jesus's actual public ministry. Next came the "oral tradition," when the story of Jesus of Nazareth would have been passed orally from person to person. During this period, there would have been little need for a written record. Jesus's disciples, followers, and other eyewitnesses were still around to offer firsthand, and undoubtedly vivid, accounts of their encounters with Jesus. Indeed, they were probably bursting with enthusiasm and eager to respond when people asked, "What did he say?" "What did he do?" "What was he like?" For some episodes there would have been multiple witnesses; for others, a handful; for a few, just one.[15] But there is no need for books when you have eyewitnesses. In any event, most of the early disciples were likely illiterate.

By the way, even at this early stage, you can already see the likelihood that differences would arise among the various oral traditions. First of all, not every eyewitness would describe an event in precisely the same way. Each would stress one thing or another, depending on what struck him or her as important. Also, as the Scripture scholar N. T. Wright has pointed out, since Jesus was an itinerant preacher, he probably would have said the same things over and over, but would have said them in slightly different ways to different audiences. "Local variations would no doubt abound."[16] So already we can see some variations creeping into the story of Jesus at this early stage, which helps to answer the question of why the Gospels don't always agree with one another.

As those original witnesses died (and it became clear that Jesus would not, as some expected, return soon), the next stage began. This required the editorial work of those who compiled the Gospels for the early church, generally known as the "evangelists," Matthew, Mark, Luke, and John. ("Gospel" is an Old English derivation of "good news." "Evangelist" is from the Greek *euangelion,* "good news" or "good message.") Over time the church settled on these four books as the approved, or "canonical," Gospels because of their wide use, theological orthodoxy, and association with the apostles.[17]

Each evangelist wrote for a slightly different audience and therefore stressed different parts of the story, leaving out what another writer would deem important or adding passages that another writer would consider less significant. During the editing process, these authors also inserted various comments and emendations, for the purposes of explanation or exhortation, that may not have been found in the original stories or texts. An author like Luke, for example, felt it necessary to explain some Jewish religious practices that might have been unfamiliar to his readers. Someone like Matthew, who wrote for a largely Jewish audience, did not.

Three of the Gospels—Matthew, Mark, and Luke—are deeply intertwined. Although there are competing theories about how they are connected, it is clear that they are. Most scholars posit Mark's Gospel as coming first, with the evangelist writing to a non-Jewish community around AD 70. Matthew's Gospel, written around 85 or 90 and addressed to a primarily Jewish audience, is an expanded and revised version of Mark, supplemented with other stories, including, for example, the narratives about the birth of Jesus. Luke, though most likely a Gentile (or non-Jew), nonetheless knew something about Jewish traditions when he wrote his Gospel roughly around the same time as Matthew; he also drew on Mark, and also supplemented his narrative with other stories. Both Matthew and Luke also relied heavily on an independent source of sayings—nicknamed "Q" by scholars after the German *Quelle,* meaning "source."

While Matthew, Mark, and Luke carefully edited their books to address specific communities of readers, their Gospels are so similar that they are referred to as the Synoptic Gospels, because they include numerous passages that can be looked at together (Greek *synopsis,* "view together").

The Gospel of John, written somewhat later, most likely for Christians in the eastern Mediterranean area in the late first century, is markedly different from the Synoptics. John's narrative introduces several well-known characters who do not even appear in the other three Gospels, including Nicodemus, the man born blind, the Samaritan woman, and Lazarus. Few of the episodes of Jesus's public ministry recorded in John mirror those in the Synoptics.

Jesus *himself* seems different in the Gospel of John. No longer the earthy spinner of homespun parables or the down-to-earth carpenter at home with Galilean fishermen, John's Jesus often can seem like an omniscient sage who speaks solemnly, even oracularly: "I am the way, and the truth, and the life."[18] To me, the Jesus of John can seem more divine than human. As Joseph A. Fitzmyer, SJ, a New Testament scholar, writes, "What a picture of Jesus we would have, if we had only the Fourth Gospel! Would we know much about the humanity of Jesus?"[19]

Daniel J. Harrington, SJ, my professor of New Testament at Boston College, used to tell our class that the New Testament provides us with "a general outline of Jesus's life." We could, he said, imagine the evangelists sitting at their desks before various scraps of paper on which were written parables and proverbs, discussions with the disciples and debates with religious leaders, as well as healing stories and other miracles. Gathering them together, they would stress one thing and omit another in order to provide a complete story.

But not *entirely* complete—or one designed for scrupulous accuracy. That's not to say that the Gospels aren't true or accurate. Rather, careful readers will discover some continuity problems. Overall, the Gospels agree with one another on both story and sequence. This is often the case with the Synoptics, where Jesus's words are often repeated verbatim and his actions are nearly identical. When Jesus calls a tax collector named Levi (or Matthew), he utters the same words in all three Synoptic Gospels: "Follow me."[20]

But in some places, the evangelists—who were not what we consider today to be professional historians—do not agree on important details. Jesus makes only *one* journey to Jerusalem in the Synoptic Gospels, while he makes several in John. The story of Jesus's birth in the Gospel of Matthew describes Mary and Joseph as living in Bethlehem, fleeing to Egypt, and then moving for the first time to Nazareth, while Luke has the two living *originally* in Nazareth, traveling to Bethlehem in time for the birth, and *then* returning home again. Mark and John have nothing of such traditions. In some Gospel passages Jesus offers his parables without explanation, despite the seeming inability of the disciples to understand. In others, he explains things to help them understand. ("The seed is the word of God."[21]) In one telling of the Beatitudes, Jesus says, "Blessed are you who are poor." In another, "Blessed are the poor in spirit."[22] More crucially, some of the Resurrection stories are substantially different. In some accounts, the Risen Christ appears as a material being; in others he can apparently walk through walls.

Sometimes these differences reflect the different intentions of the evangelists. Luke, for example, evinces a great deal of concern for the poor in his Gospel (and so may have chosen to write "you who are poor" rather than "the poor in spirit"). But at other times the reasons behind the differences in the Gospels are not as easy to understand.

So what did Jesus really do? What did he really say? Based on the four Gospels, most of the time we are able to tell. But, occasionally, it's difficult to determine with absolute precision.

The various presentations of the events in the New Testament, then, can sometimes be difficult to "harmonize," even for the devout Christian. So it's important to use one's faith *and* reason when reading Scripture, in order to understand the story, its context, and its meaning the best we can. The evangelists won't agree at all times because of the different resources at their disposal, the particular needs of their communities, and what they felt was most important. None of them, by the way, thought that talking about Jesus's childhood or young adulthood was important—as modern-day biographies their works would be poorly reviewed! But they weren't writing a biography or a history; they were writing a religious document to help people understand and believe in Jesus Christ.

BUT WHAT HAPPENS WHEN, even assuming the varying intentions of the writers, the Gospels are hard to *believe*? For me, that's not been an issue, but as we begin our pilgrimage into Jesus's life we need to look at belief and disbelief. And the story of the Annunciation is a good place to start. How did it happen? If you were there, what would you have seen?

Was the Annunciation at all like the various artistic interpretations? Was the angel a winged creature, as in a Botticelli painting, clad in a rose-colored gown, gently grasping a lily, and kneeling at the feet of Mary, whose whole body withdraws from the encounter?

Was it like the movies, as in Franco Zeffirelli's 1977 TV miniseries *Jesus of Nazareth,* where we see the angel appearing as a shaft of light, but we hear only the startled Mary's side of the conversation?

Was it like what we experience in our prayer? Once on retreat I prayed with this passage, and as the angel walked over the dry ground of Nazareth, I imagined grass growing in his footprints. He entered Mary's house, grasped her hand, and told her the news. Mary paused for a long while before answering the angel, thinking deliberately. Despite her fear, she was able to say yes, because she thought not only of the difficult things that might come her way, but also of the good. She trusted that God would be good to her and then joyfully rushed to her cousin Elizabeth to say, "I'm going to have a baby!"

The sources of this Gospel passage are difficult to pin down. For one thing, only Mary could have been the source of the story of her meeting with the angel. John Meier says this in *A Marginal Jew:* "While Mary might theoretically be the ultimate source for some traditions in the Infancy Narratives, grave problems beset the claim that she is the direct source of any narrative as it now stands. To begin with, Mary cannot be the source for all the infancy traditions in both Matthew and Luke; for, as we shall see, Matthew and Luke diverge from or even contradict each other on certain key points."[23]

In other words, if Mary were the source, why didn't Matthew include the story of her angelic encounter in his narrative of Jesus's birth? The Gospel of Matthew focuses instead on Joseph, who receives the news of Mary's birth in a dream.

Why this divergence? Matthew may have highlighted Joseph because of his desire to emphasize Jesus's connection to King David—which comes through Joseph. Another possibility for the divergence was suggested to me by the New Testament scholar Amy-Jill Levine, author of *The Misunderstood Jew,* a study of Jesus's Jewish roots: Matthew's Gospel tells us that Joseph's father is named Jacob. Matthew's Joseph is a dreamer of dreams, just like the earlier Joseph, the son of another Jacob, from the Book of Genesis. By focusing on Joseph, Matthew may have wanted to show Jesus's symbolic connections to the history of Israel.

Perhaps both accounts are accurate: Mary was visited by an angel, and Joseph learned of it in a dream.

Perhaps, then, Luke got the story of the Annunciation exactly right, having heard the story from Mary or from someone who heard it from her. After all, Mary was alive during her son's public ministry and presumably for some time after the early Christian community began. Why couldn't she have passed along the story?

Perhaps it happened differently, say, in a dream. Again, why not? Or perhaps the story of the angel was the only way that Mary could communicate an otherwise unexplainable encounter with the divine. Often people have to resort to metaphors to describe a dramatic encounter with God: "It was like a dream, but I was awake." "It seemed as if I heard God's voice, but not exactly." "It was like feeling the words, but they were as clear as anything I've ever heard." Mystical experiences are hard to verbalize.

Joseph Fitzmyer answers our question bluntly: "What really happened? We shall never know."[24] We do not have direct access to Mary's experience. And never will—except through what Luke tells us.

After meditating on this passage for many years, I have come to believe that either Mary met Gabriel precisely as the passage describes or she had a unique encounter with the divine that could be expressed only in terms of a heavenly messenger—an understanding based on the Jewish tradition of angels. Her experience, which she "treasured" and "pondered" in her heart, as Luke says later, was communicated to the disciples after the death and resurrection of her son, when it could be more fully appreciated.[25] The story was passed orally from person to person, but especially treasured by the community for which Luke wrote, and so he included it in his Gospel.

But is it possible to believe that this event could have happened just as Luke describes it?

Let me be clear: *yes.* God can do anything. If God can create the universe from nothing, then causing a young woman to become pregnant in a miraculous way seems a small thing. The modern mind may have a hard time believing in the miraculous, but such belief lies at the heart of the Gospels. Unless you want to follow Thomas Jefferson and scissor out whatever makes you uncomfortable or forces you out of the realm of what you consider possible, then you are invited to believe in changing water into wine, healing the sick, and raising the dead. A miraculous pregnancy is not beyond God.

Other stories in Jesus's life may seem easier to accept, and this may have been true for the early church as well. Why? Because, unlike with the Annunciation, there were witnesses, sometimes one or two people, sometimes dozens, to report what happened. And sometimes, as in the case of the Feeding of the Five Thousand, there were, well, *five thousand* to attest to what they had seen. That particular miracle is sufficiently astounding to be included in all four Gospels.[26]

Nothing described in the New Testament is beyond the power of God. Mary understood this. And so when the angel said, in whatever way he said it, "Nothing will be impossible with God," the young woman said yes.

NOW THAT WE HAVE a sense of what the Gospels are, how they were written, and how important it is to study them, you can see how reading them relates to faith. Yes, the Gospels were written by four different people in four different ways for four different audiences, but they all recount the same story: the life, death, and resurrection of Jesus. As modern believers and seekers, when we read a Gospel, we strive to understand its context, not poke holes in the narrative. We read a story not to pick it apart, but to encounter Jesus. In that way, we read in the light of reason and with the eyes of faith. And even those readers who are not Christian, or who are not seeking to dedicate their lives to Christ, might consider bracketing issues of possible contradiction and read the texts generously.

That brings us to the final part of the Annunciation. A few years ago I was discussing this passage with a friend, a Catholic sister named Janice. We were talking about how this narrative mirrors the life of the believer: God initiates the conversation; we fear; God re-assures us and tells us what will be required; we doubt; God points us to past experiences and helps us to trust; we say yes; and finally we are able to bring into the world, with God's grace, something new.

"You're forgetting the most important part," she said. "Then the angel left her!"

Janice was right. Then came for Mary the time of faith. Who knows if before the Resurrection she ever had an experience as transformative as the Annunciation? The Gospel of Luke tells us that Mary "pondered" all these things in her heart. It may have taken many years for things to become clear.

Profound spiritual experiences usually engender feelings of con-fidence and trust. But as time passes, you may begin to wonder if those events were real. Or you may never again have an experience as profound. When Mother Teresa's journals were published in 2007 as *Come Be My Light,* many readers were shocked to discover that after a series of mystical experiences early in her adult life, the rest of her days passed with little sense of God's presence in her prayer. Mother

Teresa spent the remainder of her life meditating on those earlier experiences, treasuring them in her heart.

Mary lived long enough to see her son perform wondrous deeds. She was present at the Wedding Feast at Cana, when Jesus turned water into wine, and she also would have been witness to him after the Resurrection. Yet in those intervening years, when Jesus was an infant, then a child and an adolescent, she may have asked the same questions that believers ask today: "Did that really happen? Was that really God? How can I believe?"

The Gospel of Luke tells us that, after the Annunciation, Mary rushed to spend time with Elizabeth, who was carrying John the Baptist in her womb. It's hard to imagine that Mary would not have discussed her experiences with Elizabeth, a trusted older woman, and with her husband, Zechariah, a devout man steeped in the Jewish Scriptures. Both would have listened carefully as Mary told her strange story, reflecting on Mary's experience in light of the Jewish traditions. But even with the support of the wise Elizabeth and her learned husband, Mary may still have questioned.

In time, on Easter Sunday, Mary received the ultimate answer. In time, so do we.

But first comes trust.

THE ANNUNCIATION
Luke 1:26–38

In the sixth month the angel Gabriel was sent by God to a town in Galilee called Nazareth, to a virgin engaged to a man whose name was Joseph, of the house of David. The virgin's name was Mary. And he came to her and said, "Greetings, favored one! The Lord is with you." But she was much perplexed by his words and pondered what sort of greeting this might be. The angel said to her, "Do not be afraid, Mary, for you have found favor with God. And now, you will conceive in your womb and bear a son, and you will name him Jesus. He will be great, and will be called the Son of the Most High, and the Lord God will give to him the throne of his ancestor David. He will reign over the house of Jacob forever, and of his kingdom there will be no end." Mary said to the angel, "How can this be, since I am a virgin?" The angel said to her, "The Holy Spirit will come upon you, and the power of the Most High will overshadow you; therefore the child to be born will be holy; he will be called Son of God. And now, your relative Elizabeth in her old age has also conceived a son; and this is the sixth month for her who was said to be barren. For nothing will be impossible with God." Then Mary said, "Here am I, the servant of the Lord; let it be with me according to your word." Then the angel departed from her.

CHAPTER 3

Bethlehem

"She gave birth to her firstborn son."

A FEW PEOPLE WARNED George and me away from Bethlehem. Its location in Palestinian territory was said to be dangerous. But once we reached the Pontifical Biblical Institute, the Jesuits told us not to worry. Besides, there was never any question about going. I didn't care if it might be dangerous: I had to see it. Who knew if I would ever return to the Holy Land?

The best route, said Father Doan, was to take the Number 21 "Arab bus" from the Damascus Gate, an impressive arch in the city walls flanked by two crenellated stone towers. In ancient times a highway led from this gate to the capital of Syria. So early one morning George and I walked a now familiar route into the Old City: exiting the main gate of the Pontifical Biblical Institute, passing through a *luxe* apartment complex, and padding down a set of broad limestone steps. In just a few minutes we reached the Jaffa Gate, the entrance nearest the Jesuit residence. A few minutes later we passed over the invisible border that delineates the Jewish section from the Arab section and found ourselves across from the Damascus Gate, surveying a phalanx of idling white buses.

We were the only non-Palestinians aboard the Number 21. The bus reminded me of the minivans that I frequented during my two-year stay in Nairobi, complete with raucous music, ancient shock absorbers, and chatty passengers. During our thirty-minute trip, we could easily see the Wall, the massive barrier separating the Palestinian territories from Israel. As we entered Bethlehem an Israeli soldier boarded and swiftly checked our passports. The ease with which we entered Bethlehem surprised me. Leaving would be a different story.

We told the bus driver that we would like to see Manger Square, where the Church of the Nativity is located, and he helpfully dropped us off at the nearest stop. When we alighted from the bus, we were instantly surrounded by gesticulating cabdrivers, like bees to flowers, each energetically offering to drive us into town. Doan had recommended this arrangement, so we accepted the offer of a friendly Palestinian man, short of stature, whom I will call Aziz.

Aziz was garrulous and helpful, but also slightly pushy—not surprising for someone supporting his family on a taxicab driver's income. Although George and I told Aziz that we most wanted to see the Church of the Nativity and Shepherds' Field (where an angel announced the birth of the Messiah), Aziz insisted that there were many other places nearby that were worth a visit. "Well worth it! Well worth it!" he said.

As anyone who has traveled abroad (or at home for that matter) will tell you, there is no little danger involved in entrusting yourself to an eager cabdriver. But George and I were in an adventurous mood.

"*First* we go to Shepherds' Field!" he said. Aziz's yellow cab raced through the narrow streets of Bethlehem and, in a few minutes, deposited us at the entrance of Shepherds' Field.

As should not have surprised us in the Holy Land, there are *two* Shepherds' Fields, one run by the Greek Orthodox Church, the other by the Franciscans. Correctly intuiting that we were not Orthodox, Aziz had driven us to the second locale. Shepherds' Field was not what I had imagined: that is, rolling green hills where friendly shepherds grazed their fluffy white sheep, who bleated cutely before a picturesque view of the Little Town of Bethlehem. That's what comes from seeing too many Christmas cards.

Today Shepherds' Field boasts an impressive garden with tall palm trees and flowering bushes. Down a hill, the tumbledown ruins of a small Byzantine-era church perch on a parched promontory overlooking the dusty plains surrounding Bethlehem. Amid the ruins are an altar and a few metal benches, which make up a simple chapel for pilgrims. There were no sheep. On this day, a few feet away, archaeological digs were covered with metal roofs.

Was this where shepherds "watched their flocks by night," as Christmas carolers would have it? In his guidebook, Murphy-O'Connor concludes that any historical significance of the location is "unlikely," though the church was built on a site occupied by nomadic shepherds in the first century.[1] As we stood on the windswept bluff overlooking the city, the sun raining down heat, I thought, *Well, you never know.*

In fact, Drew had told me that one of his happiest memories from his many visits to the Holy Land was watching, from the vantage point of Shepherds' Field, a shepherd lead a mixed flock of goats and sheep down the opposite hill, past an Israeli settlement then being built, and away into the Judean wilderness.

After a series of improbable detours that took us to the desert, to Herod's palace-fortress, to a lonely monastery, and to the edge of heat stroke, Aziz deposited us at Manger Square.

THE BEGINNING OF THE familiar Nativity narrative in Luke's Gospel, which recounts the story of the events commemorated in Bethlehem, locates the birth of Jesus in history, a chief concern of Luke. "In those days a decree went out from Emperor Augustus," he begins. So we are somewhere between 27 BC and AD 14. More specificity: Quirinius was governor of Syria, says Luke.[2]

The decree orders "all the world" to their own cities for a census. And because Joseph was "descended from the house and family of David," he travels to David's city, Bethlehem, with his wife. By this time Mary is pregnant. Luke does not say how long the couple stayed in Bethlehem, but while they were there she gave birth to her first-born (*prōtotokos*) son. The Greek word does not necessarily mean that Mary had other children, though the Gospels will later speak of Jesus's "brothers and sisters."[3] Luke is simply telling us that this was Mary's first child.

Did Luke the historian have all his facts straight? For the Gospel of Matthew tells a different story. In his version, Mary and Joseph were natives of Bethlehem, and so it was natural that Mary would give birth there. It wasn't until *after* Jesus's birth that they moved to Nazareth, after the death of the murderous King Herod, who, according to Matthew, sought to put to death every male child under the age of two in the area of Bethlehem, to eliminate the threat of the newborn Messiah.[4] Murphy-O'Connor notes this about Luke's version: "Their long residence in Galilee gave Luke the impression that they had always lived there, and he had to find a reason which would place them in Bethlehem at the moment of the birth of Jesus."[5] So we have two Gospel accounts, but the same place of birth: Bethlehem.

Luke tells us that Mary "laid him in a manger, because there was no place for them in the inn." The word *manger* comes from the French verb "to eat" and is simply the wooden stand that holds animal feed. The one who will feed the crowds in the Multiplication of the Loaves and Fishes, who will call himself the "Bread of Life,"[6] is born in a *manger*.

But there's a potentially more interesting word in this passage. The word used in most Christmas pageants—"inn"—is in the original Greek *kataluma,* which can also be translated as "guest room" or "lodging area."[7] So we might envision a room in a house or even an open space where travelers lodged. Thus, some scholars suggest this interpretation: since there was no room in the "guest room," the baby was placed in a manger in another part of a house, most likely the ground floor, where animals were typically kept. Perhaps, then, the familiar image of the manger in a wooden stable is inaccurate. Either way, as New Testament scholar Luke Timothy Johnson notes, "The transient condition of the parents is clear."[8] Raymond E. Brown, SS, emphasizes this in his massive book *The Birth of the Messiah,* perhaps the most extensive study on the topic. The Gospel image of the manger has less to do with poverty and more to do with the "peculiarity of location caused by circumstances."[9]

Another ancient tradition holds that Jesus was born in a cave, a detail that first appears in the second-century writings of St. Justin Martyr and in an apocryphal gospel, *The Protoevangelium of James.* Caves are still common in the area around Bethlehem, and many houses in antiquity were built around or above them; the rough spaces were used for stabling animals. Murphy-O'Connor suggests that we can imagine Joseph taking Mary into his house (or, say, his parents' house) away from the confusion of the main living space. Later on, St. Jerome, writing in 396, spoke of "the cave where the infant Messiah once cried," and the first church commemorating the birth of Jesus (the forerunner of the Church of the Nativity) was built over a cave.

THE PRESENT-DAY CHURCH OF the Nativity is a squat, buff-colored, fortress-like edifice built on the site of the fourth-century church mentioned by St. Jerome. Its byzantine history is summed up by the physical appearance of the church's main entrance, which clearly shows three stages of development—that is, the doorway was made progressively smaller and more difficult to enter, and the outlines of the larger, more ancient doors can easily be seen. Visitors can discern first, a large sixth-century opening (a wooden lintel is still embedded in the church wall); second, a smaller archway fashioned by the Crusaders; and finally, an even smaller entrance, from the Turkish and Ottoman periods, which was designed to prevent looters from entering the church with ease. Today the entrance to the great church is a three-foot-high doorway.

Thus, to enter the Church of the Nativity, one must bow or kneel. As a result, the paving stone has been worn smooth, with a marked indentation made by millions of pilgrims. Strangely, I found this entrance, called the Door of Humility, more moving than the church's interior. As I entered the building on my knees, I thought not only of how God had lowered himself to enter into our humanity, but also, more specifically, how Jesus had lowered himself so much that he assented to be crucified.

THE LONG, HIGH-CEILINGED INTERIOR was jammed with people. Far from the gleaming marble space that I anticipated, the Church of the Nativity, with its smooth stone floor and timbered roof supported by massive columns, appeared dilapidated. Its walls and woodwork were dusty, understandable for a building dating from the sixth century. But knowing that the structure dated back to the time of the emperor Justinian imbued the gritty setting with a meaning that transcended the grime. I couldn't wait to see the actual spot where Jesus was born. I anticipated being deeply moved. But where was it?

We made our way through the crowds and inched ahead in an ill-defined line with hundreds of tourists. Soon George got antsy, bothered by the crush. "I'll see it later," he said. I was already finding it a spiritual challenge to maintain a reverent attitude while being elbowed every few seconds by my fellow pilgrims. Gradually the throng carried me, like a twig in a river, to the main altar in the upper church. In a few minutes, the crush grew more intense as people spied our target: a narrow archway behind the main altar. Trying not to step on toes, I gingerly walked down a shallow stone staircase, squeezed my way through the arch, and was in the Nativity Grotto.

The Nativity Grotto was the only place where one of my original objections to visiting the Holy Land—the touristy sites would turn me off—proved justified. The crowd squished itself around two spots, with nearly everyone snapping photos or filming videos. The first, to the immediate right, was the traditional site of the birth of

Jesus. Behind a small arch were the remains of a cave. Under an altar that stands in the front of the cave is the holy site, marked by a large silver star affixed to the stone floor and illumined by several hanging lanterns. I knelt down to kiss the cold stone and said a prayer. A few feet away is the Chapel of the Manger, where by tradition Mary laid her baby. I kissed that spot as well and prayed for my family: my mother, my sister, my brother-in-law, and my two nephews.

Upon rising, I was immediately surrounded by pilgrims talking loudly, snapping photos, taking videos, gesticulating wildly, jostling one another, and reaching into crinkly plastic bags for a water bottle or candy bar. Over the years I've visited many other crowded religious sites—Lourdes, for one—but had never found it so difficult to pray. Why? Perhaps nowhere else did the visitors seem so blasé as they did at the Nativity sites. Maybe it was just this particular crowd on this particular day, but most people were strolling around and chatting as if it were Disneyland. I wanted to say, "Wait a minute! Remember where you are!" On the other hand, who knows what was going on inside of them? Fortunately, the rest of the Holy Land was infinitely more prayerful.

When I stepped back into the cavernous interior of the church I found myself confused. This ancient holy place, where Christian pilgrims had come to pray for millennia, where I had expected to be moved to tears, left me cold. I spied George sitting in a pew by himself. With his eye for the bizarre, he pointed out something hanging from the church's ornate chandeliers. Apparently in keeping with Western traditions they were hung with garish red Christmas ornaments. "Ho! Ho! Ho!" he said.

I laughed aloud, but couldn't stop thinking about this confusing place, at once holy and off-putting.

CONFUSION MAY HAVE BEEN what Mary and Joseph felt, though we are not told explicitly. Luke's Gospel is more intent on describing the physical surroundings of the Nativity: the crowded lodgings, the common manger, the bands of cloth in which the child was wrapped. He says nothing about the emotional state of either Mary or Joseph. Compare that to his vivid description of the shepherds in the field, to whom the angel announces Jesus's birth: "They were terrified." But perhaps Luke does not need to state the obvious. Whatever the circumstances of the birth (a trip into Bethlehem or living in Bethlehem already), confusion would have been natural for the couple.

Recently I read a series of meditations by Adrienne von Speyr, a twentieth-century Swiss mystic, in which she describes insights into the lives of the saints that came to her in prayer. Although she was obviously not in Bethlehem at the time, and although the Catholic Church is notoriously reluctant to pronounce on "private revelations" (experiences in private prayer), what von Speyr wrote about St. Joseph seemed sensible: "Joseph, the righteous man, is involved in something that at first frightens him; he does not understand it. But then grace brings him a certain understanding, even if it remains incomplete."[10]

We haven't talked much about Joseph yet. But that's not unusual when it comes to the Nativity story. In many Christmas scenes (whether classical paintings or cheap Christmas cards) Mary's husband is sometimes shunted off to the side or stuck in the back of the scene, behind a shepherd. Joseph is often portrayed as a wizened old man, balding and stooped, looking more like Mary's father than her husband.

Why this relative lack of attention to Joseph, especially since he can be a powerful figure not only for fathers, but also for all Christians?

Joseph has presented a delicate problem for the Catholic Church over the past two millennia. The miracle of the Incarnation was not only that God became human, but also that this was accomplished through a virgin. Naturally, Mary is one of the stars of the Nativity story, at least in Luke's Gospel. But the emphasis on Mary's virginity may have made her marriage to Joseph an uncomfortable reality—

after all, if they were married, didn't that mean that they had sex? That flew in the face of an early tradition in the church—Mary's perpetual virginity. So Joseph ended up in the background.

Some scholars have posited this as one reason that Joseph is portrayed as elderly in so many paintings, even though some experts estimate he was around thirty years old at the time of Jesus's birth. Lawrence Cunningham, a professor of theology at Notre Dame and author of *A Brief History of Saints,* told me in a conversation, "Nine times out of ten in Christian art, Joseph takes on more of father-protector role rather than a husband. That was a way of solving the sexuality problem." Cunningham noted that in some paintings, Joseph is shown dozing off in the corner of the stable or even leaving the scene of the Nativity entirely, "out of modesty."

We can't blame Western artists for giving Joseph short shrift. They didn't have much to go on. Joseph is given no lines to speak in any of the Gospels and is not mentioned by name anywhere in Mark's Gospel. Significantly, he is absent during Jesus's public ministry and even at the Crucifixion, where, by contrast, Mary is featured prominently. This has led many scholars to conclude that he died before the end of Jesus's earthly life. In the Church of St. Joseph in Nazareth is a moving stained-glass window entitled *The Death of Joseph,* a rare scene in Christian art. The dying man lies in a bed, his right hand held tenderly by Jesus, his left by Mary.

So what do we know about Joseph? Apart from his trade—he's called a *tektōn* in the Gospels, which is usually translated as "carpenter" but is more likely a general craftsman—not much. But Pheme Perkins, a professor of New Testament at Boston College, told me that we can draw some interesting conclusions if we read the Gospels carefully.

"The most obvious assumption in antiquity would have been that Joseph had been married before and was a widower," Perkins told me. "Most likely, an arrangement was made for him to find a young wife." This is the basis for the Catholic tradition that Jesus's "brothers and sisters," mentioned in the Gospels, were from Joseph's first marriage. (Mainline Protestant churches are generally more comfortable with the possibility that Mary could have given birth to other children after Jesus.)

Given that Mary seems not to have been forced for economic reasons to remarry after her husband's death, "Joseph must have been a good provider," Perkins said. She is not certain that his portrayal as an elderly man in so many works of Christian art necessarily had to do with issues surrounding sexuality. "We usually make revered figures older," she said. "If you look at most of the paintings of St. Peter and St. Paul, they look older, no matter what stage of life they're in."

Though most of Joseph's life goes unmentioned in the Gospels, he carried out an exceedingly important task: helping to raise the Son of God. During the first years of Jesus's life, and perhaps into his young adulthood, he would have learned much of what he knew about the Jewish faith—its beliefs and practices, its history and ethics—from his mother *and* his foster father. Perhaps the skills Jesus learned alongside Joseph in the carpentry shop—patience, hard work, creativity—were put to use in his later ministry. In this way Joseph represents the holiness of the hidden life, doing meaningful things without a great deal of fanfare.

Joseph's actions during the Nativity story offer a powerful model for Christians. The Gospel of Matthew describes him as a "righteous man" who does what God asks of him after his initial confusion. After discovering Mary's pregnancy, Joseph thinks of "quietly" ending their marriage plans, so as not to disgrace her. But the Gospel of Matthew tells readers that an angel reassures the clearly confused Joseph in a dream: "Do not be afraid to take Mary as your wife," says the angel, who then explains the unusual circumstances of the birth. "The child conceived in her is from the Holy Spirit."[11]

In both the Old and New Testaments, dreams are privileged ways in which God communicates with people. In the Book of Genesis, Jacob dreams of a ladder reaching up to heaven, with angels ascending and descending.[12] Jacob's son and Joseph's namesake, the Joseph of Genesis, receives messages in dreams about his future and later, as a servant in Pharaoh's court, becomes an interpreter of dreams.[13] In my experience as a spiritual director, I have noticed how dreams are sometimes means through which God can communicate difficult truths, which the conscious mind might not be ready or able to grasp. And in my own life, I've had several revelatory dreams that, though they didn't predict the future or tell me that my wife was going to miraculously conceive a child, seemed indeed gifts from God.

Joseph faced an agonizing decision. But with God's grace he moved from confusion to a process of discernment and finally to acceptance. In this way he mirrors Mary more than we might initially suspect. While the sequence is different for Mary and Joseph, both face confusion, both have vivid experiences of God, both are confronted with a never-before-made decision, both assent to God's will, and both then prepare themselves for a life that will be, needless to say, confusing.

Matthew, by the way, may also have been more intent on describing Joseph's role because of the evangelist's desire to present Jesus as the fulfillment of the Old Testament. His Gospel begins with a lengthy genealogy starting with Abraham, continues through David, and ends up with Joseph. In this way Joseph is a symbol of both continuity (the continuation of the royal line of David and the placement of Jesus in the long line of Jewish prophets) and discontinuity (the unique way that Jesus's birth will come about and the utter newness of his ministry).

During the latter part of the Christmas story, the Holy Family leaves their homeland. Again in a dream, Joseph is told to flee from Bethlehem to Egypt to escape the rage of Herod, who will order the slaughter of all male children under two years of age. "Now after they [the wise men] had left, an angel of the Lord appeared to Joseph in a dream and said, 'Get up, take the child and his mother, and flee to Egypt, and remain there until I tell you; for Herod is about to search for the child, to destroy him.'"

Throughout the entire story, the personality of Mary's husband shines through, wordlessly. "Here is a model of someone who represents all the virtues in the Hebrew Bible," Perkins told me. "He is asked to do something shocking, but because he's righteous, he follows God's guidance."

Joseph was responsible for protecting Mary and her son in extreme conditions. Perkins calls him a "model for how people can follow God through difficult times."

HOW DID JOSEPH DEAL with these difficult times? By pushing on in the midst of confusion. Matthew describes God communicating with Joseph through two dreams, first to explain Mary's pregnancy and then to direct him to Egypt. "But," as von Speyr intuits, "he will never fully comprehend what happened with Mary the Virgin."[14]

This makes sense. Even in the light of direct revelation from God, Mary and Joseph could be forgiven for feeling confused. What soon-to-be mother and soon-to-be father do not feel confusion? And if normal parents feel addled, how much more confused must have been Mary and Joseph, parents of the most unusual child in history? I imagine them trudging to Bethlehem, loving and supportive of one another, trusting and hopeful in God, but worried. Did they keep their feelings to themselves, or did they share them? Perhaps they said to one another, trying to understand things: "Tell me, Mary, more about your experience with the angel." Or "Tell me again about your dream, Joseph."

So they were probably wondering, confused, and possibly frightened. Frightened of not finding lodgings in time, of the physical complications in an era when women often died in childbirth, and of their ability to care for the child whom they knew would be different.

Those emotions may have continued after the child's birth. One of the most common emotions that new parents have often shared with me is fear. How will I know what to do? How will I provide for my child? What happens if he or she gets sick? When my first nephew was born I remember being seized with a welter of emotions. Joy first of all. But also—and this surprised me—fear. Would he remain healthy? Would an accident befall him? Would he live?

Last year, while visiting my mother in her retirement community, I was asked to take my seven-year-old nephew to the indoor pool. Matthew loves to swim; on the way to the pool, he raced past an elderly woman, almost knocking her over, and shouted, "I'm going to the *pool!*" But every time he leapt joyfully into the water I worried: Would he get hurt? And when he shouted, "Uncle Jim, watch this!" and flipped backward from the pool's slippery edge, I thought: *Don't hit your head!* Fear. And this was only an hour in a pool.

The next week, I asked a father of three children if he ever felt the same. "Yes," said my friend. "I love being a father, but I'm afraid almost all the time."

Had Mary and Joseph known precisely what their son's future would hold, they might have been even more afraid. I've always wondered if Mary or Joseph had much intimation of Jesus's future. After all, they knew that this child was destined for something special, even if they did not fully understand. Did they fear the entrance of this holy boy into a sinful world? Were they consumed with worry about their son's future?[15] Did they cast their minds back over what had happened to prophets in the past? If so, this did not prevent them from carrying out what God had asked them to do.

Fear is often identified as a stumbling block in the spiritual life—in Jesus's time as well as ours. "Do not be afraid!" Jesus says, more than once. In fact, "Do not be afraid" may be what Jesus most often tells us not to do. The angels say the same to the shepherds in the field. But *confusion* seems less worthy of attention, although we feel it just as frequently. "Don't worry about being confused!" would be an equally consoling message from God. We can take as our models Mary and Joseph, who had the right to be the two most confused people in history, who were confronted with something utterly baffling, but did what God was asking of them anyway.

Mary and Joseph do three simple but essential things: they listen, they trust, they love.

IRONICALLY, THE BIRTH OF Jesus was meant to *lessen* confusion for the rest of the world.

"God meets us where we are." That's what my first spiritual director told me frequently. In other words, God comes to us in ways that we can understand and appreciate, even if only partially or incompletely. For someone who delights in relationships, experiences of God might come through a conversation with a close friend. For a parent, through the smile on the face of an infant. For an active person, in working among the poor in a homeless shelter. For an introspective person, by meditating on Scripture. God meets us where we are.

God could have come to the world in any way that God desired. We may be so conditioned to the story of the birth of Jesus in humble circumstances that we forget that this was a choice. God could have come to us as a powerful ruler, born into a family of wealth and privilege. To push the theological envelope further, God could have come as a disembodied voice speaking from the heavens.

But God wanted to meet us where we are. So God came, first of all, as a human being, as something—someone—other men and women could approach. God is not only a flaming bush, a pillar of fire, or even a mysterious cloud, as God is described in various places in the Old Testament. God is one of us.

Second, God came in the least threatening of human states: a baby. God entered our world screaming and crying, dependent on someone to change him, feed him, nurse him, and care for his bodily needs. God came helplessly into the world to help us.

Finally, Jesus came from an unremarkable background. The Son of God was nothing special by outward appearance or by human standards. One might be awed by a great ruler or a learned scholar, but not by a simple craftsman. When Jesus began preaching, people in his hometown said, "Is not this the carpenter?"[16] In other words, "Who, *him*?"

God comes to the world as a human being, at the risk of confusing Mary and Joseph, so that the rest of us will not be confused. Confused about God? Look at Jesus. See what he does. Listen to his words.

How can we respond to the entrance of God into our lives? In much the same way that Mary and Joseph did, and as parents do today: by protecting and nurturing something unique. Faith needs to be nurtured. This does not mean that we need to shelter our faith from the world, by closing ourselves off from the concerns of modern life. Rather, as Mary and Joseph did for Jesus, we are invited to respond to the gift with reverent care. We are called to nourish our faith (with prayer, worship, reading, service, and spiritual conversations) in the same way Mary and Joseph were called to nourish the Infant Christ.

ON THE WAY BACK from the Church of the Nativity, Aziz announced that he would drive George and me to the Milk Grotto, a small cave-cum-chapel where Mary is supposed to have nursed Jesus during the Holy Family's escape into Egypt.

It's odd stumbling upon a popular pilgrimage site that you've never heard of. You feel that you should know much more about it than you do, which in this case for me was nothing. At first I suspected that the chapel was merely a medieval invention, but a brochure in the church, officially Magharet Sitti Mariam, the Grotto of the Virgin Mary, noted that the pilgrims have been coming here since the fourth century. Over the cave itself is a modest church with an ornate façade, also fashioned from white stone, which was constructed by the Franciscans in the nineteenth century.

Pious legend has it that a drop of Mary's milk fell to the ground, turning the cave the milky white color that persists today. It remains a popular destination for women hoping to give birth; hopeful women scrape some limestone powder off the wall and even, said one pamphlet, mix the powder with water and drink it.

The grotto was empty and cool. After the crowds at the Church of the Nativity, I was grateful for the quiet. George sat down on a small stone bench and closed his eyes; I sat down on another bench, rested, and prayed. Silence was elusive in the famous Church of the Nativity; ironically, in this church that I had never heard of, boasting a legend that I found extremely unlikely, I felt nearer to God. I thought not only of Mary and Joseph's confusion but also their fatigue. I wanted to stay there all day.

But there was still one more stop on our agenda, or at least one person's agenda. "You must visit my friend!" said our cabdriver. Aziz had talked all day about a friend who ran a curio shop. He threaded his car through Bethlehem's narrow streets and squeezed into a tiny parking space. He vaulted out of the driver's seat, walked down the street, pounded on a metal door, and waited a few moments until a balding man in a long white robe came out and shook his hand. "You are *welcome!*" Aziz said to us.

Having spent two years in Kenya helping to run a refugee-made handicrafts shop, I could see that Aziz's friend was offering us some high-quality wares. And given the poverty of many Palestinian families, I figured that this would be a good place to purchase some of the most popular of Holy Land souvenirs: olive-wood carvings. For all we knew, Aziz received a small kickback for any visitors he brought to the isolated shop. But we didn't care. Why not patronize a struggling merchant and a hardworking cabdriver?

As I was deciding on what to select, George motioned me over to a shelf of merchandise. He held up an unusual Nativity scene. Placed between the Holy Family and the Wise Men was a barrier, a thin block of wood. The owner explained, "That is the wall that blocks off the Palestinian territories. Jesus was a Palestinian, just like us."

After George and I loaded up on olive-wood sculptures, Aziz drove us to the Bethlehem checkpoint, run by the Israeli border police. The checkpoint consists of a series of high stone walls, metal barricades, and turnstiles, each one patrolled by a guard. The guards thoroughly searched both men and women, and even small children, vigorously patting them down before permitting them to leave. Palestinians working in Jerusalem must pass through this checkpoint every day. A relative calm prevailed the day of our visit, but I knew that many days were not calm, for while most Israelis argue that the barrier is a necessary security precaution, the Palestinians see it as a humiliation, a despoliation.

We crossed the parking lot, where the bus to Jerusalem awaited. "It's easier to get into San Quentin than out of Bethlehem," said George, the Catholic chaplain at the prison.

During the ride back to Jerusalem on the Number 21 bus, I thought about exits and entrances. The image of the Door of Humility stuck with me, as did the legend on a small sign near the entrance to the Church of the Nativity:

> We are hoping that: If you enter here as a tourist,
> you would exit as a pilgrim.
> If you enter here as a pilgrim,
> you would exit as a holier one.

As I mentioned, you have to kneel to pass through the Door of Humility. That action is a striking image of the life of belief. For humility is the gateway to faith. Without it, we rely simply on our own efforts, without recognizing our dependence on God. Without it, we rely simply on our own reason, without opening ourselves up to the possibility of the miraculous. Without it, we cannot fully enter into the world that God has in store for us.

Paradoxically, our model in this is God, who humbled himself by becoming one of us, who entered our world by passing through the body of a young woman who was probably writhing on the floor of a stable, a cave, or a little room. In a way, Mary was a Door of Humility as well.

Humility is the key to almost everything in the spiritual life. And I hope that one day I might be a holier, in other words, humbler, pilgrim.

George and I made it home just in time for Mass.

THE BIRTH OF JESUS
Luke 2:1–20
(See also Matthew 1:18–25)

In those days a decree went out from Emperor Augustus that all the world should be registered. This was the first registration and was taken while Quirinius was governor of Syria. All went to their own towns to be registered. Joseph also went from the town of Nazareth in Galilee to Judea, to the city of David called Bethlehem, because he was descended from the house and family of David. He went to be registered with Mary, to whom he was engaged and who was expecting a child. While they were there, the time came for her to deliver her child. And she gave birth to her firstborn son and wrapped him in bands of cloth, and laid him in a manger, because there was no place for them in the inn.

In that region there were shepherds living in the fields, keeping watch over their flock by night. Then an angel of the Lord stood before them, and the glory of the Lord shone around them, and they were terrified. But the angel said to them, "Do not be afraid; for see—I am bringing you good news of great joy for all the people: to you is born this day in the city of David a Savior, who is the Messiah, the Lord. This will be a sign for you: you will find a child wrapped in bands of cloth and lying in a manger." And suddenly there was with the angel a multitude of the heavenly host, praising God and saying, "Glory to God in the highest heaven, and on earth peace among those whom he favors!"

When the angels had left them and gone into heaven, the shepherds said to one another, "Let us go now to Bethlehem and see this thing that has taken place, which the Lord has made known to us." So they went with haste and found Mary and Joseph, and the child lying in the manger. When they saw this, they made known what had been told them about this child; and all who heard it were amazed at what the shepherds told them. But Mary treasured all these words and pondered them in her heart. The shepherds returned, glorifying and praising God for all they had heard and seen, as it had been told them.

CHAPTER 4

Nazareth

"Jesus increased in wisdom and in years."

ON THE DAY WE visited Nazareth, Sunday Mass was about to begin in the Basilica of the Annunciation. George and I found some empty spots in the hard wooden pews just as the procession started, and we tried to comprehend an unfamiliar language. But although I speak only a few words of Arabic, it proved easy to follow the familiar parts of the Mass. The sounds and cadences, I realized, were also closer to Jesus's original language—Aramaic—than English. I closed my eyes and wondered what Jesus's actual voice sounded like.

Afterward, we visited the Church of St. Joseph, a modest structure built in 1914 atop the remains of a medieval church. That earlier church was itself located on top of what tradition claims to be the carpentry workshop of Joseph. Tradition may claim it, but most scholars do not. In *The Holy Land* Murphy-O'Connor bluntly calls it a "pious tradition that has no foundation."[1] So much for that. On the other hand, Murphy-O'Connor notes that remnants of a first-century village have been excavated at the site, and evidence of silos, olive presses, and areas for storage are visible.

The pious tradition of the location of the workshop may have no foundation, but Jesus's youth, adolescence, and young adulthood in this town do. He was known during his public ministry as "Jesus of Nazareth," and he spent most of his life here.

Yet oddly, between his birth and his entrance into public ministry there is only one incident from his life mentioned in the entire New Testament. When Jesus was twelve years old, his family went on a pilgrimage to Jerusalem for Passover. On the way back, as Luke tells us, Mary and Joseph realized that the boy was not with their traveling party. This is not as callous as it may seem. It was natural in a group of pilgrims that included extended families for a parent to assume that the child was with another relative. Frantic ("in great anxiety," says Luke), Mary and Joseph rushed back to Jerusalem where they found the twelve-year-old in the Temple, calmly speaking with the Jewish teachers there. "Why were you searching for me?" says the precocious boy. "Did you not know that I must be in my Father's house?"[2]

With that vignette Luke offers us a glimpse not only of Jesus's intelligence, but also of his natural affinity for the religious world. His attraction to the Temple may be similar to a young student gravitating to a particular musical instrument or a certain sport. "Of course I would be here," he seems to say to his parents—and to us. "Where else would I be? I love it here."

From that point until his baptism at age thirty the Gospels offer a single sentence to describe his life. After Jesus is found in the Temple Luke writes: "And Jesus increased in wisdom and in years, and in divine and human favor." What a sentence! One verse encompasses eighteen years. The time between Jesus's being lost in the Temple and his baptism by John at the Jordan River is cloaked in mystery and is often referred to as the "Hidden Life."

That elision can be frustrating for believers who want to know as much as they can about Jesus. His birth is afforded more Gospel lines than his childhood, adolescence, and young adulthood combined. But again, the Gospels were not written as historical documents (that is, as we understand biographies today), but as faith documents. Consequently they are not concerned as much with Jesus's youth as with his public ministry. So that part of his life remains almost totally obscure.[3]

Nonetheless, running through the history of Christian spirituality is a strong current of devotion to the Hidden Life. And in Catholic circles, the person most closely associated with the Hidden Life is also, not surprisingly, associated with Nazareth. Charles de Foucauld, a nineteenth-century French aristocrat and soldier who abandoned a life of privilege for an austere existence in the North African desert, may be fairly called the Apostle of the Hidden Life.

Born in 1858 to a noble family, the Viscount Foucauld squandered an immense fortune and entered the French military in 1881. After being posted to Algeria, Charles was dismissed for "indiscipline and notorious conduct," in this case taking a prostitute with him and passing her off as his wife. When his regiment was posted in Tunisia, he rejoined them. The viscount's time in the military would be short-lived, but his sojourn in North Africa awakened a lifelong interest in the region. After permanently resigning from the army, he undertook an exploration of Morocco under the auspices of the French Geographical Society.

The piety of the local Muslims sparked in Charles a new interest in his Catholic faith, which led to a pilgrimage to the Holy Land. There he became fascinated with the spirituality of Jesus's Hidden Life. It dawned on him that the "life of Nazareth," the ordinary existence that Jesus led before his public ministry, could be followed by every person as a path to holiness. So Foucauld gave away all his possessions and entered a Trappist monastery in Syria; he later moved to Nazareth to work as a gardener at a monastery of Poor Clares, a women's religious order. But this still did not satisfy him, so he returned to North Africa, where he lived among the Tuareg people in Morocco. There Charles hoped to found his own religious order, whose members would embody the spirituality of the Hidden Life. Though greatly respected by the locals, he was killed by Tuareg rebels in a botched looting in 1916.

Seemingly Charles "failed" in his life, but after his death several religious orders, including the Little Brothers of Jesus and the Little Sisters of Jesus, were founded on his inspiration. During my time working in Kenya, I came to know a community of Little Sisters who lived down the street from the Jesuit community in Nairobi. Their lives consisted, as Charles would have hoped, in doing "ordinary" work—as maids and factory hands, farmers and cleaning women— and spreading the Gospel in everyday circumstances.

During our visit to Nazareth I was delighted to spy on our map a tiny rectangle marked "Charles de Foncauld Monastery." Was this (misspelling and all) the convent where he had worked as a gardener? It was only a few blocks from the Basilica of the Annunciation, so after peering at the ruins of Nazareth, George and I set out to find it. After losing our way several times, I stopped at a souvenir shop and asked the owner, who spoke French, if she could direct us to the Charles de Foucauld monastery.

"Mais oui, le grand philosophe!" she said. The great philosopher, Michel Foucault. Evidently shopkeepers are well-read in Nazareth.

When I said, *"Non, non. Charles,"* she shook her head.

"Le monastère?" I asked hopefully.

"Ah," she said, and motioned vaguely down the street.

A formidable stone wall running the length of the block surrounded what appeared to be a monastery. I wasn't sure if this was the Poor Clare monastery where Charles had lived or a men's religious order that had named their monastery after Charles. There was no sign, but we rang the rusty doorbell beside a stout wooden door set deep into the stone wall. No answer. We went around the corner, walked down a hill, and rang the bell at a high metal gate.

"This is a school," said the caretaker who opened the gate only a crack. "The monastery is up there."⁴

We returned to the original entrance, knocked again, and waited again. *"Tant pis!"* George said. Too bad. But I wanted desperately to gain access.

Many of us wish that we could gain access to the story of Jesus's years in Nazareth. But like those monastery walls, the New Testament keeps that part of Jesus's life hidden from view.

I am fascinated by the Hidden Life. On the one hand, it is marvelously mysterious: we know very little about what Jesus did during the years in Nazareth. At the same time, it's not an insurmountable mystery. We have plenty of solid biblical, archaeological, and historical studies that can tell us a good deal about life in first-century Nazareth. And recently there has been a veritable explosion of findings about ancient Galilee. As a result, there is a surfeit of books about the level of influence of Roman and Greek culture on Galilee, the sociological and economic situation at the time, first-century Jewish religious practices, what the archaeological finds say about family life in the region, and, more broadly, daily life in Jesus's time.

But there's another reason I'm drawn to the Hidden Life, and it's similar to what attracted Charles de Foucauld: In Nazareth Jesus's life was most like our own. None of us is going to be preaching and performing miracles—at least not as Jesus did—but all of us live everyday lives, as Jesus did in Nazareth, being taught and cared for by our parents, loving and squabbling with our families, playing with our friends, learning what it means to be an adult, and in time earning a living. Was Jesus any less the Son of God when he was doing ordinary things? No.

But what *was* Jesus's life like during his thirty years in Nazareth?

THERE ARE A NUMBER of superb scholarly studies on life in ancient Galilee and, more specifically, first-century Nazareth, then a tiny town in southern Galilee. Drawn from archaeological research and a variety of historical sources, together they paint a picture of a largely agrarian society, populated mainly by the lower classes and the poor, in the midst of an abundantly fertile region. Even during our pilgrimage to Galilee in the blazing heat of late August, the area was dotted with gnarled olive trees, tall date palms, and all manner of crops. During the wetter months, the landscape bursts into colorful bloom—or so we were told! The Jewish historian Josephus, writing a few decades after the time of Jesus, described one strip along the Sea of Galilee's northwest shore as the most productive parcel of land in all of Israel.[5]

Despite the fertile land, though, the region of Galilee on the whole remained, as archaeologist and New Testament scholar Jonathan L. Reed describes, "on the fringe of the Roman Empire, both geographically and politically."[6] Roman roads avoided it until the second century. So it was something of a backwater. As for Nazareth, most scholars estimate that anywhere from two to four hundred people lived there in Jesus's day.[7] Thus, Nazarenes lived in a backwater of a backwater.

Today the ruins of the houses in Nazareth are scant, but the archaeological evidence has revealed small dwellings built with local stones (basalt or limestone) that were stacked roughly atop one another. The floors were of packed earth and the roofs thatched, constructed over beams of wood and held together with mud. Two or three homes were clustered together around an open courtyard, where much of the cooking would have been done. Also in the courtyard might be a common cistern and a millstone for grinding grain. Animals might have been penned here as well. When I worked in Jamaica as a Jesuit novice, I saw similar arrangements: in the poorer parts of Kingston, families lived in small houses clustered together around a "yard" where common activities were performed.

In Nazareth, the small rooms that were closed off were used for shelter, sleep, sex, and, as the theologian Elizabeth A. Johnson, CSJ, notes in her book on Mary, "giving birth and dying."[8] Evidence from the rooms points to little privacy for the inhabitants, but a great sense of community. Needless to say, in such a tight-knit community Jesus would have been very well known—his friends, his habits, his ways of speech, his likes and dislikes. This insight will become important later on and explains the expressions of shock from the people who knew him: "Is not this the carpenter's son? Is not his mother called Mary? And are not his brothers James and Joseph and Simon and Judas? And are not all his sisters with us?" say the crowds in Matthew's Gospel.[9]

What kind of food was prepared in the open-air courtyards? The diet in Nazareth at that time would have been mainly grains, vegetables, and some fruits, along with olives and olive oil from the plenteous trees in the area, with the occasional drink of milk or cut of meat if the family had access to animals. Salted fish was an occasional luxury. A stew of lentils and a few seasonal vegetables might be ladled onto some pita bread for a meal, along with some welcome fruits and cheese or yogurt.[10] A decent but not always reliable water source was situated at the edge of the village, at a place now called the Well of Mary.

Garbage and sewage would often have been tossed outside the house into alleyways between the small couplings of homes, much as it is today in parts of the developing world. During my time working with the Jesuit Refugee Service in Nairobi, I saw how those living in the city's slums were forced to live without water and toilets. They likewise had no choice but to deposit their garbage and sewage in small canals that ran through the slums. These foul streams and rivulets, which had to be stepped over every few feet, overflowed during the rainy seasons and stank all times of the year. It is one of the most pitiable aspects of life for those who are desperately poor.

Clothing in the Nazareth of Jesus's time would have been simple. Most men would have worn a loincloth, a tunic, and a cloak made of either linen or, most likely, wool, probably colored in some way. Women would have worn similarly simple clothing. All of the material for clothing would have been spun, woven, and sewn by the women of the town, with the wool taken from the flocks of sheep that grazed on the nearby hills.[11]

In her aptly named book *Stone and Dung, Oil and Spit,* a fascinating study of the details of Jewish daily life in Galilee and Judea in the time of Jesus, Jodi Magness, an archaeologist and professor of early Judaism, reminds us that Westerners tend to view the ancient world through a "highly sanitized lens." In even the most sophisticated cities conditions were "filthy, malodorous and unhealthy" by contemporary standards. "If we could be transported back in time," writes Magness, "it is unlikely that most of us would survive exposure to the widespread dirt and diseases, to which we lack immunity."[12]

As a result, the quality of the health of the inhabitants of Nazareth was far below modern standards. John Dominic Crossan and Jonathan L. Reed, scholars of the historical Jesus, sum up the conditions in the town during Jesus's time in a sobering few sentences:

> Most skeletal remains predictably show iron and protein deficiencies, and most had severe arthritis. A case of the flu, a bad cold, or an abscessed tooth could kill. Life expectancy, for the luckier half that survived childhood, was somewhere in the thirties. Those reaching fifty or sixty were rare.[13]

Many of the few hundred inhabitants of Nazareth, most belonging to extended families, depended upon farming to feed themselves and pay taxes, using the method of "polycropping," or diversifying plantings to avoid becoming overly dependent on a single crop. The area was perfectly suited for the Mediterranean dietary triad of grain, olive, and grape. Larger families helped with the work on the farm, but it was not a secure living; one drought or paltry harvest could mean famine. Elizabeth Johnson summarizes the ways to earn a living: laborers were "peasants who worked their own land, tenant farmers who worked land belonging to others, and craftspersons who served their needs."[14] In that last category of craftspersons, we can include Joseph and Jesus.

The primary role of adult, married women was to care for the home and tend to children; they also worked in the fields when needed. Younger sons from large families or those born out of wed-lock might attempt to find work as a soldier or even turn to banditry. (Perhaps Jesus was drawing from stories of families in Nazareth when he spoke of prodigal sons.) Women living without the protec-tion of a father, husband, or son might work independently in baking or textiles, hire themselves out as servants, or in more desperate cases turn to prostitution.[15] Life was hard, and people lived peril-ously close to the edge, economically and socially.

People did not travel afar much, since it was both dangerous and expensive. When they did—for example, for the pilgrimage to Jerusalem—they did so in larger groups so as to ward off bandits. Life was, as Crossan and Reed say, "predominantly local."[16]

Adding to the burdens of this life was the class system under which the vast majority of the populace labored. Much of what the land produced, and the income earned, went to support the ruling elite—in this case both Herodian and Roman authorities—through a system of taxation. There were triple taxes: first, the tithe, or 10 percent, that went to the Temple in Jerusalem; second, tribute to the Roman emperor; and third, payment to the local Jewish king, in this case Herod. Thus, because of the vagaries of weather and crop yields, poor health, and these triple taxes, families were liable to fall into debt and financial ruin.

The populace was overlaid with a complicated hierarchy made up of not only rulers but a governing class that consisted of members of the court, as well as merchants and some priests. And although the two "top classes" (the rulers and the governing class) comprised only 1 percent of the population, they took in not less than half of the income of the region.[17] Just below the top classes were the merchants and priestly classes. At the very bottom were the outcasts.

Just above the unclean were the peasants, who worked the land, and the artisans. Interestingly, the artisan class, because they did not have the benefit of a stable plot of land, likely ranked somewhere below the peasantry. Jesus's family was in the artisan class and likely near the bottom rung of the economic ladder. He would have known what it meant to be poor, and to dwell among those eking out a living in arduous circumstances, at the whim of the weather, illness, and one's overlords.[18] He would have also known what it meant to live in a world of interconnected relationships, where the artisan would have helped out the farmer, the older woman her pregnant neighbor, and the one with extra food the family whose crops had failed. "All archaeological evidence from the Roman period," say Crossan and Reed by way of summing up, "points to a simple peasant existence in Nazareth."[19]

What about the religious practices in this area? Even though the Gospels refer to "Galilee of the Gentiles" (that is, a land of non-Jews) and there were tensions between the high priests in Jerusalem and local Galilean priests, archaeologists are reasonably certain that Galilee was firmly Jewish.[20] "Archaeological excavations in and around Galilee show that the Galileans were Jewish, not a mixed blend of Jews and Gentiles," writes Reed. "Galilee was overwhelmingly Jewish at the time of Jesus."[21]

Though part of the Roman colony of Palestine, the Jews of the area were distinguished from their Gentile neighbors by laws directly governing their day-to-day lives. This meant proper observance of the Jewish laws ordering practices such as the purification rituals for the body and hands, religious fasting and dining observances (including which foods were considered impure), keeping the Sabbath, clothing and burial customs, and avoiding people considered "unclean."[22] All of these observances provided a way to worship God not only with the spirit, but also with the body. Jesus would have been raised in such a system of laws and customs and would have been instructed on what and whom to avoid. He would later challenge some of these customs, to the horror of some of his fellow Jews.

Overall, Jesus lived the first thirty years of his life in a marginal Jewish hamlet. Significantly, Nazareth is not mentioned anywhere in the Old Testament. Nor is it mentioned in the Talmud, which lists sixty-three other villages in Galilee, or in the writings of Josephus, who names forty-five other Galilean villages. "Can anything good come out of Nazareth?" asks Nathanael.[23] In that Gospel passage Nazareth is, quite literally, a joke.

And yet, just four miles from Nazareth was Sepphoris, a bustling city of thirty thousand, which was being rebuilt at the time by Herod Antipas. The city's extensive ruins show an amphitheater seating three to four thousand people, courts, a fortress, a royal bank, and houses with frescoes and gorgeous mosaic floors; it was a cosmopolitan place where Greek would have been spoken.[24] Jesus's hometown, by contrast, was a place of subsistence only, very unlike other larger towns with a greater Roman and Greek influence. The modest remains of Nazareth today stand in stark contrast to clear residues of affluence in Sepphoris. One archaeological team wrote about Nazareth: "The principal activity of these villagers was agriculture. Nothing in the finds suggests wealth."[25]

There is a lively scholarly debate over whether Jesus might have sought work in the growing city of Sepphoris, attracted by the demand for good carpenters or craftsmen, and therefore whether he would have been exposed to Greek and other cultures. The city called by Josephus "the ornament of all Galilee" was only an hour-and-a-half walk from Nazareth.[26]

"He doubtless knew Sepphoris," writes E. P. Sanders in *The Historical Figure of Jesus*. Then why is this great town, so close to Nazareth, not mentioned in the Gospels? Reed hazards a guess: perhaps its Hellenized culture and affluent citizenry did not appeal to Jesus. Sanders writes that since Jesus viewed his ministry as primarily directed toward the Jews in the villages and small towns, cities like Sepphoris were not a high priority.[27] Or perhaps like the rest of the Hidden Life, his visits are simply not mentioned in the Gospels.

It is impossible to know whether Jesus visited Sepphoris as a youth or adolescent, but to my mind, in the years that this curious young man lived in Nazareth and later as a craftsman seeking work,

it would have been odd for him *not* to have visited the growing cosmopolitan city at least a few times and been exposed to the multilin-
gual and multicultural world of Romans, Greeks, and fellow Jews.
During his visits Jesus would have seen some of the wealthier, more
lavishly furnished homes in Sepphoris, so different from the relative
hovels of his friends and family in Nazareth. Perhaps the contrast
between the wealth of Sepphoris and the poverty of Nazareth influenced Jesus's later comments on income disparity. Perhaps he even
picked up a few Greek words and phrases, which would serve him
well later in life. Two of his disciples, Philip and Andrew, have Greek
names, another indication of the mélange of cultures around the Sea
of Galilee.

Also, though Nazareth itself was a backwater, it was in the
middle of a complex series of roads and trade routes in Lower Galilee, and its proximity to Sepphoris would have placed it in the midst
of an "urbanized and urbane" milieu, again arguing for some so-
phistication or at least some exposure to a sophisticated milieu for
Nazarenes.[28] Crossan writes that despite its size, the town's residents
"lived in the shadow of a major administrative city [Sepphoris], in
the middle of a densely populated urban network, and in continuity
with its hellenized cultural traditions."[29]

Crossan argues against the picture of Jesus, then, as a country
boy unfamiliar with anything outside his town. Moreover, Jesus
would have also made the pilgrimage to Jerusalem for the major religious festivals of the year, along with his family, and would have been
further exposed to life outside of Nazareth.

Still, as Sanders notes, Jesus was not an "urbanite." Trips to Sepphoris would have been for work, not to imbibe the Greek culture.
Village life was dominated by work; when his work was finished,
a carpenter plying his trade in a nearby town would have packed up
his tools and gone home. And as for language, as a resident of the
tiny hamlet of Nazareth, besides his studies in Hebrew, Jesus would
likely have known only a smattering of Greek. In his book *Greco-*

Roman Culture and the Galilee of Jesus, Mark Chancey concludes, "[E]n-thusiastic claims about the high number of Galileans proficient in Greek are difficult to support," probably more so in a small town like Nazareth.[30]

Jesus's native language was Aramaic. The Gospels, though writ-ten in Greek, record several traces of Jesus's mother tongue. Many scholars believe that some of the most "authentic" of Jesus's words are those in Aramaic, preserved by the original listeners, then passed on by oral storytellers, and finally carefully recorded by the evange-lists. We hear Jesus say to a little girl thought to be dead, *"Talitha koum!"* ("Little girl, get up!"). And to the ears of a deaf man, *"Eph-phatha!"* ("Be opened!"). He tells people that they will be condemned if they call someone *rhaka* ("fool"). Jesus's anguished last words, ut-tered from the cross, are in Aramaic: *Elōi, Elōi, lema sabachthani!* ("My God, my God, why have you forsaken me?").[31] So he was an Aramaic speaker, and almost certainly one with a distinctive Galilean accent. Interestingly, Peter is suspected of knowing Jesus during the Passion apparently because people recognized his Galilean accent.[32]

As for Jesus's education, Meier notes in *A Marginal Jew* that, al-though Jesus may not have had what we consider formal education, he may have grown up in a culture that was more literate than we might suspect. While literacy was not the lot of everyone in Galilee, the fact that Jesus was able to read from the Scriptures suggests that he was literate. And, given that his teaching was "imbued" with the outlook and language of the sacred texts of Judaism, says Meier, "it is reasonable to suppose that Jesus's religious formation in his family was intense and profound, and included instruction in reading bibli-cal Hebrew."[33]

And as my time in East Africa reminded me, many of the poor who interact with people from a variety of different ethnic backgrounds and linguistic groups learn to speak a number of languages—despite poverty and a lack of formal education. There-fore, it's reasonable to conclude that Jesus's everyday language was

Aramaic, that he knew Hebrew, and that he perhaps spoke a smattering of Greek. But that he was literate made him atypical in the
first-century world. "Jesus comes out of a peasant background,"
says Meier, "but he is not any ordinary peasant."[34]

But there is another kind of education: that of work. Which
brings us to the tantalizing word *tektōn,* the sole evidence we have of
Jesus's Hidden Life. During the time between the ages of twelve and
eighteen, it is likely that Jesus was apprenticed to Joseph as a *tektōn,*
a word usually translated as "carpenter." But the romantic view of
the boy in a tastefully appointed workshop with a full complement
of tools hanging primly on the wall is unwarranted. Joseph and Jesus
probably worked in the hot sun, plying their trade, and lugging their
tools overland to surrounding villages and towns to support the
family. Jesus's status as Mary's firstborn (*prōtotokos,* as Luke tells us
in the infancy narratives) meant that he would have also received,
according to Meier, "special attention" not only in his religious education, but also in training for a trade.[35]

Meier surmises that the size of Jesus's family (Mary and Joseph,
four "brothers" and an indeterminate number of "sisters") probably
necessitated that they obtain some of their food from a plot of land.[36]
Interestingly, in his parables and stories Jesus frequently makes use
of images *not* from carpentry, which one would expect, but from
farming—the sower and the seeds, the mustard seed, and the weeds
that grow up alongside the wheat, for example.[37] Does this mean that
Jesus spent more time in the fields than we suspect? Perhaps. His
use of agrarian terms may also have made sense when preaching to
crowds primarily made up of farmers, listeners who were more familiar with the flower and the stalk of wheat than with the saw and
the adze.

Meier's *A Marginal Jew* provides a superb description of what it
meant to be a *tektōn* and what Jesus would have done during those
eighteen years. Meier chooses to translate the word as "woodworker."
The term itself may have been used derisively, perhaps because it

designates a person on the lower end of the social scale. We can find traces of that derision in the Gospels. In Mark, the earliest Gospel, people ask of Jesus, "Is not this the *tektōn*?" Writing later, Matthew seems to find the comment so bothersome that he transfers the occupation to Joseph: "Is not this the son of the *tektōn*?" Luke, even later, dispenses with the occupation altogether: "Is not this Joseph's son?" So does John: "Is not this Jesus, the son of Joseph?"[38] Jesus's trade seems not to have garnered much respect, even in the Gospels.

While Elizabeth Johnson notes that the Gospels use the word *tektōn* to "designate a carpenter, a stonemason, a cartwright and joiner all rolled into one," Meier focuses mainly on the woodworking and attempts to reconstruct his work.[39] His passage on Jesus's working life deserves to be quoted in full:

> Some of Jesus's work would have been carpentry in the narrow sense of the word, i.e., woodwork in constructing parts of houses. But in Nazareth the ordinary house would have had walls of stone or mud brick. Wood would be used mostly for the beams in the roof, the space between beams being filled in with branches along with clay, mud and compacted earth. The people of Nazareth could not have afforded the use of wood to build whole houses, or even the floors in them. However, doors, door frames, and locks or bolts were often made of wood, as at times were the lattices in the (few and small) windows. Beyond carpentry in this sense Jesus would have made various pieces of furniture such as beds, tables, stools, and lampstands (cf. 2 Kgs 4:10) as well as boxes, cabinets, and chests for storage. Justin Martyr claimed that Jesus also made "plows and yokes." While this is probably an inference by Justin rather than a relic of oral tradition, it does tell us what work a person from Palestine—which Justin was—would attribute to a *tektōn*. . . . Thus while Jesus was in one sense a common Palestinian workman,

he plied a trade that involved, for the ancient world, a fair level of technical skill. It also involved no little sweat and muscle power. The airy weakling often presented to us in pious paintings and Hollywood movies would hardly have survived the rigors of being Nazareth's *tektōn* from his youth to his early thirties.[40]

But even the sharpest historian's tools cannot craft a complete look at daily life in Nazareth, for, as with those who are the desperately poor even today, life wasn't all toil, filth, and misery, despite the crushing economic systems and the difficult physical conditions. Archaeological evidence of small stone dwellings for extended families also indicates the likelihood of close relationships and an ingrained feeling of belonging—to the family, to the extended family, and to the village. Living and working in close proximity to one another, whether in the fields or in the tightly packed houses of a small village, would have fostered a strong sense of community, particularly if Nazareth was seen by outsiders, as Nathanael's comment suggests, as a joke. Strong religious beliefs would mean an awareness of a person's reliance on God, a sense of gratitude for the blessings in life—a timely rain shower, an unexpectedly good crop, a baby delivered in good health—and the knowledge that God is part of everyone's daily life.

While Jesus's life in Nazareth would be considered hard by most modern standards, it was surely not a life without its moments, perhaps many moments, of joy and laughter.

This was the world out of which Jesus stepped—a world of poverty, hardship, and toil. But also a world of close-knit and religious families who relied on one another in tough times. And this was the background of the man who would soon speak to the people of Nazareth, who thought, falsely, that they knew all there was to know about him.

THIS BOOK IS MEANT to introduce you to Jesus Christ. And one way to know Jesus better is by understanding not only his words and deeds as recorded in the Gospels, but by thinking about what his life might have been like before his public ministry began. Thanks to archaeology, that life is becoming less hidden. So even from that short exploration of daily life in Palestine what spiritual lessons might we draw from the thirty years of Jesus's life in Nazareth?

More specifically, how might Jesus's daily life in Nazareth have influenced his later ministry? And how might his "ordinary" life intersect with our own?

First of all, *Jesus understood the lives of those on the margins from firsthand experience.* When Jesus meets the poor during his public ministry and treats them with compassion, and when he directs his followers to care for the poor, it is not simply the stance of someone looking down from on high, as a wealthy person might pity the homeless man he passes on the way to the office. Rather, it is the stance of the person who himself came from a poor town, and who may have felt that compassion for years. Jesus's love for the poor came not only from meditating on the Scriptures, from seeing injustice in the world around him at the time of his ministry, and from his divine connection to the Father, but also from his life in Nazareth: his youth, adolescence, and early adulthood.

Even if he never once journeyed to Sepphoris (which is hard to imagine about a curious boy and then a carpenter eager to earn his daily bread), Jesus would have been acutely aware of the income disparities in Galilee, the taxes levied on the people, and the way that something as random as drought can wipe out a year's earnings. Jesus knew the precariousness of human life. He would also have seen how the class system forced many poor people to see themselves as powerless.

Imagine someone growing up in a backwater town and being forced to witness his social group as not only indigent, but subject to slights and insults. As an adult that person might naturally want to lift his people from such indignities. (Once on a retreat I imagined a young Jesus passing by a poor man being harassed by a wealthy land-lord, and feeling anger.) Again, Jesus's emphasis on the dignity of the poor and marginalized ("Blessed are you who are poor!") may have found its foundation not simply in what he saw as an adult, but in his experiences as a young man.

Second, and more basically, *Jesus understood human life—all the messy physical realities of being human.* Jesus wasn't simply God playact-ing at being human. Here's an earthy example: Last year a vicious stomach flu tore through my Jesuit community. Despite vigorous hand washing, it hit me one night. Without going into details, it was the sickest I had ever been—even including my time in East Africa. As I hunched over the toilet for the fifth time that night, I had a surprising thought: *Jesus did this.* Admittedly, he did not contract a norovirus in a Jesuit community, but Jesus certainly got sick. He got hungry. He ate. He drank. We know, explicitly from the Gospels, that he got tired, as when he falls asleep in a boat on the Sea of Gali-lee. The physical realities of human life were not unknown to him.

Nor were the emotional ones. As a fully human person, Jesus felt the full range of human emotions. He could be, for example, joyful. That little children wanted to be near him shows a sunny personal-ity.[41] (Generally speaking, children are not drawn to the morose.) He had a sense of humor, as evidenced by the playful exaggeration and clever figures in his parables and stories (the man who builds a house on sand, for example, or the parent who would give a child a stone instead of bread, elements that would have drawn some laughter in his day).[42] Jesus might even have been playful: after all, he seems to bestow nicknames on some of the disciples.[43]

Jesus feels the more "difficult" emotions too. He can grow agi-tated, even tetchy at times. "You faithless and perverse generation, how much longer must I be with you? How much longer must I put up with you?" he says to the disciples at one point.[44] He speaks sharply to the Syrophoenician woman who asks for healing for her daughter. He weeps over the death of his friend Lazarus. He feels anguish in the Garden of Gethsemane. And these are just the incidents recorded in the Gospels.

Even from what little we know about life in Nazareth in Jesus's day, we can reasonably posit other emotions: he loved Mary and Joseph; he treasured the members of his extended family; he enjoyed friendships as a child, adolescent, and young adult. As a *tektōn* he probably worked alongside fellow Nazarenes, helping stonemasons build a house, traveling over the hillsides with fellow carpenters to chop down trees, or walking back to his village from a job and seeing some of his neighbors at their daily tasks, and then spending a few minutes enjoying some lighthearted conversation. In Nazareth Jesus surely knew friendship. He led a fully human emotional life.

To that end, a third point: *Jesus understood family life.* Now, it is almost certain that Jesus was celibate. How do we know this? For one thing, the Gospels talk about Jesus's mother and "brothers and sisters," so if he had a wife it would be odd *not* to mention her.[45] Meier also suggests that being unmarried was seen as undesirable for most rabbis of the time, and even though Jesus was not technically a rabbi, it would have been strange for the Gospel writers to *concoct* a story that he was celibate if he was in fact married.[46] The Gospels' silence about a wife and children likely means that Jesus had neither.[47]

What are some possible reasons for Jesus's remaining unmarried? He may have intuited that once he started his ministry, it would be short or even meet a disastrous end. As a Jew, he knew the fate of other prophets. Jesus may have foreseen the difficulty of caring for a family while being an itinerant preacher. Or perhaps his celibacy was another manifestation of his single-hearted commitment to God. After sifting through the facts, Meier lands on the last reason: "The position that Jesus remained celibate on religious grounds [is] the more probable hypothesis."[48]

But that does not mean that he did not understand married life—he lived with Mary and Joseph and knew married friends in Nazareth (by the time Jesus was thirty most of his male friends would have married)—or family life—he lived with his four "brothers" (James, Joses, Jude, and Simon) and his (at least two but perhaps more) "sisters." He and his cousins (or siblings) probably lived in the same small stone house in Nazareth among a tight grouping of houses filled with other relatives. His "brothers" and "sisters" played together, fought together as any family members do, and wept together when Joseph died.

Thus when Jesus told stories about, say, a wayward son being welcomed home by his father, these insights may have been colored by his own experiences. And when he entered a family home in Galilee for a meal with friends, when he visited the house of Peter and his wife in Capernaum, when he dined with Martha, Mary, and Lazarus at Martha's house in Bethany, he understood their world. Families and extended families were a central part of the culture of Jesus's time, and so he understood them.

Jesus understood the emotional life of intimate friendships too. We can assume that he—as a fully human person—experienced the normal sexual urges as he matured, most likely experienced the typical adolescent crushes, and perhaps fell in love. At some point Jesus would have had to undergo a serious discernment about what it meant to be a good friend and share intimacy while remaining celibate. All of this flows from love, and we can see traces of Jesus's deep loving friendships in not only his patient affection for the disciples, but also his encounters with people like Mary, Martha, and their brother Lazarus, who is described at one point to Jesus as "he whom you love."[49] He must have been a loving and kind friend to both men and women, capable of great intimacy and affection.

Finally, *Jesus understood work*. This cannot be emphasized enough because it is so often forgotten.

Jesus does not simply stride onto the world stage at his baptism, having spent the last thirty years praying, wandering dreamily through the countryside, or idly examining a piece of olive wood when the mood struck him. Besides the daily chores of helping his family run a house, he would have probably spent many years (upward of, say, fifteen years) working as a *tektōn* with Joseph. And if Joseph died early, as it seems he did, Jesus himself might have taken over the family business. Did Jesus run Joseph's business with the men in his extended family? If so, could that kind of working together have influenced his ministry? Could that have helped him understand what it meant to make plans, to motivate a group of adults, to calculate the cost of a venture? Or did he work alone, and learn how to make difficult decisions on his own?

Jesus was a worker, and that work must have influenced his outlook on life. As I mentioned, Meier notes that Justin Martyr, a second-century theologian, gives voice to the tradition that calls him a maker of yokes. In Jesus's day only the most talented *tektōn* would have been able to fashion a good yoke for oxen (perfectly made to fit the team of oxen, so that it caused no chafing or discomfort). When Jesus said, "[M]y yoke is easy and my burden is light," did people of his day, who knew what an easy yoke was, smile to themselves and say, "Yes, he did make good yokes"?[50] Was he subtly playing on their knowledge of his background?

Think of the values that a carpenter needs. You need persistence to carry out physically taxing labors. Imagine Jesus not simply delicately sanding a small table, but cutting down trees, carrying the heavy logs back to his house, and fashioning planks for lintels and doors, all the while lugging tools all over Galilee. You need patience for slowly waiting for the wood to dry. You need a sense of fairness, for charging your customers a fair price. And if you are working alongside other laborers—builders, stone carvers, roofers, masons, and so on—who would also be constructing houses, you need an ability to cooperate and even to lead. All these traits would serve him well later in his ministry. They were useful tools.

Many of Jesus's parables are about work and workers: the man who is paid more than what others consider his fair share; the farmers in the vineyard; the person who calculates the cost of a venture, and so on. These parables came from someone who knew the notion of a fair day's work. He understood the kind of work that women did as well, having watched his mother, women in his family, and other women in the village at their labors. The brief parable of the woman cleaning her house to find one lost coin may have come from watching his mother at her daily chores.[51]

Though they are not many, there are tantalizing signs of Jesus's *tektōn* background in some of his sayings. In the Gospels of Matthew and Luke, Jesus compares those who act on his words to a house builder who has "dug deeply and laid the foundation on rock." When a flood comes, the house stands firm, "because it had been well built." By contrast, the foolish person, who does not put into action Jesus's words, is like the person who builds a house on sandy ground. When storms come, the house washes away.[52] Was Jesus drawing on his knowledge of building—more specifically, of helping to build houses in and around Nazareth? Would his hearers have known him as a reputable builder?

When Jesus tells his listeners, "No one who puts his hand to the plow and looks back is fit for the kingdom of God," is he referring to something that the *tektōn* would have made—a plow?[53] Are these echoes of his work in this familiar line of Scripture?

Finally, in each of the Synoptic Gospels, during his last days in Jerusalem, Jesus refers to those who would reject him by saying, "Have you never read in the scriptures: 'The stone that the builders rejected has become the cornerstone; this was the Lord's doing, and it is amazing in our eyes'?"[54] It is a powerful image, but there are multiple images of rejection in the Old Testament upon which Jesus could have drawn. Why did he choose this one? Perhaps its relation to the art of building held special appeal to the *tektōn*.

In the messy and beautiful physical realities of the human person, in the craziness and sublimity of family life, and in the toil and satisfaction of the working life, Jesus knew the world.

Soon the world would know him.

NOW FOR SOME SPECULATION—ON Jesus's consciousness, or, we might say, self-consciousness. Here we are entering into more of an imaginative exercise, because while we can study the archaeology of first-century Galilee, we cannot gain access to the mind of Jesus, other than through what is revealed to us through the Gospels. Still, it's worth thinking about as we seek to understand him. So let's look at how the Gospels portray the knowledge of Jesus.

First, did Jesus learn? This question is fraught with theological difficulties. The main dilemma is: Since he is divine, doesn't he know all things? Some passages in the Gospels show Jesus having a knowledge surpassing human understanding. When he is faced with a dead girl, he proclaims, "The girl is not dead but sleeping." And in the Gospel of John he says, "The Father and I are one," which clearly implies divine knowledge. However, Luke notes that as a young man Jesus "increased in wisdom," which just as clearly implies a growth in human understanding and knowledge. The Greek word is *proekopten:* Jesus "progressed" in wisdom.[55] Why would he have to progress in wisdom if he knew everything?

In the Gospel of Mark, Jesus indicates at least one thing that he doesn't know: "Heaven and earth will pass away, but my words will not pass away. But about that day or hour no one knows, neither the angels in heaven, nor the Son, but only the Father." The passage seems to imply limited knowledge on the part of Jesus.[56]

Any answers to "What did Jesus know?" depend on whether we focus on his divinity or his humanity: God's knowledge is limitless, and human knowledge is limited. But since we're looking at Jesus's ordinary life in Nazareth at this point, let's consider his human consciousness. As a youth, Jesus was probably curious. What child isn't bursting with questions about everything? We can imagine him asking questions of Mary and Joseph: "What's that?" As an adolescent, he would have sought answers to larger questions: "Why do people die?" As an adult he would have been interested in the lives of those around him: "Why must we give so much to Herod?" His teachers in Nazareth would have instructed him in his Jewish faith, including how to read Hebrew. And Joseph would have trained him in the art of being a *tektōn*.

But not everything about Jesus's learning is wholly speculative. At least one passage in the Gospels shows Jesus as open to learning. After the Syrophoenician woman asks to have her daughter healed, he says, "It is not fair to take the children's food and throw it to the dogs." But when she responds, "Sir, even the dogs under the table eat the children's crumbs," Jesus seems to change his mind. "For saying that, you may go—the demon has left your daughter."[57] He seems to learn something from the woman. Perhaps he is moved by the love she evinces for her daughter—so great is it that she risks another harsh comment. So it seems that even after beginning his public ministry Jesus is open to learning from others.

Jesus also may have "progressed," to use Luke's word, in understanding his vocation. Once again, we face a dilemma. Did the Son of God always fully comprehend his unique purpose? Did he understand it from the day of his birth, or at least from the time he gained self-awareness?

One possible approach, based on several passages in the New Testament, is that Jesus may have grown in his understanding of his mission, step by step, until finally grasping it completely. After all, his first miracle, the Wedding Feast at Cana, seems a reluctant one. When the wine runs out, his mother encourages him to come to the aid of the hosts. But he says to her, rather sharply, "Woman, what concern is that to you and to me? My hour has not yet come."[58]

In response, his mother calmly says to the servants, "Do whatever he tells you." Mary seems to grasp his call before he does, perhaps because she's had more time to meditate on it. I've often wondered how much Mary and Jesus discussed his future and shared their thoughts about his unique vocation. In his book *To Know Christ Jesus,* F. J. Sheed wonders why we so often think of them as "tight-lipped and inarticulate, each pretending not to know that the other knew."[59] Perhaps this was the moment when Mary invited him to embrace the path that God had set out for him.[60]

After his mother's encouragement, Jesus grasps what is required of him. More confident now, he tells the steward to fill the earthen jars with water. But it is not water that comes out; it is wine: his first miracle.

Later, Jesus is bursting with confidence in his vocation. "Lord, if you choose, you can make me clean," says a leper. "I do choose!" says Jesus. "Be made clean!"[61]

Near the end of his earthly life, in the Garden of Gethsemane, Jesus must confront for the final time what God intends. "If it is possible," he prays, "let this cup pass from me."[62] But through intense prayer, he realizes that his impending suffering is what God the Father is asking of him. Here, it seems to me, he fully understands his vocation. To me, several Gospel passages seem to show a growth in his understanding of his identity, which reaches its ultimate point in his surrender to God on the cross, and ultimately is brought to fulfillment in the Resurrection.

As Elizabeth Johnson writes, perhaps even Jesus himself was surprised on Easter Sunday, when "his ultimate identity burst upon him with all clarity."[63]

PERHAPS IT STILL MAY be hard to see Jesus's life as like your own. Likewise, the culture of first-century Nazareth may seem almost incomprehensible. In his book *Jesus of Nazareth,* the Scripture scholar Gerhard Lohfink reminds us how strange Jesus would appear to us today:

> He would—probably to our profound horror—look quite different from the way that we had imagined him. He would be neither the sovereign Christ of the Byzantine apses nor the fettered man of sorrows of Gothic art nor the Apollonian hero of the Renaissance. His Aramaic language would be comprehensible to only a few specialists. A lot of his gestures and postures would seem strange to us.

We would sense he lived in a different civilization and a different culture.[64]

Nonetheless, because of what we know of the human person and what we can know about the Hidden Life, we can begin to identify intersections with our own lives.

Many of us protest that we are just too ordinary to be holy. Our lives feel far from the extraordinary life of Jesus of Nazareth. And so we sadly speak of our "just" lives. I'm just a student. I'm just a mom. I'm just a businessman. But for most of his life, Jesus was just a carpenter in a little nowhere town. Meier calls him "insufferably ordinary." This is why his townspeople and family and friends were so shocked when he began his public ministry: "Is not this the carpenter?"

Jesus shows us the inestimable value of ordinary time. As the Jesuit theologian John Haughey comments, during Jesus's time in Nazareth God fashioned him into "the instrument God needed for the salvation of the world."[65] In Nazareth Jesus speaks to the meaning and worth of our ordinary lives.

Soon the *tektōn* who had been hidden in the small town would begin his public ministry, step onto the world stage, and decisively change human history.

But before that, he had one more place to visit.

THE HIDDEN LIFE
Luke 2:51–52

Then he went down with them and came to Nazareth, and was obedient to them. His mother treasured all these things in her heart.

And Jesus increased in wisdom and in years, and in divine and human favor.

CHAPTER 5

Jordan

"Do you come to me?"

ALL FOUR GOSPELS TELL us that before Jesus launched his public career, he first went to visit his cousin John, who was baptizing on the Jordan River.

But where, exactly? The Jordan River runs from the northernmost part of current-day Israel southward through the Sea of Galilee and finally empties into the Dead Sea, a course of 156 miles. As with many sites in the Holy Land, there are multiple candidates for the location, each hotly vying for authenticity—and tourism.

The Gospels aren't much help on this particular question. Both Mark and Matthew say that John was baptizing "in the river Jordan" at a place accessible to people from Jerusalem and Judea. Luke says, even more vaguely, that John went into "all the region around the Jordan." John's Gospel is more specific, locating the spot at "Bethany across the Jordan," a site otherwise unmentioned in the rest of the New Testament.[1] Recent excavations, however, on the eastern bank of the Jordan River have uncovered twenty churches, as well as caves and baptismal pools from the Roman and Byzantine periods, and this Jordanian site now claims to be "Bethany beyond the Jordan."

Before traveling to the Holy Land, I hadn't a clue where John did his baptizing. Unlike my fascination with the Hidden Life, I'm not as curious about the precise details surrounding the Baptism of Jesus. At one point during our drive from Jerusalem to Galilee,

I remarked to George, as I examined our map, "Oh, I see, in this area the Jordan River marks the boundary between Israel and . . . *Jordan.*"

"Please tell me you didn't just realize that," said George. "You *do* know that the West Bank means the West Bank of the Jordan River, don't you?"

"Oh please," I said, feigning intelligence. My knowledge was definitely of the human sort.

We visited the baptismal site on the way back from Galilee, en route to Jerusalem. On a blisteringly hot day, after another colossal breakfast at the Mount of Beatitudes hostel, we bade farewell to Sister Télesfora and made an early start. After four days in Galilee, we had seen almost all of what we wanted to see.

IT WAS A SPUR-OF-THE-MOMENT decision to visit the place (or at least one claimant to the place) where Jesus was baptized. Before George and I left Jerusalem, Father Doan told us that the Israeli government had recently "demilitarized" a plot of land across the river from the "Bethany beyond the Jordan" site, which had previously been opened only a few times a year. This area on the Israeli West Bank, called Qasr el-Yahud, had been captured from Jordan in the 1967 war. Until a few months before our visit, the site, located in the middle of a heavily mined area unfit for tourists, was essentially off-limits.

As George and I zipped down Route 90 toward Jerusalem, I kept my eyes peeled. Suddenly a sign materialized: BAPTISMAL SITE.

"Let's go!" I said.

"Do you really want to?" he asked. "The last time I was here, we visited the Jordan River and it was pretty gross." He described seeing a small stream of a sickly hue trailing through the desert.

I persisted. "Wouldn't it be wonderful to renew our baptismal vows at the Jordan River?" George offered an unconvincing shrug without taking his eyes off the road. But ever the generous travel companion, as soon as we saw the turnoff for the site, he turned left.

It didn't look like the way to a holy site. A dusty path led downhill into a dry, yellow, lunar landscape devoid of greenery. We bumped over the heavily rutted road and pulled into the former military zone, now staffed by the Israeli Nature and Parks Authority. After we emerged from the car into the stunning heat, I spied a brand-new amphitheater, with long benches, located on the river bank. The lowermost bleachers of the amphitheater were underwater, to make baptisms easier.

On the opposite bank, in Jordan, stood a modest wooden pavilion; stairs led down to the water. There a baby was being baptized. The child cried the way so many about-to-be-baptized babies do, with an unmistakable combination of surprise and fury. Farther along the other bank were several lovely stone churches. The Jordanian side was far more developed than the Israeli side.

Then I saw the Jordan River. It was neon green, more like Mountain Dew than water.

"I told you it was gross," said George. The river had reached perilously low levels thanks to irrigation projects upstream and was now reputed to be highly polluted.[2]

Gingerly, I climbed down the steps a few inches from the water. "Come on," I said. "It's the Jordan River! Let's renew our baptismal promises." I playfully splashed him.

"Ugh!" he said.

I had accidentally splashed him when his mouth was open! He spat out the green water. I apologized, but felt terrible. George retreated to the car to rinse out his mouth with bottled water. After blessing myself with the Jordan water and saying a hasty prayer, I returned to the car.

Fishing into my suitcase, I retrieved an unopened travel-size bottle of Listerine. "Here, rinse your mouth out with this. It should disinfect whatever you swallowed." He used the whole bottle.

Now *I* was angry. "You didn't have to use the whole thing!"

We glowered at one another, got into the car, which suddenly seemed smaller, and slammed the doors.

How had we arrived here? I don't mean, how had we found the Jordan River? Instead, how had we reached the point where two close friends could have an argument, trade barbs, and grow sullen over a minor accident *at a holy site?*

Our anger didn't last long. Soon George was joking about it, putting his own trenchant spin on Jesus's words in the Gospel. "John baptized you with water," he said in the car, "but I will baptize you with . . . *cholera!*"

Still, the question lingered: How had we arrived here? The answer is one that I've grown more comfortable talking about, the older I get: sin. Both George and I are still liable to sin.

When I was a boy, Sister Margaret Jude taught my Sunday school class about baptism. All of us are born carrying original sin, even babies, and baptism was necessary to remove our sin. Even then, I couldn't fathom how babies could be sinful or, more to the point, be condemned for that sin if they died before baptism. But the church has softened its position on that latter point: in 2007, Pope Benedict XVI approved a Vatican report that supported "the strong grounds for hope that God will save infants when we have not been able to do for them what we would have wished to do, namely, to baptize them into the faith and life of the Church." That's what I've always believed too.

Still, original sin has always made sense to me, thanks to years of meditating on my own flawed humanity. No matter how often I pray, how many retreats I make, or how hard I try, I still sin. It is something that I bump up against daily. This is not to say that I'm a serial killer, a notorious sinner, or even a mean person. Rather, I'm aware of my sinfulness because, like everyone else, I sin. So I can say with the psalmist: "For I know my transgressions, and my sin is ever before me."[3] And I continually speak with others who also bump up against their sinfulness. As the old saying goes, original sin is the one verifiable Christian dogma.

The early church fathers called this "compunction," the recognition of one's sinful tendencies. The love of God pierces the heart (*compunctio* in Latin means "puncture") and helps us to recognize our need for conversion. Every day our human nature humbles but does not humiliate us, gently and naturally. No effort or great penances are required for us to experience our limitations and taste our sinfulness, both of which lead us to recognize our constant need for God. Thus it is a grace to know one's sinfulness.

At the Jordan I came face-to-face with sin, in a small way. This was one reason John came to baptize: to call the whole people of Israel to conversion, but also to invite individuals to recognize their need for God. The Gospels say that he was calling people to "the forgiveness of sins."[4]

Which leads to a tantalizing question: Why does *Jesus* have to be baptized?

ONE TOOL THAT NEW Testament scholars use when sifting through what is authentic and what might be a later addition by the evangelists is the "criterion of embarrassment." If something can be seen as potentially embarrassing to the early church, or to Jesus, then it is unlikely that it would have been *added*. As John Meier suggests, it is hard to imagine that the writers of the Gospels would have gone out of their way to insert something new into the story that would have embarrassed or "created difficulty" for the early church. "Rather, embarrassing material coming from Jesus would naturally be either suppressed or softened in later stages of the Gospel tradition."[5] In short, the more embarrassing an event or saying, the easier it is to argue for its historicity.

The example Meier uses to illustrate this criterion is the Baptism of Jesus. Though it's a familiar story for modern-day Christians, in many ways it might have made little sense to the early church.

Why would Jesus need to be baptized? If anything, shouldn't the Son of God be doing the baptizing?

For the early church, eager to proclaim Jesus's divinity to the world, the story would obviously have proved problematic. Reading backward, then, we can see that the evangelists seemed to be stuck with an event that would have been hard to explain to newcomers. There is little chance that they would have consciously *made up* something like this. In addition, the story is included in all three Synoptic Gospels and referred to in John, so it needs to be taken seriously.

To begin to answer the question of why Jesus presents himself at the Jordan, let's look briefly at what John was doing.

Before Jesus stepped onto the public stage, John the Baptist had a flourishing ministry, his own circle of disciples, and his own distinct style of preaching.[6] Though his message varies slightly from Gospel to Gospel, John in essence preaches repentance, announces the arrival of the "reign of God," and issues stern warnings to Israel. He uses vivid, even violent images (the ax aimed at the root of the tree, the winnowing fork that separates the wheat from the chaff, which then burns in unquenchable fire[7]) to underline the seriousness of his message and emphasize the imminence of God's reign.

In John's eyes, making a decision about the reign of God surpasses every other consideration. Jesus will largely follow John's approach. This is one reason that Jesus will not hesitate to set aside what he considers "lesser" rules and customs; for him they are subservient to the coming of God's reign, or kingdom.

Here's a not-too-shocking confession: my image of John mainly comes from the movies. In prayer I imagine him wild-eyed and unrestrained, shouting not out of anger but urgency—and perhaps that is not far off the mark. In Franco Zeffirelli's miniseries *Jesus of Nazareth,* Michael York portrays him as a fearsome prophet, hectoring the crowds. Charlton Heston is equally as belligerent in *The Greatest Story Ever Told.* And John appears much the same in *The Last Temptation of Christ,* in which André Gregory is an older but no less fierce prophet. Hollywood's John is typically (and accurately) clad the way the Gospels describe: wearing clothing of "camel's hair with a leather belt."[8] This too was symbolic, suggesting a conscious identification with the Prophet Elijah, whose return was said to presage the coming of the Messiah.[9]

Gerhard Lohfink suggests another powerful image used by John: the *location* of his baptizing. Wherever it was along Route 90, the site chosen by John was invested with meaning. By ministering not in cities or towns, but in the wilderness, and specifically where Israel once crossed the Jordan to enter into the Promised Land, John is indicating that Israel (that is, the Israel to whom he was preaching) needs a new exodus and a new entry into the Promised Land.[10] And into a new reign, soon to be inaugurated.

But why baptism? The act apparently derived from Jewish purification rituals, though it may also have had a connection to the initiation rites of some Jewish sects. You can see evidence of this in the story of the Wedding Feast at Cana, in the Gospel of John, where six stone jars filled with water stand ready for the purification rites.[11] Water in general would have connoted not only cleansing (as in a symbolic sign of repentance of sins) and life (as in the element necessary for plants and animals), but death as well, especially as it related to the great flood in the Book of Genesis. (The term *baptizō* simply means to dunk or immerse.)

Like his kinsman John, Jesus of Nazareth would also emphasize the radical nature of the kingdom of God, but he would do so largely through more poetic and nonviolent means, and through the signs and symbols about his message that were "spoken" most powerfully by miracles.[12] Jesus's words lent meaning to his actions, and his actions shed light on his words.

John Dominic Crossan suggests that Jesus also learned from John's approach and ultimate execution what would and would not work. Crossan opines that John the Baptist was hoping that God would come as a warrior who would use force on behalf of Israel, and that John's aim was to swell the ranks of repentant Jews through baptism until those ranks prompted the coming of the messianic age. Others add that Jesus also would have had a deep appreciation for John's message: many biblical scholars posit that Jesus was for a time one of John's followers.[13]

John, however, understood his place in "salvation history," though he wouldn't have used those words. He described himself as the "voice of one crying out in the wilderness" and the forerunner of the "one who is more powerful than I," whose sandals he was not worthy to untie.[14]

That brings us back to our original question: Why does Jesus feel the need to be baptized? Let's see what the Gospels have to say.

In Mark's Gospel, John the Baptist simply does it—sans explanation. Jesus "came from Nazareth of Galilee" and, upon his baptism, Jesus saw the heavens "torn apart" and the Holy Spirit descending upon him "like a dove." (The Greek is *hōs peristeran,* not a dove per se, but "as a dove" or "like a dove.") The importance here lies not so much with the appearance of a bird, as portrayed in most classical paintings, as with the presence of the Holy Spirit. The tearing open of the heavens may have served for Mark's audience as a sign of the opening of a new kind of divine-human communication. A voice from heaven then proclaims, "You are my Son, the Beloved; with you I am well pleased."

After this, Jesus is driven into the desert immediately (*euthus,* a word we will see a great deal in Mark) to begin his period of testing, or temptation. Interestingly, Mark's account of the baptism is told from Jesus's perspective. Jesus sees and hears these things, but we're not told explicitly if anyone else does. Mark's account (unlike the other Gospels) intimates that Jesus had a *private* experience of God's revelation.

Luke's description is in parts more specific, but in others more confusing. His Gospel presents Jesus as *already* baptized. Jesus is praying with people in a crowd, who have also been baptized, when the heavens open and the Holy Spirit descends on him in a slightly different way: "in bodily form (*somatikō*) like a dove." That is, the

Holy Spirit appeared, physically, as a dove. Again, the voice comes from the heavens, presumably heard by the crowd. "You are my son, the Beloved, with you I am well pleased."[15]

But there's an oddity in Luke's version. John the Baptist doesn't seem to be on the scene, for in the previous passage Luke says that John has been imprisoned by Herod. Who did the baptizing? We are not told.

The Gospel of John's version features more storytelling. As in the Synoptics, the Baptist assumes a subordinate role to the man who may once have been his disciple. The day before the baptism, John says, in response to those who asked whether he was the Messiah: "I am not worthy to untie the thong of his sandal," a menial task done for a master by a slave.

The next day, presumably at the Jordan River performing baptisms, John sees Jesus approaching and proclaims him as the "Lamb of God." It is a phrase rich with meaning—most likely referring to the use of the lamb as a sacrifice, as a means to reaffirm Israel's relationship with God, particularly during Passover.[16] The term also prefigures Jesus's sacrifice during his crucifixion, which occurs during the Passover. Despite John's earlier protestations about his subordination, he performs the baptism.

Or seems to. We're not told anything about the baptism itself, nor is there any mention of Jesus stepping into the Jordan River. John the Baptist describes the descent of the Spirit after the fact: "I saw the Spirit descending from heaven like a dove (*hōs peristeran*), and it remained on him." Then John explains, "I myself did not know him, but the one who sent me to baptize with water said to me, 'He on whom you see the Spirit descend and remain is the one who baptizes with the Holy Spirit.'"

In other words, God has somehow revealed to the Baptist that Jesus is the one he has been anticipating. The voice that in the Synoptics came from the heavens speaks to the Baptist directly. What John has awaited, God provides. Overall, the Gospel of John's version subordinates the Baptist and also clearly identifies—early on and publicly—Jesus's divine identity, rather unlike the Synoptics, where Jesus's identity will be something of a secret.[17]

Only in Matthew is the big question raised. John the Baptist tries to prevent (in some translations "forbid") the baptism, and he says bluntly to Jesus: "I need to be baptized by you, and do you come to me?" And only in Matthew does Jesus provide an answer of sorts: "Let it be so now; for it is proper for us in this way to fulfill all righteousness."

What does Jesus mean by "fulfilling all righteousness"? Does this answer John's question—or ours? The Greek phrase is *plērōsai pasan dikaiosunēn,* which can be translated as fulfilling, bringing about, or completing "all righteousness," a kind of accord with God's will. It is an obscure answer that may have confused both John the Baptist and the early readers of Matthew's Gospel.

While some argue that Jesus's words refer to the later tradition of Christian baptism or to a fulfillment of the Old Testament, Jesus may simply be referring to the kind of life to which John's disciples have pledged themselves, one "producing good fruit," as John says earlier in Matthew. Notice that John the Baptist says nothing about Jesus's sinlessness. Nor does Jesus. Jesus freely presents himself to be baptized by John, though he is sinless; and John freely baptizes him, though he feels unworthy to do so.

Jesus somehow came to realize that baptism was what God the Father desired for him—to fulfill "all righteousness." Perhaps this meant publicly aligning himself with John's ministry. Perhaps before he began his own ministry, he wanted, in a sense, to pay tribute to that of his cousin, as a way of underlining his solidarity with the Baptist's message. Jesus may also have wanted to perform a public ritual to inaugurate his own ministry.

But there is another possibility, which is that Jesus decided to enter even more deeply into the human condition. Though sinless, Jesus participates in the ritual that others are performing as well. He participates in this movement of repentance and conversion not because he needs it, but because it aligns him with those around him, with those anticipating the reign of God, with the community of believers. It's an act of solidarity, a human act from the Son of God, who casts his lot with the people of the time. It has less to do with *his* original sin, which he does not carry, than identifying with those who carry that sin, as George and I experienced at the Jordan. The divine one is fully immersing himself, literally in this case, in our humanity.

It reminds me of a line from a biography of another radical, St. Francis of Assisi, the thirteenth-century saint whose own decisive act came when he walked away from the wealth of his father, a cloth merchant, and did so in a public way: by stripping naked in the public square in Assisi. The biographer Julien Green wrote that his dramatic gesture was a "juridical act," according to medieval mentality. "From now on, Francis, with nothing to his name, was taking sides with the outcast and the disinherited."[18]

At the Baptism, Jesus was taking sides with *us*. God stood in line.

Theologians often speak of Jesus as "taking on" the sins of humanity.[19] In his book on baptism, *Everything Is Sacred,* Thomas J. Scirghi, a Jesuit theologian, compares Jesus's sense of sin to the shame that parents might feel if their child were guilty of criminal behavior. There is no sin on the parents' part, but they often feel the weight of the suffering that was caused by their child. As the Protestant theologian Karl Barth wrote, perhaps no one was in greater need of baptism than Jesus, because of this "bearing" of our sins.[20]

For those present, three elements would have invited them (and invite the reader) to imagine, in Harrington's beautiful phrase, "a new possibility of communication" between God and humanity. The first is the opening of the heavens; second, the dove-like descent of the Spirit; and third, the voice. Interestingly, the voice identifies Jesus in three ways that would have been familiar to the early church: "My Son" (reminding people of the Davidic king, who was thought of as God's son), "the Beloved" (as in the story of Abraham and Isaac, his "beloved son"), and the one with whom God is "well pleased" (echoing a line from Isaiah describing "God's servant"). As Harrington writes, "At the outset of Jesus's ministry, he is identified in terms of biblical figures that provide types for his own person and activity."[21]

AFTER THE INCIDENT AT the Jordan, Jesus is described by the Synoptic Gospels as being "led" into the desert. The Gospels differ slightly on the precise wording, but the overall sense is that Jesus is irresistibly moved by the Holy Spirit to do this. Mark's Gospel uses the strong word *ekballei,* the same word that will later be used for Jesus's "driving out" of demons. He is "driven," "thrust forth," or in one translation "hurled" into the desert.[22]

The Gospels also depict Jesus fasting for forty days and forty nights, which is probably not to be taken literally, but is instead an ancient way of expressing "a long time." Ellis Winward and Michael Soule write in *The Limits of Mortality* that a human being could survive at most thirty days without food and water and be conscious for no more than twenty-five.[23]

Clearly Jesus was tested during his time in the desert, though interpretations of what happened vary. Traditional representations—in the fine arts, literature, and film—often depict Satan appearing physically. Others surmise that Jesus experienced these tests, or temptations, within himself.

Essentially, in the desert Jesus is tempted to assume a life of power, security, and status, in contrast to the humble and austere life of service he will choose. Mark's Gospel simply states he was tested: "He was in the wilderness for forty days, tempted by Satan." In Matthew and Luke we read the familiar incidents of Satan tempting him in three ways: to turn stones into bread (to feed himself); to throw himself from the highest tower of the Temple (to prove God's love); and to worship Satan (in return for power and wealth).[24]

While understandings vary of what Jesus's time in the desert involved, it is not an episode we can dismiss as irrelevant. William Barclay suggests that Jesus told the story of this episode to his disciples (how else would they know of it?), so it should be taken seriously.[25]

Biblical narratives of this chapter in Jesus's life are complicated and obscured for the modern person by centuries of paintings that depict miniature demons and hellish animals tempting him. (In Martin Scorsese's film *The Last Temptation of Christ*, Jesus is tempted by, in order, a snake, a lion, and a flame.) So it may seem an exotic chapter in his life. Yet this incident may not be so difficult to understand; this aspect of Jesus's life is more accessible to us than we might initially imagine. Ready to begin his divine mission, Jesus was subject to some human temptations.

The first temptation, in which the devil says, "If you are the Son of God, command these stones to become loaves of bread," is a physical one, but it is for more than food. It is a temptation saying, "Sacrifice everything for your physical needs, not just for food but for anything you crave—because you deserve it. Your body, your comfort, your physical well-being come before anything else." Jesus does not denigrate or disparage his body, but he knows that it cannot always come first. As the Franciscan writer Richard Rohr often says in lectures, this temptation reminds us that our "false selves" usually press for the satisfaction of our immediate wants. Yet those wants are seldom what we really need.

It is also a temptation for Jesus to do a miracle for *himself*, which he never does in the New Testament.

The second temptation, to throw himself from a high perch of the Temple and let God save him, is saying, "Show everyone how great you are. Show people that God loves you the best. You're on top." It is the opposite of what Jesus wants for himself—and for his followers. Not a community of superiors and subordinates, but a community of equals.

Finally, the third temptation, the offer of what he could rule—"all the kingdoms of the world and their splendor"—if he would bow down to Satan, is a temptation for power at any cost. "Do anything to acquire and hold on to power—power at work, at home, over all others. Grab it and be willing to sacrifice compassion and charity to keep it." But Jesus decisively rejects this temptation as well. His power will come in humility, his leadership in service.

In the desert Jesus is tempted to give in to selfish desires. These are the same types of temptations that we face regularly, even if the circumstances are not so dramatic.

Notice that in each of these three temptations there is an element of good. It's always harder to be tempted by pure evil, which is easier to spot and reject; the true temptation is the seemingly good one. For example, it is a good thing to feed oneself and care for one's body.

It's easy for us to listen to the voices that do not come from God; those voices can sound appealing. Likewise, sometimes it feels more natural to dwell in the darkness than to turn toward the light. We hear voices that tell us we are unworthy of God's love, that nothing will change, that all is hopeless. We hear the voice of, as one of my spiritual directors called it, the Hinderer. We tend to turn more toward our inner "demons," who tell false stories about us and subvert our identities, rather than turning toward God, who knows our true story, our real identity.

Jesus realizes the need to turn away from those dark voices, and he does so with the help of his Father. Jesus is driven into the desert, much as we are driven to reflect on our lives in times of testing and struggle. But he is not alone, and neither are we. The same power that helped Jesus in his desert helps us in ours.

In the end, Jesus rejected these temptations and returned to Nazareth to commence his ministry. Though sinless, he was not free from temptations. Once again, Jesus fully participates in our humanity, aligns himself with us, and completely immerses himself in the human condition.

WE BEGAN THIS CHAPTER with a brief consideration of original sin, an idea that drives much of the theology behind the Christian practice of baptism. George and I bumped into our own sinfulness at the Jordan River. And at the same place (roughly) Jesus aligned himself with sinful humanity, decisively inaugurating his public ministry.

But though this act of baptism was a vivid demarcation in Jesus's life, it would be a mistake to separate the Jesus who was born in Bethlehem, raised in Nazareth, and worked as a *tektōn* in Galilee, from the man who preached and healed. It would be a mistake to separate the young (pre-baptism) Jesus from the adult (post-baptism) Jesus. The event at the Jordan River did not create a new person. If we hope to understand something about his "after," it is essential to think about the "before."

To know Jesus, then, we are invited to think of him not simply as the preacher and healer, but as the boy, the adolescent, and the young adult. Only then will we be able to appreciate him as fully human.

Denigrating the "before" is common in the spiritual life. After a conversion experience, one is tempted to set aside, downplay, or reject one's past. In Thomas Merton's biography *The Seven Storey Mountain,* the former dissolute student turned Trappist monk largely characterizes his former life as bad, and his life in the monastery as good. Of the "old" Thomas Merton, he said ruefully, "I can't get rid of him."[26] In time Merton would realize how misguided a quest that is: there is no post-conversion person and pre-conversion person. There is one person in a variety of times, the past informing and forming the present. God is at work at all times.

As Thomas Scirghi notes, the sacrament of baptism *reorients* us.[27] For the disciples of John it marked their willingness to be converted, to experience *metanoia,* a Greek word meaning a change of perception, a change of heart. Water symbolized both life and death. So baptism was seen as a dying to an old life and being born into a new one. For the early Christians too, it would have marked a radical change and, more than we might be able to grasp today, a new way of life.

Yet the temptation for anyone who has changed, grown, or moved on from what seemed a less satisfying part of life, is to think of the old person as dead, as Merton did. It took me years to realize how limiting this approach can be, because it closes us off from seeing grace in our past. It is not that I believed that my childhood was a model of original sin, that I was a wicked teenager or an unredeemed young adult. Rather, after entering the Jesuit novitiate, I slowly began to believe that all that had gone before was not as valuable as what had come after. I had undergone, to use an overused word, a "conversion" and so had put on the "new man," as St. Paul says. This was indeed true. But I felt no need for the past, and sought to find God only in the present and in the future. In doing so I was negating all the good that God had done for me in the past.

Sometimes we close the door to our past, thinking that since we have "progressed," the past has little to offer. But we need to keep the door to our past open.

A few years ago, I received an e-mail that floored me. A friend from college had discovered a photo of our group of friends standing together on the steps of the run-down off-campus house in which we lived for two years. One of those friends, named Brad, had been killed in an automobile accident during our junior year. The photo shocked me. Seeing my friends, seeing Brad, and seeing myself smiling alongside him, opened a door that had been kept firmly shut. Until then, I had judged my past as less important than my present, seeing it as a place where God had not dwelt. But there was visible proof: surrounded by my good friends, I was smiling and happy. Had I forgotten these beautiful moments? Had I judged them of little value? Perhaps the Gospel writers thought the same: Why would anyone want to know about Jesus's early life?

And just a few days before writing this chapter, one of my best friends from childhood sent me three photos of myself in the fifth grade. This was even more startling, for they were photos I had never seen, from a time that I thought was lost, over forty years ago. It was as if God were offering me a clear window into my past. In the full-color photos, I was playing with friends during recess at our elementary school. Outside, in a spot near a green field that I recognized immediately, in whose tall grasses I used to hunt for grasshoppers, we were climbing over one another to build a human pyramid. The three photos showed a progression of six boys having fun: climbing atop one another, successfully completing the pyramid, and then tumbling over one another as our shaky pyramid collapsed. In each photo I had an immense smile on my face.

If you had asked me if I had a happy childhood, I would have said yes. Deep down, though, I might have said to myself, "But my life wasn't meaningful until I entered the Jesuit novitiate, until I fully accepted God." The door to that part of my life I had closed, or kept only slightly ajar. Those smiles reminded me that God was with me all along, forming me. As God is doing in every moment of our lives.

All of our lives are important, even the parts of our past that we have ignored, downplayed, or forgotten. If we open the door to our past, we will discover God there, accompanying us in both happy and sad moments.

Jesus of Nazareth is not simply the man who preaches and performs miracles. Jesus is not a person who, after his baptism, forgets his old life to start anew. Like all of us, he is more than that. He is the boy who played with his friends in Nazareth, and maybe even made human pyramids with them, laughing all the while. He is the adolescent who asked questions and wondered where his life would lead. He is the adult who worked as a *tektōn* for many years in his hometown.

We usually think of Jesus as the preacher and healer. But that is only part of his life. Before his visit to the Jordan River, he was a person with a graced history, whose details may always remain sketchy to us, but that nonetheless remain a part of him.

By contrast, the people of Nazareth saw Jesus only as the boy, the adolescent, the *tektōn*. They were unwilling to see him in any other way. We will soon see how misguided that was.

THE BAPTISM OF JESUS
Matthew 3:13–17
(See also Mark 1:9–11; Luke 3:21–22; John 1:29–34)

Then Jesus came from Galilee to John at the Jordan, to be baptized by him. John would have prevented him, saying, "I need to be baptized by you, and do you come to me?" But Jesus answered him, "Let it be so now; for it is proper for us in this way to fulfill all righteousness." Then he consented. And when Jesus had been baptized, just as he came up from the water, suddenly the heavens were opened to him and he saw the Spirit of God descending like a dove and alighting on him. And a voice from heaven said, "This is my Son, the Beloved, with whom I am well pleased."

CHAPTER 6

Rejection

"Is not this the carpenter?"

"LISTEN TO THIS," I said to George as we were driving to Nazareth. I had just read a surprising comment in Murphy-O'Connor's by now indispensable guide to the Holy Land: "Slender evidence suggests that a Judaeo-Christian community survived in Nazareth during the C2 and C3 AD." And a fourth-century pilgrim reported few visitors. That seemed bizarre. One would expect Jesus's hometown to have been the scene of a *flourishing* Christian community in the second and third centuries, given the town's significance.

That may explain the modest archaeological site we found a few feet away from the Basilica of the Annunciation. The excavation's main features were a few traces of the foundations of houses dating from the first century. Perhaps no one in the second and third centuries bothered to preserve evidence of the village from Jesus's day, and few in the fourth century considered those remains important enough to warrant a visit. Or perhaps the small site reflects the size of the village or, more simply, the impermanence of the poorly constructed buildings.

Among the ruins in Nazareth may be the remnants of a first-century synagogue, the site of one of the most important events in Jesus's life and one of my favorite Gospel passages. After Jesus's time in the desert, Luke reports that he returned to Nazareth and preached in the town's synagogue. What he says was so offensive to the people that they expelled him from his hometown, but not before some of them tried to kill him.

But if any traces of the synagogue remain from that time, they have not been uncovered. The earliest evidence for a synagogue dates from later, around the second or third century. Or perhaps the remains lie underneath today's Synagogue Church in Nazareth, built on a spot venerated since the sixth century, near the Basilica of the Annunciation.

While it's not surprising that the ruins have not been located, I was surprised to read this conclusion in *Excavating Jesus* by John Dominic Crossan and Jonathan L. Reed:

> Luke also presumes that a tiny hamlet like Nazareth had both a synagogue building and scrolls of scripture. The first presumption is most unlikely and . . . no evidence for a first-century synagogue building was discovered at Nazareth.[1]

Unlikely? How could a Jewish town, even a small one, not have a synagogue?

After some inconclusive research, I decided to call Professor Reed himself in his California office. The expert in first-century archaeology was friendly and helpful, and his answer made sense. "A Jewish village of that size at that time," he told me, "would not have had a synagogue building." Reed's conclusions were based on excavations of towns of similar size in the region. "The very few synagogue buildings at the time were located in towns five or ten times larger than Nazareth."

Then where would people in Nazareth have gathered? "Outdoors!" he said immediately. "Perhaps they congregated in an open space in the village, or in a courtyard owned by someone in the village who was wealthy enough to build a house with a courtyard." Reed envisions this Gospel narrative along the lines of the Sermon on the Mount, with Jesus preaching in the open air.

Wherever the location, Luke reports that Jesus was ejected from Nazareth, his hometown for roughly thirty years, for what he said.

IT'S EASY TO THINK of Jesus as being admired—at least up to his Passion, when he is rejected by almost everyone. And overall this was true. Jesus was sought after, popular, as in the original Latin *popularis*—belonging to, or accepted by, the people. When considering Jesus's enormous appeal, we might recall the disciples who immediately abandoned their old lives to follow him, the grateful men and women he had cured of illnesses, the delighted parents of healed children, the forgiven sinners turned into followers, and the great crowds who followed him from town to town, who hung on his every word—and on his person too. Frequently people simply wanted to *touch* Jesus.

Consequently, Jesus, frequently beset by crowds, often sought to "withdraw." "He entered a house and did not want anyone to know he was there," says Mark's Gospel. Matthew also mentions his frequent desire to escape from the crowds, and even the disciples, in order to pray. Following the death of John the Baptist, he "withdrew . . . to a deserted place by himself." After the Multiplication of the Loaves and Fishes, Matthew tells us that Jesus suspected the crowds wanted to make him king, so he "went up the mountain by himself to pray." The Gospel of John says after that same miracle, "he withdrew again to the mountain by himself." Luke's Gospel frequently emphasizes Jesus's desire to pray. At one point, beset by "many crowds" seeking to hear him and be healed, Luke tells us, "But he would withdraw to deserted places and pray."[2] This must have happened time after time. Although these passages are often deployed by preachers and spiritual writers to illustrate Jesus's love of prayer, they also reveal his popularity.

During our pilgrimage, this facet of Jesus's public life was made clearer after seeing the close confines in which he worked. His base of ministry was the small town of Capernaum, on the northern end of the Sea of Galilee. In and around Capernaum, Jesus performed many miracles, among them the exorcism of a possessed man in the synagogue and the feeding of the multitudes. Just outside the town today, on a sidewalk along the shoreline of the Sea of Galilee, sits the *Petra Haemorroissae,* the "Hemorrhage Stone," a waist-high granite monument that commemorates Jesus's healing of a woman with a hemorrhage, a story that appears in all three Synoptic Gospels.[3] On his way to a synagogue official's house, Jesus is stopped by a woman "who had been suffering from hemorrhages." All she wants is to touch "the fringe of his cloak." She does so, and she is healed instantly.

This story is often taken as a representation of the variety of individuals healed by Jesus (the daughter of a synagogue official and a desperate woman) and of Jesus's great power (the woman needs only to touch his clothing). But the story also shows his astonishing magnetism. He is on his way to one healing when someone clamors for *another* one. It reminds me of the scene in the film *Jesus Christ Superstar* where crowds of people desperately stretch out their hands and sing, "Touch me, touch me, Jesus!"

Near Capernaum, in the rocky hills overlooking the sea, is the Eremos Cave (after the Greek word for "hermit"). In a rough opening in the hillside, where there is barely enough room for a person to stretch out, tradition says that Jesus took refuge from his popularity.

But Jesus wasn't always popular. Immediately after his time in the desert, he returns to Nazareth. And this story of unpopularity speaks to me in a special way.

WITH DECEPTIVE CALM, LUKE begins the story of Jesus's return to Nazareth. After his stay in the desert he goes back to Galilee "filled with the power of the Spirit." News of him (*phēmē*, "fame") spreads throughout the surrounding territory, and he begins teaching in the synagogues in Galilee, where he was praised by everyone. (For our purposes, let's assume that there was some sort of gathering space—either indoors or outdoors—which I'll call a synagogue. The word means, after all, "an assembly.")

Then he returns to Nazareth, "where he had been brought up." One day he goes to the synagogue on the Sabbath day, "as was his custom." Luke portrays Jesus as an observant Jew, a pious believer who frequents the synagogue. Nothing out of the ordinary here.

His presence in the gathering would have been quite ordinary. By age thirty Jesus must have been well known in the small town as not only a pious man, but also a reliable tradesman, perhaps like his father Joseph. When they saw Jesus stand up in the gathering on the Sabbath, some of those in attendance in Nazareth may have thought, *There is my friend Jesus. I wonder what he'll say. He always has something interesting to say about Scripture.* Or, *I wonder where Jesus has been for the last few weeks. Someone said something about the desert. He's probably thinking about joining the Baptist—he's always been devout.* Or, *There is Mary and Joseph's son. I remember him when he was a little boy, and even before, when there was all that trouble over his birth.* Or perhaps, *There's my carpenter. I haven't seen him for a few weeks. I wonder when he's going to start that job!* (Remember that in the Gospels people in the area refer to Jesus more frequently as "the carpenter" than they do "the rabbi.")

The carpenter follows the standard practice of the day for Jewish men: he stands up to read a passage from Scripture and then sits to comment on it. At that time the Sabbath services included a reading from the Torah (the first five books of the Bible) and then from the Prophets. The *chazzan,* or attendant, in the synagogue would have passed Jesus the scroll. Then again, Crossan and Reed in *Excavating Jesus* wonder if Nazareth would have been wealthy enough to afford scrolls. Perhaps, then, we can assume that Jesus read from a piece of text before him or recited it from memory. But again, nothing out of the ordinary.

Jesus reads aloud a passage from the Book of Isaiah that might have been well known to the people in his hometown as a prophecy of the coming Messiah, though this was a somewhat ambiguous term in Jesus's day. (In general, the Messiah was the one sent by God to usher in a new era of God's powerful rule.) Talk of the Messiah was in the air. Jesus reads these words: "The Spirit of the Lord is upon me, because he has anointed me to bring good news to the poor. He has sent me to proclaim release to the captives and recovery of sight to the blind, to let the oppressed go free, to proclaim the year of the Lord's favor."[4]

Then Jesus rolls up the scroll, hands it back to the attendant, and sits down. "The eyes of all in the synagogue were fixed on him," says Luke. Why? Were they simply waiting for him to comment on this passage or anticipating something especially inspiring? Perhaps they had heard of Jesus's reputation as a kind of holy man. Their later reaction, however, shows that they weren't expecting what he would say at all.

What he says is extraordinary: "Today this scripture has been fulfilled in your hearing." In other words, "I am the fulfillment of the Scripture you just heard." "Today" is an important word for Luke. The breaking into human history of the reign of God is not happening in some far-off time, or in some distant land, but right now, and as Jesus is saying, not in some distant land, but before your very eyes. Today and here.

Not all first-century Jews believed in the coming of the "messianic age," when God would usher in an era of peace. But this belief and hope were in the air. Among those who did believe, there was general agreement that the age would arrive through an individual: the Messiah (*Mashiach* in Hebrew, "the anointed one"; in Greek, the *Christos*). And the selection that Jesus read, describing God's promises to his people—the nations will cease warring, the sick will be healed, captives will be freed—was, as Amy-Jill Levine notes, associated with the messianic age.[5]

All this is associated with the "kingdom of God" or the "reign of God," to which most New Testament scholars point as the crux of

Jesus's teaching.[6] This sometimes surprises people who assume that his central message was loving your enemies or offering forgiveness or helping the poor. But though all of those are central to his message, they are not *the* central message: the reign of God was.

IRONICALLY, TWO THOUSAND YEARS after Jesus introduced this message, scholars are still unclear about precisely what he meant. For one thing, the phrase more or less originated with Jesus. It appears in very few places in the Old Testament. For another, Jesus seems to have described the reign of God in some places as a future event, in others as already present.[7]

So when, where, and what was this reign of God?

On the one hand, the reign of God is already realized in Jesus's own presence among the people; on the other, it's not completely here because, as anyone can see, vengeance, injustice, and suffering still endure. Theologians refer to this idea as the "already but not yet." But even that elegant phrase cannot encompass Jesus's idea of the "time" of the reign. In Jesus's day, most people delighted in paradoxes, so there was no reason for Jesus to have to specify any particular time. E. P. Sanders writes:

> It may help if we think of Jesus—or any other first-century Jew who wished to talk about God's rule—as having the option to combine in various ways *here, there, now* and *later*. . . . There is no difficulty in thinking that Jesus thought that the kingdom was in heaven, that people would enter it in the future, and that it was also present in some sense in his own work.[8]

Nor did Jesus have in mind a clear-cut definition. The reign of God ("reign" is a better translation of the Greek *basileia* than "kingdom," which implies a geographic place) encompasses many realities: the reversal of unjust suffering, the pouring out of rewards on the faithful, and the joyous participation of believers in the heavenly banquet.⁹ But exactly where, what, how, and especially when, were obscure to Jesus's listeners, and remain obscure to us. The reign of God is a reality that cannot be grasped fully, nor can it be contained in the language of a strictly worded definition. This is why Jesus used poetic means to describe it—called parables, as we shall soon see.

But in Nazareth, as Luke describes the event, Jesus is saying clearly: "The reign of God is here, because I am here."

IT TAKES A MOMENT for his words to sink in. The experiences of those in Nazareth that day may be similar to times in your life when an astonishing statement takes a while to register. After a few seconds of shock, you say, "Did she say what I *thought* she said?" When I first told a few college friends, over dinner at a New York restaurant, that I was leaving my job at General Electric to enter the Jesuit novitiate, they paused for several moments before speaking. "What?" said a friend. "What?" When the waiter came to take our order, he asked, "Do you need more time?" My friend said, "Yes, a lot more time."

Initially, those in the synagogue appreciate what Jesus says. "All spoke well of him and were amazed at the gracious words that came from his mouth," says Luke. The Greek is beautiful: *ethaumazon epi tois logois tēs charitos*. Literally, they marveled at the words of grace.¹⁰ Some are amazed that the local *tektōn* knew so much. "Is not this Joseph's son?" they ask.

In Mark's version, written closer to the original events, the amazement among the people in Nazareth is even more pronounced. Mark's vivid account, which occurs later in Jesus's ministry, after some of his miracles, recounts questions that indicate a rising astonishment: "Where did this man get all of this?" What is this wisdom that has been given to him? What deeds of power are being done by his hands!" Then comes almost an explosion of shock: "Is not this the carpenter, the son of Mary and brother of James and Joses and Judas and Simon, and are not his sisters here with us?" In Matthew, the questions are similar, though Jesus's identity is changed to "the carpenter's son."

In both cases, the people are thunderstruck. How can someone like this—*like us*—say these things?

Mark's and Matthew's versions, then, explain something that Luke omits, for in Luke the mood suddenly shifts without explanation. Matthew and Mark, however, say, "And they took offense at him." The Greek is *eskandalizonto:* literally, they stumbled on this. The root word is *skandalon,* a stone that one trips over, from which we get the word "scandal." They cannot get over the fact that someone from their hometown is saying and doing these things. They move quickly from amazement to anger. Jealousy may have played a role as well.

Jesus anticipates their desire for miracles and predicts their inevitable reaction. You will tell me, he says, "Do here also in your hometown the things we have heard you did at Capernaum." (This is somewhat confusing in Luke, since Jesus does not move to Capernaum until later, so perhaps Luke has moved this story farther ahead in his narrative of Jesus's life.) "Truly I tell you, no prophet is accepted in the prophet's hometown." Jesus seems to be quoting from a popular saying as well as drawing on what his townsfolk would have known of the fate of the Jewish prophets.

Mark's earlier version is more poignant—you can almost feel Jesus's sorrow in having to say what he is about to say. In Greek his words could be translated as "A prophet is not without honor except in his native land (*patridi*), and among his relatives, and in his own house (*oikia*)." Imagine the combination of sadness and pity he must have felt uttering those words before his closest friends and his family.

For Mark and Matthew, the story ends there. Matthew says that Jesus is unable to perform "many deeds of power" because of their lack of faith. Mark says that he cured "a few sick people" and was amazed by their lack of faith in him. Then Jesus leaves.

Luke's version, however, continues. If Jesus's words weren't enough to anger those in the synagogue, he reminds them of the story of Elijah, the prophet who during a time of severe famine and drought helps not a single Israelite, but a woman in Zarephath, a non-Jewish town. What's more, another prophet, Elisha, cured Naaman, another non-Jew, of leprosy rather than healing a Jewish person with leprosy. In so many words, Jesus is comparing himself to the great prophets from Israel's past and reminding people that these two prophets took their messages to outsiders.[11] "Without faith you cannot expect any miracles," he seems to be saying, "so don't expect me to stick around."

As if to underline his prophecy, Jesus uses the forceful term "Amen," a version of "I assure you," before he makes that comparison.[12] Rather than relying on a verse from Scripture or another expert on the Torah to give credence to his words, Jesus presents *himself* as the authority. To sum up: I'm telling you from my own authority that you're treating me just like your ancestors treated the prophets, so don't be surprised that I can't do any miracles here—your lack of faith is the reason. It is a challenge to the crowd.

This is the last straw. "When they heard this, all in the synagogue were filled with rage." So much so that they drive him from their midst and lead him to the brow of the hill to throw him off. But Jesus "passed through the midst of them." You can see why he would have, probably with immense sadness, felt forced to leave his hometown.

Not far from the first-century ruins of Nazareth is Mount Precipice, where the furious townsfolk are said to have brought Jesus. The steep cliff today drops off onto a busy highway. Many scholars question the location of the actual site, but given Nazareth's hilly terrain, almost any candidate is sufficiently dangerous. But if the site is legendary, the story is almost certainly not. As Harrington suggests about a passage in which Jesus is rudely rejected by those who knew him best, "This is not the kind of story that early Christians might invent."[13]

JESUS FACED REJECTION NOT because the townspeople in Nazareth were small-minded (much less because Jews of the time were any more insular than anyone else in antiquity), but because they could not accept his words. But how was he able to pass "through the midst of them"? Perhaps when Jesus looked upon the crowd, when he recognized them, and when they saw *him* recognize them, they were made aware of what they were doing.

Conceivably, the people of Nazareth pulled back from doing violence to Jesus because they suddenly saw themselves as God saw them—people unwilling to listen to the voice of a prophet. Jesus made them look at a place in their own heart, and they did not like what they saw.

Jesus also saw them as beloved children of God. He saw them in their complexity, not simply as sinful people, but also as people incapable of seeing the truth, because of the human limitations that we all share. That recognition might have been too much for them. So he could pass through their midst.

ONE POPULAR WAY FOR preachers and teachers to present this passage is from the crowd's perspective. Even when the Messiah was standing before them, they failed to see him. The people of the tight-knit village knew him so well that they couldn't imagine someone so ordinary and so familiar as the carrier of divine grace. The usual moral is: be careful not to overlook anyone as an instrument of grace.

But here is something we often overlook: Jesus knew *them*. When he stood up in the synagogue building or in the outdoor gathering space, he saw the faces of people he knew well. There were his fellow carpenters; there were his cousins; there were his mother's friends; there were his peers. Therefore, he must have known how they would respond to what he was going to say.

Imagine planning to speak to a group of friends or family—people you've known your whole life. Now imagine that you're going to tell them something alarming. Let's say you're dropping out of college, you're moving across the country, or you're breaking off an engagement. If you know them well, you probably *know* how they're going to respond. You can anticipate how each person will react.

Walking into that synagogue, the perceptive *tektōn* probably could predict how people would respond when he declared himself the Messiah. He knew that he would be rejected and even attacked, but he did it anyway.

Jesus must have expected that his controversial statement would engender strong, angry, and even violent reactions. But he seemed unbothered by the prospect of controversy. Why? Because he was fearless, independent, and free.

Jesus also does so generously. Though he challenges the crowd, he evinces no resentment toward them. After all, he is preaching "good news," figuratively and literally. The expression usually refers to the entire Gospel message. But in a homier sense, what he is saying is plain old good news—the blind will see, captives will be released, and there will be a "year of the Lord's favor."[14] It's a contrast from the fire-and-brimstone message of John the Baptist. Surely, this is good news. But the people were still angry.

Luke Timothy Johnson suggests that the townspeople were furious not simply because Jesus proclaimed himself as Messiah, but also because he declared that his ministry would not be done in Nazareth and, what's more, that he would bring his mission to the Gentiles, the non-Jews. "He is not acceptable in his own country because his mission extends beyond his own country," says Johnson.[15] It is likely that Jesus knew how a message of openness to the Gentiles would be received in his hometown. Nonetheless, he is fearless.

How was he able to do this? First, his courage flowed from the grace that came from his Father in heaven. But second, it may have come from Jesus's freedom from any desire for approval from the people in Nazareth. Jesus did not need their approval; he needed only to be true to himself. This is not to say that he did not love his family and friends in Nazareth or that he somehow held the people in the synagogue in contempt—Jesus was compassion personified. Rather, he didn't need them to agree with him, approve of him, or even understand him. Nazareth was neither the locus of nor the reason for his ministry.

Jesus was also wise enough to know that he could not change them. If they didn't listen to him, perhaps people elsewhere would. This may be why Jesus spent most of his time in Capernaum, not Nazareth.

Jesus did not feel the need for approval from the synagogue, the town, or his family. In short, he didn't need to be liked.

FOR MANY YEARS I struggled with the desire to be liked. And a few years ago I came to my annual retreat with two related problems on my mind. The first was that a person in my Jesuit community had taken an active dislike to me. Of course I knew that not everyone would love me or even like me, but that another Jesuit would despise me (believe me, he did) was disconcerting. He treated me with great contempt, at times refusing to speak to me. (Yes, religious communities are not perfect.) The second issue was the feeling that I must speak out about a controversial issue in the church, which would probably earn me enmity. (It doesn't matter what issue; the controversy is long gone.)

Both challenges turned on my need to be liked. So my spiritual director recommended the Rejection at Nazareth for my prayer. It was easy to imagine the crowd shouting Jesus down, at the tops of their voices, and to see the looks of hatred on their faces.

Meditating on that passage helped me realize how frightened I was of rejection. And thinking of Jesus's courage in Nazareth helped free me of something that had long kept me bound. Whenever I thought of saying or doing something that might have seemed controversial or unpopular I often wondered, *What will people think?* It's a dangerous snare—you can easily end up paralyzed with inactivity, bound by the chains of approval.

Jesus was the opposite: entirely free. Perhaps this came from his intimate relationship with the Father, with whom he was united in prayer. Perhaps this came from his relationships with Mary and Joseph and the rest of his extended family, who offered him the parental love that characterizes many self-confident people—to the point where he felt comfortable disagreeing with or even angering them. Or perhaps it came from his understanding that his mission was of supreme importance, that proclaiming the coming reign of God was more important than whether a few people from his hometown disagreed with, disliked, or rejected him.

Jesus's freedom sprang from an unwillingness to let other people's opinions determine his actions. If he had succumbed to what other people thought, he never would have spoken in the synagogue, he never would have healed anyone, he never would have stilled a storm. He never would have raised anyone from the dead, for fear of offending those in authority. He never would have opened his mouth to proclaim the Good News.

Relying on family, friends, and the larger community can be salutary. It helps us in problem-solving, consoles us in times of sorrow, and magnifies our rejoicing. The support of our family, the advice of our friends, and the wisdom of the community also keep us humble, because we are reminded that we don't know everything.

But an overreliance on other people's opinions can paralyze us. For many years, I tailored some of my actions not only to fit what was generally accepted, but to gain for myself others' approval. *Don't say that; it's too controversial. Don't do this; people won't like you. Don't wear that; people won't think you're cool.* Many of us know that temptation. In some social gatherings I used to wonder, *What can I say to get people to like me?*

How paralyzing that was! Because any action will win approval from one person and earn contempt from another. Gradually, this overweening desire to be liked put severe limits on my freedom. But the Rejection at Nazareth freed me from that self-made prison. It felt as if God were asking me on that retreat: "Must everyone like you? Mustn't the desire to be liked by everyone die? Doesn't it need to die if you are to have any sort of freedom?"

Once I realized this, I felt a palpable liberation from worrying about the fellow who disliked me in my community, and from my fears over whether anyone would disapprove of what I wrote. Of course, I still need correcting at times. Like anyone, what I say and do requires careful discernment. People may dislike or disapprove of our actions for good reasons. As my novice director told me, "Just because you're being persecuted doesn't mean that you're a prophet. It may mean you're wrong!"

But the story of the Rejection at Nazareth enabled me to reject the need for approval. Now I worry far less about being loved or even liked. Jesus in Nazareth freed me from that particular prison. The *tektōn*'s freedom gave me the freedom to be free. As he said on that day, he had come to "proclaim release to the captives."

Including, in a way, this one.

THE REJECTION AT NAZARETH
Luke 4:16–30
(See also Matthew 13:54–58; Mark 6:1–6)

When he came to Nazareth, where he had been brought up, he went to the synagogue on the Sabbath day, as was his custom. He stood up to read, and the scroll of the prophet Isaiah was given to him. He unrolled the scroll and found the place where it was written:

The Spirit of the Lord is upon me,
because he has anointed me
to bring good news to the poor.
He has sent me to proclaim release to the captives
and recovery of sight to the blind,
to let the oppressed go free,
to proclaim the year of the Lord's favor.

And he rolled up the scroll, gave it back to the attendant, and sat down. The eyes of all in the synagogue were fixed on him. Then he began to say to them, "Today this scripture has been fulfilled in your hearing." All spoke well of him and were amazed at the gracious words that came from his mouth. They said, "Is not this Joseph's son?" He said to them, "Doubtless you will quote to me this proverb, 'Doctor, cure yourself!' And you will say, 'Do here also in your hometown the things that we have heard you did at Capernaum.'" And he said, "Truly I tell you, no prophet is accepted in the prophet's hometown. But the truth is, there were many widows in Israel in the time of Elijah, when the heaven was shut up for three years and six months, and there was a severe famine over all the land; yet Elijah was sent to none of them except to a widow at Zarephath in Sidon. There were also many lepers in Israel in the time of the prophet Elisha, and none of them was cleansed except Naaman the Syrian." When they heard this, all in the synagogue were filled with rage. They got up, drove him out of the town, and led him to the brow of the hill on which their town was built, so that they might hurl him off the cliff. But he passed through the midst of them and went on his way.

CHAPTER 7

Galilee

*"And immediately they left
their nets and followed him."*

ON THE FIRST MORNING of our stay in Galilee, we visited one of the sites I most hoped to see during our pilgrimage. I had stumbled upon the place in a guidebook just a few weeks before our departure. It was called the Seven Springs. There, on a northern corner of the shore, seven freshwater streams pour into the Sea of Galilee. And while the water level is lower than it was during Jesus's day, the terrain probably looks much the same as it did in the first century. Waves lap over dark rocks, tufts of grasses dot the beach, and the lack of tall trees affords an unobstructed view of the blue-green water. You can see all the way across to the hills on the other side.

In the Gospels, by the way, the Sea of Galilee is also called the Sea of Tiberias (after a large city on its banks), Lake Gennesaret (from the Hebrew word for "harp," describing the lake's shape), or sometimes just "the lake." You can imagine my embarrassment when I discovered that what I thought were three separate lakes were one. Until a few weeks before our trip, I kept checking maps to figure out how the three biblical bodies of water were connected, before my friend Drew politely set me straight. It is one lake, about thirteen miles long and eight miles wide at its widest point.

On the day of our visit, dozens of people splashed about in the Sea of Galilee, and a large Orthodox Jewish family was enjoying a sort of holiday at the Seven Springs. The scene was the opposite of what I had expected—an ornate shrine, a little church, or even a grand basilica. But there was nothing but the sea. The boisterous crowds made for a pleasant atmosphere. Dipping my fingers into the water, I made the Sign of the Cross.

The Seven Springs is the traditional site of the Call of the First Disciples, where Jesus, just beginning his ministry, invites four Galilean fishermen to accompany him. Many pilgrims believe that the Seven Springs is the story's locus, for as Luke tells the tale, Jesus meets up with the fishermen just as they are "washing" their nets. The freshets that flow into the Sea at this precise spot make it a logical place for those fishermen's task.

The rushing streams and the breaking waves make the Seven Springs a surprisingly noisy place. With the washing of the nets, the commotion of fishing boats being hauled onto shore, the men unloading their catch, the rolling surf, and the burbling springs, Jesus's appearance might have surprised the otherwise preoccupied Galileans.

Speaking of surprises, here's a problem with the Gospels: We've heard the stories so many times that it's easy to overlook their overriding strangeness. We've lost the ability to be surprised by them. As one writer said, they become like old coins, their edges smoothed away.[1] The Call of the First Disciples is one such story. But if you read it with fresh eyes, it reveals itself as an unsettling tale. How could four men walk away from everything—their jobs, their families, their entire way of life—to follow a carpenter who says only a few words to them?

MARK TELLS THE STORY in sure, swift strokes. He begins with Peter (who's still called Simon) and his brother Andrew. Both are hard at work, plying their trade along the shore of the Sea of Galilee. According to several ancient writers, the Sea of Galilee was home to a thriving fishing industry, its shores heavily populated. The area was also something of a crossroads in between the Hellenized (that is, Greek-influenced) cities to the east and the Jewish towns and settlements to the west. Perhaps this is one reason that Jesus was attracted to the locale: he could be assured of meeting people from all over the region. Mark's Gospel will portray Jesus going back and forth across the lake, perhaps symbolizing his mission to both Jews and Gentiles.[2]

So the romantic idea of Jesus passing a group of men silently mending their nets on a quiet seashore may be inaccurate. Perhaps Jesus came upon them in the midst of crowds of fishermen, busy on the bustling shoreline.

Indeed, Mark paints an active scene. Peter and Andrew are casting their nets into the sea. (John's Gospel tells us that Peter and Andrew are from Bethsaida, only a few miles away, and that Andrew was a disciple of John the Baptist.[3]) The pair's activities are common even now. A few minutes after George and I visited the Seven Springs and piled back into our car, we spied two small figures on the shoreline, facing the sea, making motions with their arms, apparently throwing something into the water.

"What are they doing?" said George. "Can you tell?"

"I can't believe I'm saying this," I said, "but they're . . . casting their nets."

Mark adds, somewhat superfluously, "for they were fishermen." The cynical reader might say, "No kidding." But Mark and the other Gospel writers often use what Scripture scholars call "Semitic repetition" to underline a point, sometimes telling the same story two different ways. Besides, their profession, as we will see, is not of passing interest. It bears repeating.

In Mark's account Jesus has just finished his sojourn in the desert. Without fanfare the carpenter from Nazareth strides up to Peter and Andrew, probably greets them, and says words that will change everyone's lives. Most Christians know the famous quote in the following translation: "Follow me and I will make you fishers of men."

The Greek is *Deute opisō mou, ka poiēsō humas genesthai haleeis anthrōpōn.* The first part of Jesus's invitation might be better translated as "Come after me," which may have reminded Mark's original audience of the Jewish practice of the student walking behind the teacher. Many scholars say that already Jesus is making a break with tradition. Normally it was the student who sought out the teacher. Here, the master chooses.

The master also *makes.* The second part of the Greek, "And I will make you to become fishers of people," shows what Jesus has in mind for these fishermen. The verb *poieō* ("to make or do") is the root of the words "poem" and "poetry," and this passage beautifully conveys a sense of creation.[4] After calling them into relationship with him, Jesus will "make" or fashion his disciples into something new and beautiful. John Meier in *A Marginal Jew* calls it a "command-plus-promise."[5]

Some Christians familiar with the term "fishers of men" are often surprised that the Greek used is a form of *anthrōpos* (that is, people: *anthrōpoi*), and not of *anēr* (men: which would be *andres*). Jesus's ministry will not be limited to men. As his ministry unfolds, the disciples will see that Jesus's net is large enough to include a fantastic variety of people, often the very fish that are the least expected by those doing the casting.

Where did Jesus's odd choice of words come from? Meier notes that while metaphors connected with fishing were common in the ancient Mediterranean world, the phrase "fishing for people" (or any other similar phrase) appears nowhere in the Old Testament. When the metaphor of fishing for human beings (or using a hook as bait) is used, it is used negatively—for example, God's catching a wicked person or group of people.[6] Nor does that particular phrase appear elsewhere in the New Testament—that is, Jesus does not employ the metaphor for any other person or group of people. In other words, it seems to be a phrase that Jesus originated—for this particular group of men. Thus, says Meier, "it was tied to specific persons in a specific situation."[7] It is an early example of how Jesus tailored his message and his words to his audience.

The invitation is also open-ended. Jesus does not tell Peter and Andrew *how* they will "fish for people." He does not say, "Come after me, and I will make you fishers of people by doing the following things: I'll preach, I'll perform miracles, I'll ask you to assist me in my ministry, and then I'll suffer, be crucified, and be raised from the dead after three days, and finally, after my resurrection, you'll be charged with spreading my message to the ends of the earth."

No. Jesus's call is—like many calls—appealing but also confusing. As the angel asks of Mary at the Annunciation, Jesus asks the disciples to assent to something mysterious.

It's not just his choice of words that is unusual; it's the very calling of disciples. As I mentioned, at the time rabbis didn't call followers; followers and students sought out the teacher. Nor does Jesus say something like, "Come and learn the Torah with me," the normal impetus for seeking a teacher. Nor were Peter and Andrew asked to "serve" their teacher, another Jewish custom. Finally, in another break with tradition, Jesus didn't ask them to stay in a particular place to be his disciple. No, they would be on the road. "Follow me" was meant in a physical way as well. All of this would have been odd for Jews of the time.[8]

Jesus's unusual choice of words would have been instantly memorable to his listeners. Even for devout Jews it would not have been the expected metaphor—he turns a negative metaphor on its head. Jesus is also speaking their language—notice that the carpenter doesn't choose an image from his own trade ("Follow me and we will build the kingdom" or "Follow me and we will sand down the rough edges of humanity"). Instead, he uses their own life to call them to a new one. Several New Testament scholars told me that the phrase may also be an indication of Jesus's playful humor—telling professional fishermen that they would be, absurdly, "fishing for people." Overall, it is an original request, "strikingly different, not to say shocking," says Meier.[9] Strange.

Stranger still is their response: *Kai euthus aphentes ta diktua ēkolouthēsan autō.* "And immediately they left their nets and followed him." The expression *kai euthus*—"and immediately"—will occur many times in Mark's Gospel, giving everything a sense of urgency in his fast-paced tale of Jesus. Decisions need to be made immediately. The two leave their nets and follow—the Greek *ēkolouthēsan* connotes not simply following a person's teaching (as today some might say they are followers of the teachings of Gandhi or Nietzsche) as much as following the individual. It implies a personal relationship with Jesus. Follow me—but also join me, live with me, eat what I eat, meet whom I meet. Share in my life.

Farther down the shore, Jesus meets up with James and John, the sons of a man named Zebedee, working on their nets. Jesus calls them—once again *euthus,* immediately. But James and John are not washing their nets after a fishing voyage. The most common translation is that they are "mending" their nets, but "preparing" may be closer to the Greek, with James and John readying their nets for an upcoming fishing trip, suggestive of a new beginning. They too leave behind their father and the "hired men" in the boat. And while Jesus calls them together, he does not call them as an unindividuated mob: "Hey, all you anonymous fishermen working on the shore—come with me!" These are individual calls.

WE MAY HAVE HEARD this story so many times the fishermen's responses seem foreordained. Of course they follow him, we think. That's what disciples *do.* But their decision was by no means an easy or obvious one. After all, they had commitments and responsibilities; they were settled. We know, for example, that Peter was married, because the Synoptics tell us about his mother-in-law.[10] And for those who think that they were dirt-poor fishermen with nowhere to go (and so it would have been easy to leave their crummy business behind), we should remember that fishing in Galilee was often profitable; the lake's fish were exported considerable distances. One commentary calls Capernaum an "important trade center."[11] James and John are leaving behind a boat with "hired men," which indicates that Zebedee's business was at least successful. Likewise, Peter and Andrew were working together—a family business.

In addition to the commitment to a job, there is the obligation to family as well: Peter is married; James and John are leaving behind their father. (That Peter leaves his wife—unless he is a widower and caring for his mother-in-law—inserts an element of confusion into the story. What happens to her? The Gospels are silent.[12]) And who is to say that Zebedee hadn't pinned his hopes on his sons taking over the family business? Duty to their father would have been paramount—not simply as a professional obligation, but as a reflection of the filial piety so prized in those days. In their book *Let the Little Children Come to Me,* a study of childhood and children in antiquity, the authors note that there was an expectation that sons would continue their father's work, and that such continuation was seen as a sign of true obedience.[13]

Finally there are ties of habit and security. Most likely their families had lived and fished on the shores of Galilee for generations. The historian Henri Daniel-Rops notes that not only had fishing on the Sea of Galilee existed since "beyond the memory of men," but that even the names of the towns along the shore highlighted the importance of the industry.[14] Bethsaida means "the fishery" or "fishing town," and the Greek name for Magdala was Tarichaea, or "dried fish."[15] Fishing was the raison d'être of these towns.

Galilean fishermen often worked together in groups—most likely family groups—pooling their resources not only physically, for the fishing voyages, which required a great deal of human labor, but also financially, to purchase the boats and equipment needed for their trade. There were two methods of fishing. The first was the use of a seine, or dragnet, weighted down and drawn behind a boat. Jesus would use this kind of net as an image of the kingdom in which the dragnet catches all sorts of fish, which God will sort out.[16] The second method made use of a smaller casting net, of the type George and I saw, which could be deployed from the shore or from a boat, flung out by hand into the sea. Notice that there is no mention of a boat in Peter and Andrew's case; James and John are in their father's boat.

This may indicate that the second pair was slightly more well-off; larger dragnets were the more profitable way of fishing.[17] But that does not mean that they were wealthy. Reed suggests that the father of James and John "probably owned a modest house, a boat, and some nets, and occasionally hired a few day laborers who were worse off. But in general fishermen were a motley crew."[18] The ruins of the houses on the shores of the Sea of Galilee attest to the fact that the fishing industry was no "financial bonanza."[19]

Overall, Peter and Andrew, James and John were accustomed to this way of life, and they were accustomed to this way of life *together.* Luke says that James and John were business partners with Peter.[20] The four, then, knew one another well. Perhaps that's why Jesus called them together—intuiting that it would be easier for them to come with their brothers and friends.

And while it is true that Jesus doesn't call them as an undifferentiated mob, he does call people to work together with him as a *group,* an early indication of the communal element of his ministry. Jesus could have worked alone, or he could have selected a single person— say, Peter or Andrew or Mary Magdalene—as his assistant, but instead he calls many people to labor with him. Inviting people to work together is a constitutive part of Jesus's ministry, and it reflects his keen understanding of human nature—and perhaps his own need for a group of friends around him. Later we will see that when Christ rises from the dead he will appear to the disciples individually, but more often to a group. The New Testament scholar John R. Donahue, SJ, calls his activity "radically social."[21]

Still, even with their common call, it must have been hard for the fishermen to leave behind their ways of life. In that way, these Galilean fishermen were like many of us. It's difficult to let go—even harder to let go based on a few words from a stranger. Each of these men was enmeshed in a variety of very real commitments. The nets they were holding are a marvelous image of the intricate ties that bound them to their old lives—their entanglements.

What accounts for the immediate conversions of these four fishermen? How were they able literally to drop their "nets"—all that entangled them—and follow Jesus?

FIRST, *they may have been waiting for the Messiah.* As practicing Jews, the Galilean fishermen would have probably known passages in the Old Testament that spoke of the coming Messiah, from "the region of Zebulun and Naphtali," where Capernaum is located.[22] These men lived during a time when, and in a place where, the Messiah was expected.

Second, *they may have heard of Jesus before he set foot in their town.* During my time working with the Jesuit Refugee Service in East Africa, I met many young Sudanese refugees who had fled their country after a brutal civil war. In the face of great peril, they had walked many miles from the deserts of Sudan to northern Kenya, where they stayed in refugee camps; from there they found their way to Nairobi. There, they sought out a Catholic sister named Luise, who ran a scholarship program for refugee children. They all knew her name. "All I knew when I left Sudan," a young boy told me, "was that I needed to be finding Sister Luise." Her name had traveled many miles.

Perhaps Jesus's name had traveled too, from nearby towns to Capernaum. On one retreat, I imagined the fishermen aboard their boat avidly discussing Jesus, just as he was approaching them. Perhaps overhearing them speculate, he decided that it was the right time to issue an invitation to those curious men: "Follow me."

Third, *the fishermen may have been interested in Jesus, but were awaiting an invitation.* In Luke's version of this story (when Jesus calls Peter following a miraculous catch of fish), Jesus has just healed Peter's mother-in-law. That miracle would have made Peter more open to Jesus's message; it would also have made Jesus more compelling. The fishermen may also have witnessed other miracles as well, ones that went unrecorded.

Still, the fishermen may have wanted to join Jesus, but did not feel worthy of the task. They may have been attracted to Jesus's message, but unsure if he would accept them as followers. Perhaps each felt that someone who was "just a fisherman" wouldn't be welcome. Jesus gave them the chance with his personal invitation.

Fourth, *they may have already met Jesus.* An even simpler explanation may be one found outside the Synoptics. The Gospel of John lists Andrew as a disciple of John the Baptist, who hears the Baptist refer to Jesus as the "Lamb of God." Andrew then introduces his brother to the man he names as the Messiah: "He brought Simon to Jesus."[23] Conceivably, Jesus met the two fishermen near the Jordan River, traveled to Capernaum to call them decisively, and then called James and John.[24]

Fifth, *perhaps Jesus had resided in Capernaum longer than the Gospels indicate.* In the Gospel of Luke, after the rejection at Nazareth, Jesus "went down" to Capernaum, where he may have already spent some time. Mark's account has Jesus moving directly from his Baptism to the Temptation to the Calling of the First Disciples at the Sea of Galilee. After this, he settles in Capernaum, which seems to have become his home base.[25]

The timing here is confusing, but Jesus might have dwelled in their village for a few weeks or months. So the disciples could have been talking about their mysterious new neighbor as they plied their trade on the bright waters or as they mended their nets.

Sixth, *his personality was probably so magnetic that it swept away doubt or fear.* Think of holy people you have heard, seen, or met. Think of people like Mother Teresa, Pope Francis, or the Dalai Lama, whose charisma is unmistakable. Even those who are not religious may feel an attraction to them. Holiness calls to a deep part of us, a part we may not understand, because we are naturally attracted to holiness. And if people are attracted to those men and women, imagine the irresistible charisma of the Son of God. The fishermen may have been responding to his magnetic personal holiness.

Seventh, *Jesus's invitation is powerful and direct.* This is a particular characteristic of his call. Again, many sources note that in Jesus's time it was unusual for a rabbi to seek out disciples. John Donahue told me, "In the rabbinic tradition, a student approaches a rabbi and asks to become a disciple. In the Greco-Roman world also potential students sought out a teacher." But here the teacher does the inviting. And it is much more than a call; it is close to a command, brooking no dissent. Jesus doesn't say, "Would you like to follow me?" but "Follow me."[26] And he offers them a tantalizing and mysterious promise—to "fish for people."

That still doesn't entirely explain the wholehearted response of the fishermen. No matter what the time sequence, or when they first met him or heard of him, at some point Jesus of Nazareth said to them, "Follow me."

The question remains: Why did they say yes?

Perhaps *because they were ready.*

Jesus of Nazareth may have come at a time when each was ready for something new. Peter, Andrew, James, and John may all have known that it was the right time to begin a new chapter in their lives. The ancient Greeks had two words for time: *chronos,* the tick-tock chronological time that we are more familiar with; and *kairos,* the right or opportune moment. We also know what these *kairos* moments are like: tired and dissatisfied with our lives, we're waiting for someone to say that it is okay to change. For the fishermen on the shore, this was their *kairos* moment.

As I was writing this chapter, a young man came to see me. Dave, as I'll call him, was working in a successful financial business, but felt an ardent desire to work with the poor. A few months earlier he had taken advantage of an unexpected opportunity to volunteer at an orphanage in the developing world, and he had found the experience transformative. In a long conversation Dave shared how much he loved working with the children, and more generally how he was powerfully drawn to work with those in need. After his stint overseas he returned to his work in finance. His current job, he said, was dull, but when he talked about his time at the orphanage, his face lit up. Now he was looking for a change. He was waiting, expectant, ready. If someone had walked in the door that day with an invitation to leave it all behind, with a promise for something new, he would have dropped everything. It would have been the *kairos* moment for him. Dave was ready.

There are many ways of being "called." Many people think that being called means hearing voices. Or they feel that since they have never had a knocked-me-off-my-feet spiritual experience that they have not been called. But often being called, as my friend from the financial-services industry discovered, can be more subtle, manifesting itself as a strong desire, a fierce attraction, or even an impulse to leave something behind.

When I was working for General Electric, after having graduated from the Wharton School of Business, I gradually found myself growing more dissatisfied with my work. One night after a long day, I saw a television documentary about the Trappist monk Thomas Merton. Something in that documentary—especially the look of contentment on Merton's face—spoke to a deep part of me, a part that had never been spoken to. Though I wouldn't have described it in these terms at the time (for I didn't speak in that language), it called to me, and promised me something new.

But the call isn't the province simply of priests or members of religious orders. All sorts of people feel powerfully drawn to vocations of all kinds: education, medicine, art, and business, for example.

God calls us in another way: to be the people we were meant to be. God creates us as unique individuals with our own gifts. And so we are already the people God made us to be. At the same time, God continually invites us to greater and greater freedom, asking us to drop the nets that entangle us in our old ways of doing things, ways that no longer are healthy for us, ways that keep us from being more loving.

In such times we can hear the voice of God. Perhaps we are stuck in a relationship characterized by mutual recrimination and hatred. It has ensnared us. Or we are tangled up in the uncharitable way we treat others, trapped in the net of unkind words and selfish motives that we have woven. Or maybe we're just lazy, and our nets are the familiar ties that keep us living the same way we always have. Or we feel that we can never undo the wrong things that need to be undone, like a fisherman cursing over his tangled net.

Then we experience something that seems to promise something new. For me it was, of all things, a television documentary. For Dave, my friend in the financial-services industry, it was the experience of working in an orphanage. For someone else it might be something heard in a conversation, something read in a book, something seen in a movie. This is just as much of a call as the one Jesus issued at the Sea of Galilee. But, as I mentioned earlier, Jesus's invitation to the fishermen was open-ended. It's usually unclear what the future will bring. All that is clear is the call.

We need to listen carefully for those calls and not grow so entangled in our daily lives that we miss them. An open and attentive stance will help us hear better and make it less likely that we block out God's voice. What if Peter and Andrew and James and John had been closed-minded or too busy to listen to Jesus?

At the beginning of the book I pointed out the two main ways of looking at Jesus—the Jesus of history and the Christ of faith. It's important to know all that we can about the historical person who called Peter, Andrew, James, and John. But it's also important to be open to the ways Jesus calls us today. It is not enough simply to know what Jesus said by the Sea of Galilee. We must also be ready to hear his voice in our own lives.

We must be receptive to the ways that God calls us—today, tomorrow, or ten years from now—so when we hear God say, "Follow me," we will be ready to drop our nets. And follow.

THE CALL OF THE FIRST DISCIPLES
Mark 1:16–20
(See also Matthew 4:18–22)

As Jesus passed along the Sea of Galilee, he saw Simon and his brother Andrew casting a net into the sea—for they were fishermen. And Jesus said to them, "Follow me and I will make you fish for people." And immediately they left their nets and followed him. As he went a little farther, he saw James son of Zebedee and his brother John, who were in their boat mending the nets. Immediately he called them; and they left their father Zebedee in the boat with the hired men, and followed him.

CHAPTER 8

Immediately

"What have you to do with us,
Jesus of Nazareth?"

THE MORNING AFTER WE arrived in Galilee, I rose early to pray in the garden of the Mount of Beatitudes. On a simple wooden bench I leaned against a tall eucalyptus tree and imagined Jesus walking on these very grounds. I had a sore back, but the grooves in the eucalyptus tree fit my back as if it had been placed there by some divine massage therapist. After breakfast, George and I decided that first we would visit Capernaum, which was within sight of our Franciscan hostel.

During our pilgrimage we visited Capernaum twice.[1] But I could have spent days there. (My journal for our first day there uses the word "amazing" three times on one page.) Excavations in Capernaum have revealed the foundations of houses from the time of Jesus, and one site has been venerated as the home of St. Peter from as early as the fourth century. In *The Holy Land* Murphy-O'Connor suggests that the town had little to recommend it to Jesus other than it was Peter's home. (Capernaum is only a few feet from the shore, not a bad place for fishermen and their families to settle.) At the time, the little town stretched for about three hundred meters along the sea. When we visited it was an oppressively hot day, and the sea sparkled under the bright sun.[2]

Bargil Pixner, a Benedictine monk, scholar, and longtime resident of Israel, estimates that Capernaum had roughly one thousand to fifteen hundred inhabitants when Jesus ministered there. It was a "frontier town" guarded by a large Roman garrison under the direction of a centurion. The garrison also provided support for the tax collectors whose job it was to collect tariffs from those who caught fish in the lake. The custom house of Matthew, the tax collector, was probably in the area. Murphy-O'Connor notes that since Luke records the synagogue as having been built by the Roman centurion, the townspeople may have been too poor to afford to construct a synagogue.[3]

Today in Capernaum you can visit a newer synagogue, probably from Byzantine times, which is said to have been built over the first-century synagogue in which Jesus preached. You can stand on that site, look out at the Sea of Galilee, and wonder about the story that happened there two thousand years ago.

For me, Capernaum was like a dream. Here was the view of the sea that Jesus must have seen every day. Here was the sky under which he lived. Here were the birdsongs he must have heard. I was filled with a sense of the *reality* of Jesus.

It also raised a multitude of questions. Why did he move from Nazareth to Capernaum? Or, more broadly, why to the Sea of Galilee? After being booted out of Nazareth, why not move, say, to Jericho, Jerusalem, or Bethlehem? The most convincing answer came from Father Doan, over dinner one night at the Pontifical Biblical Institute. The Sea of Galilee was a trading crossroads, with people coming and going from all over the region, crisscrossing the lake, buying and selling fish, a place of great traffic. Here, perhaps Jesus thought, he could reach many different kinds of people. And perhaps as a crossroads the area might be more open to new ideas.

Or perhaps he just found the sea, as I did, beautiful. Both George and I spent a lot of time in prayer, looking out at the sea. I could have stayed in Capernaum forever.

DURING MY JESUIT PHILOSOPHY studies at Loyola University Chicago, I studied Greek. My first course was Introduction to Ancient Greek, taught by an energetic young Greek professor and archaeologist named Paul Rehak; the second was a one-on-one tutorial focused on the Gospels, taught by Wendy Cotter, CSJ, a Catholic sister and New Testament scholar. Gradually, I learned the brand of Greek called *koinē,* or common Greek, used in the New Testament.

One of the first passages I translated with Wendy was from the Gospel of Mark: the electrifying story of Jesus healing a man in the synagogue at Capernaum. (In Luke, the story takes place immediately after the Rejection in Nazareth.) Buried within that story was an unusual phrase that has stayed with me, almost twenty-five years after first encountering it.

Jesus and his disciples enter Capernaum, after having left Nazareth. The small town will now be his base. (Matthew calls it *tēn idian polin,* "his own town."[4])

On the Sabbath, Jesus goes to the synagogue *euthus,* immediately.[5] He has decided to begin his ministry in the place of teaching and instruction. Once again Mark's use of *euthus* gives Jesus's life a breathless, urgent quality. The impression is of a man who felt he had a great deal to do, and perhaps not a great deal of time in which to do it.

Immediately before this, in the Gospel of Mark, Jesus has just called on Peter, Andrew, James, and John by the Sea of Galilee. It's easy to imagine the scene: the erstwhile fishermen, still unused to the role of disciples, trying to keep pace with Jesus; the curious onlookers in the synagogue wondering what their new neighbor will say; and others trying assiduously not to pay undue attention to this upstart. At the time, anyone with sufficient learning could be invited to teach in the synagogue; one needn't have had any sort of formal ordination or official credentials.[6]

So the fact that Jesus spoke in the synagogue indebted no one to show him any special honor. But ignoring Jesus will prove impossible. As in Nazareth, those in the synagogue in Capernaum are "astounded" at his teaching. (The Greek word *explēssonto* is variously translated as "struck with panic," "amazed," "astounded," or "overwhelmed with astonishment.") Such a dramatic response is another characteristic of Mark's portrait of Jesus. Surprise, wonder, fear, awe, astonishment, amazement, or similar reactions from the crowds and the disciples occur again and again in his Gospel. Donahue and Harrington note that this establishes a rapport with the reader, who would also be amazed by what he or she was reading.[7]

What it felt like to be in the presence of Jesus is difficult for the Gospels to convey. But Mark tries. People are amazed not simply by his miracles, but by what he says. Such descriptions and the frequent use of words like "astounded" give us a glimpse into his incredible charisma.

Then, *euthus* again, something dramatic happens. A man with an "unclean spirit" enters the synagogue or makes himself known to the crowd. In the Jewish tradition, "unclean" is one way of speaking about the demonic. It means something out of place in a spiritual sense, not in order, and in this case something opposed to the holy.[8] Mark will also use the word "demon," the Greek way of speaking about the same reality.

The possessed man sees Jesus and cries out, *Ti hēmin kai soi, Iēsou Nazarēne?*

It's a mysterious mix of words about which translators differ. A strictly literal translation would be: "What to us and to you?" It is sometimes rendered as "What have you to do with us?" Another translation has, "What is there between us and you?"[9] Or, "What have we to do with you?"[10] Or perhaps, "Who are you to us?" The use of the plural "us" is also a frightening tipoff to readers, indicating that the man is possessed by many demons, like the Gerasene demoniac in a later chapter, who shouts at Jesus, "My name is Legion; for we are many."

When I first read this passage with Wendy Cotter, I was immediately taken by the force of that hard-to-translate question, as if the jumble of words reflected the man's incoherent rantings. This striking phrase reminded me of times when I was so angry I could hardly speak, could barely get the words out. The possessed man virtually spits his words at Jesus. Even his use of "Nazarene," which some translate as "you Nazarene" captures some of his contempt. "Who the hell are you to us?" could be a modern translation.

Then, strangely, the possessed man says, or shouts, something sensible. "I know who you are, the Holy One of God." Here, in the first chapter of Mark, someone speaks the identity of Jesus. "Have you come to destroy us?" The demons who inhabit the man intuit something essential about Jesus.

The onlookers must have been baffled. They must have asked themselves, "Yes, who *is* this?"

On a retreat years ago I wondered if perhaps the demon was trying to tempt Jesus through pride—that is, "I know who you are: the Holy One of God. Tell everyone else who you are." If this is so, Jesus, as in the desert, rejects this temptation.

Jesus confidently rebukes the spirit and orders him to leave the poor man. "Be silent," he says (literally, "muzzle yourself"), "and come out of him!" The spirit throws the man on the ground and with a great cry comes out of him.

The people are again "amazed" and give voice to what they were probably wondering all along: "What is this?" They marvel at the exorcism and Jesus's teaching, which, the crowd says, comes "with authority."

The teaching and the healing are inextricably connected. Jesus's deeds lend authority to his words, and authenticate them: someone who can drive out demons is surely someone to listen to, and what he says must be true. And his words help to explain his deeds; since his preaching is about the reign of God, his healings must somehow be a manifestation of the coming of that reign. As Raymond Brown writes, "Teaching and an exercise of divine power in healing and driving out demons are united in the proclamation of the kingdom, implying that the coming of God's rule is complex."[11]

The crowd also must have marveled at the *way* the exorcism was accomplished: without any of the complicated incantations or rituals that other wonder-workers used—without even a touch. This man did this with just his words. Jesus's speech is more powerful than the demonic power. And his words effect what he says.

No wonder they were amazed.

HERE IS A CRITICAL question to ask about the Gospels: How is an intelligent, rational, modern-day person to understand tales about possessions? For healings and exorcisms are an important part of Jesus's ministry. As Meier says in *A Marginal Jew*:

> The statement that Jesus acted as and was viewed as an exorcist and healer during his public ministry has as much historical corroboration as almost any other statement we can make about the Jesus of history. Indeed, as a global affirmation about Jesus and his ministry it has much better attestation than many other assertions made about Jesus, assertions that people often take for granted.[12]

To understand what Jesus is doing we have to examine what he's confronting. Who does Jesus encounter when meeting someone with an "unclean" spirit or possessed by a "demon"?

William Barclay proposes two sensible possibilities. Either we relegate demonic possession to the realm of primitive thought and conclude that this was a way of understanding illness in a prescientific era, or we accept the action of the demonic both in the New Testament and today. And, notes Barclay, in the case of the former, we still need to plumb Jesus's actions. Did Jesus know more about such things than did the people of his time? On the one hand, Jesus is fully divine and so may have enjoyed an awareness unknown to any of his contemporaries—or to us. On the other hand, if we say that he somehow understood more about science and medicine than others, we're contradicting the belief that Jesus was fully human, with a human consciousness, and that he needed to be taught something before he could know it.

Here's one way to think about it. First, some of the possessions in the Gospels seem rather to be the manifestation of physical illness. I'm not speaking about Jesus healing someone who is truly under the sway of demonic forces, but about the healing of those called "possessed" who are in reality suffering from a purely physical ailment. There is, for example, the compelling story of a distraught father, told in all three Synoptic Gospels, who brings to Jesus a boy who is called epileptic.[13] The father's love for his son and his anguish over the boy's illness will resonate with anyone who has seen a child suffer.

Desperate, the father kneels at Jesus's feet and describes the condition: "Lord, have mercy on my son," he says, "for he is an epileptic and he suffers terribly; he often falls into the fire and often into the water."[14] But when the boy is healed, Jesus is described as giving a "rebuke" to "the demon," which came out of him "instantly."

So here the ancient mind attributes to a demon what we now attribute to a physiological condition. It conflates possession with illness.[15] That would be an example of Barclay's first possibility.

Still, Jesus heals the boy of a terrible condition that has caused great suffering to him and his father, which is the point of the story. It remains miraculous.

But there are some Gospel stories that still, two thousand years later, do not lend themselves so easily to scientific explanations—stories in which the demon is able to identify Jesus as the Messiah at a time when others around him (including his closest followers) still have no clue; stories in which the demons speak of themselves, oddly, in the plural, as when they identify themselves as "legion"; stories in which the demons enable people to do frightening physical feats, such as bursting through chains. These accounts still have the ability to send a shiver up our spines, for there is something decidedly otherworldly about them.

In our own day too, there are some credible stories of possessions that defy rational explanations. Since entering the Jesuits, I have read about and heard reports from rational and reliable witnesses who have assisted at exorcisms and who have seen terrifying things that defy logical explanation. Perhaps someday we will have further scientific explanations, but to my mind the possibility of possessions is not hard to believe. Understanding it is quite another thing.

From an infinitely less threatening vantage point, I've done enough spiritual counseling to witness the effects of evil in people's lives—evil that is more than something from within them and that seems to exhibit similar characteristics from person to person. That is, there is a certain *sameness* to the way that people describe this force. St. Ignatius of Loyola, in his classic sixteenth-century text *The Spiritual Exercises,* once delineated the three ways that the "enemy of human nature" acts: like a spoiled child (making a person act childishly, selfishly, refusing to take no for an answer), like a "false lover" (tempting the person to conceal bad motives or sinful behaviors), or like an "army commander" (attacking a person at his or her weakest point). Such descriptions ring true for those who have experienced them.

I believe in the presence of evil as a real and coherent force opposed to God and one that can sometimes overtake people, but not necessarily in the popular conception of the devil. As C. S. Lewis said, when asked if he believed in the devil, "I am not particular about the hoofs and horns. But in other respects my answer is, 'Yes, I do.'"[16]

No matter how you envision the power of evil, there is an important theological point in this Gospel story. Jesus enters into a struggle that goes beyond his healing of the boy. Harrington writes, "Jesus is engaged in a battle with cosmic significance. He struggles against and overcomes the chaotic forces of nature, Satan, sickness, and death. In this respect his acts of power are part of his mission to proclaim and make present the kingdom of God."[17]

And no matter how you understand some of these possession stories, the point is that the crowds saw a man named Jesus heal a person who was either sick or possessed. Either way it's not surprising that Mark describes the crowds who have witnessed the exorcism as *ethambēthēsan,* amazed. It was amazing and still is.

DESPITE PEOPLE'S LACK OF direct experience with exorcisms these scenes prove surprisingly easy for people to meditate on. To begin with, they are easy to imagine. People have seen enough dramatic portrayals to concoct an image of the violent person spitting imprecations at Jesus. Also, almost all of us feel at some point that we would like God to rid us of our "demons." We're not "possessed" like the poor man in the story, but we desperately want Jesus to rid us of whatever seems in opposition to God's desires for us. We feel that something is not in the right place, out of order, opposed to the holy.

On one retreat, I imagined the enthusiastic new disciples entering the synagogue in Capernaum and jockeying for position. Suddenly the demoniac enters—from outside the synagogue—racing in and throwing himself before Jesus. The crowd is terrified. Since the disciples are new, they probably are too. Jesus is not.

The incident seems a harsh, almost violent, one. The demoniac spits out his curses at Jesus. Jesus shouts, "Be silent, and come out of him!" and with a loud cry the demon immediately throws the man on the ground. In response, the astonished congregation bursts into loud shouts of praise, of confusion, of wonder, all the while talking and gesticulating, trying to understand what they have seen. It is a noisy scene.

But maybe it wasn't that way at all in Capernaum.

At one point in Matthew's Gospel, Jesus describes himself as "gentle and humble in heart."[18] So perhaps in the synagogue that day Jesus acted more quietly than we suspect. Isn't it possible that when Jesus saw the terrible force that consumed the man, he first paused in silent pity, as any compassionate person would do when faced with such torment? Maybe Jesus simply turned to the man and said quietly, "Come out of him."

That passage from Matthew may also give us a glimpse into Jesus's inner life. Despite his fiery preaching, his passionate opposition to oppression, and, yes, his physically tossing the merchants out of the Temple, Jesus describes himself as "gentle." Another translation uses "meek." So perhaps when confronting the unclean man, Jesus was calmer than we normally picture him.

During another retreat, I imagined Jesus slowly removing his prayer shawl, standing up, and approaching the man in utter silence before ordering the spirit out of him. Some of the most effective responses to anger and violence can be a confident peace and a quiet trust in God. Maybe that's what astonished the crowds.

"WHO ARE YOU TO us?" was the English-language translation that Wendy Cotter and I finally settled on during our tutorial in New Testament Greek. Who is God to us? One answer is compassion, forgiveness, and mercy, even when we feel we deserve them the least.

Jesus's healing of the man in the synagogue was immediate. Our own healings, however, usually don't happen *euthus*. And this is a source of sadness for many of us. We desperately long for something as instantaneous as what Jesus offered to the man. And I'm not talking simply about physical healings.

For many years I've struggled with a variety of sinful patterns and selfish attitudes: pride, ambition, and a selfishness that is masked as self-care. And I've worked hard—through prayer, spiritual direction, and even therapy—to rid myself of, or at least to lessen, these "demons." But moving away from deeply rooted tendencies is a long process that takes work and requires patience. Conversion takes time. Most of all, you must trust that God wants you to change every bit as much as Jesus wanted to help the man in the synagogue.

Yet I still sin. I try to avoid vanity, but I find myself vain, despite myself. I try not to be mean-spirited, but sarcastic words fly out of my mouth as if of their own accord. In prayer I wonder: *Where does this come from? Why am I still like this? When will these demons leave me?*

St. Paul's words return to me: "For I do not do the good I want, but the evil I do not want is what I do."[19]

Once I was so frustrated about an unhealthy aspect of my personality that I knelt on the floor and begged God to change me as quickly as Jesus had changed the man. As in the case of the unclean spirit, what reason would God have for not exorcising that part of me? Why wouldn't God do this *euthus*? After an hour, waiting, I rose from the floor, the same person as before.

A few months later, I was speaking to a spiritual director, lamenting this. Why wouldn't God heal me as quickly as Jesus had healed the man in the synagogue? Who was God to me, if God couldn't do this?

The spiritual director pointed to a tree outside his window. "See that tree?" he said.

I nodded.

"What color is it?"

I knew he was leading me to an obvious answer that I couldn't yet see.

"Green," I said. "It's a green tree."

"In the fall it will be red," he said.

And I knew this. I had seen that very tree in the middle of a New England autumn. It was a glorious scarlet.

"And no one sees it change," he said.

Conversion happens most often in a slow, deliberate, and mysterious way, like a tree changing colors in the fall. And often you can't see the change in yourself.

But change comes. About ten years after I entered the Jesuits, I realized that I no longer was as envious of others as I had once been. Certainly I still fall prey to that tendency, but before entering the Jesuits, envy was something I confronted daily—sometimes hourly. Over time, with prayer and reflection that led to greater self-understanding, it had evaporated. One day I noticed it simply wasn't there. It was grace, and it had as much to do with God's desire to heal me as it did with my "working" on it. For if we open ourselves to the workings of grace, God will heal us of whatever prevents us from living fully and freely. To me, this is the meaning of conversion.

Ti hēmin kai soi? "Who are you to us?" We can ask that question of God today, just as the man in the synagogue asked it of Jesus centuries ago. And we can hear the same answer, spoken in the language of faith: God is the possibility of healing, conversion, and, most of all, of new life.

THE HEALING OF THE MAN WITH THE UNCLEAN SPIRIT
Mark 1:21–28
(See also Luke 4:31–37)

They went to Capernaum; and when the Sabbath came, he entered the synagogue and taught. They were astounded at his teaching, for he taught them as one having authority, and not as the scribes. Just then there was in their synagogue a man with an unclean spirit, and he cried out, "What have you to do with us, Jesus of Nazareth? Have you come to destroy us? I know who you are, the Holy One of God." But Jesus rebuked him, saying, "Be silent, and come out of him!" And the unclean spirit, throwing him into convulsions and crying with a loud voice, came out of him. They were all amazed, and they kept on asking one another, "What is this? A new teaching—with authority! He commands even the unclean spirits, and they obey him." At once his fame began to spread throughout the surrounding region of Galilee.

CHAPTER 9

Gennesaret

*"Go away from me, Lord,
for I am a sinful man!"*

IN THE FIFTH CHAPTER of Luke's Gospel, Jesus preaches to a crowd by Lake Gennesaret—also known as the Sea of Galilee and the Sea of Tiberias. As I've already confessed, before visiting the Holy Land I thought that these were three separate bodies of water, and I imagined Jesus cheerfully strolling from one to the other.

There were a great many other things I didn't know about the region. For one thing, how close everything was. Many of the places where Jesus performed his miracles were just a mile or two from Capernaum. In one morning you could walk from the scenes of the Call of the First Disciples to the Multiplication of the Loaves and Fishes to the Healing of the Woman with the Hemorrhage. It was no wonder that Jesus was besieged by crowds. Not only was he performing miracles, but he was doing so in a confined geographic space.

The Gospel of Luke tells us that the crowd is "pressing in on him." This is not surprising, since Jesus has just healed the man in the synagogue at Capernaum and, afterward, healed Simon's mother-in-law. Perhaps being pushed back closer to the shoreline by the people, Jesus stumbles upon fishermen who are cleaning their nets. Given that they would clean their nets *after* fishing, the reader knows that they have just completed a night of hard work. Jesus steps into Simon's boat and asks him to push out from land so that he can teach. In the boat, Jesus sits down, the traditional posture for a teacher of the time. This small detail in Luke's Gospel indicates Jesus's confidence.

When he is finished preaching, Jesus asks Simon to go into the deep water and let down his nets. Not surprisingly, Simon is dubious. "Master" (*epistata*), he says, using a term showing respect for Jesus's authority, "we have worked all night long but have caught nothing. Yet if you say so, I will let down the nets." Simon's full humanity is on display; he oscillates between a natural doubt ("Are you kidding?") and faith ("If you say so").

Simon is willing to try again, a good trait for a disciple—or anyone for that matter. For those who wonder why Jesus would have chosen the hardheaded and impetuous Simon (whom he will later name Peter) to run his church, here is an early indication: "You want me to try again? In this same boat we were just fishing from? If you say so, Jesus."

He may also have been encouraged by having listened to Jesus's preaching. What Jesus preached from the boat goes unrecorded, but perhaps it so impressed Peter that the fisherman was filled with confidence in the carpenter. Still, you can imagine him doubting even as he unfurled his sail.

Scholars term this a "call narrative" and, as you can tell, it is similar to the Call of the First Disciples as told in Mark and Matthew.[1] Certain key elements are the same; for example, the story takes place on the Sea of Galilee, while Peter and his friends are plying their trade. But Luke tells the story differently, and may also be combining two tales—the story of the call, which Mark and Matthew recounted, and the "work of power" that is about to happen.

Peter and the so-far-unnamed others let down their nets, which are suddenly filled to the bursting point—so much that the boat almost sinks and they have to call on their partners to help. It's easy to imagine the commotion: the boat suddenly leans to one side and begins to take on water, the fish flop noisily in the nets as the men strain to hoist them aboard, the other fishermen hurriedly row over

to help their friends, and the men shout exultantly after a long night
of catching nothing. Incidentally, the rationalistic interpretation
that Jesus saw a shoal of fish that the fishermen had missed seems
unconvincing here. It's a stretch to imagine the carpenter spotting
something that the experienced fishermen had overlooked.

Once on retreat I prayed with this passage and imagined the
sudden lurch of the boat as the school of fish banged into the net,
and Jesus's smiling response to this great miracle: "What's in the net,
Simon?" And I could imagine Simon's response: a combination of
fear, wonder, and hope. That dramatic lurch changed his life. In fact,
Jesus may have needed something dramatic to convince the head-
strong Peter to join him.

Peter's response is deeply moving. He falls to his knees and says,
"Go away from me, Lord, for I am a sinful man!" Luke notes that this
gesture came from "amazement" (*thambos,* or religious awe before
the holy). Peter now calls Jesus not simply Master (*epistata*), but Lord
(*kyrios*).

Peter wasn't the only one astounded by what he saw. Luke now
tells us that others were present. All who were with him "were
amazed," including James and John, sons of Zebedee, who are called
"partners" with Peter. The word used for partners is *koinōnoi,* which
can also be translated as "sharers." Luke Timothy Johnson notes that
the image of the soon-to-be-apostles already working together, and
pooling their resources, sets the stage for the community of disciples
they will soon become.[2]

Standing before Peter, Jesus says, "Do not be afraid, Simon.
From now on you will be catching people." That's "people" again—
anthrōpous.

Luke ends the story abruptly: "When they had brought their
boats to shore, they left everything and followed him." This is not
just a physical following, as if they simply walked in single file behind
Jesus. The Greek *ēkolouthēsan* connotes a spiritual following, the
total commitment of the disciple to the teacher.

We've already considered how the fishermen might have been able to leave everything to follow Jesus. But what lies behind Peter's seemingly strange behavior aboard the boat? Isn't it odd to move so quickly from telling a person to leave to wanting to follow him? More basically, why would Peter ask Jesus to "go away"? Why would *we*?

OVERWHELMED BY THE MIRACLE of the immense catch, Peter is "amazed," falling to his knees before the Lord. Peter seems painfully aware of his sinfulness, of the distance between himself and Jesus. In the bright sunlight of God's love, Peter sees his shadow side. So he utters an utterly human response: "Go away from me, for I am a sinful man."

We can try to imagine Peter's possible frame of mind when he asked Jesus to leave him, but it is just as important to understand why *we* say to God, "Go away from me."

Let's look at some possible reasons.

First, *unworthiness*. Many people struggle with feelings of inadequacy or shame. "Why would God want to be in a relationship with *me?*" they ask. This happens even in the face of overwhelming evidence that God desires to be part of their lives. People growing in awareness of the spiritual life often tell me about powerful experiences in prayer—for example, being moved by a passage from Scripture or sensing the presence of God in nature. But when I suggest that God is speaking to them through these experiences, they recoil. "That's ridiculous," they sometimes say. "It's impossible that God would want to communicate with me. I'm too sinful."

Well, of course you're sinful. We are all sinners, but sinners loved by God. And God still desires to enter into a relationship with each of us.

A few years ago I was co-directing a parish retreat with a woman named Mary. The weekend's theme was learning from the lives of the saints. During one presentation Mary told the group the story of

Dorothy Day, the American-born founder of the Catholic Worker movement, who had in her young adulthood undergone an abortion. Mary said to the group, mostly women, "Imagine all the good that would never have gotten done if Dorothy Day had said: 'What could God do with me? I had an abortion.'" Feelings of inadequacy are human, as Peter shows us, but we are invited to see them in the light of God's love.

A second reason we push God away is *fear*. Fear of the Lord is healthy, even praised in Scripture. The Book of Proverbs calls it "the beginning of wisdom."[3] As God's creatures, we must be in awe and reverence of the Creator of the Universe. Sometimes we overlook this aspect of our faith, but it probably wasn't difficult for Peter to summon up that emotion when he felt the boat lurch to one side.

Our appreciation of the role of simple human fear in the apostles' lives may be limited by an overfamiliarity with the Gospels. We might be so used to these stories that Jesus's display of power is predictable or even boring. Well, of course, Jesus can cause a huge catch of fish; that's just what he *does*. But to Peter and "all who were with him," the event must have been absolutely terrifying. Peter, who knew the sea well, was a professional fisherman and had just been out fishing all night; he *knew* there are no fish around.

Imagine a friend being able to control nature. Imagine your friend suddenly being able to make a storm gather overhead with the snap of his fingers. Seeing him command the elements would be deeply unsettling and understandably frightening. It would seem that all you know about nature has been shaken to its core; and you would now fear your friend, who seems to possess this bizarre power.

We might be frightened of God's power even if it doesn't manifest itself in such dramatic ways. During a retreat a few years after I entered the Jesuits, I was praying about the challenges of chastity. How would I ever deal with feelings of loneliness, how could I endure a life without a significant other? Suddenly, *euthus,* as if a switch had been turned on, memories of love cascaded into my mind.

I remembered being loved by so many people: this Catholic sister I knew well, this priest who had helped me through a rough patch, this friend who had been a part of my Jesuit life. All examples of how I had been loved—always, but especially as a Jesuit. It was an answer to my questions about chastity. But the point is this: I couldn't believe the speed with which it happened, and at the time I felt not gratitude but *fear*—that God seemed to be answering my prayer so directly and immediately.

Fear of the Lord is natural. But it must be coupled with an understanding of God's love, for Jesus performs miracles not simply to show his power, but to show his love.

The third reason is *fear of change*. People starting out in the spiritual life often share a common image of God: the Evil Trickster. Some young adults, for example, have said to me, "Well, I feel God is inviting me to be more loving, forgiving, and open. But I fear what will happen if I say yes." They worry that they will be taken advantage of by others or that they'll be labeled as doormats. Or they fear that once they let go of their old ways—whether or not those ways have been effective or healthy—they will be lost. Basically, they fear that by following God's invitation, things will go wrong.

Often this image results from envisioning God the way we see other authority figures. If your father or mother was a demanding taskmaster, you may unintentionally ascribe some of those attributes to God. Likewise, if you have experienced authorities as untrustworthy, you may have a hard time trusting God.

So I often ask people, "What is your understanding of God? Is God the Evil Trickster who wants to lure you down the garden path to trick you and bring you to ruin?" Challenged intellectually, they often realize how misguided that image is: "Of course not!" God desires the best for us. As the Book of Jeremiah says, "For surely I know the plans I have for you, says the Lord, plans for your welfare and not for harm, to give you a future with hope."[4]

More generally, we might fear change per se. What will happen if I follow Jesus? What will it mean to abandon my old ways? How will I change? Fear of change may have been one of the reasons Peter says, "Go away from me." We may also fear not changing *fast* enough. We grow impatient with the slow process of conversion. Remember that no one sees the trees change color. Change happens if we're open to God's grace, but it happens in God's time. It took time, after all, for Simon to become Peter.

Fourth is *fear of intimacy*. We often fear real intimacy not only with one another, but also with God. What would it mean to let someone into our inner lives? Peter, a hard-nosed fisherman, may have feared intimacy with this itinerant preacher, someone from outside of his family circle, outside of Capernaum. But, again, the intimacy that Jesus offers is motivated by love. And even then, we can feel fear.

Now, notice Jesus's response to Peter's emotional "Go away from me!" Not only does Jesus *not* depart from Peter; he calls Peter to join him in his mission: "From now on you will be catching people." Jesus comes not to drive people away, but to call us to join him, if we are willing to follow, no matter who we are—single, married, or vowed; rich or poor; old or young; liberal or conservative; lay, clergy, or religious; gay or straight.

This is an important message to those who, for whatever reason, feel as if their churches are saying to them, "Go away!" Some divorced and remarried Catholics tell me they feel this way. Some gays and lesbians do as well. So do some women. But Christ's message is not only a call to conversion, but one of inclusion, a message that welcomes us into the community and restores us to it. Even if you're made to feel unworthy and are tempted to say, "Go away!" Christ says, as he did to Peter, "Join me in my great mission."

Despite what must have been some fear, Peter still follows Jesus. The Gospels can be seen, at least in part, as the story of Jesus's friendship with his disciples: one party is always faithful, the other parties not as much. Peter continues to sin in the weeks and months to follow. Nonetheless, Jesus continually calls him to conversion.

Jesus knows Peter's weaknesses and calls him anyway. Jesus calls us anyway too, in spite of our weaknesses.

In fact, Jesus ultimately may have called Peter to lead the church because Peter was painfully conscious of his own weakness. He would never forget how far he fell, how much he failed—and so he would remember to rely on God's strength, not his own. How many of us must learn, sometimes multiple times, to acknowledge our weakness and to trust in God.

As Jesus stood on Lake Gennesaret, he may have guessed that Peter was not only bold, persistent, and courageous; he was also weak enough to be a good leader.

LET ME RETURN TO those Christians who feel marginalized from their churches and to those who sometimes feel discouraged or scandalized by what their churches do.

It is important to remember that the church did not die and rise from the dead. Jesus did. Especially in times of difficulty and scandal, we need to be reminded that our faith is not in an institution but in a *person:* Jesus. Certainly we experience Christ in and through the church and certainly the church is the "Body of Christ" on earth. And I don't in any way deny or minimize the importance of the church. But the church does not save us. Jesus does. It is Jesus, not the institution, who has called you into relationship with him. Even though we may feel as if the church is saying "Go away from me," those words never pass from Jesus's lips when he meets sinful people.

For those who feel scandalized because of sins committed by members of the church, it is also important to remember that the church has always been imperfect. Dorothy Day once said, "I love the Church for Christ made visible, not for itself, because it was so often a scandal to me."⁵

Once again, this is not to drive anyone away from the church. Most of my adult life has been dedicated to the church. But the church is made up of people who fail, who sin, and who commit grave error, even crimes. The church has been imperfect since its beginning. Christians who read this Gospel passage from Luke know that all three of these men will fail Jesus at crucial moments. James and John will misunderstand him when they proclaim that they want to be "first" in the kingdom of heaven. More seriously, Peter will fail Jesus three times during the Passion. The initial enthusiastic response on the shore of Galilee draws us into a human tension between fidelity and failure, which will be repeated over and over as the disciples' pilgrimage unfolds.

It is our pilgrimage too. In belonging to a church, we sometimes feel unworthy of membership. We also feel, at times, that the church is unworthy of the one who founded it. We walk both a pilgrimage of power in the light of the Resurrection and a pilgrimage of powerlessness in the face of sin. We have the benefit of knowing all this now. Peter did not. He said yes to Jesus with utter trust, having seen what Jesus could do. But he could not have known to what shores his yes would take him.

WHAT WAS PETER THINKING as he rowed back to the shore? On one retreat, I realized that after Jesus said, "From now on you will be catching people," Peter and the disciples still needed to return to shore. There was ample time for him to decide to say no to Jesus's offer. To have second thoughts. Peter must have wondered when he saw the astonishing, alarming, unbelievable catch of fish, *Is this really happening?* For he is no longer seeing things as they are in the natural world, but as they are in the reign of God. Now he has to make a choice about how he is going to see.

F. J. Sheed has a wonderful insight about this miracle. Peter, he notes, had already seen other miracles—the healing of his mother-in-law, for instance. Perhaps he was also present at the Wedding Feast at Cana, traditionally Jesus's first miracle, as recorded in the Gospel of John. But these phenomena—healing bodies and making wine—were outside Peter's experience. "But fish were different: he knew all about fish. This miracle hit home to him as the others had not."[6]

As Peter rowed or sailed back to the shore, he may have considered everything that he would have to give up: his livelihood, his family, everything he knew. He must have had doubts. As Peter strained against the waves on Lake Gennesaret, he must have asked himself whether he would be able to leave so much behind. He must have toggled between worry about the future and amazement over the miraculous catch of fish.

I imagined being in the scene and asking Peter, "How could you do it?" And in my prayer he seemed to point to the net and say, "Just look at all those fish!"

All of us need to leave things behind in order to follow God. For some of us, it is addictive patterns of behavior, for others an overweening emphasis on our own success, for others the adulation of the crowd. It helps sometimes to look not just at what we're leaving behind and what God promises us, but also at what God has shown us *already*.

Just look at all those fish.

THE MIRACULOUS CATCH OF FISH
Luke 5:1–11

Once while Jesus was standing beside the lake of Gennesaret, and the crowd was pressing in on him to hear the word of God, he saw two boats there at the shore of the lake; the fishermen had gone out of them and were washing their nets. He got into one of the boats, the one belonging to Simon, and asked him to put out a little way from the shore. Then he sat down and taught the crowds from the boat. When he had finished speaking, he said to Simon, "Put out into the deep water and let down your nets for a catch." Simon answered, "Master, we have worked all night long but have caught nothing. Yet if you say so, I will let down the nets." When they had done this, they caught so many fish that their nets were beginning to break. So they signaled to their partners in the other boat to come and help them. And they came and filled both boats, so that they began to sink. But when Simon Peter saw it, he fell down at Jesus' knees, saying, "Go away from me, Lord, for I am a sinful man!" For he and all who were with him were amazed at the catch of fish that they had taken; and so also were James and John, sons of Zebedee, who were partners with Simon. Then Jesus said to Simon, "Do not be afraid; from now on you will be catching people." When they had brought their boats to shore, they left everything and followed him.

Chapter 10

Happy

"Rejoice and be glad."

Blessed were we to be staying at the Mount of Beatitudes hostel. Not simply because of the air-conditioned rooms, the titanic breakfasts, the proximity to so many sites in Galilee, or even the gracious Franciscan hospitality, but something else: the ease of prayer. Whenever we emerged from our hotel we stepped on holy ground: the spot where Jesus, by tradition, preached the Beatitudes during his Sermon on the Mount. And in case we ever forgot, tour buses rumbled into the parking lot every few hours, from early morning to late afternoon.

The Church of the Beatitudes, the centerpiece of the complex, was surrounded by a lush garden filled with date-palm and cypress trees and carpeted with scented flowers and bougainvillea. A few days into our stay, George and I decided to spend the morning praying. So shortly after dawn, I sat on a bench and leaned against a tall eucalyptus tree.

Naturally, I prayed about the Beatitudes. It would have been almost impossible not to. Scattered throughout the garden were small granite markers, six inches off the ground, featuring lines from Matthew's version of the Beatitudes: *Beati Pauperes Spiritu, Quoniam Ipsorum Est Regnum Caelorum,* read a sign almost obscured by red flowers. "Blessed are the poor in spirit, for theirs is the kingdom of heaven."

Tʜᴇ Bᴇᴀᴛɪᴛᴜᴅᴇs ᴀʀᴇ ᴛʜᴇ series of Jesus's statements that begin with "Blessed are," found in both Matthew and Luke, which offer different versions of Jesus's list. In the Gospel of Matthew, the Beatitudes begin what is commonly called the Sermon on the Mount: "When Jesus saw the crowds," writes Matthew, "he went up the mountain; and after he sat down, his disciples came to him. Then he began to speak, and taught them, saying: 'Blessed are the poor in spirit . . .'"

On a mountain, but where? As I've mentioned, scholars debate and sometimes despair over finding the precise locations of Jesus's miracles and speeches. Daniel Harrington says about the Sermon on the Mount that "attempts at determining the exact site are useless."[1]

Jerome Murphy-O'Connor arrives at the same conclusion and employs some ingenious sociological deduction to explain the current location of the Mount of Beatitudes. It was inevitable, he wrote, that the well-watered and shady spot on the shores of the Sea of Galilee where pilgrims picnicked in Byzantine times would become identified as the scene of many feeding miracles, including the Multiplication of the Loaves and Fishes. "Then," he adds tartly, "it became convenient to localize the Sermon on the Mount on a small hill nearby."[2] So conceivably I was praying miles from the real location.

Still, somewhere on the western side of the Sea of Galilee, on a rise (unless the evangelists were using the mountain as an allegorical place of revelation—that is, comparing this incident to the revelation of the Torah to Moses on Mt. Sinai), the Gospel of Matthew tells us that Jesus named those he considered blessed.

Matthew's version of the Sermon on the Mount, however, includes more than just the Beatitudes. Stretching leisurely through chapters 5 to 7, it continues with some condemnations against the rich and complacent as well as many other teachings—on judging, anger, adultery, serving two masters, anxiety—and it also includes the Lord's Prayer. Most likely these are a collection of sayings from

Jesus gathered into one place in Matthew's narrative. By contrast, Luke scatters some of these same teachings throughout his Gospel in various places.

Luke also situates the sermon elsewhere. Jesus has just come down from the mountain, after naming the twelve apostles. From there, with a "multitude" in tow, he stops on a "level place," where he heals many people before beginning to preach. As he often does, Luke connects the ministry of healing with the ministry of the word: one gives authority and meaning to the other. Because of this "level place," Luke's version is often known as the Sermon on the Plain.[3]

In both cases "crowds" or "multitudes" follow the Teacher. In Matthew, Jesus goes up the mountain in sight of the crowds and begins to instruct the disciples. But this does not exclude the crowds, who presumably are listening in. Luke's narrative refers to the "great crowd" of disciples (*ochlos polus*), then a "great multitude" of people (*plēthos polu*), and finally a "crowd" (*ochlos*). In Luke, Jesus has just called the Twelve so the sermon serves as a set of operating instructions for them, with the crowds listening in.

In both cases, though, many people are around. Jesus intends his message for a large audience. And Matthew and Luke are implicitly saying, "That includes you."

"Blessed are," Jesus says, and he names those whom he favors.[4] In Matthew's version they are: the poor in spirit, those who mourn, the meek, those who hunger and thirst for righteousness, the merciful, the pure in heart, the peacemakers, those who are persecuted for righteousness' sake, and those who are persecuted, reviled, and slandered because they follow Jesus. Now, the entire Sermon on the Mount, as gathered together in Matthew, was probably not delivered in full on that one day. More likely it is a compendium of Jesus's teachings. The Beatitudes might have been easy for a large crowd to hear, but as William Barclay notes of the entire sermon, "Anyone who heard it in its present form would have been exhausted long before the end."[5]

Luke's version is more compact. Jesus blesses the poor (instead of the poor in spirit), the hungry, those who weep, and those who are persecuted because they follow Jesus. In both Gospels all will receive a reward. Consider the passage in Luke:

> Blessed are you who are poor, for yours is the kingdom of God.
> Blessed are you who are hungry now, for you will be filled.
> Blessed are you who weep now, for you will laugh.
> Blessed are you when people hate you, and when they exclude you, revile you, and defame you on account of the Son of Man. Rejoice on that day and leap for joy, for surely your reward is great in heaven; for that is what their ancestors did to the prophets.

These groups, variously forgotten, marginalized, downtrodden, persecuted, or simply hopeless, are to be rewarded. But when? Now or later? Once again, we are faced with a question about the "timing" of the reign of God. On the one hand, the kingdom of God *belongs to* the poor. So, already. On the other, mourners *will* be comforted, and the ones who are persecuted will receive their reward *in heaven*. So, not yet.

Many scholars speak of the Beatitudes as an eschatological promise; that is, these groups will be showered with blessings by God in the future.[6] Another interpretation is that Jesus reveals these people as *already* blessed—he praises and welcomes them specifically into the reign of God. They are blessed now because Jesus blesses them. In his book *Jesus of Nazareth,* Gerhard Lohfink underscores this radical immediacy. Jesus, he believes, is not saying that mourning or being hungry is a blessing—nor is he in this discourse promising those groups blessings merely in the afterlife (though these would surely come). The turning point is already here: "God's intervention is about to take place and . . . it is especially the hopeless who will experience God's hope and salvation in a measure beyond all telling. . . . He promises the poor and beaten down in particular that they will participate in the reign of God."[7]

Here, then, are Jesus's favored ones. In his comfort of and care for them, Jesus is drawing on many of the Hebrew Scriptures that point to the poor and oppressed as those deserving special attention.[8] But Jesus goes beyond that, elevating them in his reign and offering them as models of discipleship. They provide a partial sketch of character traits, attitudes, and virtues befitting disciples.[9] Thus, the Beatitudes work on multiple levels and in multiple times: as a template for discipleship in the present (be humble now); as an indication of those who are favored (God loves the humble); and as a promise of future reward (God will reward the humble).

For all these reasons the Beatitudes are often called the Gospel within the Gospel.

WHAT WAS IT LIKE for the original listeners to hear the Beatitudes? Since we are not Aramaic-speaking Galileans in the first century who intuitively understand the milieu in which Jesus was preaching, the best answer may be: Who knows? However, we know something about what it meant to be poor, hungry, and persecuted at the time, so we can posit a few reactions.[10]

First: surprise. Those on the bottom are promised a place on top. Jesus's upside-down vision represented a complete transformation of society as his listeners knew it. Those who had suffered much must have been consoled.

Another reaction, among the wealthy or powerful, might have been shock. If the reign of God was to be given into the hands of the poor, for example, what did that mean for those with money and power? Certainly they had heard of this before, in the Hebrew Scriptures, but the urgency of Jesus's words may have sparked fear. How could such a radical social transformation happen without violence?

Although Jesus intends that everyone (the multitudes) participate in the reign of God, there must have been some who found threatening what we normally consider comforting words. Even today, with so many lines from the Beatitudes embedded in our literature and culture, Jesus's list of favorites retains its power to shock.

A few of the groups Jesus praises would still win praise today—for example, the "pure in heart." The Greek is *katharoi tē cardia,* literally, the "clean of heart." The word had multiple meanings in Jesus's time: clean, like recently washed clothes; clean, like grain that has had impurities removed; or clean, like a substance that has never been adulterated—like wine that has not been mixed with water.[11] Mostly this term relates to pure motives rather than to ritual or sexual purity. People not acting out of excessive self-interest, whose inner and outer lives correspond, like those in the Psalms with "clean hands and pure hearts," are the subject of his blessing.[12] It's a challenge to be "clean of heart," because even in our most selfless moments we may act from mixed motives. But the general meaning—a person of integrity—would be praised today. So if Jesus were to say today, "Blessed are people of integrity," he would probably get a hearty round of applause.

Other lines might be met by stony silence. Even when we distinguish between groups promised consolation or justice (the poor, the hungry, mourners) and groups praised for their behavior (the pure in heart, peacemakers, those who hunger for righteousness), Jesus's words disturb, because many of those Jesus singles out for praise are sneered at today. Think about our common perceptions of some of these groups.

Let's start with the poor. Often today they are seen as lazy, an embarrassment to society, or simply nonentities. By the way, the word Luke uses—*ptōchoi*—may refer not simply to the indigent or even the working poor, but to something more specific—beggars. The word is connected to the root *ptōssein,* meaning to crouch or cower, the way that many beggars do. Perhaps to reclaim the full power of Jesus's words we can hear him say, "Blessed are the beggars." Have you ever walked past a group of homeless people and thought, *Blessed are they?*

How about the "poor in spirit"? Many Christians find it hard to appreciate this Beatitude, because almost any translation implies the opposite of what Jesus means. Several years ago during a Bible study class in a parish, I asked the group what they thought of when they heard the term "poverty of spirit." A woman's hand shot up. "Someone who doesn't believe in God?" Paradoxically, to be poor in spirit is to be rich in faith. It indicates a person whose humility allows him or her to grasp the fundamental reliance on God. But even armed with that understanding, we sense that this Beatitude is still a threat. Humility is an unpopular virtue.

"Meek" may be an even more unpalatable word, conjuring up a simpering milquetoast, someone afraid to stand up for himself or herself, a person devoid of self-confidence and self-respect. When was the last time you heard someone say, "I really like that guy. He's so meek"?

What did Jesus mean? The Greek *praeis* is a complicated word with several possible meanings: self-control over one's passions; obedient or domesticated, as in an animal; or gentle. To understand Jesus's likely intent, it may help to look at the Hebrew that was the antecedent of the Greek. (Remember, like all the evangelists, Matthew had to translate Jesus's Aramaic or Hebrew into Greek.) Jesus probably had in mind the word *anawim*.[13] The *anawim* were not simply the meek, but those who were so poor, or weak, that they knew they depended utterly on God. So, poor *and* humble, a combination of two traits not highly prized today.[14]

How about the merciful? The Greek *eleēmones* is the virtue of being generous or forgiving in excess of what is expected—that is, having mercy. But let's return again to the Hebrew or Aramaic. Jesus likely used a variant of the word *chesed*. That word popped up frequently in my Old Testament classes, and every time it did the professor would invariably say that "mercy" doesn't do it justice. Barclay describes this virtue as follows: *"Chesed, mercy,* means the ability to get right inside other people until we can see things with their eyes, think things with their minds, and feel things with their feelings."[15]

How often do we do that? Anyone who gives others the benefit of the doubt, tries to identify with someone on the opposite side of the theological or political spectrum, or forgives after having been horribly wronged is often seen as naive, lacking in self-respect, or, worse, a traitor. "You're forgiving *him*?" Today too, many respect not mercy, but revenge.

How about the peacemakers? Nearly all of us would praise those who work for peace. The Hebrew *shalom,* which Jesus likely used, means more than the absence of violence; it is the state of the highest good for all people. But there is about peacemaking a sense of the quixotic. Do you really think you can bring peace to your family, your workplace, your church, a country torn by violence? Most people would shake their heads and say, "Good luck!"

In popular thought, then, some of the groups named in the Beatitudes are thought of as lazy, cowardly, foolish, and gullible—basically, losers. In fact, one of the phrases in Luke's list refers specifically to those who are set aside: "Blessed are you when people hate you, and when they exclude you, revile you, and defame you on account of the Son of Man." The word for "exclude" is *aphorizō,* and it has the sense of being set aside, excluded, marked off from others by a boundary—that is, "marginalized." Embedded in the Beatitudes is the recognition that some disciples will be thought of as people who don't matter.

All this reminds me of my visits to the French shrine of Lourdes. Briefly put, Catholics believe that in 1858 the Virgin Mary appeared to a poor young girl named Bernadette Soubirous beside a filthy grotto near the Gave River in a small town in southern France. During one apparition, Bernadette was told to "bathe in the waters." Not there, said the vision, when the young girl began walking toward the river. Confused, Bernadette started digging a few feet away from the riverbank. There she uncovered a bubbling spring of clear water, which proved to possess remarkable healing powers for some people in the town. Since then physicians have authenticated sixty-seven inexplicable cures of various illnesses in Lourdes, and the shrine attracts millions of pilgrims each year.

Every evening in Lourdes a huge procession draws as many as ten thousand people to pray the Rosary. Rain or shine, the procession begins by the river and ends in front of the massive gray church that now rises over the grotto. In the closing moments of the procession, the crowd gathers in a large plaza before the church. Then the crowd parts, like the Red Sea, to make way for the sick, for those who have journeyed to Lourdes for healing. Hundreds of men, women, and children—who suffer from the final stages of cancer, various forms of paralysis, and every variety of incurable disease—are pushed in wheelchairs and carts to the front of the crowd to receive a blessing. Some look on the edge of death; others lift their heads with difficulty, limbs twisted; others nestle in their mother's or father's arms. These are the *malades,* the sick.

In Lourdes, the sick come first. Never have I seen this without thinking about the Beatitudes. These are the ones who Jesus singles out in the Sermon on the Mount and elsewhere in his ministry: "The last will be first."[16] The ones on the bottom are on top. The ones who are ignored are celebrated. The ones who are pushed aside are given pride of place. The ones in the back of the line get the best seats. Blessed are they.

THIS DOES NOT MEAN that Jesus was making a blanket statement about the inherent goodness of poverty or mourning per se. We must, for example, distinguish between the voluntary poverty of the disciple and the involuntary poverty of the person struggling to make ends meet. Having worked with the poor in both the inner cities of America and the slums of Africa, I know that poverty in and of itself is not "blessed." Likewise, Jesus is not saying that mourning day and night for the rest of your life is desirable. What he's saying is more subtle.

Consider his words "Blessed are the poor." Besides reminding us that the poor are blessed by a God who promises justice for the oppressed, Jesus is also turning our attention to the way the poor live in relationship with God.

While one cannot overgeneralize about those who are poor, I can say this, based on my experience over the last twenty-five years: many people who live in poverty are more conscious of their reliance on God than are their wealthier counterparts. During my two years in Kenya, I noticed this many times. There the refugees with whom I worked taught me a great deal about God. Without wealth, status, or power, their natural dependence on God was ever before them. And the refugees would regularly express thanks to God for small blessings—a found coin, getting over a cold, a conductor forgetting to ask them for their bus fare. "God is good!" one Rwandese refugee would say whenever life went her way. Their almost constant, and constantly voiced, gratitude was a blessing for me—and a spiritual lesson.

So was their generosity. Almost to a person, the refugees were unbelievably generous with what little they had. Once I was invited to a Ugandan refugee's small shack in the slums of Nairobi for an afternoon visit. Loyce had been given a small grant from the Jesuit Refugee Service to purchase a sewing machine, so that she could work as a seamstress from her home. Upon my arrival, I discovered that Loyce had cooked a full meal with beef, peanuts, and rice, which must have cost her a week's earnings. When I protested, Loyce said that this was simple hospitality.

The next year, after returning to the States, I was invited to give a talk to a small group of wealthy people in a tony apartment in Manhattan around dinnertime. After speaking for an hour, I was offered a glass of water and a few crackers. Then the group—I'm not making this up—went out for dinner without inviting me along. "Good night, Father!"

I remembered my meal in the slums with Loyce. Ironically, the topic of my talk that night was life in East Africa.

We cannot lump together all the poor (or all the rich). Even categories like "the poor" and "the rich" are misleading. Not every poor person is grateful or generous. And grinding poverty is an evil. But Jesus of Nazareth, who had grown up in a poor village, knew that we can often learn much from the poor. Jesus's comments about poverty are frequent in the Gospels: over and over he asks us to care for the poor—it is a litmus test for admission into heaven—so it is always surprising to me when Christians set aside this teaching.[17] But Jesus is saying that more than helping the poor and more than working to combat the systems that keep them poor, we must *become* like them—in their simplicity, generosity, and dependence on God.

So we are not only to care for them, we are to become poor ourselves, to strip ourselves of all that keeps us from God. In this reliance on God, the poor are our models. And so blessed are they.

The Beatitudes are not just a promise of reward for those who suffer unjustly and a prediction of the turnabout of the status quo. They also paint a portrait of the person Jesus wants us to be.[18] Several of Jesus's themes in the Beatitudes are repeated elsewhere in the Gospels. "Blessed are the poor" means not simply that the indigent will be rewarded, but that simplicity of life is important. ("It is easier for a camel to go through the eye of a needle than for someone who is rich to enter the kingdom of God."[19]) "Blessed are the poor in spirit" means not simply that they will be rewarded, but that humility is important. ("The greatest among you will be your servant."[20])

Jesus was inviting the multitudes, and us, not only to hear a promise of future reward to those who suffer, but to embody certain virtues now. In doing so we become the people he intends us to be, participate in his reign, and become his disciples. And so we are blessed.

As I SAT IN the garden on the Mount of Beatitudes, I wondered, *What would it mean to live the Beatitudes?* A phrase that I once heard on a retreat came to mind: A Person of the Beatitudes. Since I first heard that expression, I've tried to become that person—humble, merciful, gentle, peacemaking, seeking justice for others—and have tried to move closer to the vision of personhood Jesus was describing. But I still have far to go.

It's obvious when you meet a Person of the Beatitudes. The most recent example is someone I met a few years ago, a young Jesuit who is, funny enough, named Luke, who worked with me at *America* magazine. Luke lives simply and tries to be poor. All Jesuits take vows of poverty, but Luke lives more simply than most, with very few possessions; and when I met him he had just completed a stint working with the poor on a Native American reservation in South Dakota. Luke was also meek (he never shouted or bullied people); poor in spirit (when I once suggested some major changes to an article he was writing, he accepted them willingly, eagerly, even cheerfully); and merciful (he thought nothing of spending his Christmas Eve driving an elderly Jesuit many miles to spend time with his family). Most of all, he hungered and thirsted for righteousness (Luke was an active member of the Catholic Worker movement).

One day Luke told me that he was fasting for a week. That weekend he was planning to attend a protest march for peace and had committed himself to eating no solids, only drinking juice, as a spiritual preparation. Beatitude-wise, that meant he was hungry too. I mentioned this to the person with whom he shared an office, who professed surprise. His office mate had no idea Luke was fasting. Had that been me, I would have probably found some way to make sure everyone knew! But a Person of the Beatitudes—poor, poor in spirit, meek, hungering for justice, peacemaking—doesn't need to do that.

The Beatitudes are a vision not only for the end times, or for society, but for us. We become who Jesus hopes us to be, as a people and as individuals. So we are blessed.

MAYBE MORE THAN BLESSED. During my time in East Africa, I once attended a weekend retreat that took as its theme the Beatitudes. Held in a small parish center near Mt. Kenya, the retreat was led by Anthony Bellagamba, IMC, an Italian priest who had spent many years in Africa.

One day, as black-and-white colobus monkeys skittered across the roof, Father Bellagamba invited us to think about how the Beatitudes influenced our work with the poor. In my retreat notes I wrote down the questions that made a special impression on me: "Do you show superiority when dealing with them? Do you affirm them? Do you help them obtain their identity?" The Beatitudes, he said, can also relate to the way we look at ourselves: "Do you show mercy to yourself by being patient with yourself?"

At one point he explained that the word "beatitude" comes from the Latin *beatus,* meaning "blessed."

"No kidding," I said cynically to the Jesuit sitting beside me.

"But do you know what else it can mean?" asked Father Bellagamba.

"Happy!" he said with a big smile.

When we translate the original Greek, Father Bellagamba said, we can use either "blessed" or "happy." The Greek *makarioi* carries both meanings, while the English "blessed" conveys only a sense of being approved by God—fortunate, welcomed, holy.[21] But Jesus offers something else to the downtrodden, oppressed, and forgotten. He promises them, and all who follow him, happiness. Incidentally, my friend Luke is a pretty happy guy.

Imagine how different Christian spirituality would be if the Beatitudes were translated with the word "happy." Imagine that when we heard those readings we heard a long list of happiness. "Happy are the merciful." "Happy are the pure in heart." "Happy are the peacemakers." But that's what Jesus was saying that day in Galilee, and to us today.

Does that sound odd? Remember that Jesus promises that those who mourn will laugh. And remember what, at the end of both versions of the Beatitudes, Jesus says to those who are persecuted. According to Matthew, "Rejoice and be glad." Luke is even zestier: "Rejoice on that day and leap for joy." Another translation is "Rejoice on that day and dance!" Jesus ushers us into a space of happiness, now.

So it's conceivable that the main reaction of the original hearers of the Sermon on the Mount is something we tend to overlook in the Christian life: happiness. On that day, wherever the mountain was, I'll bet that the poor were delighted to hear themselves included in Jesus's vision. I'll bet that the forgotten were happy that Jesus was promising them a place at the table. I'll bet that the oppressed were joyful to be elevated, finally.

And I'll bet Jesus was smiling when he said it. For happy was he.

THE BEATITUDES
Matthew 5:1–12
(See also Luke 6:20–23)

When Jesus saw the crowds, he went up the mountain; and after he sat down, his disciples came to him. Then he began to speak, and taught them, saying:

"Blessed are the poor in spirit, for theirs is the kingdom of heaven.

"Blessed are those who mourn, for they will be comforted.

"Blessed are the meek, for they will inherit the earth.

"Blessed are those who hunger and thirst for righteousness, for they will be filled.

"Blessed are the merciful, for they will receive mercy.

"Blessed are the pure in heart, for they will see God.

"Blessed are the peacemakers, for they will be called children of God.

"Blessed are those who are persecuted for righteousness' sake, for theirs is the kingdom of heaven.

"Blessed are you when people revile you and persecute you and utter all kinds of evil against you falsely on my account. Rejoice and be glad, for your reward is great in heaven, for in the same way they persecuted the prophets who were before you."

Chapter 11

Capernaum

"They removed the roof above him."

DID JESUS HAVE A house? That's something I wondered about during our stay in Galilee. With so many stories about Jesus walking from town to town and his comment that the "Son of Man has nowhere to lay his head," until recently I imagined that the itinerant carpenter either slept by the side of the road with his disciples or simply bunked at the houses of friends—like with Martha and Mary in Bethany or with Peter by the Sea of Galilee.[1] But one passage about Jesus's time in Capernaum, his base for ministry, includes a tantalizing phrase.

Mark paints the early days of Jesus's ministry as a flurry of activity in Capernaum and the surrounding towns. And prominent in Mark's second chapter is the dramatic story of the healing of a paralyzed man. When recounting that same story, the Gospel of Matthew notes that it takes place in "his own town." Luke, on the other hand, leaves the location vague; he places Jesus simply in Galilee. But Mark says that people had heard that Jesus was *en oikō*, in the house or in a house. But some translations use "at home."[2] People had heard that he was at home. Did this mean Jesus owned a home?

Some scholars say that this Greek phrase could refer to the house of Peter and his brother Andrew, the ruins of which you can see in present-day Capernaum.[3] About this first-century structure Jerome Murphy-O'Connor notes: "[T]he hint that the room was put to some type of public use is confirmed by the great number of graffiti scratched in the plaster walls. Some of them mention Jesus as Lord and Christ."⁴ Crossan and Reed note that the graffiti in this simple first-century "courtyard" house was scrawled in Aramaic, Hebrew, Greek, Latin, and Syriac. "The very fact that the room was plastered and graffitied," they write, "makes it totally unlike any other in Capernaum, or elsewhere in Galilee, and demonstrates that this one-time room in a private residence was held in special regard by many people only a century after Jesus's activities in Galilee."⁵

The site was venerated by early Christians, who built a small church there, a structure mentioned by at least one fourth-century pilgrim. Today, over the ruins of the modest, octagonal, basalt-stone church, roughly fifteen feet in diameter and standing some three feet high, hovers an enormous modernist church perched on metal pylons: the Church of St. Peter's House. It looks like a gray spaceship has landed atop the original structure. On the floor of the steel-and-glass church is a window through which pilgrims peer directly into the ruins of the much older church and the original dwelling below.

Is this the site of Peter's house? Murphy-O'Connor concludes that, although it is impossible to know for certain, evidence of veneration from before the time of Constantine argues for its authenticity: "The most reasonable assumption is the one attested by the Byzantine pilgrims: namely, that it was the house of Peter in which Jesus lodged (Mt 8:14)."⁶

In that case, was Jesus's house a few feet away from Peter's in Capernaum? It would have made sense for Jesus to have a permanent dwelling. Then again, perhaps it makes more sense for the man who asked his followers to give up all they had to own nothing of his own.⁷ Either way, Jesus made his "home" among the houses of Capernaum. And by tradition the door was open to all guests.

Capernaum is described at various times in the Gospels as a *polis* ("city"), though archaeologist Jonathan Reed points out that this may be simply a loose term for any town or village. Mark notes that Capernaum had a toll house, and other evangelists suggest the presence of a small garrison under the command of Herod Antipas, which argues for a town of some importance.[8] But archaeological finds indicate that the town, which probably held around a thousand people, was a "simple peasant and fisherman's village."[9] Unlike wealthier towns in Herod's territories, Capernaum did not have an outdoor market, or *agora*. Nor were any of its streets paved. Indeed, no wider than six to ten feet, the crooked and disorganized passageways were more like alleys than streets.

In *Excavating Jesus,* Crossan and Reed invite us to imagine walking around Jesus's home base in Galilee: "You could easily manage your way around Capernaum by keeping to the spacious shoreline, or you could cut through the village in spaces left between clusters of courtyard houses. Passageways and streets ran in slightly crooked and curved lines with wider spots used to work on a boat, hang and mend fishing nets, or set up goat and sheep pens."[10] Overall, they describe the village as "a step up from Nazareth, but many, many steps down from Sepphoris or Tiberias."[11]

What did homes in Capernaum look like in Jesus's time? Akin to those in Nazareth, they were small, usually one or two rooms, built with the rough, dark, local basalt stone—still evident in the ruins today—and held together with mud or dung. Few of the houses had more than one story, and if they did, the poor construction techniques made the walls susceptible to collapse.

From the total lack of any remains of stone arches, vaults, or rafters and an absence of roof tiles in the excavations, archaeologists have concluded that the houses were topped off with a flat, thatched roof, made from sturdy wooden crossbeams, filled with brushwood, and packed together with clay. Grass often grew atop the roof.[12]

That roof plays an important part in the marvelous story of the paralyzed man, told in all three of the Synoptic Gospels.

IN MARK'S TELLING, JESUS has returned to Capernaum and is either "in the house" or "at home," where he is swamped with visitors, the crowd spilling into the courtyard. As I've mentioned, the places where Jesus did his miracles around the Sea of Galilee were very near one another. So reports that many in the area had heard of him are easy to understand.

Thus, as the Gospel of Mark tells us, in the house there was no room for the crowd, "not even in front of the door." It's easy to imagine the crush of people straining to see and hear and even touch the wonder-worker. After all, in Mark's account Jesus has just healed a man with leprosy. Then and now, people are desperate for not only a physical healing but someone who preaches with authenticity. Word would have spread like wildfire within the confines of the small towns clustered along the shoreline.

In the midst of Jesus's preaching, four men arrive carrying a paralyzed man on a *krabattos,* a mat or pallet. A *krabattos* was used by the poor as a bed, but also could have been used by the paralyzed man for begging. (During my time in Nairobi, some of the refugees wove such straw mats and indeed some of these mats were used, as in Jesus's time, by beggars.[13]) The man's desperate condition is made clear by Mark, and he would have been doubly desperate: not only could he not walk (or conceivably even move), but his lameness might have been considered by some to be the result of sin.

The four men have a problem. They are unable to get near Jesus because of the crowd. This may simply reflect the crush of people. But, as we will see later with the story of Zacchaeus, a short man who must climb a tree to see Jesus "because of the crowd," the phrase may serve to remind us that the "crowd" can prevent us from getting close to God in a variety of ways.

Not able to reach Jesus because of the crowd, the man's friends do something daring—and desperate. Clambering onto the roof, they hoist up their friend and begin tearing apart the roof. (The roof was a place to rest and relax, so there was usually a stairway leading up to it.) The Greek says, marvelously, that the four "unroofed the roof" (*apestegasan tēn stegēn*), ripping off the mud and thatch. In Luke's later version of the story he alters the wording for his readership. In his account the men remove "tiles," which would have been more familiar to his cosmopolitan audience. But Mark's description is more accurate.[14]

In her beautiful poem "Cure of the Paralytic," Irene Zimmerman, OSF, tells the story in the voice of one of the friends, who remembers, "We lowered the litter / and swung ourselves down / in a rain of dust and straw."[15]

The men's love for their friend has always moved me. They care for their friend so much that they carry him on his *krabattos,* which must have taken a great deal of effort on their part. They love him so much that they are willing to make a spectacle of themselves. If any of your loved ones has ever had a serious illness, you know that you would do *anything* if it meant a possible cure. And they want him to meet Jesus so much that they risk angering Jesus (or Peter) by destroying an important part of the house. But no matter—these men want healing for their friend.

A few years ago in Lourdes, I met a woman whose middle-aged husband was crippled with a muscle-wasting illness. As we sat one afternoon beside the Gave River, I commented on how difficult it must have been to travel from the United States to France with someone with disabilities. "I didn't care what it took," she said to me, "I was going to bring him here, come hell or high water." It is this kind of love—a physical love, a love that *does* something—that the man's friends demonstrate.

Commotion must have ensued. In the middle of the crowd's straining to see and hear and touch Jesus—people probably were already on edge—the four friends climb onto the house, tear apart the roof, and lower their friend into the overwrought crowd. We can imagine people being shocked. "Stop!" "Jesus is speaking!" "What are you doing to his roof?" Some may have been infuriated by the rude intrusion into the house. But perhaps some, seeing the man's condition, sensed the generous motives of his friends. Did they stretch out their arms to help the man down? There was probably a good deal of arguing and directing: "No, this way!" "Hand him to me!" "Don't let him fall!"

Jesus experiences strong emotions, but they have nothing to do with the roof. The man new to Capernaum is affected not simply by the plight of the paralyzed man, but by the loving faith shown by his *friends*. Jesus must have been able to recognize the effort it took for these men to carry their paralyzed friend all the way through town (or perhaps from a neighboring town) to see him. This evokes a response from Jesus. Mark says, "When Jesus saw their faith, he said to the paralytic, 'Son, your sins are forgiven.'"[16]

Jesus seems moved to see people demonstrate such faith in him so early in his ministry. In Mark's Gospel, faith is intimately related to Jesus's abilities to perform miracles; later Jesus will say that he could not perform any miracles in certain towns because of their lack of faith. As Thomas D. Stegman, SJ, a professor of New Testament at Boston College, reminded me, Jesus's power to heal remains the same no matter where he is. "The question is," he said, "are people willing to receive the gift he is offering?"

Faith moves the friends of the paralyzed man to break through boundaries—social and physical—in order to find healing for their friend. Overall, faith is also intimately coupled with love and compassion: the friends' love for their infirm friend, Jesus's compassion for the friends, and finally his compassion for the paralyzed man.

As I mentioned, illness in Jesus's time was widely thought to be a result of sin. And paralysis was closely related to lameness, an impurity in the Old Testament, a stain that meant exclusion from some social settings. Thus the forgiveness of sins would have been a signal blessing for the man and the cause for celebration.

But not everyone is happy. The scribes who are present, perhaps attracted by the crowds or intent on investigating Jesus's activities, are bothered. Mark reports that the scribes say "in their hearts" that only God can forgive sins. In the Greek it is unclear whether Jesus is declaring that *he* is forgiving sins or pronouncing that *God* had forgiven them and he is acting as a kind of proxy for God. The scribes' reaction, however, shows that they think Jesus is presenting *himself* as the agent of forgiveness.

Somehow, Jesus perceived "in his spirit" what they were thinking. Now, to understand that Markan phrase we don't need to think of Jesus as a mind-reader. Rather, he may be showing a keen grasp of his surroundings. If a person says or does something shocking, the faces of those nearby often convey their reactions. "Who does he think he *is*?" say their faces.

Mark recounts their concerns, which are religious in nature: "Why does this fellow speak in this way? It is blasphemy!" But *houtos,* the Greek word used for "fellow," is derogatory. It can be translated not as "Why does this rabbi or teacher speak blasphemy?" but "Why does this *guy* speak blasphemy?"

Blasphēmein meant to insult someone or injure a person's reputation. In the Gospels it connotes profaning the name of God, and of course has much earlier roots in Jewish law. (The Book of Leviticus prescribes stoning as the punishment for that sin.) When Jesus offers the paralytic forgiveness, he is taking upon himself the prerogative of God. Besides, forgiveness of sins would normally require a confession of sins, along with some sort of reparation. The paralyzed man has done nothing.

But, as noted in *The Jewish Annotated New Testament,* it is inaccurate to portray Judaism as a harsh, rule-based community that restricted forgiveness and to paint the scribes as maleficent, though they are sometimes portrayed that way in the Gospels. For one thing, Judaism had a variety of ways of understanding the forgiveness of sins, and for another, the early Christians themselves engaged in shunning sinners.[17] So a black-and-white, good-versus-evil portrait of Jesus versus scribes and the Pharisees (two distinct groups with distinct roles) is inaccurate.

That kind of approach can also lead us to ignore not only the Jewishness of Jesus but the beauty of the Jewish law, which, as E. P. Sanders notes, "brings the entirety of life . . . under the authority of God."[18] We should also remember that the scribes, devout Jews bound to interpret the Law, no doubt were caught off guard by Jesus's offer of forgiveness. Who wouldn't be?

Still, Mark reports a definite controversy, and it is just as important not to water down the threat brought by Jesus's ministry. One of the reasons Jesus was crucified is that he posed a clear threat to certain powerful groups in his time. A bland, unthreatening Jesus who never ruffled anyone's feathers would not have posed a threat to some of the Jewish leaders, nor would he have been executed by Rome.

In this account, Jesus then responds to the doubts of the scribes. Now the passage moves into what scholars call a "controversy story," in which Jesus contends with religious or civic leaders. As he does on many occasions, Jesus poses a clever question. In this case it is not a rhetorical or indirect one, but a clear challenge.

Which is easier, he asks: to forgive sins or to say, "Stand up and take your mat and walk"? That puts the scribes in a bind. If they say, "Forgiving sins," they are belittling what is rightfully God's work. If they say, "Healing a lame man," they are publicly declaring that it is easy for Jesus to heal, thus supporting claims about his divinity.

The crowd must have been thrilled: "He is going to heal him, right here!" The scribes must have been worried: "He is going to heal him, right here!"

Mark recounts Jesus's dramatic words and includes some stage directions: "'But so that you might know that the Son of Man has authority on earth to forgive sins'—he said to the paralytic—'I say to you, stand up, take your mat and go to your home.'"

And immediately—*kai euthus*—the man rises and picks up his mat. But he does not return home *euthus*. Instead, he goes out "before all of them so that they were all amazed." The newly healed man wants to show everyone, including his four friends, what God has done for him. All are amazed—*existasthai,* literally, standing outside themselves. They are beside themselves! Then they glorify God—a subtle rejoinder to the scribes who suspected Jesus of blaspheming against God. What joy there must have been, among the crowd, in the healed man, and among his faithful friends.

Then comes a phrase that always makes me smile, because it seems at once so honest and so utterly understated. The onlookers say, "We have never seen anything like this!"

For the most part, Matthew and Luke hew closely to Mark's narrative. Luke, however, ends his story this way: "Amazement seized all of them, and they glorified God and were filled with awe, saying, 'We have seen strange things today.'" Robert F. O'Toole, SJ, a Lukan scholar, told me that Luke's ending to many miracle stories is "joy, wonder, blessing, and praise," a fitting tribute to the works that God does in our lives. Any thoughts of the roof, of blasphemy, or of the man's sinfulness are swept aside in the wake of God's power.

Was Jesus intending to heal the paralyzed man from the moment he was lowered into the crowd? It's impossible to know, but to my mind, yes. Otherwise the man is reduced to a prop in a controversy with the scribes. It seems more likely that, if Mark's recounting is accurate, Jesus first intended to offer him forgiveness and then physical healing, conceivably as a sign of what was equally as important as the ability to walk. That is, he was implicitly saying to the crowd: "You think that a person's physical infirmities are bad? Sin is worse. First, therefore, I will forgive whatever sins he has committed."

But why did the man need forgiveness? Was Jesus simply recognizing that all of us are in need of forgiveness? Very likely. Was Jesus implying that the man's condition was the result of some hidden sin, as was often thought at the time? Less likely. In the Gospel of John, Jesus comes upon a "man born blind" and he is asked, "Who sinned, this man or his parents, that he was born blind?" Jesus's answer is blunt: "Neither this man nor his parents sinned."[19] That is, illness is not a punishment, despite what some believed in Jesus's time.

And not just in Jesus's time. Last year, a friend called me to share a wrenching story. She was suffering from an inoperable brain tumor and had received a visit from a group of women from her church, who told her that her illness was the work of the devil. My friend was shocked and hurt. These women may have meant something entirely different, but my friend heard their words as a condemnation, and an accusation that she had somehow brought this on herself— and their words stung. I reminded my friend of the story from the Gospel of John, where Jesus decisively rejects this line of thought. Who sinned? "No one."

So again, why the need for forgiveness for the paralyzed man?

ON A WEEK-LONG RETREAT at a Trappist monastery in Massachusetts, I was offered an imaginative answer. My friend Jim is a former Jesuit and has been a Trappist monk for more than twenty years. That week he served as my retreat director. One late afternoon in February, with a light snow swirling outside the windows of the monastery, I spoke with him about this passage, sharing with him much of what I described in this chapter: the love of the paralyzed man's friends, the likely reactions of the crowd, and how I could connect the friends' actions with the concept of Christian community.

Often, when we are in trouble, or doubting, or struggling, we rely on others to carry us to God. Just as often we must do the carrying, to help friends who are struggling. This is one of the many benefits of organized religion, as we all need others to help us find God. Even though we may disagree with others and find life in a community occasionally annoying and sometimes scandalous, we need others, because the community is one way that we are carried to God, especially when we are too weak to walk to God on our own.

But I wondered about the paralyzed man. He may have felt shame for his illness or for being unable to support himself. Maybe his friends carried him in spite of himself. Sometimes when we are too embarrassed to approach God, someone must bring us there— even drag us there. Many times when I am discouraged, demoralized, or angry at God, it is friends who remind me of God's great love and who carry me to God. We cannot come to God without others.

This may be what evoked Jesus's compassion. He recognizes the man's dark feelings, and so he says, in essence, "Whatever you think you may have done to make this happen, you are forgiven." William Barclay believes that Jesus is saying, "God is not angry with you. It's all right." Jesus is showing him how God truly looks at us, and it's often not the way we *think* God looks at us. While the scribes are horrified that a human being is doing the forgiving, the friends may have danced for joy.[20]

But I wondered aloud, "Why did Jesus feel the need to forgive the paralyzed man? Could he not have said that the man had *not* sinned, as Jesus did in the case of the blind man?"

Jim told me that one day as he prayed over this Gospel passage a story came to him. Of course he admitted it's highly unlikely that it happened in this way, but our conversation reminded me that the people in the Gospels were real people who had full lives before and after they encountered Jesus. They are not mere literary characters or allegorical figures, but individuals with histories. Jesus steps into the rich and complicated lives of people in first-century Palestine, as God steps into our own.

The man was a roofer in a nearby town, said Jim. One day he is working on a job with his friends, and from atop the house he spies the owner's beautiful wife. A good man and faithful husband, he still finds himself staring. So fraught does the situation become that the roofer thinks of quitting the job, but he can't—his family needs the money. One day, overcome with passion, the roofer sleeps with the beautiful woman. Immediately he is consumed with guilt over what he has done to his wife.

The next day he returns to the job and, while working atop the house, slips and falls through the roof onto the hard dirt floor. He is paralyzed. Instinctively, the roofer blames himself for his sin. His friends carry him home to his wife, who suspects what has happened (for she knows the beautiful woman). But she cares for her husband out of love.

When his friends visit him a few days later, they tell him about the wonder-worker who lives in Capernaum. But he resists. Weighed down by shame, he feels unworthy of seeing Jesus. But his friends carry him there, unroof the roof, and lower him before Jesus. Jesus himself has already heard the story of the roofer in the nearby town, and he has pity on the paralyzed man. This is why Jesus tells him to go home. Jesus knows he will not only rejoice in being able to walk about, but in being freed from his sins. The man rushes home to kiss his loving wife and hug his children.

In both Mark's original narrative and Jim's imaginative retelling, sin and paralysis are connected: sin can paralyze us, preventing any forward motion. We are stuck until we are able to be forgiven, until we meet God in some way, or until our friends take pity on us, unroof our world, and let in the light.

THE HEALING OF THE PARALYZED MAN
Mark 2:1–12
(See also Matthew 9:1–8; Luke 5:17–26)

When he returned to Capernaum after some days, it was reported that he was at home. So many gathered around that there was no longer room for them, not even in front of the door; and he was speaking the word to them. Then some people came, bringing to him a paralyzed man, carried by four of them. And when they could not bring him to Jesus because of the crowd, they removed the roof above him; and after having dug through it, they let down the mat on which the paralytic lay. When Jesus saw their faith, he said to the paralytic, "Son, your sins are forgiven." Now some of the scribes were sitting there, questioning in their hearts, "Why does this fellow speak in this way? It is blasphemy! Who can forgive sins but God alone?" At once Jesus perceived in his spirit that they were discussing these questions among themselves; and he said to them, "Why do you raise such questions in your hearts? Which is easier, to say to the paralytic, 'Your sins are forgiven,' or to say, 'Stand up and take your mat and walk'? But so that you may know that the Son of Man has authority on earth to forgive sins"—he said to the paralytic—"I say to you, stand up, take your mat and go to your home." And he stood up, and immediately took the mat and went out before all of them; so that they were all amazed and glorified God, saying, "We have never seen anything like this!"

CHAPTER 12

Parables

*"He began to teach them many
things in parables."*

HERE'S A STORY SPANNING several decades. It shows why it sometimes takes a long time for people (including me) to understand a
Gospel story.

The first chapter happened when I was a Jesuit novice. Twenty-
five years ago, during the first month in the novitiate, I read about a
place called the Bay of Parables. While I can't remember what book
this was, I remember the vivid impression it made.

In the Gospel of Luke, Jesus finds himself so hemmed in by
crowds that he climbs aboard a boat and asks Peter to row out into
the Sea of Galilee, so that he can preach from the boat.[1] The Gospels
of Mark and Matthew also report incidents of Jesus's preaching from
a boat.[2] In Galilee, said this book, there is still a place known as the
Bay of Parables, where that Gospel passage most likely happened.
Near the shoreline is a naturally occurring amphitheater, where
people would have been able to sit comfortably to listen to Jesus;
moreover, the unique acoustics of the site made it easier for the large
crowd to hear Jesus.

The notion that people could identify exactly where a particular
Scripture story happened captivated me. I remember thinking, *Cool!*
But the explanation baffled. Why would Jesus get into a boat to address a crowd? (I imagined the carpenter standing up in the boat,
wobbling, and falling into the water.) Why wouldn't he stand on

the shoreline? Because of its oddness the tale of the Bay of Parables stuck with me.

The second chapter of my story: A few years later, I was on a summer vacation at a Jesuit house outside Boston, in a town on a bay that empties into the Atlantic Ocean. After breakfast, a few Jesuits would sit on the broad lawn that overlooks a harbor and spend a relaxing morning reading books or chatting. One morning, we heard a commotion in the harbor, which turned out to be the ruckus from a sailing school for some boisterous kids. The distance between us and the group of miniature sailboats was about a mile. To my surprise, we could easily hear the kids talking (or whining) as if they were only a few feet away: "I don't know how to fix my *rudder*!" "My sail isn't *working*!" You could also hear the frazzled instructor encouraging her students: "No, do it *this* way!"

I remarked how amazing it was that we could hear their voices so clearly. One older Jesuit said, "Well, of course. Sound travels over water very easily. You remember that story of Jesus preaching from the boat, right? That's one reason he did it that way. It was probably easier for the crowds to hear him."

His casual insight delighted me. It reminded me that some of what we may not "get" in the Gospel often turns out to have a real-life explanation, once we think about the context of the story. Perhaps because I felt that I'd been let in on a kind of secret, I had a renewed desire to learn more about that story, and about the Gospels.

Finally, the third chapter: George and I arrive in Jerusalem about a decade after my encounter with the noisy sailing school. At dinner on the first night, Father Doan, the Jesuit superior at the PBI, asks me what we'd most like to visit. The first place I want to see, I tell him, is the Bay of Parables.

Doan replied, "The what?" Now, here was a Jesuit priest who has lived in the Holy Land for years. "I've never heard of it."

Okay, I thought, *maybe it's the* one *place he hasn't heard of.* George looked doubtful.

A few days later, we made the four-hour drive to Galilee and found our way to the Franciscan hostel on the Mount of Beatitudes. After we settled ourselves in our rooms, Sister Télesfora asked us, "So, Fathers, what would you most want to see?"

"The Bay of Parables!" I said.

"The what?"

When I described it, Sister Télesfora shook her head and furrowed her brow, as if I were deluded. Or insane. And she is not simply a Franciscan sister—she also teaches New Testament Greek, so she would presumably know about the site.

George rolled his eyes and said afterward, "It's like you were asking about Santa's workshop at the North Pole."

A few hours later, we made our way to Tabgha, the traditional site of the miracle of the Multiplication of the Loaves and Fishes, and we prayed briefly in the small chapel there. Afterward, in the gift shop, I noticed one of the Benedictine monks, screwed up my courage, and asked, "Do you know where the Bay of Parables is?" I fully expected him to say, "The what?"

Instead, he said in a heavy German accent, "*Ja, ja!* Zee Bay of Pah-rables!" He stumbled in English, so I called over George, who speaks German. "It's verry cloze to here," he said.

The monk grabbed a small map from beside the cash register and scribbled some directions. Then George translated his German. "Just walk along the road and you'll see . . . an opening in the bushes. Then go down into the bush and you'll see . . ." George paused, looked at the man, looked at me, and then asked him to repeat a word. George said to me, querulously, "I think he said to follow the stones . . . painted *purple*?"

"*Ja, ja!*" he said excitedly. "*Wie-o-let.* Wie-o-let paint on zee rrocks."

So under the blistering hot sun—it must have been 110 degrees— George and I followed his map and, sure enough, almost tripped over several boulders marked with violet bars.

"Wie-o-let," said George dryly.

As we walked farther into the dry grass, a handful of wood hyraxes, squirrel-size rodents, scurried around our feet and zoomed up the low trees.

Immediately (*euthus!*) the ground dropped away from us, and we found ourselves on the rim of a natural amphitheater. People had likely stood here and listened to Jesus preaching from the boat. Or, as is often said in the Holy Land, "If it didn't happen here, then it happened a few hundred yards from here." As I gazed on the blue-green water sparkling under the sun, I could easily picture Jesus sitting in a boat just a few hundred feet from where we were standing. I couldn't stop smiling when I realized what we had found.

"Zee Bay of Pah-rables," said George.

Then I saw something that amazed me even more. All around us was this: rocky ground, fertile ground, stony ground, and even a thorn bush.

DOES THAT SOUND FAMILIAR? In the Parable of the Sower, Jesus tells the story of a farmer who goes out to sow and whose seed falls on different kinds of ground. Told in all the Synoptic Gospels, the parable illustrates (among other things) the way that Jesus's message is received, in both his day and our own.[3] Jesus even explains the parable at length in the Synoptics. The rocky ground represents those who hear the word, but do not allow it to take root; when trials come they "wither away." The thorny ground is an image for those who hear the word, but the "cares of the world" and "lure of wealth" choke it off, and the seed produces no yield. But the fertile ground represents those who hear the word, accept it, and bear great fruit, "in one case a hundredfold, in another sixty, and in another thirty."[4]

As I stood under the broiling sun, I was gobsmacked to see rocks, thorns, and fertile ground. No one planted the thorn bushes, carted in topsoil, or arranged the stones to make the locale look as it did in Jesus's time, as if we were in a theme park called Jesus Land. They were just *there*.

It dawned on me that when Jesus used objects from nature to convey his message—seeds, rocks, birds, clouds, water—he may not have been talking in generalities, but about these things *right here*. Not "Think about rocky ground," but "Look at *that* rocky ground." Not "Those people are like thorns," but "Those people are like *those* thorns." It grounded the Gospels, and Jesus, in a way that I never could have imagined. It made me think more about the way Jesus drew on nature in his parables.

Then I remembered another insight I once heard about this passage. The Parable of the Sower may refer not only to which individuals are open, or not open, to receiving the Gospel message. It may also refer to those *parts* of ourselves that are open, and not open. Can you see your whole self as the field and consider what parts are fertile, what parts are rocky, and what parts are choked with weeds?

Where, for example, are you open to God's word in your life? Perhaps you are easily able to find God in your family. That may be your good soil. Where is your rocky soil? Perhaps you are compassionate at home but less so at work, stubbornly clinging to old grudges. That aspect of your life may be unyielding, and God's word cannot penetrate the soil of your soul. What part of your life is choked with weeds? Perhaps you desire to follow God but are obsessed with wealth, which chokes off the fruitful growth that God might wish.

To continue the metaphor, God may want to dislodge a few rocks and pull out some weeds in order to clear a space for God's word to take root. This may take the form of a friend confronting you on some selfish behavior, a sudden recognition of your own stubbornness, or even a period of suffering that opens you to God in a new way. God plows, unearthing the good soil where God's word can be planted, take root, grow, and flourish.

Facing the Sea of Galilee, I wondered about the people who, in

Jesus's day, sat where I was standing now. What did they think when they heard these parables for the first time? I thought about how glad I was that I had listened to Drew and come to the Holy Land. I thought of all of these things as I stood at the Bay of Parables.

I also thought about C. H. Dodd.

In our Introduction to the New Testament class, Father Harrington began our discussion of the parables by quoting a definition from the Scripture scholar C. H. Dodd, which was memorable in its precision. In his book *The Parables of the Kingdom,* Dodd defines a parable as "a metaphor or simile drawn from nature or common life, arresting the hearer by its vividness or strangeness, and leaving the mind in sufficient doubt about its precise application to tease it into active thought."[5]

The Greek *paraballō* means "to place one thing beside another." As Harrington notes, "A parable is a form of analogy that seeks to illuminate one reality by appealing to something better known."[6] The complex reality of the reign of God, the main theme of Jesus's preaching, is illuminated by something as simple and familiar as a mustard seed. But Jesus used this device creatively, and he spun out parables in many forms. Some are elaborate stories with multiple characters. "There was a man who had two sons," begins his Parable of the Prodigal Son. Others are the briefest of metaphors: "The kingdom of heaven is like a treasure hidden in a field."

The parables are poetic explanations of spiritual concepts impossible to comprehend fully. The reign of God is far too rich to be encompassed by any one definition, no matter how theologically accurate. True forgiveness is impossible to explain in a few words, no matter how well chosen. And where a strict definition can close down a person's mind, a story is more likely to open up the imagination. Jesus saw the benefit of telling a parable about a shepherd seeking out a lost sheep and allowing the hearers to "tease" out the underlying meaning for themselves. When people find meaning in stories on their own and discover the truth for themselves, it's easier for them to make the message their own.

The parables are endlessly rich, and Jesus's brilliant use of these images remains unmatched. As an experiment, try coming up with a parable of your own and you'll see how difficult it is to create one that is short, fresh, memorable, easily understood, and open-ended enough to allow a person to enter more deeply into the mystery of the reign of God.

But beyond that, the parables, says N. T. Wright, are not simply information about the reign of God; they are "part of the means of bringing it to birth." Jesus's frequent use of parables was intended to jump-start the reign, not just by giving people something to think about, but by inviting them to live in the new world being created.[7]

Many of the parables also go against the expectations of the audience and are therefore subversive, as in the Parable of the Good Samaritan, when the man from a hated ethnic group was ultimately revealed to Jewish listeners as the good guy who cares for the stranger.[8] Jesus thus forced his listeners—gently, through stories and images—to confront their prejudices about others and their preconceptions of God. "The deep places in our lives—places of resistance and embrace—are not ultimately reached by instruction," writes the Protestant theologian Walter Brueggemann. "Those places of resistance and embrace are reached only by stories, by images, metaphors and phrases that line out the world differently, apart from our fear and hurt."[9]

Jesus grasped all this about the parable form—either through divine inspiration or through the human experience of having lived among the people of the region and knowing how to speak with them. Besides, if Jesus *had* given an abstruse philosophical lecture to the predominantly peasant audience, they wouldn't have understood him. And if he had taken an hour to explain a complex theological point to farmers worried about returning to their crops, they would have just walked away. Far better to grab them with a provocative story or a piquant metaphor.

Or to draw on what is happening in the here and now that might illuminate the reign of God. As Jonathan Reed notes, the construction of the nearby towns of Sepphoris and Tiberias for people far wealthier than those living in Capernaum and the smaller towns might have increased people's awareness of income disparities. So Jesus's stories about the rich and the poor would have been applicable in general, but the presence of the towns then being built by Herod Antipas would have given the stories added punch. Archaeologists have found that the well-built houses in Sepphoris were far more lavish than the single-room dwellings found in Capernaum and Nazareth; in wealthier towns houses were covered in roof tiles and had frescoed interiors and occasionally mosaics. The building of Tiberias and Sepphoris, notes Reed, meant the "accentuation of social stratification" to people living in poorer towns.[10] So Jesus's listeners might have heard Luke's parable about the rich man who lives in comfort while the poor man starves outside his door and thought, *Yes, just like in Tiberias and Sepphoris.*[11]

More basically, Jesus uses things (rocks, birds, seeds) and people (the farmer planting his crops, the woman sweeping her house, the son who wastes money) that were part of everyone's daily life. As John Donahue writes in *The Gospel in Parable,* "The parables manifest such a range of images that the everyday world of rural, first-century Palestine comes alive in a way true of few ancient cultures."[12]

You can almost see the people nodding in agreement as Jesus spins out earthy tales of people, places, and situations they would have known well. One of the challenges for current-day readers, then, is to learn as much as we can about that time, so that we can better understand these wonderful tales and metaphors. As Gerhard Lohfink says, Jesus's parables betray a "deep love for reality."[13] All the more reason to understand the historical reality of Jesus's world.

ALMOST TWENTY YEARS AGO, I worked with the Jesuit Refugee Service in Nairobi, Kenya. My job was to help refugees begin small business to help them support themselves and their families. One day I was driving my jeep outside of the city, near the Rift Valley, to visit a farmer who had started a cattle farm with some assistance from JRS. As I wound my way up a steep mountain pass, I was transfixed by the verdant green grass that carpeted the hillside. Suddenly, seemingly from nowhere, a lone white sheep clambered down the hillside and darted in front of my car. I swerved to avoid hitting it (there were no other vehicles around). Then I watched the sheep gingerly climb down into the valley on the right side of the road.

Just then, from my left, a figure darted across the road. It was a young Maasai shepherd. In the Maasai culture the youngest boys, sometimes as early as five, tend the sheep; the older ones herd goats; and the oldest, including men, take care of the cattle. The shepherd dashed in front of my idling car. Barefoot, he smiled and waved to me as he passed. He scrambled down the side of the hill in pursuit of the sheep, raising clouds of dust, calling loudly all the while. I watched him climb down the hill for a few seconds. Then I looked up and saw the rest of the flock, about twenty or thirty sheep, up the hill on my left.

How stupid! I thought. *He's leaving behind the whole flock for that one sheep.* Then something dawned on me, and I laughed out loud. It was the Parable of the Lost Sheep in action! In its entirety the parable reads as follows, in Matthew:

> What do you think? If a shepherd has a hundred sheep, and one of them has gone astray, does he not leave the ninety-nine on the mountains and go in search of the one that went astray? And if he finds it, truly I tell you, he rejoices over it more than over the ninety-nine that never went astray. So

it is not the will of your Father in heaven that one of these little ones should be lost.[14]

If God pursues us with even half the energy as that young Maasai boy, then humanity has nothing to worry about.

That concise parable is just one example of Jesus's use of an image that his listeners would have known well, a shepherd who loses a sheep from the fold. Now, as a person who had never seen a shepherd outside of the movies before coming to Kenya, I had no clue that a shepherd would leave a flock behind. But notice that Jesus says *"Does he not* leave the ninety-nine?" He's not telling his original audience something new; he's drawing on what they already know. That is also clear in Luke's version: "Which one of you, having a hundred sheep," he asks, "does not leave the ninety-nine?" His listeners also know that the search for the sheep is not always successful: the audience grasped the importance of the words "if he finds it."

The story would have spoken to them of God's profound desire to find us, especially those who are in any way lost, or one who is, as in Matthew's version, a *planōmenon,* a "wandering one." There is a palpable sense of God's pity on the one who inadvertently wanders off. How often this happens in our lives; we find ourselves, almost without realizing it, far from God and from others. But there is no judgment here, only compassion.

Luke's version adds a touching note. "When he has found it, he lays it on his shoulders and rejoices. And when he comes home, he calls together his friends and neighbors, saying to them, 'Rejoice with me, for I have found my sheep that was lost.'" With this physical detail Luke evokes both the psalmist's imagery of the shepherd who cares for his sheep and the pastoral practice of the time.[15] (Ancient statuary shows shepherds carrying sheep in the same way.) This deeply personal addition sounds like something Jesus and his listeners would have seen often. Thus, Jesus offers from his listeners' everyday lives an image that powerfully evokes God's love for them.

In Luke and Matthew, Jesus explicitly connects these parables to God's rejoicing over the finding of "one sinner who repents," which is greater than God's joy over the ninety-nine who "need no repentance," as Luke says. To illustrate, he offers yet another image, one of a woman who has ten coins, loses one, and sweeps the entire house to find it.

It is not beneath Jesus to speak about common things, so intent was he on conveying the message of the reign of God. If talking about sheep does the trick, he'll tell a story about a shepherd. If talking about a woman searching for a coin helps, he'll talk about her.

His use of parables, then, parallels the gracious entrance of God into our human existence. Just as it was not beneath Jesus to approach his listeners in ways they could understand, so it was not beneath God to come in a way that we can understand—in Jesus. With a parable Jesus says, "Do you want to know what the reign of God is like? Let me tell you a story." In Jesus, God says, "Do you want to know what I am like? Let me *be* a story for you, the story of Jesus." In a sense, Jesus is the parable of God.

Stories, which human beings seem hardwired to remember, are also more likely to "stick" than definitions are. When preaching at Mass, I will often relate a real-life anecdote to illustrate a point. Inevitably, that's what people remember most. "Oh, I *loved* that story about your nephews!" someone will say afterward. The challenge is offering stories that make the point but don't detract from it, a challenge that Jesus mastered perfectly.

Wit is another important element of Jesus's parables. This may seem surprising to those of us who read his parables with a straight face, but we often miss the earthy humor inherent in the stories. Humor is culture bound and time bound; since we don't live in Jesus's day, we can't fully appreciate the humor embedded in the parables, which would have made them memorable to those who first heard them. Father Harrington told me that for people in first-century Palestine some of Jesus's stories would have been "hilarious." The idea, for example, that someone would build a house on sand instead of solid ground would have struck people as terribly funny.[16]

We may also overlook the humor because, unlike the first audiences, we've heard these passages multiple times—often delivered in dry and didactic ways. And even if we recognize the humor, we're still too familiar with the stories. So we are probably underestimating the surprising and amusing impact they would have had on the first-time hearers in first-century Palestine.

The parables, however, are not simply stories, or even funny stories. As Harrington notes, in each parable something unusual surfaces: a huge harvest, an immense mustard bush, an enormous amount of bread, a pearl discovered by accident.[17] There is always a twist, often a shocking, jarring, or even incomprehensible turnabout. Some parables are hard to grasp; and some, once grasped, are hard to accept. But Jesus meant them to be provocative—the kingdom of God demanded an urgent, all-or-nothing, do-it-now response—so the parables retain their power to provoke and shock.

And confuse! Even today the most familiar parables may baffle us. There is strong evidence that Jesus himself did not expect all his listeners to grasp the parables. One of the most difficult passages in the Gospels, much discussed by Scripture scholars, comes in Mark, when the disciples ask Jesus bluntly why he speaks in parables. His answer was most likely as mysterious to them as it is to us:

> "To you has been given the secret of the kingdom of God,
> but for those outside, everything comes in parables; in order
> that
>> 'they may indeed look, but not perceive,
>> and may indeed listen, but not understand;
>> so that they may not turn again and be forgiven.'"[18]

Here Jesus is quoting a passage from Isaiah, which speaks of those who are deaf and blind to the word of God.

Some scholars say that "in order that" is better translated as "because." In other words, some do not grasp the parables because they are hard-hearted. But even given that translation, it is still a troubling passage. An almost identical explanation occurs in Luke and Matthew.[19]

Did Jesus not want people to understand him? I put that question to John Donahue. He noted that those mysterious verses in Mark may best be understood in terms of the Messianic Secret—that is, an example of Jesus's teaching his disciples privately. Father Donahue explained that in the ancient world there were many instances of private teaching to "insiders." Also, Jesus exhibits a kind of restraint, holding back, as it were, from fully revealing things to everyone at every opportunity. But it was still hard to imagine Jesus not wanting most of his listeners to understand.

"Most likely," he told me, "Jesus did not *expect* everyone to understand his teaching." Donahue noted that the first use of the word "parable" comes in the third chapter of Mark, in a setting where his family thought he was crazy.[20] "Then Jesus tells a parable to his adversaries, and the section concludes with his saying that his mother and brothers are 'outside,' while the true family 'inside' are those who do the will of God."[21] It is an indication that the parables were meant to be understood mainly by his inner circle.

Donahue reminded me that parables are never fully "understood" anyway. Speaking about "understanding" is a bit rationalistic, he said. "A better phrasing would be 'enter into the mystery of the kingdom of God.' Remember C. H. Dodd's saying that a parable 'teases.' To my mind, a parable is a question waiting for an answer, and it does not really 'exist' until it is 'appropriated,' but it is never really 'understood.'"

Adding to the often baffling quality of the parables is another striking feature: we encounter characters Gerhard Lohfink terms "immoral figures."[22] In the Gospel of Matthew, for instance, Jesus tells the story of a man who discovers a treasure hidden in a field.[23]

Upon discovering it, he sells all he has in order to purchase the field. Preachers often use this parable as a way of stressing the overriding value of the reign of God—we should be willing to part with anything to attain it.

We may be so familiar with this parable that we overlook something: the man does not tell the rightful owner of the field what he has found! As heroes go, he is a devious one. Lohfink points to several such immoral figures whose presence underscores the urgency of the reign of God. Some of the characters in the parables stop at nothing to get what they want. Jesus seems to be saying that one must be single-hearted in one's pursuit of the kingdom, even as much as the unscrupulous man pursuing that treasure—no matter what.

OVER TWO THOUSAND YEARS after parables were introduced to the crowds in Galilee, debates over their meaning continue. Not long ago, Barbara Reid, a Dominican sister and professor of New Testament at Catholic Theological Union in Chicago, provided a unexpected explanation about one of the most familiar Gospel parables. In the process she provoked my Jesuit community into a lively conversation about a story we thought we knew.

In the Parable of the Talents, in both Matthew and Luke,[24] a wealthy man entrusts his servants with his fortune before going away on a journey. To the first servant (or slave), he gives five talents, to the second two, and to the third one. As Matthew recounts the story, the wealthy man gave each one funds "according to his ability." By the way, here is a possible instance of Jesus's playful use of hyperbole: a *talanton* was a huge amount of money, equivalent to roughly fifteen years of wages, so the man is turning over to his servants a ridiculous amount of wealth. The audience would have perked up upon hearing about the largesse of such a generous, trusting, or possibly naive master.

When the master (*kyrios,* or lord) returns, he discovers how well each servant has cared for the money. The first one proudly reports that he has invested the money and has earned five more talents. The master praises him lavishly, "Well done, good and trustworthy slave; you have been trustworthy in a few things, I will put you in charge of many things; enter into the joy of your master." The second slave has likewise invested, turning his two talents into four; he is similarly praised by the master.

The third slave, however, did not invest the money at all. In fact he buried it—literally, in the ground. Why? "Master," he says, "I knew that you were a harsh man, reaping where you did not sow, and gathering where you did not scatter seed; so I was afraid, and I went and hid your talent in the ground. Here you have what is yours."

The master is enraged. Not simply because he's been insulted as a "harsh" man (*sklēros,* hard or severe), but because the servant has failed to increase the man's wealth—even though he was not instructed to invest it. The master taunts him: "You knew, did you, that I reap where I did not sow, and gather where I did not scatter? Then you ought to have invested my money with the bankers." He instructs the other servants to *take* the man's one talent and give it to the one with ten. "For to all those who have, more will be given, and they will have an abundance; but from those who have nothing, even what they have will be taken away." The master then punishes the slave, throwing him into "outer darkness," where there will be "weeping and gnashing of teeth."

Why is the servant punished so cruelly? After all, he didn't lose the money; and no one told him he was supposed to invest it. Besides, he might have lost money if he had. For most readers today, the harsh treatment is shocking. It's also poignant, writes Donahue: the poor man is describing what he thought was a prudent action and then almost *proudly* returns the original to the master. How sad it is to imagine someone who thinks he is doing a good deed punished instead and to see his world shattered.[25] Is Jesus holding up this unfortunate person as a model of foolishness? What's going on?

The most common interpretation, which you will hear advanced in most sermons and homilies, is that the parable is a warning to those who do not use their "talents" in life. Perhaps because the word "talent" in English automatically carries that meaning, most preachers inveigh against "burying our talents" and encourage us to do the best we can with our "God-given talents," or there will be hell to pay.

But most parables cannot be exhausted by a single interpretation. For his part, Donahue surmises that the problem with the third servant is the way he reflexively judges his master, assuming he is a "hard" man, when the master has done nothing to justify this charge. Indeed, to entrust such a large sum demonstrates an almost exorbitant level of generosity and trust. Additionally, the third servant names his motivation for hiding the talent as fear.

"It was timidity that spelled his downfall," writes Donahue in *The Gospel in Parable,* "which was not warranted by anything known directly about the master." The servant views his master as "hard" though he had been treated fairly. Falsely imagining himself as a victim, the servant created a situation in which he became "with tragic irony" a real victim. In a sense, the man created a "master" of his own making, rather than letting the master be himself.[26] Perhaps we are to take from this story not the idea that we are to "use our own talents," but rather the idea that we are to let God be God.

That same lesson can be drawn from a similar parable, in which a master pays laborers who have worked only one hour the same wage that he pays to those who have worked a full day.[27] Many current-day readers also find this parable, usually called the Parable of the Laborers in the Vineyard, nearly scandalous. That someone working for just an hour would be paid the same as someone working many hours more seems unjust. The story never fails to annoy the capitalist mind. But the master has an answer to those who question him: "Are you envious because I am generous?" The lesson here may be: Let God be generous. As with the timid servant in the Parable of the Talents, the angry laborers have already decided the master is ungenerous.

But the interpretation of the Parable of the Talents that prompted discussion in my community was even more unusual than Donahue's. Barbara Reid believes that a key to the parable is remembering that Jesus was not operating in a capitalist system in which wealth could be increased by investment.[28] At the time, she suggests, people would have believed in a "limited good," where there was only so much wealth to go around and where increasing one person's wealth meant taking it away from another. "One who amassed large amounts for himself would be seen as greedy and wicked," she writes. The third servant, she believes, is the *honorable* one, because he refused to cooperate with a system in which the master continues to accrue large amounts of money while others are poor.

Reid sees the parable as a warning "about the ease with which people can be co-opted by an unjust system," while also encouraging disciples to expose unfettered greed. She believes that the last verse shows what happens to those who "blow the whistle" on the rich and powerful. The disciples therefore are not to take the man going on a journey as a stand-in for God and not to take the parable as an encouragement to use their "God-given talents." Although this is an important lesson, Jesus's listeners may not have understood the parable in that way, since "talent" did not have the connotation that it does in English.

In Reid's view, this parable, like many other parables, is about the need for the disciples to be faithful during the time between Jesus's departure and his coming again and to go against the prevailing attitudes. "In contrast to slaves, who live in servile fear of a greedy master who metes out cruel punishment to those who will not go along with this program for self-aggrandizement, Jesus's disciples live with trust in God, whose equitable love emboldens them to work for justice here and now while awaiting ultimate fulfillment."

When I first came upon Reid's interpretation I had to read it three times. It was almost the opposite of the traditional explanation.

So which is it? While my money is on the traditional explanation, the parables will never give up all their meaning. That's why I enjoy preaching about them. Nothing so riles up an audience as a parable that they don't "get" or "like." That's what C. H. Dodd meant when he said they "tease" the mind into active thought.

"That parable really seemed to bother the congregation," I once told the pastor of a church after a homily I had preached.

"Good!" he said.

Saying that the parables may be difficult to grasp, however, does not mean that Jesus did not intend for listeners to get the point. Even the most open-ended parable was designed to convey a message, if only to his inner circle, and even if they failed to grasp that message on the first hearing.

To that end, let's look at perhaps Jesus's most famous parable and think about how it might tease our minds into active thought about the reign of God. Perhaps you can imagine yourself standing by the Bay of Parables listening to Jesus, alongside the original hearers of these stories, surrounded by the rocks and the grass and the bushes and the thorns and saying to your companions, "What in the world does he mean by *that*?"

"THERE WAS A MAN who had two sons," said Jesus, in the best short-story intro in history.[29] "The younger of them said to his father, 'Father, give me the share of the property that will belong to me.'" Immediately Jesus's listeners would have perked up. The young man is asking for an early distribution of his inheritance, which is tantamount to saying to the father, "I wish you were dead." *Rotten son!* the listeners would think.

Sometime later, the son moves to a far country, where he squanders all he has "in dissolute living." The Greek *asōtōs* is sometimes translated as "careless living," but "debauchery" is closer to the mark. After he spends his wealth, a famine grips the land, and the now impoverished man hires himself out to a swineherd, who gives him a job feeding pigs.

Tending the pigs of a Gentile would have meant that the man was as alienated as a Jew could possibly imagine.[30] In his poverty, he envies the pigs: "He would gladly have filled himself with the pods that the pigs were eating; and no one gave him anything." Not surprisingly, the man comes to his senses (*eis heauton de elthōn,* literally, "came to himself"), apparently repents, and remembers his father's farm, where the hired hands have more than enough to eat.

Either out of honest remorse or simple hunger, the man decides to apologize and say, "Father, I have sinned against heaven and before you; I am no longer worthy to be called your son; treat me like one of your hired hands." The "hired hand" is the *misthios,* the one to whom wages were due, but nothing more, certainly not a personal relationship. The son is saying to the father, in essence, "Imagine now that *I* am dead." Already Jesus's story is setting up the listeners to think about matters of life and death.

The son sets off toward home. You can imagine Jesus's listeners expecting, as in other parables where miscreants are dealt with harshly, that the younger son will be severely punished. If the steward who failed to invest was cast into outer darkness, how much more will a greedy son suffer! But while the son was still far from his home, his father "saw him and was filled with compassion."

Let's pause here. We may be so familiar with the story that we overlook something that may have surprised its original audience: at this point the father hasn't heard his son express any remorse yet. Jesus says that the father was "filled with compassion" simply upon seeing him. The Greek is the wonderful *esplagchnisthē,* he felt it in his guts—the seat of feelings in the Hellenistic world. It's the same word Luke uses to describe Jesus's emotions when seeing the hungry crowd before he feeds them in the Multiplication of the Loaves and Fishes, and that was used earlier in Luke when Jesus meets a widow in the town of Nain, whose son has just died. It is also used to describe the Samaritan's reaction upon seeing the beaten man in the Parable of the Good Samaritan.[31] We are meant to feel for people in our guts, to be moved to compassion, and to act.

Then the father does something marvelous. The English translation says that he "ran and put his arms around him and kissed him." The original Greek is far more beautiful. *Kai dramōn epepesen epi ton trachēlon autou kai katephilēsen auton* can be translated, "And running, he fell upon his neck and fervently kissed him." It recalls the tender scene in the Book of Genesis where Joseph, in service to the Pharaoh, is overcome with emotion at being reunited with his brothers (who had sold him into slavery), falls upon them, and kisses them. Joseph cries so loudly that all of Pharaoh's household can hear him.[32]

The scene of the father weeping over his wayward son is a beautiful, human scene. But it must have awakened complex emotions in Jesus's listeners. Who could fail to think of one's own father's embrace and the deep-seated human need for parental love and acceptance? At the same time, who could not feel confused by the father's apparent approval of the son's leave-taking and debauched living? What was going on?

For the shocked, more shock follows. The father calls for a special robe to be brought out—*prōtēn,* the first, the best one—and placed on the son; and he offers a ring for his finger. He orders the "fatted calf" brought out, that is, the calf fed specifically on grain (rather than left to graze in the field) and marked for special celebrations. "For this son of mine was dead and is alive again; he was lost and is found!" Luke Timothy Johnson rightly calls these "extravagant" gestures.[33]

In Luke's Gospel, this parable follows the Parables of the Lost Sheep and the Lost Coin, so early readers would have made the connection to God's seeking out and welcoming the lost. The shepherd carries the sheep around his neck in a tender gesture; the father rushes to kiss the son's neck in a tender gesture. You can feel the father's joy and his relief: My son is home! The father is prodigal—lavish, extravagant, and overly generous. The story could easily be called the Parable of the Prodigal Father.

In my work as a spiritual director, I have found few other passages that can so help people facing difficulties in their relationship with God. Often we can be trapped by our own preconceived notions of how God judges, how God reacts, and how God relates to us. Some of these come from the unhealthy ways that other authority figures, like parents or teachers, may have related to us, rather than from the ways that God actually relates to people. We end up withdrawing farther from a God of our own making, rather than drawing closer to the God who made us.

A young man once told me that he couldn't bring himself to pray because he kept imagining God judging him for not only everything he did, but also for everything he thought. Distractions in prayer, angry thoughts about a coworker, and frequent sexual fantasies were all reasons that he was sure God judged him. I invited him to think about the Parable of the Prodigal Son. As soon as the words were out of my mouth, his face became wreathed in a smile.

"I love that parable," he said. "But what does that have to do with God?"

"Everything!" I said. "Here's an image of God not from your own mind, but from Jesus's mind. Why not pray with *his* image of God?" A look of relief washed over the young man's tired features.

The story, though, may offer us an image not simply of God the Father, but of Jesus himself. For the Parable of the Prodigal Son comes in the fifteenth chapter of Luke. And how does that chapter begin? With the "Pharisees and the scribes" grumbling about Jesus. "This fellow welcomes sinners and eats with them," they say.[34] Thus the parable may be Jesus's response to that critique. Those who complain about eating with the sinful are compared, unfavorably, to the soon-to-be resentful elder son. Like most of the parables, the Prodigal Son can operate on many levels, highlighting Jesus's acceptance of sinners, the acceptance or nonacceptance of Jesus by the Pharisees and scribes, and God's acceptance of all.

But there's more to this story than even acceptance. Everyone now starts to celebrate. The father's joy is magnified in those around him. Some of Jesus's first listeners may have thought, *Well, they're celebrating now, but wait until that son gets his comeuppance!*

Those hard-hearted sentiments are now expressed by the older son, who has so far remained on the story's sidelines. The dutiful one is working in the fields when he hears music and dancing at the house. At this point, I always wonder if Jesus is not telling a parable, but recounting a tale based in real life; that small detail of hearing the music and the jealousy it sparks lends it the ring of truth. *What's that?* you can imagine the elder son thinking. *A party? Why wasn't I invited?*

The elder son discovers that his brother has returned. To add insult to injury, he learns the news from one of the slaves. He is so angered that he refuses to enter the house.

There is also some pathos evident. The father had time to have food prepared, and yet no one thinks to "search for" the elder brother. His deep emotions are understandable. So the father comes out and begins to "plead" with him. (The Greek *parekalei* could also mean "comfort.") The loving father who can forgive his wayward son would surely have understood the elder son's dark emotions, and he invites him to rejoin the family. Notice the parallels: the elder son's anger is expressed by his unwillingness to enter the house; the father's compassion is expressed by his going out of the house.[35] Now it is the elder son who is about to cut himself off from the family.

Then the elder son explodes. "Listen!" he says. "For all these years I have been working like a slave (*douleuō*) for you." What's more, "I have never disobeyed your command." Unlike, he implies, that other son. Then the coup de grâce: "Yet you have never given me even a young goat so that I might celebrate with my friends. But when this son of yours came back, who has devoured your property with prostitutes, you killed the fatted calf for him!"

In one explosive sentence, the son vents the feelings of all those who have ever felt ignored or underappreciated for their hard work. In my experience, most Christians are trying to lead good lives and therefore are more like the dutiful elder son than the wastrel younger one. We are more likely to feel the older son's emotions: resentment over not being appreciated, jealousy over the success of someone who does not "deserve" it, anger at what we deem as favoritism, and sadness at feeling excluded.

Notice how powerful emotions lead the son to exaggerate his grievances, as they often do in our lives. He speaks of the brother's consorting with prostitutes, though that has not been explicitly mentioned by either the son or the father. Hurt feelings lead him to falsely accuse his brother. His words betray his rage; when speaking to his father he calls his brother, contemptuously, *huios sou houtos,* "this son of yours." Even devout Christians fall into the elder son's trap: we do our work but secretly harbor resentment that we are not rewarded the way we *should* be treated.

This point is expertly drawn out in Henri Nouwen's *The Return of the Prodigal Son,* a book-length meditation on this parable. Nouwen, a twentieth-century Dutch Catholic priest, often drew on his own experiences to illustrate a complex Gospel passage or other Christian themes. In his chapter on the elder son comes this frank confession:

> Often I catch myself complaining about little rejections, little impolitenesses, little negligences. Time and again I discover within me that murmuring, whining, grumbling, lamenting, and griping that go on and on even against my will. The more I dwell on the matters in question, the worse my state becomes. The more I analyze it, the more reason I see for complaint. And the more deeply I enter it, the more complicated it gets. There is an enormous, dark drawing power to this inner complaint. Condemnation of others and self-condemnation, self-righteousness and self-rejection keep reinforcing each other in an ever more vicious way.[36]

When I first read those lines I thought, *Me too.* During my early Jesuit training, I lived with someone who seemed to be admired by everyone in our house. Everyone laughed at his jokes; everyone delighted when he entered a room; everyone looked forward to his presence. Or at least it seemed that way to me. Though we were friends, I grew jealous—so much so that when he was sure to be at a gathering, I felt tempted to exclude myself from the community. I felt like the older brother, trapped by envy.

The son also seems angry at the father's *joy*. I felt the same upon seeing others joyfully interacting with my brother Jesuit. Not only does the father forgive the younger son, he does it joyfully—running out, kissing him on the neck, preparing a feast. You can feel the older brother boil with rage while everyone else celebrates. It's a common response. How often do we become resentful over the good fortune of others?

The older son's anger flows not only from his jealousy, but also from his inability to forgive his brother and to forgive his father for ignoring him all those years. He seems imprisoned by his resentment. Most of us know the feeling that the wrongs done to us are unforgivable, inexcusable. But in this parable Jesus points out not simply the cost of sin to the sinner, but the cost to the wronged one of not forgiving.

Stepping out of the prison of resentment is essential for our freedom—and for everyone else's freedom. Jesus doesn't tell us if the elder brother ever reconciled with his younger brother, but if he did not, the father's joy would be incomplete and the younger son would never feel truly welcomed.

Sometimes our inability to accept another's good fortune comes from denigrating our own lives. We focus not on what we already have, but on what another person seemingly has. And usually our perceptions of another's good fortune are dangerously skewed: we tend to magnify another's blessings while minimizing our own, and we ignore someone else's struggles while exaggerating ours. Thus, as in the case of the elder son, we cannot see clearly. Envy masks ingratitude.

The father reminds the older son of just that at the end of the story. Addressing him as "my son," he says, "You are always with me, and all that is mine is yours. But we had to celebrate and rejoice, because this brother of yours was dead and has come to life; he was lost and has been found."

Like the father's forgiveness, God's love is prodigal, foolish to those who look upon life in worldly terms. But the father doesn't care if he looks foolish as he races to embrace his son. He cares only about his son. His joy leaps off the page—it is necessary to "celebrate" and "rejoice," he says, as if one word couldn't possibly describe his joy.

God's mercy is relentless, like the woman who sweeps all day looking for a single coin. It is ridiculous, like the shepherd who leaves the other ninety-nine sheep for just one. Most of all, God's mercy is joyful, like the father rejoicing in love and compassion. During those times when it seems that it's hard to forgive or that others will mock us for forgiveness, it helps to remember how lavish God is with his forgiveness of us. Remembering this may make it easier for us to be prodigal with our own mercy. And rather than finding ourselves afraid to look foolish or weak, we may forget ourselves and find ourselves running headlong to embrace the other.

We may act like the wayward younger brother and feel like the hardworking elder brother, but in the end we are called to be like the merciful father.

THE DEEP JOY THAT I felt at the Bay of Parables that day came from recognizing—as if for the first time—not only the utter reality of Jesus's human life on earth (standing in a particular spot in Galilee, in front of a particular group of people, on a particular day in the first century), but also his compassionate use of the parable. It was not beneath him to use the things beneath him to explain things above. The parable was an act of love.

There was also the joy that came from finding something I thought I'd never see and something others said probably didn't exist. My search for the Bay of Parables seemed a kind of parable about faith. It took me almost twenty-five years to find it, but once I did, I would never forget it. I'm not sure if Jesus spoke the parables from the precise spot where I stood, but it seemed reasonable to conclude that he did—given the landscape, its proximity to Capernaum, and how, as I learned a few summers before, a human voice can travel over water.

Later in the day, at the gift shop at the Mount of Beatitudes, I bought a copy of Bargil Pixner's guidebook *With Jesus Through Galilee*. Flipping through the pages I came across a photo with the caption "Bay of Parables." I laughed when I saw it.

At dinner I showed the photo to Sister Télesfora, and she laughed too. "There it is," she said. "I have never seen that!"

The delight of that day remains with me. Rather than trying to re-create it, let me share what I wrote in my journal that night in its unedited joy:

> There is almost too much to write down today. George has been great about letting me pick and choose what I wanted to do, since he has been here before. So today I said that I really wanted to find the Bay of Parables, where J preached from the boat—Pixner mentions it as well. We asked a nice OSB monk @ Tabgha who gave us a handy map. (Btw it's been broiling hot the whole time.) We parked at the side of the road and found a path marked by a purple and white set of signposts and soon we found it! Indeed, you could see the natural bowl shape of the place—a real amphitheater, and it was easy to imagine the crowds sitting down. And to think that the parables were first heard *here*. I could barely contain my joy! And to turn around and see the rocks and thorns and birds and realize that these were what he was talking about: these birds, these plants, these thorns. Overwhelming.

THE PARABLE OF THE SOWER
Mark 4:1–9
(See also Matthew 13:1–9; Luke 8:4–8)

Again he began to teach beside the lake. Such a very large crowd gathered around him that he got into a boat on the lake and sat there, while the whole crowd was beside the lake on the land. He began to teach them many things in parables, and in his teaching he said to them: "Listen! A sower went out to sow. And as he sowed, some seed fell on the path, and the birds came and ate it up. Other seed fell on rocky ground, where it did not have much soil, and it sprang up quickly, since it had no depth of soil. And when the sun rose, it was scorched; and since it had no root, it withered away. Other seed fell among thorns, and the thorns grew up and choked it, and it yielded no grain. Other seed fell into good soil and brought forth grain, growing up and increasing and yielding thirty and sixty and a hundredfold." And he said, "Let anyone with ears to hear listen!"

THE PARABLE OF THE PRODIGAL SON
Luke 15:11–32

Then Jesus said, "There was a man who had two sons. The younger of them said to his father, 'Father, give me the share of the property that will belong to me.' So he divided his property between them. A few days later the younger son gathered all he had and traveled to a distant country, and there he squandered his property in dissolute living. When he had spent everything, a severe famine took place throughout that country, and he began to be in need. So he went and hired himself out to one of the citizens of that country, who sent him to his fields to feed the pigs. He would gladly have filled himself with the pods that the pigs were eating; and no one gave him anything. But when he came to himself he said, 'How many of my father's hired hands have bread enough and to spare, but here I am dying of hunger! I will get up and go to my father, and I will say to him, "Father, I have sinned against heaven and before you; I am no longer worthy to be called your son; treat me like one of your hired hands."' So he set off and went to his father. But while he was still far off, his father saw him and was filled with compassion; he ran and put his arms around him and kissed him. Then the son said to him, 'Father, I have sinned against heaven and before you; I am no longer worthy to be called your son.' But the father said to his slaves, 'Quickly, bring out a robe—the best one—and put it on him; put a ring on his finger and sandals on his feet. And get the fatted calf and kill it, and let us eat and celebrate; for this son of mine was dead and is alive again; he was lost and is found!' And they began to celebrate.

"Now his elder son was in the field; and when he came and approached the house, he heard music and dancing. He called on one of the slaves and asked what was going on. He replied, 'Your brother has come, and your father has killed the fatted calf, because he has got him back safe and sound.' Then he became angry and refused to go in. His father came out and began to plead with him. But he answered his father, 'Listen! For all these years I have been working like a slave for you, and I have never disobeyed your command; yet you have never given me a young goat so that I might celebrate with my friends. But when this son of yours

comes back, who has devoured your property with prostitutes, you killed the fatted calf for him!' Then his father said
to him, 'Son, you are always with me, and all that is mine
is yours. But we had to celebrate and rejoice, because this
brother of yours was dead and has come to life; he was lost
and has been found.'"

CHAPTER 13

Storms

"Teacher, do you not care?"

ONE AFTERNOON, IN THE middle of our stay at the Franciscan hostel and after a full day of visiting sites on the Sea of Galilee, George and I found ourselves with a few free hours before dinner. Scouting around for a place to pray, I walked onto the veranda of the chapel that serves as the centerpiece of the complex. Overlooking the lake from an impressive height, the Church of the Beatitudes was designed in 1938 by the Italian architect Antonio Barluzzi. Its construction was funded by—of all people—Benito Mussolini, who took great interest in the Holy Land.[1]

The stone chapel, capped by a dark gray dome, is octagonal-shaped, with each of its eight sides commemorating one of the Beatitudes. I wasn't a fan of the chapel's chilly marble interior, and the Mussolini connection also made it more difficult for me to meditate. I pictured Il Duce poring over the architectural plans and pounding his fist on the table in disagreement. On the other hand, Barluzzi surrounded his chapel with a magnificent colonnaded portico, a spot that is, according to Murphy-O'Connor's guidebook, "the best place from which to contemplate the spiritual dimension of the lake; one can see virtually all the places in which Jesus lived and worked."[2]

Alone on the shaded porch, I had a commanding view of Jesus's life in Galilee. To my left I could easily see the ruins of Capernaum, just a mile or so from where I stood. Past that was Bethsaida, where Peter and Andrew lived. In front of me, across the sea, were the pinkish-gray hills of the land of the Gerasenes, where Jesus healed a demoniac. On the road beneath me was the traditional site where Jesus healed the woman with the hemorrhage. To my right were the traditional venues for the Call of the First Disciples, the Feeding of the Five Thousand, and the Breakfast by the Sea. And I was standing on (or near) the spot where Jesus had preached the Sermon on the Mount. I felt drunk with the spiritual history of the place.

I sat down, my back against the cold stone wall. The cloudless sky ranged from a bright blue overhead to the palest lavender at the horizon. A light breeze came up. For the first time in my life I was able to pray with my eyes open. In classic Ignatian contemplation you imagine yourself in various Scripture passages, trying your best to see the place in the mind's eye. But this time I had to do no imagining at all. Here it was, laid out before me. On Barluzzi's portico I could easily imagine the first-century fishermen plying their trade on the sea—because I could see beneath me, on the shoreline, fishermen casting their nets.

Suddenly a terrific wind arose, sweeping all the dry palm leaves off the portico. I laughed, because I *really* wanted a storm to blow up. Let me tell you why.

I've been a spiritual director for more than twenty years. It is one of my greatest joys.

Spiritual direction helps people notice where God is active in their prayer and in their daily lives. While it may overlap with a number of other practices, spiritual direction is neither psychotherapy (which focuses mainly on the psychological underpinnings of a person's problems), nor pastoral counseling (which focuses mostly on problem-solving in a spiritual setting), nor confession (which focuses on sin and forgiveness). Spiritual directors are trained specifically to enable a person to recognize God's activity; this means helping that person with prayer.

What topics come up in spiritual direction? Anything significant that arises in prayer, moments in your daily life when God felt close, and frustrations over how God might seem absent. Being a good spiritual director requires formal training, which includes learning how to listen well and notice where a person might be overlooking God's activity. It's not enough simply to be prayerful. St. Teresa of Ávila, the sixteenth-century Carmelite nun, famously said that if she had to choose for a spiritual director between someone who was wise and someone who was holy, she would choose the wise person. Optimally, you would like both!

My first spiritual "directee," as they're called in the trade, approached me when I had been a Jesuit for only two years. Following my novitiate, I studied philosophy at Loyola University Chicago. An undergraduate in my Introduction to Philosophy course asked if he could see me for spiritual direction. I asked my own spiritual director if I was ready. "You're ready to be a director when people start asking you," he said. It was a moving experience to hear, and see, how God was at work in this young man's life. Directing him also introduced me to a common experience: *my* faith grew, the more I saw how God was at work in someone else. It's a spiritual boost to see God's activity in others, particularly during times when you, yourself, feel dry. It's like doubting the wind and then seeing it sweep across a field of tall grass. You say to yourself, *Ah, there it is!*

The next summer I spent two weeks in a spiritual directors' training program at a Jesuit retreat house outside of Toronto, Canada. Years later, after my ordination I spent an entire summer at a Jesuit retreat house near Cincinnati, Ohio, learning about spiritual direction techniques, most of which hinge on being a good listener. "Slow, silent, and stupid," goes one mantra. Don't rush; don't be afraid of silence; and don't assume that you know what the other person means—ask.

Since then I've served as a spiritual director for dozens of people, both on a regular monthly basis and during retreats—weekends and eight-day and thirty-day retreats. It is rarely dull. In Ohio one of our instructors told us, "If you're bored in spiritual direction, it probably means that the other person is not talking about God. They might be talking about problems at work, difficulties at home, or health issues, but they're not yet talking about God. Because the Holy Spirit is never boring!"

In my experience as a spiritual director, I've noticed that a handful of Bible passages seem to help almost everyone. I've already mentioned Jeremiah 29:11, which begins, "For surely I know the plans I have for you," and invites the reader to meditate on God's provident care. But the passage that is by far the most helpful for people going through difficult times is the Stilling of the Storm. I know of no other passage that is as helpful to Christians. It has been helpful to me too.

THE STORY IS ESSENTIALLY the same in the three Synoptic Gospels, though the song begins on slightly different notes. "One day . . ." (Luke). "Now when Jesus saw great crowds around him . . ." (Matthew). "On that day, when evening had come . . ." (Mark). For purposes of clarity I'll focus on Mark's account.

Jesus asks his disciples to cross in the boat to the "other side" of the Sea of Galilee. Mark's audience will notice two things. First, Jesus's request comes at the close of a long day of preaching, from a fishing boat offshore. The crowds have just heard several parables, the last being the Parable of the Sower. Jesus will now leave them behind to sail with the disciples. Mark tells us that other boats accompany them; these may have carried the larger group of followers. (Remember that there were increasingly larger concentric circles of apostles, disciples, and followers.[3]) Perhaps Jesus will reveal something special to the smaller group. So readers may think it's a hopeful time.

Mark's audience will notice something else: it is evening. On the sea this can be a time not of anticipation, but fear.

Before the story begins in earnest, the English translation includes a charming phrase. "And leaving the crowd behind, they took him with them in the boat, just as he was." For many years I wondered about those words. What did it mean—"just as he was"? The English might be vague, but the Greek is clearer: *paralambanousin auton hōs ēn en tō ploiō.* A literal translation would be: "They took him as he was in the ship." That is, Jesus was already in the boat, so the disciples just piled in, and together they set off for the other side. But the opaque English translation unintentionally reminds us that we need to take Jesus "as he is" rather than trying to make him as we would wish him to be. The disciples often had a hard time dealing with Jesus as he was, just as we do.

Suddenly a great (*megalē*) windstorm arises on the sea, and the waves begin to swamp the boat. The Greek suggests a kind of tornado. Even today storms suddenly stir up the Sea of Galilee, the result of dramatic differences in temperatures between the shoreline (680 feet below sea level) and the surrounding hills (which can reach 2,000 feet). The strong winds that funnel through the hills easily whip up waves in the relatively shallow waters (only two hundred feet deep). Today a boating industry for pilgrims thrives on the Sea of Galilee; often boat owners will take pilgrims on a tour and even include a Mass aboard the vessels. A few former pilgrims told me that while they were aboard those tourist boats, a storm arrived without warning. Their surprise was exceeded only by the sheer pleasure of witnessing a biblical "storm at sea."

But the disciples would not have felt any pleasure. It's important to remember the terror that storms held for those in Jesus's day as well as the rich religious symbolism of water. In ancient times water was a symbol for life and a means of purification, but it also held out the potential for death and was an occasion of danger, as in the story of the Flood or the story of Jonah. The Psalms speak of God's power over the seas and also use water as a symbol of peril: "Save me, O God," says the psalmist, "for the waters have come up to my neck."[4] Raging seas and howling storms would have represented to Jesus's contemporaries chaos and danger. Jewish belief was that the sea could also be the abode of demonic forces.

On a less theological level, sea voyages were simply dangerous, as St. Paul would attest.[5] A storm at sea could be frightening even for experienced fishermen. Far worse is the storm at sea at night.

Not long after a terrible hurricane hit the East Coast of the United States and caused widespread destruction, I saw footage of a woman describing the panic she felt as the "storm surge" hit. She described the waves barreling up her street, bursting in the door of her house, and rising up to her neck; she could barely get the words out—the fear in her voice was still palpable. A cubic meter of water weighs over two thousand pounds, which explains the destruction it can cause during a hurricane or flood, crushing everything in its path. This is a window into the kind of terror that the water would have held in Jesus's day.

But in the face of the chaotic storm Jesus is calm. Beyond calm. "He was in the stern, asleep on the cushion," says Mark. What Donahue and Harrington call "untroubled sleep" signals trust in God's protection even in the direst circumstances.[6]

A word about that boat. Before I left for Israel a Jesuit friend said that the most moving part of his entire Holy Land pilgrimage was the Jesus Boat Museum. That a museum, and not a church, won that accolade recommended a visit. So one day I dragged George to the ultramodern Yigal Allon Museum, located on a *kibbutz* by the shoreline.[7]

Inside was the Ancient Galilee Boat, the remarkably well-preserved remains of a first-century fishing craft discovered in 1986, when a drought lowered the level of the lake. The artifact from the time of Jesus sits in a pristine room, gently supported by cushioned metal struts. The dark, wooden vessel, which would have included a mast, is large—almost 27 feet long by 7½ feet wide. For me the most touching feature was evidence of numerous repairs, the reuse of timbers, and a multiplicity of wood types (twelve in all), some salvaged from other boats. It suggested, as the brochure said, "a long work life and an owner of meager means." What's more: "An analysis of crew size suggests that this is the type of boat referred to in the Gospels in use among Jesus's disciples."[8]

A smaller, modern-day reconstruction of the boat in another room included a raised wooden ledge on which several people could sit. So it would have been easy for Jesus to find a place to sleep, perhaps on a cushion or a bag of sand used for ballast or comfort.[9]

But it wasn't easy for his friends to understand *how* he could sleep in the violent gale. "They woke him up," said Mark, "and said to him, 'Teacher, do you not care that we are perishing?'" Among his disciples were four fishermen, one of whom was likely the owner of the boat, and even *they* were afraid of dying. It must have been a hellacious storm.

Jesus rises up. Matthew uses *egertheis,* which conveys not simply standing, but rising to his full height to confront the storm. He "rebukes" the wind and says to the sea, "Peace! Be still!" The word Mark uses for Jesus's rebuke (*epetimēsen*) is the same used for his commands to evil spirits, and Jesus's phrasing is similar to the way he rebuked the demon in the synagogue at Capernaum: "Be silent, and come out of him!"

At once there is a "great" calm. The Greek *megalē* is the same word used for the "great" wind, highlighting both natural danger and Jesus's power over it. We can tell that the disciples are terrified, because Jesus says to them, "Why are you afraid? Have you still no faith?" A more literal translation of Mark's Greek—*pōs ouk echete pistin*—may better convey Jesus's amazement at the disciples' reaction: "How is it that you still have no faith?"

Their terror is not surprising. We're so used to some Gospel stories that they can seem predictable. But sit on the narrow wooden seats next to the disciples, and Jesus's power will render you speechless. And the disciples are frightened by not simply the miraculous—or what might seem magical—power, but what it *meant*. Controlling nature was the prerogative of God alone. The creation story in Genesis recounts God's dividing of the waters, separating the rains above and the seas below, and also exerting power over chaotic nature.[10] Jews aboard might have remembered one of many psalms on that same theme: "You rule the raging of the sea; when its waves rise, you still them."[11]

The next line is stunning: *ephobēthēsan phobon megan*. They feared a great fear.

Fear of the storm has morphed into fear of God, the awe accompanying a display of divine power, a theophany. When they next open their mouths, I imagine them having a hard time getting the words out: "Who then is this, that even the wind and the sea obey him?"

The carpenter who just offered homey parables on the shoreline reveals a supernatural command over the waters. Jesus is mighty in word and in deed. I can only imagine the disciples sitting in stupefied silence as the voyage continued, now over calm waters.

BACK TO SPIRITUAL DIRECTION. Why has this story proved so helpful to so many people I've seen through the years?

Out of all my directees only one was a fisherman! But everyone faces stormy times, when God's presence is hard to perceive. One of the most common struggles in the spiritual life is a feeling of God's absence during painful times. Even some of the saints report this. Why is this so common? Perhaps because when we are struggling, we tend to focus on the area of pain. It's natural, but it makes it more difficult to see where God might be at work in other places, where God is not asleep.

A young man, whom I'll call Aaron, once came to me for monthly spiritual direction. With palpable sorrow Aaron explained how he felt God had abandoned him after he was diagnosed with a chronic illness. His sense of God's presence, his ability to see God around him, the ease with which he had once prayed—all had evaporated. Thus, his sadness over his physical condition was exacerbated by a sense of abandonment. When I asked him if he had ever prayed about the Stilling of the Storm, he wept. Just mentioning the passage evoked tears—you could tell that he instantly connected with the disciples' feelings of abandonment.

When we next met, Aaron said that he was embarrassed about what had happened in his prayer. Imagining himself aboard the boat was easy, as was picturing the waves crashing around him. He saw the waves as apt images of his inner turmoil. But when he thought about Jesus sleeping, he said that he shouted aloud in his apartment, "Get up! Get up! Where are you, Jesus? Why don't you *care* about me?" He wept when recounting this.

After Aaron admitted his embarrassment, we talked about God's ability to handle his feelings of anger and abandonment, since God has been able to handle powerful emotions since (at least) the time of the Psalms. "How long, O Lord?" laments the psalmist. "Will you forget me forever?"[12] This is what Aaron, the disciples, and countless believers have said to God.

Expressing his emotions honestly made it easier for Aaron to talk to God honestly, and that in turn enabled him to notice God's presence in other parts of his life. Aaron's honesty didn't remove the physical pain, but it helped to reestablish an open relationship with God. For when you say only the things that you believe you *should* say, rather than being honest, any relationship grows cold, including one with God. Once Aaron was able to be open and transparent in his prayer, he felt God's presence. "Funny enough," he said, "it made me feel calm. Like the sea after Jesus stilled it."

Aboard the ship the disciples express the human tendency to fear. Were we somehow able to ask the disciples at that moment why they were afraid, they would likely scoff, "Why *wouldn't* we be afraid?" Those living along the Sea of Galilee knew what storms could do to boats, and to people. Fear made sense. Without a healthy fear of the elements, Galilean fishermen wouldn't have taken the necessary precautions to protect themselves, their boats, and their catches.

But Jesus warns against fear in the spiritual life. When it comes to God's activity, fear is, paradoxically, dangerous, because it turns us away from God. Rather than focusing on what God can do, we are tempted to focus on what it seems God cannot do—that is, protect us. Indeed, Jesus's earthly life is bracketed by warnings against fear. At the beginning of his earthly life, the angel announcing his conception says to his mother, "Do not be afraid." And at the beginning of his new life, the angel announcing his resurrection to the women at the tomb says, "Do not be afraid."

Jesus's counsel against fear reveals several truths, a few things he wanted us to know about the world, and about God.

First, *I have not come to harm you.* God's presence should not prompt fear, for God always comes in love. Second, *don't fear the new.* God's entrance into your life may mean something will change, but unanticipated doesn't necessarily mean frightening. Third, *there is no need to fear things you don't understand.* If it comes from God, even the mysterious should hold no terror. You may not understand fully what God is asking, but this is no cause to be frightened. At the Annunciation Mary couldn't foresee what her future would hold, but she was empowered to fear not. And at the Resurrection the disciples probably didn't understand what, or more precisely who, stood before them, but they soon learned not to be afraid.

A healthy fear may remind fishermen to guard against contingencies like a storm, but in the spiritual life fear can lead to the inertia of hopelessness. It can paralyze us, destroy our trust, crush our hope, and turn us inward in unhealthy ways. Unchecked, it can lead us into despair, if we conclude that only woe can come out of the present situation, which is an implicit denial of God's ability to do the impossible.

Notice that the disciples encounter fear where they are most comfortable—aboard their own boats in Galilee. Especially when God enters into our familiar surroundings, cozy places or parts of our lives where everything seems settled, we may be particularly frightened. Perhaps there is a sudden thaw in a frozen relationship. Maybe you fear this new challenge to your old ways. "What are you doing here, God?" we may say. "Don't make me let go of my resentments. I'm too settled." We may not fear the storms as much as the calm after the storm.

Even in these places Jesus says, "Do not be afraid."

THE STILLING OF THE Storm is similar to another incident in which Jesus brings calm: his walking on the water. Without delving into too much detail, we can briefly sketch out the narrative that appears in Matthew, Mark, and John.[13] In all three Gospels the story follows the Feeding of the Five Thousand on the shore of the Sea of Galilee. After feeding the crowd, Jesus immediately (*euthus*) dismisses the disciples and "makes" or "forces" them to board their boats and cross the sea. There is no indication why the journey is so urgent, unless we take the next line as an explanation: "After saying farewell to them, he went up on the mountain to pray." Perhaps his insistence was a way of saying, "I really need some time alone."

As I mentioned earlier, near the traditional site of the Feeding is a hollowed-out space on a hill called the Eremos Cave, in which Jesus may have prayed.[14] It is a small ovoid opening in the rocky hillside, perhaps five feet high by ten feet wide. The morning George and I scrambled up to see it (it's a few hundred feet from the shoreline), we found the cave empty and the dusty site barren save for an empty beer bottle sitting insolently at the opening. The cave can accommodate a single person and provides some shelter from the elements; if it existed in Jesus's day (and there's no reason to think it didn't), it would have made an ideal place for solitude.

By sunset the disciples' boat has reached the middle of the Sea of Galilee. (In Matthew, the Greek says, "many stadia away from the land"; a *stadion* is an ancient measure of roughly two hundred yards.) From his far-off position Jesus sees the disciples straining at the oars in the face of an adverse, or "contrary," wind. Matthew says the boat was being "battered by the waves."

Then "early in the morning" (or in the Greek at the "fourth watch of the night," between three and six in the morning), according to Mark, "he came towards them . . . walking on the sea. He intended to pass them by." The disciples are terrified and cry out in fear; they think they are seeing a ghost.

The one standing upon the waves greets them. "Take heart (*Tharseite*, Courage!), it is I," Jesus says simply, which may be a gently human way of reassuring them. Or it may be an echo of God's divine declaration to Moses in the Book of Exodus, "I am who I am."[15]

"Do not be afraid," says Jesus, who boards the boat. The wind ceases. To describe the overwhelming emotions of the disciples Mark writes, *lian ek perissou en heautois existanto,* literally, "very much exceedingly in themselves standing outside." That is, utterly beside themselves. Although they have just witnessed the Miracle of the Loaves and Fishes, they still do not understand who he is. Their hearts, says Mark, are "hardened."

Matthew's addition to the story is well known even to those who aren't familiar with the New Testament. Peter answers Jesus with a challenge: "Lord, if it is you, command me to come to you on the water."

Why does Peter, who often serves in Matthew as a mouthpiece for the disciples, request this? Is he looking for proof that the one speaking in the teeth of the gale is truly Jesus? Does Peter want to arrogate to himself God's prerogative, power over nature? Or is he simply curious to see if he can do what Jesus is doing? What fisherman wouldn't want command over the waters?

In response Jesus says, "Come."

Peter begins to walk on the water, but then notices the strong wind. Distracted by danger, Peter fears, begins to sink, and cries out, "Lord, save me!" much as the disciples did during the storm. Taking his eye off Jesus means that he can do nothing on his own. Jesus stretches out his hand, takes hold of Peter, and says, perhaps bemused, "You of little faith, why did you doubt?" Jesus brings Peter back into the boat, where all prostrate themselves and pronounce him the Son of God. In Matthew the disciples are more able to apprehend Jesus's identity. Once again, the disciples may have recalled the psalms that speak of God's saving those in danger of drowning.

In both Matthew and Mark, Jesus manifests his awesome power over the sea. In both instances the disciples are terrified. In both Jesus warns them against fear. But besides counseling against fear, Jesus offers another blessing desperately needed today: calm.

Let's consider this in light of the frenzied state of our emotional, mental, physical, and spiritual lives today. The more I listen to people, the more I hear them speak about their lives using the same words: overworked, overbooked, overwhelmed, stressed-out, crazy-busy, nuts, insane. "I have no time for my family." "I have no time to pray." "I barely have time to think." Now this does not describe everyone's life: the unemployed, the underemployed, the sick, those in the last stages of life. But our culture has impressed upon us the equation that the busier you are, the more important you are.

Some of this pressure may be the result of an economy in which more hours are demanded from employees. Some of it can be traced to increasing pressures from advances in technology. Newer forms of communication mean that it is easy for us to be always connected. You're never far from work or from anyone intent on contacting you. But some of our busyness is the inevitable outcome of a world where overactivity is praised. And if everyone else is busy, who are we to opt out?

Yet it may also mask a subtle form of pride. Being busy is often an indication of generosity; some people pour themselves out for others in a selfless way. But sometimes busyness is the way we prove (consciously or not) to ourselves that we are important. This tendency on an individual level is then multiplied out in the community, leading to a society in which extreme busyness is a badge of importance. It may also mask an inability to be still. What would it mean if we weren't running around like demoniacs? What would happen if we weren't overbooked? What would we do with ourselves if there wasn't some task at hand?

Not long ago I found myself in a kind of storm. Trying to be generous, I had agreed to do many talks around the country. This had been my pattern for the last several years. I enjoy speaking to groups and visiting colleges, parishes, and retreat houses, but it was becoming unmanageable.

One weekend I flew to a city several hours away and, while my hosts were delightfully welcoming, the logistics of the trip were unavoidably bollixed up. There was confusion over where I was staying, a more grueling itinerary than anticipated, no heat in my bedroom, delayed flights, stormy weather, and an ear infection that made flying agonizing. After returning home, exhausted, what Thomas Merton would call a "filthy" cold hung on for two months. The doctor said that overwork and stress had played a part.

One day, looking over my schedule for the coming year, which was packed with travel, I began to worry. Fear set in. How could I continue at this pace? But gradually, I noticed something else within me: a deep-down desire to live a calmer, quieter, more contemplative life. A great many people were counting on me for lectures and retreats. Yet the more I thought about it, the more my longing for a quieter life increased. Still, in the midst of the storm I was bewildered. Should I cancel engagements and disappoint others or continue on and disappoint myself? I promised myself that I would pray about it the next day.

Early in the morning, when I closed my eyes, the first thing I saw in my mind's eye was Jesus, clad in a light blue robe, standing silently on the sea, a glassy calm. He stretched out his hands as if to say, "Come." But unlike Peter I didn't feel the invitation to walk on the water, as if to prove something. Instead, he seemed to be saying, "Why not come into the calm?" The wind whipped around his blue garments, with the sound of a flag in the wind, but both he and the sea remained calm.

Why not come into the calm? Why not indeed? It seemed a real invitation: Come. That morning I crafted a letter of cancellation to many of the events I had already accepted. I am loathe to cancel anything, as I consider it as a breaking of my word, but the choice was either a life of storms or a life with at least a little more calm. So I was honest: I needed more quiet in my life in order to be a good Jesuit. I wrote my e-mail, took a deep breath, and hit "Send."

The responses were more understanding than I could have imagined. "Good for you!" most of them said. "I should do the same thing," wrote another. The president of a Jesuit university where I was scheduled to deliver a lecture wrote a compassionate note, averring that it's important to take care of oneself and live a contemplative life, in order that one may be of greater use to God. I felt a great calm.

Not everyone can jettison tasks in this way. A new mother or father cannot simply stop rising in the "fourth watch of the night" to change a squalling infant. A person caring for an elderly parent cannot simply walk out of that boat. But most of us know that there are some unnecessary things that prevent us from living more contemplatively, extraneous tasks and events and dates and appointments and things that can be thrown overboard. Do you have to make everyone happy by agreeing to every request? Must you say yes to something else you cannot possibly do—on the job, at your children's school, or in your family? Aren't there a few things that you can drop overboard?

Can you hear Jesus inviting you to more calm in your stormy life? Even Jesus needed to take time alone to pray.

Reading this you might fear. What would it mean for the storms to cease and for you to live more contemplatively? The disciples knew this fear. Even when things grew calm on the Sea of Galilee, when one would think that their fear would lessen, it only *grew*.

Jesus gently guides us away from fear, and he calls to us, as he did to the disciples, inviting us onto the calm waters of life.

Listen to him. He says to you, "Come."

THE STILLING OF THE STORM
Mark 4:35–41
(See also Matthew 8:18; 23–27; Luke 8:22–25; John 6:16–21)

On that day, when evening had come, he said to them, "Let us go across to the other side." And leaving the crowd behind, they took him with them in the boat, just as he was. Other boats were with him. A great gale arose, and the waves beat into the boat, so that the boat was already being swamped. But he was in the stern, asleep on the cushion; and they woke him up and said to him, "Teacher, do you not care that we are perishing?" He woke up and rebuked the wind, and said to the sea, "Peace! Be still!" Then the wind ceased, and there was a dead calm. He said to them, "Why are you afraid? Have you still no faith?" And they were filled with great awe and said to one another, "Who then is this, that even the wind and the sea obey him?"

CHAPTER 14

Gerasa

*"Night and day among the tombs
and on the mountains
he was always howling and bruising
himself with stones."*

EARLY IN OUR STAY at the Franciscan hostel, I asked Sister Télesfora about the surrounding geography. I pointed vaguely to the opposite bank of the Sea of Galilee, where the rolling hills looked like folded cloth, and said, "What's over there?"

"Oh," she said airily, "the land of the Gerasenes."

"You're kidding," I said. "Is that really where the story of the Gerasene demoniac happened?"

Raised eyebrows indicated that she was not kidding. "That's the other side," she said.

Immediately I remembered the story of Jesus and the disciples crossing in a boat to what the Gospels called the "other side," which had always seemed vague. It's hard to imagine the other side when you don't know any side at all. Once again, the force of being here, where Jesus was, almost floored me.

George seemed startled. "Oh, I really want to go there," he said. "That story is really important for me."

FOR ME TOO. IT is a stunning story, both touching and disturbing, found in all three Synoptic Gospels. It recounts the healing of a strange man who hurts others and himself. Its power to shock has been undimmed by two thousand years: the tale is called by modern Scripture scholars both "eerie" (Barclay) and "bizarre" (Meier).

Matthew, Mark, and Luke place the tale immediately after the Stilling of the Storm. Jesus and the disciples have sailed to the "other side" of the Sea of Galilee, to the "country of the Gerasenes," according to Mark. Before Jesus even steps off the boat, we must navigate our way through some textual difficulties.

Here's why: Other ancient copies of the Gospels speak of the land of the "Gadarenes" and still others, the "Gergasines."[1] This is a hotly disputed phrase, because the name does not correlate with the most likely site. Gerasa (modern Jerash, located in what is now Jordan), a large city in the region, is located roughly thirty-seven miles southeast of the sea. As we will soon see, this makes it an impossible candidate for the place. Or perhaps Mark simply intended to describe the general area between Gerasa and the Sea of Galilee.[2] But although Mark may have gotten the name of the town wrong, he is clear about the importance of the general location: Jesus is setting foot for the first time in "pagan" territory.

"Immediately," says Mark, as Jesus is still disembarking, a possessed man confronts him. The man, who has been living in the tombs that were cut into the limestone rock of the nearby mountainside, is possessed by an "unclean spirit." (Later, Mark refers to him as a *daimonizomenon,* or demon-possessed man.) Living in burial sites was, according to rabbinic literature, a sign of madness.[3] Interestingly, the word "tomb" is mentioned three times in only a few sentences, setting up Jesus's conflict not only with a demoniac, but, in a sense, with death.

The madman possesses terrifying physical strength: "No one could restrain him any more, even with a chain; for he had often been restrained with shackles and chains, but the chains he wrenched apart, and the shackles he broke in pieces; and no one had the strength to subdue him." Donahue and Harrington point out that the Greek's proliferation of negatives—literally, "No one" (*oudeis*),

"not even" (*oude*) with a chain, "was ever" (*ouketi*) able to bind him—
heightens the coming conflict with Jesus. That is, Jesus is about to
do something that no one else can do. No one. Ever.

Then comes an achingly poignant description: "Night and day
among the tombs and on the mountains he was always howling and
bruising himself with stones." It is easy to hear in this story echoes of
people we know who seem intent on harming themselves, and indeed
anyone who engages in self-destructive behavior through addictions,
compulsions, or habits. Probably the man desperately wanted to be
free of these demons, but had no idea how to free himself. His cries
(*krazōn,* to shriek) are those not just of a frightening man, but of a
frightened man.

The man rushes up to Jesus in what must have been a terrifying
scene, clambering down from the dusty mountainside, probably falling headlong, terrifying the disciples and onlookers. If this occurred
shortly after the storm at sea, it would have happened as night was
falling—or even in the dead of night. As Barclay notes, "The story
becomes all the more weird and frightening when it is seen as happening in the shadows of the night.["]4 The disciples, still recovering from Jesus's rebuke of the storm, have stepped onto unfamiliar
ground, in the dark, and are now confronted by a dangerous, violent,
probably lethal figure.

Then, touchingly, the crazed man prostrates himself before
Jesus in a gesture of worship or respect. It seems to be the man who
does this, not the demons. The poor man knows he is powerless to
heal himself and hurls himself before Jesus.

But then the demon spits out his threat to Jesus, crying out
again in a loud voice: "What have you to do with me, Jesus, Son of
the Most High God? I adjure you by God, do not torment me." It
is the same furious cry, nearly word for word, that Jesus first heard
from the possessed man in the synagogue at Capernaum: "*Ti hēmin
kai soi Iēsou?*" "What have you to do with us?"5 And here: "*Ti emoi
kai soi Iēsou?*"

Jesus's first exorcism on Gentile soil will mirror that in the Jewish synagogue: his power is equal in both settings. And as in the synagogue, the demon already knows the Messianic Secret. The demon identifies Jesus, even though the disciples failed to grasp this in the Multiplication of the Loaves and Fishes and at the Stilling of the Storm.

The possessed man's conflicted behavior points to a deeply divided self. He prostrates himself before Jesus, but then screams at him. He asks Jesus to swear "by God" that he won't be tortured, even as he is possessed by demons. The most succinct description comes from Donahue and Harrington: "The words of the demoniac show the inner division and turmoil he suffers."[6]

Why has the demon said these things to Jesus? Mark tells us that Jesus had already said to the demon, "Come out of the man," prompting the demon's response. Then Jesus addresses the demon again, directly, asking, "What is your name?"

In the ancient Near East, names held great significance and power. In the Book of Genesis, God renames Abram as Abraham, signifying a divinely ordained change in identity. Jesus will rename Simon as Peter, a sign of his new life and mission. Moreover, knowing a person's name was believed to give someone power over that person.

This is one reason that, when Moses asks to know God's name, the answer is, "I am who am." In other words, "That is my business."[7] Moses has no right to access the "power" of knowing God's name. Thus, when Jesus asks the demon's name, he poses a direct threat. "What is your name?" means "Let me have power over you."

The scene always brings chills to my spine and reminds me of the scene in the film *The Exorcist* when the psychiatrist addresses the demon within the possessed girl, Regan, whom he has hypnotized. "I'm speaking to the person inside of Regan now," he says. "If you are there, you too are hypnotized and must answer all my questions. Come forward and answer me now." After a growling Regan writhes on the bed, he asks, "Are you the person inside of Regan? Who are you?" This is Jesus's question.

Jesus receives an answer: "My name is Legion; for we are many."
What a chilling statement—there are many demons within the man.

There are a number of interpretations of this famous name.
First, Mark may simply be reporting what transpired, with the
"legion" as a colloquial expression for "many." Second, the demon
may use the word to avoid giving Jesus his precise name.[8] Third, it
may relate to the Roman legions. "Legion" is a Latin word for a military unit of around six thousand men. It was also used by Greek and
Aramaic speakers of the day, what scholars call a "loan word," bor-
rowed directly from another language. The Greek word in Mark is
simply a direct transliteration of the Latin *legion*.[9] The word could
also be a not-so-subtle reference to the presence of Roman forces in
Palestine. On the other hand, as Donahue and Harrington point out,
Jesus is not expelling Romans from Jewish lands here, since he was
in Gerasa, a largely Greek city. However, if he is on the "other side"
of the Sea of Galilee and still near Jewish territories, the word may
still evoke the image of Roman legions and their own "possession" of
Palestine.[10]

The demons beg Jesus not to send them out of the country, but
rather to send them into the herd of pigs nearby. The Greek word for
"beg," *parakalein,* is used not only for someone in need who begs, but
also for an "inferior" speaking to a "superior." The begging shows us
who is already in charge.

At that time, the notion that the demons would want to have
some place to reside (rather than being sent to an everlasting place of
damnation) was common.[11] The introduction of pigs also reminds us
of the pagan setting of the story and, also, the sense of uncleanness,
because Jews were forbidden to keep pigs or use them for food.[12]

Jesus gives the demons permission to enter the pigs. Immediately the unclean spirits enter the swine, and the entire herd (two
thousand, says Mark) rushes down the precipice into the sea and
drowns. This is one reason for the confusion over the location. If the
original story took place in the town of Gerasa, the pigs would have

had to run a marathon thirty-seven miles to the sea.[13] Once again, though, Mark may simply have been referring to a general region.

In a sense, the demons—who *asked* to be cast into the pigs—are the agents of their own destruction. Nonetheless, Jesus is shown as the quietly powerful one who liberates the man from what had kept him bound. Also, in contrast to the terrifying rantings of the man, Jesus speaks few words and, having recently fallen asleep on the boat, is an emblem of calm—in the midst of storms both physical and emotional. Mark may also want readers to see the destructive power of the demons as mirroring the destructive power of the sea, which figures into the previous passage. Both have now been decisively conquered by Jesus.

News of Jesus's astonishing feat is told by the swineherds both in the city and in the country. Some time afterward people returned to see the man "clothed and in his right mind." No longer naked (which we can infer from the "clothed" comment) and no longer deranged, he is restored to the community. No longer living among the tombs, he is symbolically restored to life. In most translations, onlookers are described now as "afraid." But the original Greek (*ephobēthēsan*) also conveys the sense of being awestruck by the power of Jesus.

Strangely, having been witness to a stunning miracle, the people plead (*parakalein* again) for Jesus to leave the area. It is the opposite of the request of the demons, who ask if they can stay. Why is this? On one hand, the swineherds were probably angered by the loss of their revenue. On the other hand, people in the pagan region might have been terrified by this Jewish wonder-worker's power. (Not to mention the sight of two thousand pigs floating in the water.) We'll return to that question.

Later, as Jesus is boarding the boat to return to the western shore, the former demoniac returns. The man begs (*parekalei*) Jesus if he can "be with him." It's easy to conjure up a quiet scene, with the water placidly lapping at the sides of the boat, a striking contrast to the turbulent episode that has just happened. Violence has been replaced by peace.

As in many cases, the man is not called to be a conventional disciple, that is, to leave everything behind. Instead, Jesus says, "Go home to your friends, and tell them how much the Lord has done for you, and what mercy he has shown you." The man is restored not just to the community at large, but more specifically to his friends. He is sent with a mission: to tell the story. There is a practical aspect to this command as well. Jesus commissions the man to spread the Good News to his people. Mark tells us that in this area, called the Decapolis—a federation of ten cities east of Samaria and Galilee— the story of Jesus's power spread.

For the readers of Mark's Gospel—who were both Jewish *and* Gentile Christians—the tale of Jesus's first interaction in pagan lands would have been an especially important lesson. And for the next generation of Christians, the story would have been used as a reminder of Jesus's outreach to those in non-Jewish communities. His power has no boundaries. Neither does his love.

Mark ends his story eloquently: *Kai pantes ethaumazon.* And all were amazed. All marveled. All were astonished.

SISTER TÉLESFORA GAVE US the name of the town now associated with the Gerasene demoniac, Kursi, on the "other side" of the Sea of Galilee, opposite from Capernaum. In Talmudic texts it was called Kurshi and identified with pagan worship. It is only about five hundred meters east of the sea, which would make rushing into the sea easier for the frenzied pigs.

George and I weren't sure what would greet us in Kursi, since so few people had mentioned the town to us. Plus, there was the devilishly complex problem of authenticity, as I mentioned. Like other scholars Murphy-O'Connor points out that the three different names for the place (the "land of the Gerasenes, Gadaranes, Gergesenes") are "suspicious," which means that it is difficult to claim that any one place is authentic.[14] But in this place, more than at any other site we visited, any questions of authenticity seemed to vanish.

We drove one afternoon to a site devoid of visitors. The sole caretaker greeted us and told us to feel free to explore the ruins of the monastery and the surrounding grounds. She told us that we would be able to see where the miracle happened "by standing on a rock behind the monastery."

The ruins of Kursi were discovered in 1970, when road work uncovered the walls of a fifth-century church and monastery. Built of a dark gray mottled stone, the complex includes what appears to be community space for the monks, outdoor workspace (including an olive press), and a church with a baptistry. On the floor are dusty mosaics arranged in complicated geometric patterns.

Though I'm no expert, the presence of a Byzantine monastery seemed to heighten the possibility that from ancient times Kursi was considered the place of the miracle. Later I checked Murphy-O'Connor, and he confirmed my hunch: "The Byzantine date of the material suggests that this was identified as the precise site of the Gospel miracle."[15] (I was pleased that the expert agreed with me!)

We wandered around the monastic ruins and examined the mosaics. I wondered aloud where the view of the famous hillside would be. But as we exited the site, the hills immediately—*euthus*—loomed up, so close it seemed that we could almost touch them. The dusty brown hillsides were dotted with trees and low bushes, and higher up—easily seen with the naked eye—were the caves, or tombs, that pockmarked the landscape. "Just like I pictured it," said George.

Scholarly controversies aside, everything fit. The topography lent itself to the Gospel story. The tombs were far enough up the mountainside that the poor man would have felt a sense of distance and isolation. It would have been easy for people to avoid the terrifying man living on the hillside, but the tombs were not so far that the people wouldn't have heard the man's shrieks. I could picture the pigs rooting around on the gentle slopes, and it was easy to visualize the herd rushing into the sea. The sea level was higher in antiquity (modern-day irrigation has caused a drop in the level), and so the distance between the scrubby hillside and the shoreline would have been shorter than it is today.

The wind blew strongly while we stood there in silence, the only pilgrims. All at once, I could see in my mind's eye, and almost hear, the thundering herd rushing headlong to the sea.

George and I stood there for some time. A rickety metal staircase attached to the side of the mountain allowed visitors to go closer to the tombs. I knew that the story meant a great deal to George, so I withdrew to allow him to pray in the mountains and near the tombs.

WHO HASN'T FELT LIKE the demoniac at some point? In fact, as I was writing this book, I reviewed the journals I kept during my annual retreats to refresh my memory of experiences in meditating on certain Gospel passages. And on the first page of the first journal, begun only a few months after entering the novitiate, I scribbled some notes about my "demons." At age twenty-eight, I was just beginning to explore my interior life in earnest and to understand how God was trying to free me:

> I still have many demons lurking in me. Despite God's best efforts, fear, anxiety, and worry still hide within me, and make their appearance at very inopportune times—like the beginning of a retreat. Unfortunately, all of them are very real. Fear of getting sick, anxiety over what would happen if I did get sick, in general worrying.

At the time, I was consumed with worry over an upcoming stay in Kingston, Jamaica, where I would work among the poor as part of my Jesuit training. Never having spent time in the developing world, I was terrified of contracting some rare illness. These were my demons at the time, and I begged God to rid me of them.

At various points early in my Jesuit training, I grew so frustrated with the things that so obviously kept me bound, kept me unfree, that I would lie on the floor, asking God to "rid me" of my demons. It sounds overwrought, but I was growing increasingly aware of the unhealthy parts of my personality that made me into a fearful and anxious person. I would beg Jesus to heal me *now*. Lying on the floor, I would wait for instantaneous healing, like that received by the Gerasene demoniac. It was easy for me to feel like the demoniac. And I could hear his cries in my own.

It is also easy to see signs of "demons" in others, particularly those who engage in long-term, sometimes lifelong, self-destructive behavior. I have several friends who have been alcoholics, overeaters, and addicted to drugs; a few friends have faced long-term emotional problems. They aren't evil of course, but all of them longed to be freed from their "demons." In their own ways, they cried out in pain, not so differently from the demoniac centuries ago.

The Gospel story suggests that some of the possessed man's friends and family may have tried to help him. Perhaps the chains were used not so much to prevent him from harming others as from harming himself. Generally in the New Testament those close to possessed persons try to seek healing for them. But some of his family and friends, and others in the land of the Gerasenes who did not know him, probably avoided the terrifying man, compounding his sense of isolation.

It is often the same in our lives. Self-destructive behavior can be frightening, and people withdraw out of fear of being harmed; they also withdraw because they are afraid of what someone else's torment might reveal about their own lives. Many of us would prefer not to recognize that we too contain a "legion" of demons that seem to have power over us. So we avoid the people on those mountainsides.

It is likewise frightening to confront your own powerlessness.

How painful it is to see someone you love harm himself or herself. How much we want liberation for the person. But how impotent we often feel when we try to help them, when we look for some way in which to heal them.

In the story of the Gerasene demoniac, the man's family and friends seem far away. Unlike in other situations, there is no mother or father to beg Jesus for healing. There is no group of friends to carry the man to Jesus's house and lower him through the roof. Perhaps the demoniac's friends have stopped attempting to help him after many years of trying in vain. Or perhaps they are like people today who, in the interests of self-preservation, pull away from the person who is bent on self-destruction. A man who is father to several children may want to help his troubled brother, but his first responsibility is to the welfare of his own children. So he withdraws from his brother and his "demons."

This is understandable. Often families and friends are encouraged by professional counselors to pull away from "toxic" personalities; in some cases this may be the only way that the family and friends can maintain their own mental health. The friends and family of the Gerasene demoniac probably tried various methods of healing—they may have already taken him to exorcists. But nothing worked, and now the man was left alone. "No one had the strength to subdue him" also means "no one could help him."

Maybe that's why he has become so self-destructive, "bruising himself with stones." Others reject him, so he rejects himself further. The man's physical strength is also an indicator of the implacability, the persistence, and the rootedness of the demonic presence.

As in the Gospel story, only God has the power to liberate fully. And, as in the Gospel story, we need to name our own demons—we need to say, "I am vain" or "I am greedy" or "I have this addiction" in order to open ourselves to healing. Naming or acknowledging our sinful patterns is the first step to healing.

In my own life, I began to be freed from my demons after years of retreats, spiritual direction, psychotherapy, conversations with friends, hard work, and grace. Of course I'm not fully free; my gradual healing has not been as dramatic, nor as complete, as the healing of the Gerasene demoniac. But Jesus the Liberator always calls us to new life—to come out of our tombs.

Such healing is often performed with great calm. Often I see Jesus's calm response to the loud, even violent behavior of the man reflected in the eyes of the best spiritual directors. When I have spat out my worst demons in their presence, they have reacted with that same imperturbable calm. The calm itself is a kind of healing.

Still, it's hard to seek out healing. The turmoil that we see in the man, the divided heart that we witness, parallels our being torn between not wanting to spend another moment with our demons and fearing the means by which we might be healed. What would I have to do to be healed? Will it be painful? Yet if we take a chance, emerge from our tombs, prostrate ourselves before God—not in a subservient way, but in a way that acknowledges God to be our "higher power"—and ask for healing, God can free us.

God's healing power is also frightening. Sometimes we act like the swineherds of the region. Rather than desiring to be with the one who heals, we ask him to leave. Now, on a literal level, the swineherds may simply have been infuriated by the death of their pigs; Jesus had just made it more difficult for them to earn a living. But on an allegorical level, the swineherds represent all those who fear change, even for the good. They stand for all those who fear leaving the tombs.

As I was writing this chapter, it dawned on me that during our time in Kursi, I hadn't asked George what was so meaningful to him about the Gerasene demoniac; I didn't want to intrude on his meditations. So I wrote him to ask.

George said the passage was one of the two key experiences of prayer that he had during his Long Retreat, also known as the Spiritual Exercises of St. Ignatius Loyola, a four-week retreat that invites a person into the life of Jesus through imaginative prayer. Jesuits make the Spiritual Exercises at least twice—once as a young novice and later at the end of their training. My friend's experience with this story during his novitiate would continue to "shape and define" his life as a Jesuit over the next twenty-five years. During that retreat, George wrote in his journal:

> Jesus invited me to look into the tombs all around me, the cemetery of bad memories that I chose to dwell in most times. And what was there? Nothing, just dust and dry bones—the fears and pains I am most afraid of are dead things. They cannot hurt me anymore. They are dead and I am alive.

George did not know that he would soon enter a two-year period of depression that he described as the most painful time of his life. It began when he stopped using alcohol to numb his feelings. Over time and with some help from his brother Jesuits, caring counselors, and "friends in recovery," he was finally able to "get up out of the tomb" he was living in and "begin to live again." The "gift of depression," as he called it, has helped him to connect with the men and women he has ministered to as a prison chaplain. I'll let him end this chapter in his own words:

> Their prison cells are like that dark tomb, and I know from my own experience how terrifying and lonely that tomb feels. But I also know that Jesus called me from the darkness just as powerfully as he called the tormented man in Gerasa from the tombs in which he was trapped. Prison ministry has been for me a way of witnessing to the power of God to free us from ourselves—from the shame and hurts and traumas

and resentments we have endured, to real freedom, to what Alcoholics Anonymous calls the Sunlight of the Spirit.

THE GERASENE DEMONIAC
Mark 5:1–20
(See also Matthew 8:28–34; Luke 8:26–39)

They came to the other side of the lake, to the country of the Gerasenes. And when he had stepped out of the boat, immediately a man out of the tombs with an unclean spirit met him. He lived among the tombs; and no one could restrain him any more, even with a chain; for he had often been restrained with shackles and chains, but the chains he wrenched apart, and the shackles he broke in pieces; and no one had the strength to subdue him. Night and day among the tombs and on the mountains he was always howling and bruising himself with stones. When he saw Jesus from a distance, he ran and bowed down before him; and he shouted at the top of his voice, "What have you to do with me, Jesus, Son of the Most High God? I adjure you by God, do not torment me." For he had said to him, "Come out of the man, you unclean spirit!" Then Jesus asked him, "What is your name?" He replied, "My name is Legion; for we are many." He begged him earnestly not to send them out of the country. Now there on the hillside a great herd of swine was feeding; and the unclean spirits begged him, "Send us into the swine; let us enter them." So he gave them permission. And the unclean spirits came out and entered the swine; and the herd, numbering about two thousand, rushed down the steep bank into the lake, and was drowned in the lake.

The swineherds ran off and told it in the city and in the country. Then people came to see what it was that had happened. They came to Jesus and saw the demoniac sitting there, clothed and in his right mind, the very man who had had the legion; and they were afraid. Those who had seen what had happened to the demoniac and to the swine reported it. Then they began to beg Jesus to leave their neighborhood. As he was getting into the boat, the man who had been possessed by demons begged him that he might be with him. But Jesus refused, and said to him, "Go home to your friends, and tell them how much the Lord has done for you, and what mercy he has shown you." And he went away and began to proclaim in the Decapolis how much Jesus had done for him; and everyone was amazed.

CHAPTER 15

Tabgha

"And all ate and were filled."

ON OUR VERY FIRST day in Galilee, after the four-hour, lost-in-the-desert drive from Jerusalem, and as soon as we checked into the Franciscan hostel, we rushed out to see where Jesus had been.

George and I piled back into the car, took out the map, and set our sights for the nearest holy site, easily accessible by the highway that encircles the Sea of Galilee. In five minutes we reached Tabgha, one of the most important sites in Galilee, the traditional location for the Multiplication of the Loaves and Fishes. Its name is a variant of the Greek *Heptapegon,* meaning "Place of the Seven Springs." Nearby, seven freshwater springs flow into the sea, marking where Jesus is said to have called the first disciples.

Before leaving the States, several friends suggested staying at a well-situated hostel at Tabgha run by the Benedictines as part of their monastery there. "It's right on the sea. And you know about the famous Benedictine hospitality," said a Jesuit friend. "But it's *really* hot." His description was validated upon my emerging from the car. Our own hostel was on a breezy mount, but Tabgha was at ultrasultry sea level. It was absurdly hot and ridiculously humid. I wondered if Tabgha was actually Greek for "furnace."

At the center of the monastery complex in Tabgha sits a simple stone chapel, a reconstruction of a fifth-century edifice. The Church of the Multiplication of Loaves and Fishes, built over the Byzantine-era church, was completed in 1982. Its airy interior, with a high-timbered ceiling and creamy stone floor, is furnished with plain wooden pews. A small portion of the church—a few stones in the atrium, a frieze in the apse—date from the original structure. A gorgeous mosaic on the floor featuring a playful design of birds, plants, and flowers is one of the artistic gems of the region.

Of greater spiritual significance is another artwork, also preserved from the original structure. On the floor before the altar, a brown-and-white mosaic depicts two fish flanking a wicker basket filled with a few loaves, in reference to what happened here. The image is a popular symbol of Galilee; reproductions of the design on cups and plates and mugs and T-shirts proliferate all over the region.

The stone church was empty when we arrived. A heavy red curtain cordoned off the interior from the steamy air outside, making the room cool. I was happy to have time to pray.

It was my first time praying in Galilee, and I was overwhelmed simply to be there. I was moved to tears upon realizing I was where not just any miracle occurred—I had been to Lourdes and many other shrines associated with miracles of the saints—but never before a miracle of *Jesus*. In my journal that night I wrote, "It put all the other miracles in their place . . . so foundational and life changing."

THE MULTIPLICATION OF THE Loaves and Fishes is actually an umbrella title for two miracles: the Feeding of the Five Thousand and the later Feeding of the Four Thousand. And that first story is the only miracle (apart from the Resurrection) recorded in all *four* of the Gospels. It appears not just in the Synoptics, but the Gospel of John as well.

Even though all four Gospel writers found this event worthy of extended description, the miracle of how Jesus fed an enormous crowd with a few loaves of bread and some fish is sometimes watered down.

Over the years I have heard homilies explaining away the story as follows: When the crowds gathered on the hillside, the disciples told Jesus that there wasn't enough food to go around. So Jesus asked them to distribute what they had (depending on the Gospel, either five loaves and two fish or seven loaves and some small fish). Jesus blessed the small amount of food and gave it to his disciples, who distributed it to the crowds. Touched by the disciples' generosity or moved by Jesus's sharing what little he had, the crowd brought out the food they had been secretly carrying all along and shared it with one another. At the end of the meal, because so many had shared with one another, there were twelve baskets left over. So, in fact, it was a miracle of sharing. As some preachers will say, "And isn't that just as miraculous as if Jesus had multiplied the loaves and fishes?"

To which I answer, No.

This easy-to-digest interpretation reflects the unfortunate modern desire to explain away the inexplicable. Donahue and Harrington refer to that particular explanation, which began circulating in the nineteenth century, as the "nice thought" interpretation, which has found its way into mainstream Christian spirituality and preaching.[1] The two judicious scholars then issue a caution rarely found in a Bible commentary: this is one way *not* to interpret the passage. The "nice thought" interpretation reflects a tendency to downplay miracles in the midst of a story that is filled with the miraculous. Indeed, almost one-third of Mark's Gospel is devoted to Jesus's miracles.

Other examples of this rationalizing tendency that I sometimes hear are as follows: The Resurrection wasn't about a truly resurrected Jesus; rather, the disciples gathered together after the events of Good Friday and had a powerful "shared memory" of Jesus and thus experienced him as present in a new way. (How a shared memory could account for the disciples moving from abject terror to a readiness to give their lives for Jesus goes unexplained.) Likewise, Lazarus wasn't dead when Jesus raised him (though the Gospels make it clear he had been in the tomb four days); he was just sick. And, according to these interpretations, the people Jesus healed were suffering from purely psychosomatic illnesses. Thus Jesus's compassionate presence cured them of whatever psychological problems led to their illness. (This may be true for a few cases, since the evangelists' descriptions of the precise illnesses are at times vague, but I cannot believe, for example, that a withered hand or leprosy was psychosomatic.)

Another popular idea is that miracles are simply part and parcel of stories about powerful figures in antiquity, and so those miracles are to be expected in any retelling of the lives of people in that era. But though people in ancient times believed in the possibility of miracles, Lohfink points out that stories about major personalities who performed miraculous healings were "extremely rare in antiquity and well-attested 'miracles' were even more uncommon." Surveying the Gospels he concludes, "Jesus is depicted as definitely a miracle worker, and a great many miracles are attributed to him, something that is unique in antiquity."[2]

To my mind, many of the interpretations that seek to water down the miracle stories reflect an unease with God's power and Jesus's divinity, discomfort with the miraculous, and, more basically, an inability to believe in God's ability to do anything.

The idea that sharing food would have so flabbergasted Jesus's followers that all four evangelists would make room for it in their Gospels, with two going so far as to record two variations (feeding four thousand and feeding five thousand) is hard to fathom. Only one other miracle narrative appears in all four Gospels: the Resurrection. That provides a gauge for how dramatic, memorable, and important the Tabgha event was for the disciples and the early church. Certainly sharing was a significant part of the life of Jesus and his followers, and it was a characteristic virtue of the early church.[3] But the theory that the food was not the result of a miracle but of sharing fails to explain the prominence of the story in the Gospels. Nor does that interpretation jibe with the disciples' complaints to Jesus about the lack of food.[4] If people had brought food and were hungry, they would presumably have taken it out—and eaten it.

As Lohfink writes, these types of explanations, which seek to make things credible for modern audiences, reflect a desire to explain away all that we cannot understand. The principle can be summarized as follows: "What does not happen now did not happen then either. If no one today can walk on a lake, Jesus did not walk on water."[5] Harrington suggests that such an attitude also assumes that historical events can and should be interpreted only through the realm of earthly cause and effect, with no supernatural explanation, and that there are no unique historical figures.[6] When we take this approach, we are in danger of reducing Jesus to the status of everyone else, when in fact he was, as Lohfink says, "irritatingly *unique*." It is the discomfort with Jesus's divinity that I mentioned in the introduction.

So let's look at this miracle, symbolized by that simple fourth-century mosaic of two fish and a basket of bread, which waits on the floor of that Benedictine church in Tabgha, as if still prepared for its encounter with the irritatingly unique Son of God.

SCHOLARS DIFFER OVER WHY two versions of this story—the Feeding of the Five Thousand and the Feeding of the Four Thousand—appear in the Gospels.[7] One explanation is that there were two distinct events (which differed in a few details, such as the amount of food available as well as the number of the people who were fed). Thus, Mark and Matthew, who include both accounts, were simply recounting two stories about two separate feedings, the first in a predominantly Jewish area, the second in Gentile territory. Most scholars, however, believe that there were two *versions* circulating of one story, and that Mark and Matthew included both in their narratives, not wanting to discount either tradition. (Repetition was not as much of a literary sin as it is today.) One argument for that view is that the second time the miracle occurs in Mark and Matthew, the disciples seem to have forgotten about the first time![8]

For the sake of clarity, then, let's look at the first story (the Feeding of the Five Thousand) as it appears in the Gospel of Mark, the earliest form available to us. But we'll also examine the other versions to see what they might tell us about Jesus.

In the sixth chapter of Mark's Gospel, the twelve apostles have just returned from the assignment that Jesus had given them, during which they had "cast out many demons" and exercised the ministry of teaching.[9] They report their successes to Jesus, and it's easy to imagine them energized and even a little giddy. In response, Jesus says to them, "Come away to a deserted place all by yourselves and rest a while."[10] Jesus isn't one to drive on punishingly until collapse; both he and his followers frequently retreat from the crowds. Also, Mark explains that the presence of hordes of people meant that the apostles had no chance to eat after having returned. So they were hungry.

In Matthew and Mark, Jesus's "withdrawal" is linked to another event, the execution of John the Baptist by King Herod. After the ruler beheads the prophet, Matthew reports that John's disciples took the body and buried it, and then "they went and told Jesus." So Jesus may have had two practical reasons for withdrawing: rest for his disciples and a desire to avoid the murderous wrath of Herod. After his public baptism by John, he would have been clearly associated with the prophet. But Jesus judged that his hour had not yet come. And we can imagine a more personal reason: Jesus was grieved by the death of his friend and possible mentor. All these reasons moved Jesus to spend time alone.

Jesus and the disciples board a boat and sail to the deserted place, which Luke locates as Bethsaida, on the northern shore of the Sea of Galilee. But the crowds, seeing them depart, "hurried there on foot from all the towns and arrived ahead of them." That little sentence offers yet another sign of Jesus's magnetism. Saying that he was "popular" doesn't convey the people's almost physical desire to be in his presence. They want healing and preaching, but they also want *him*.

When Jesus and the disciples come ashore, he catches sight of all those who have run ahead to be close to him. As Mark tells us, he had "compassion for them, because they were like sheep without a shepherd." Mark's readers would have seen in this an echo of the Good Shepherd in the Book of Ezekiel, who both tends his flock and teaches them.[11] Such parallels with the Old Testament would have enabled readers to understand, in the lovely phrase of Raymond Brown, "God's total plan."[12]

One can imagine Jesus seeing a crowd hungry for answers and healing, and wanting them to know all the good that God has in store for them. Have you ever known someone who was lost, hopeless, or despairing, and you desperately wanted that person to find hope? This may be a window into Jesus's emotional response. The Greek is vivid—again the word *esplagchnisthē*—Jesus felt this in his guts. Out of compassion he begins to teach them "many things." Luke adds that Jesus also "healed those who needed to be cured."

He must have spoken for some time, because Mark next tells us that "when it grew late" the disciples offer Jesus some unsolicited advice. Here we are in a desolate place, they say, it's late, and the crowd has nothing to eat. Send the people away, say the disciples, so that they can go somewhere and buy something to eat. The Greek is almost an order: "Send them away!" On the one hand, it is a sensible, reasonable request. There were too many people to feed, and perhaps the crowd was grumbling about the lack of food. Maybe the disciples feared a riot. On the other hand, it is the opposite of Jesus's reaction. When he sees a group of people in need, he wants to spend time with them. The disciples want to send them away.

Jesus's response may be a rebuke to their uncaring attitude: "You give them something to eat," he says. The Greek is an imperative: *Dote autois hymeis phagein!* "You yourselves give them something to eat!" The disciples counter that this is impossible. It would take two hundred denarii—a denarius was a day's wages—to feed such an immense crowd. Jesus asks them to find out how many loaves of bread and fishes they have. After checking, they report back: "Five, and two fish." These are probably preserved or dried fish. It is this meager supply that is depicted in the ancient mosaic in the church in Tabgha.

Then Jesus invites everyone to recline, as if for a banquet. The English doesn't capture the Greek phrase *symposia symposia,* indicating a formal dinner party (and perhaps reminding readers of the *symposia* of the Greek philosophers, an occasion for teaching). The repetition of the word means something like "group by group." Mark notes that they sat down in groups of fifties and hundreds, which underscores the vastness of the crowd. The disciples must have been—as they often are—flummoxed. Where is Jesus going with this?

Two charming comments color the scene. Jesus asks everyone to recline on the *chlōrō chortō,* the "green grass." It is probably close to Passover, and the grass is lush after the winter rains. The Gospel paints a verdant picture of sheep without a shepherd, ready to be fed in fertile fields. Mark also says that Jesus has them sit *prasiai prasiai,* again a repetition, here of a marvelous word meaning "flower beds."[13] They are arranged together like flower beds, in an orderly manner; some scholars suggest that the image of flower beds derives from the varied colored robes in the crowd. The description underscores the gentle, pastoral setting, as in a painting by Constable or Poussin.

What Jesus does next is something we frequently discussed in our graduate classes in liturgy. "Taking the five loaves and the two fish, he looked up to heaven, and blessed and broke the loaves, and gave them to his disciples to set before the people; and he divided the two fish among them all." These actions—take, look to heaven, bless, break, and give—most of which will reappear in the Last Supper, will later be incorporated into early eucharistic celebrations, and later still, the Mass. The blessing would have been the traditional Jewish blessing, praising God; the breaking of the loaves was reserved for the head of a Jewish family.[14]

Here we find another possible reason why all four Gospels include the story—other than its miraculous character. Even as early as Mark (around AD 70) readers would have drawn parallels to the church's eucharistic meals. One commentator notes that the eucharistic celebrations would have made the story of the loaves and fishes "common property in all the Christian communities."[15] In other words, each of the evangelists wanted to include the event in his retelling, because for each of the audiences the story carried special meaning as an antecedent to the communal worship they knew so well. As Meier notes, "In any of the Synoptic Gospels, the only occasion outside the feeding miracles when Jesus acts as the host of the meal, takes bread, gives thanks or pronounces a blessing, breaks the bread, and gives it to his followers is the Last Supper."[16]

Mark offers an understated description of the miracle itself. In a terse sentence and with no description of the astonishment the disciples normally feel, he writes: "They ate and were filled." Literally, everyone was satisfied, with the Greek suggesting a superabundance of food that enabled everyone to eat as much as they might have wanted. To hammer home the point, Mark tells us that twelve baskets of food were left, and that those who had eaten "numbered five thousand men." Matthew adds, more inclusively, "besides women and children."[17] Overall, though, the Synoptics mainly agree on the retelling of this dramatic miracle.

John's version is slightly different, highlighting the crowd's astonishment and offering more detail. Briefly put, John tells us that it happened near the time of Passover, names the disciples present, and even describes what kind of bread was used.[18] Jesus asks Philip how all the people are going to be fed. "He said this to test him," says John, "for he himself knew what he was going to do." Another detail: Andrew, Peter's brother, says to Jesus, "There is a boy here who has five barley loaves and two fish. But what are they among so many people?"

Such touching details help us picture the disciples stumbling upon an unsuspecting boy carrying a basket of food, perhaps for his family. Or, as I imagined it on a retreat, Andrew spots the boy and pulls him out of the crowd. The boy tries valiantly to keep hold of the basket, so as not to spill the precious contents as he is guided toward Jesus. Andrew was a practiced fisherman, and I imagine him steering through the crowd as easily as he navigated the Sea of Galilee. Finally brought into Jesus's presence, the boy looks into the carpenter's eyes, and wonders.

John too paints a bucolic picture, with "a great deal of grass in the place." In John the connection to the Eucharist is even clearer because Jesus *eucharistēsas,* he "gives thanks." As in the Synoptics, all five thousand eat and have their fill.

The main difference, though, is the response to the miracle. As in the Synoptics, a "large crowd" has followed Jesus, but in John because of healing he has done. John often stresses Jesus's performing "signs" (*sēmeia*) that point not only to his own divinity, but reveal other meanings: here, for example, a foretaste of the heavenly banquet to which all are invited and which Jesus used in his preaching as a symbol of the reign of God.[19] Especially in John the miracles have an educative purpose. In the Synoptic Gospels Jesus's mighty works tend to depend on the faith of the people; in John's Gospel, Jesus's signs prompt faith.

And so, "When the people saw the sign that he had done, they began to say, 'This is indeed the prophet who is to come into the world!'" The Messianic Secret, that is, Jesus's asking his disciples not to disclose his identity, is not secret here at all. They get it.

Mostly. For after his great sign Jesus intuits that the crowd is eager to "make him king." The crowd understands that they have seen something extraordinary, but they don't understand that the miracle is a sign of Jesus's love, not an invitation to shower him with honors or set up a political system with him as its head.

So Jesus withdraws from them to the mountain. The Greek is haunting: *eis to oros autos monos.* To the mountain himself alone.

EVEN NEWCOMERS TO THE New Testament will easily appreciate the rich theology of this passage. Old Testament parallels abound, which the Jewish people in Jesus's time surely appreciated more readily than do current-day audiences. Just as the Israelites, for example, were fed "in the wilderness" with water from the rock and with manna, Jesus feeds his followers in "a deserted place."[20] The feeding also parallels the nourishment that Jesus gives to his disciples in the form of his teaching. It prefigures the distribution of the bread and wine at the Last Supper. The bread symbolizes Jesus himself: nourishing, satisfying, available to all. "I am the bread of life," as Jesus says in the Gospel of John, "Whoever comes to me will never be hungry."[21] In his series *Jesus of Nazareth,* Pope Benedict XVI offers an extended meditation on the "bread motif" in the Gospels, linking Moses and manna to Jesus and the loaves and fishes and paralleling the giving of the Torah with Jesus's total gift of himself.[22]

Food betokens a host of other spiritual meanings. It is satisfying, as is God's love. The sharing of food is a communal event, underlining the community aspect of faith. "Table fellowship" was an important aspect of Jesus's ministry. Some of our happiest hours and most intimate moments are spent at the table with family and friends. Moreover, for many Jews, one major image of the world to come is of a magnificent banquet, where a meal is shared with the patriarchs.[23] Food is also about giving, sacrificing, and sharing; someone must labor to grow it and expend time and effort to prepare it. Food requires work and sacrifice. Someone also needs to do the feeding, in this case Christ. Overall, it is a gift.

Bread and fish, like the bread and wine at the Last Supper, are also simple elements. In his parables Jesus takes everyday images to teach verbally. At the Multiplication of the Loaves and Fishes he takes everyday foodstuffs to teach physically. Once again, God comes to us in ways that we can understand. Jesus uses physical objects—bread, fish, wine, water—in ways that do not go against nature, but rather perfect nature, taking what is already here and creating something new. He uses food to show us how the world should be: everyone filled and satisfied.

Despite Jesus's desire to help his friends understand the reign of God, it must have been close to impossible for the disciples to make sense of things—even if they recalled the Old Testament passages and grasped the link between being fed and being taught. Witnessing the seemingly bottomless baskets of bread and fish would have been astounding. Seeing how he had fed so many with so little would have been confusing. The miracles reveal the identity of Jesus, they teach us something, but they cannot be fully "understood." In the Synoptics, the miracles are often referred to as *dynameis,* "acts of power" that so astonish onlookers that they frequently exclaim, "We have never seen anything like this."

In the Gospel of John they are signs that point to something greater, beyond the crowd's—or our—comprehension. These symbolic actions inaugurate new meaning, something never before experienced. Lohfink phrases it elegantly when he says that the signs "create space for the reign of God and allow it to come."[24]

GOD TAKES SMALL THINGS and makes them great. That was clear at Tabgha. It's also evident in our daily lives and in our prayer. This was illustrated for me just a few years ago in, of all places, a hotel conference room.

A group of Catholic school principals and teachers had invited me to direct a day-long retreat for their group, just outside of Boston. In the afternoon I led them through a "guided meditation" using some techniques of Ignatian contemplation, which encourage us to imagine ourselves in a Scripture scene.

For our meditation I used John's account of the Multiplication of the Loaves and Fishes, since it was the Gospel reading for the coming Sunday. First I read the passage aloud, so that people were familiar with it, and then I asked a few questions based on the five senses as a way of sparking people's imaginations. *Sight:* What does the crowd look like? What does Jesus look like? *Hearing:* Is the crowd grumbling about hunger? Can you hear the waves breaking on the shore? *Feeling:* How does it feel to sit on the green grass? Are you hungry? *Taste:* What does the bread taste like? The fish? *And smell:* Can you smell the fresh air coming off the sea?

Simple questions like these can help a person picture the scene. Then I read the passage again and invited them to envision themselves on the shore of the sea as participants, as part of the crowd. Ignatian contemplation doesn't require you to do anything bizarre, merely that you imagine and trust that God can work through that imagining.

After thirty minutes of silence I asked the group to open their eyes and invited them to share what they experienced in their prayer. Many were drawn to parts of the story they had never noticed before. One young teacher noticed that the miracle was a communal event, taking place in the midst of the group, and she linked that to the communal aspect of faith, which she could sometimes overlook. Experiences of God come not just in quiet moments of solitary prayer, but together with others.

The crowd in Tabgha may be the largest group with whom Jesus spends time, which underlines the communal aspect of his ministry and serves as a reminder that religion is not simply a solitary affair. A solipsistic God-and-me approach can lead to a skewed spirituality, closed off from the nourishment that a group can provide.

One woman's comments remained with me. "I never knew that there was a little boy there!" Frankly, until I had read the passage aloud that day, neither had I. But there it is in John: "There is a boy here who has five barley loaves and two fish."

"I've been a Catholic my whole life, and I must have heard that passage dozens of times during Mass," she said. "But I never noticed him." Her attention was drawn to the boy with the loaves and fishes, and she saw for the first time that a child provided the basis for Jesus's miracle. So we discussed what she thought God might be asking her to notice. Perhaps it was an invitation to notice, in a new way, the children with whom she worked. Or to see how God can make something great from something small. Or to pay attention to blessings she had overlooked in her life, as she had previously overlooked the boy.

Who knows where this boy came from or why he brought Jesus his food. It seems improbable that he would have brought all that food for himself to eat. Perhaps his mother and father, standing in the crowd, overheard Philip complaining about the lack of food and said to the boy, "Give our food to the Master, son." Perhaps the parents were members of Jesus's larger group of followers. (Scholars posit a series of expanding groups: the Twelve, the disciples, and then the followers.) Perhaps among these were a couple and their son.

It was probably easy to overlook the young boy in the middle of the throng on the shores of the Sea of Galilee. The disciples apparently didn't bother to ask his name; or, if they asked, they didn't bother to pass it along to the evangelists; and if they did pass it along, the evangelists didn't bother to record it. After the boy steps on the world stage and offers his bread and fish to Jesus, he recedes into obscurity, leaving behind only a miracle.

One of the more common experiences of those who work in spiritual ministries is hearing a grateful person tell you how something you barely remember doing changed his or her life. How something you believed to be small became something big for someone else. Sometimes in a homily I make a brief aside about, say, suffering, and afterward a parishioner will say through tears, "That was so helpful, Father. It's just what I needed to hear today." It may have been the right time for that person to hear—a *kairos* moment—so she is naturally more open to the message. But those experiences are also examples of God's multiplying what few loaves and fishes we can offer, whether on the grass at Tabgha or inside a church in New York City.

We are invited to trust that the few loaves and fishes we bring will provide nourishment, even if we cannot see the results. After working for two years in Kenya with refugees, helping them start small businesses with modest financial grants, I could see many successes in the refugees' lives: flourishing businesses, families lifted out of poverty, men and women given new hope. Many times, though, the refugees would gradually lose touch with our office, and I had to trust that whatever help we had furnished—spiritual or financial— was somehow bearing fruit.

We also may feel that our efforts are inadequate. We try to help our friends and family, but nothing seems to work. We try to fix our children's lives, but it doesn't seem to help. We try to seek forgiveness, but others are still resentful. We try to encourage our friends, but they still seem disconsolate. We try to love, but it doesn't seem enough.

But Jesus accepts what we give, blesses it, breaks it open, and magnifies it. Often in ways that we don't see or cannot see. Or will not be able to see in this lifetime. Who knows what a kind word does? Who knows what a single act of charity will do? Sometimes the smallest word or gesture can change a life. A few years ago I told a Jesuit priest how what he had said to me on retreat helped me through a tough time. When I repeated what he had told me—word for word—he laughed and said he didn't even remember saying it. Yet his loaves and fishes had been multiplied.

Other times we are privileged to witness this abundance. Richard Rohr, the Franciscan priest and spiritual writer, recently told me a story. He had received a letter from a man he had met only once, decades before, and who wanted to visit him at his home in New Mexico. "What you said changed my life," he wrote, "and I'd like to say thank you." Richard wondered what he had said all those years ago. The man drove a great distance, and when he arrived, Richard escorted this now-middle-aged man into the parlor.

"When I was in my twenties," the man explained, "I was in a crisis and didn't know what I wanted to do in life, and do you remember what you said to me?"

Richard did not.

"You said, 'You do not need to know.' Every time I get confused, I remind myself of that." He told Richard how that phrase had become his life's mantra in all business situations and relationships and in marriage. It had made him a happy man, he said.

Richard laughed when he told me that story. "And I don't even remember saying that!"

God can take any small offering that we make—a kind word, a brief visit to a hospital, a quick apology, a short thank-you note or e-mail, a smile—and multiply it.

GOD DOES THE SAME in our spiritual lives as well, providing enormous nourishment from what seems like a fleeting event, a passing comment from a friend, a brief sentence in a book, or a few words in Scripture.

Often I've read a word or phrase in the Bible that offers consolation entirely out of proportion to what might be expected. During one retreat, I read the story of the Rich Young Man, in the Gospel of Mark, and something caught my eye.[25] In the story Jesus meets a wealthy man who asks Jesus what he must do to inherit eternal life. Jesus reminds the man of his obligation to follow the Law and then lists the Commandments. The man, portrayed by Mark as a good person, tells Jesus that he has kept these commandments "since my youth."

I had heard this story dozens of times. In fact it was one of the Gospel passages that prompted me to enter a religious order. But when I read the next line, it was as if I had never seen it before. Jesus, I knew, was about to tell the man to give up all his possessions in order to be able to follow Jesus.

It is a difficult story for many Christians, because it is often interpreted as meaning that they must divest themselves of all they own—at least the *best* disciples must. But even in Jesus's time, not all of his followers were called to do this. Martha and Mary, after all, entertain Jesus in their house. As I see it, Jesus is asking the man to let go of whatever prevents him from hearing God's voice. It is an invitation to simplicity, but an even greater one to freedom.

So I knew this story and was ready for Jesus to utter his famous next line: "You lack one thing; go sell what you own and give the money to the poor, and you will have treasure in heaven; then come, follow me."

But before Jesus opens his mouth, Mark writes, "Jesus, looking at him, loved him, and said . . ."

Jesus "loved him"? Where did that come from? I had heard this Gospel story dozens of times. How had I missed that line? I scoured the retreat house library for a Greek New Testament, opened up to the Gospel of Mark, located the passage and was shocked to read: *Iēsous emblepsas autō ēgapēsen auton:* "Jesus, looking at him, loved him."

Those three words—Jesus loved him—led to several hours of meditation. They altered the familiar story and thus altered how I saw Jesus. No longer was it the exacting Jesus demanding perfection; it was the loving Jesus offering freedom. Now I could hear him utter those words with infinite compassion for the man. Those three words changed the way I saw Jesus and his commands. I didn't even think of them as commands any longer, but rather as loving invitations. For Jesus always acts out of love. I couldn't believe how something so small—three little words—had provided such abundance in prayer.

Later in the story of the Rich Young Man, Jesus explicitly offers a promise of abundance: for everyone who leaves behind something, as the rich young man was called to do, he or she will receive "a hundredfold." More abundance.

This may be one reason so many of Jesus's parables are about things growing. The tiny mustard seed, so minuscule that it is hard to see with the naked eye, grows into a bush so large—sometimes as high as six feet on the shores of the Sea of Galilee—that birds can build their nests in it. A sower scatters seed, and when some of it falls onto fertile ground its crop yield is a hundredfold.[26] And the real work of multiplication is done quietly and mysteriously by God. How amazing it must have been for the farmers at the time, without our understanding of biology, to see the seed germinate, push forth its green shoots from the earth, grow leaves, and finally produce its yield, all under God's providential care.

Lohfink also suggests that the small seed, almost hidden from view, shows "not only the unstoppable growth of the reign of God but also the shockingly minute and hidden character of its beginning." The seed grows even as we cannot see God's work upon it. And the only response to this marvelous phenomenon is trust.[27] Overall, the reign of God *grows*.

ALL WE NEED TO do is bring what little we have, generously and unashamedly. At Tabgha, the disciples seemed embarrassed that there was not enough for the crowd and were about to send everyone away hungry. But Jesus knew that whatever there is, God can make more of it. But first we are asked to offer our loaves and fishes, no matter how inadequate they may seem. Only then can God accomplish the kind of true miracle that occurred at Tabgha.

THE MULTIPLICATION OF THE LOAVES AND FISHES
Mark 6:35–44
(See also Matthew 14:13–21; Luke 9:12–17; John 6:1–15)

When it grew late, his disciples came to him and said, "This is a deserted place, and the hour is now very late; send them away so that they may go into the surrounding country and villages and buy something for themselves to eat." But he answered them, "You give them something to eat." They said to him, "Are we to go and buy two hundred denarii worth of bread, and give it to them to eat?" And he said to them, "How many loaves have you? Go and see." When they had found out, they said, "Five, and two fish." Then he ordered them to get all the people to sit down in groups on the green grass. So they sat down in groups of hundreds and of fifties. Taking the five loaves and the two fish, he looked up to heaven, and blessed and broke the loaves, and gave them to his disciples to set before the people; and he divided the two fish among them all. And all ate and were filled; and they took up twelve baskets full of broken pieces and of the fish. Those who had eaten the loaves numbered five thousand men.

CHAPTER 16

Bethesda

*"There is a pool, called in Hebrew Beth-zatha,
which has five porticoes."*

RELIGIOUS LEGENDS SOMETIMES HAVE a strange way of turning out to be true. The best-known example may be the discovery of what is now almost universally accepted as the tomb of St. Peter. It was reputed to lie directly underneath the great dome of St. Peter's Basilica in Rome, though many scholars had judged this location doubtful and most likely inauthentic.

It was believed that the Galilean fisherman ended his earthly life in the great city in AD 64 after being martyred by the Roman authorities. St. Peter is said to have asked to be crucified upside down, considering himself unworthy of ending his life as Jesus had. The basilica in his honor was also known to have been built atop a site—the Vatican Hill—occupied by a church since the time of Constantine in the fourth century. But whether the actual remains of Peter lay there was an open question.

In the 1930s and 1940s, however, a series of archaeological finds under St. Peter's Basilica led to the discovery of the tomb of a man in his late sixties, near graffiti that included the word *Petrus*. Over time, the Vatican examined sufficient evidence to conclude that the bones of St. Peter had been located. The collection of the man's bones was largely intact, except for the feet, which were missing—not surprising given that the easiest way to remove a body crucified upside down would have been to chop off the feet first.[1]

Locations reputed to be only "legendary" or based on "popular piety" often turn out to have a basis in fact.

Why is this? Well, it's human nature to remember important places and to pass these memories along to descendants. This is particularly the case in the Holy Land. In Jesus's day, people didn't move around much; a family may have stayed in the same town for generations. Thus, if Christians in those early centuries visited Nazareth or Bethlehem and asked about important sites in Jesus's life, it's not unreasonable to think that his extended family (or their children or grandchildren) would not only have been in the area, but would also have remembered, say, the location of his carpentry shop. To take another example, Peter's descendants would have surely known the location of his house in Capernaum. These locations would have been treasured by pilgrims and knowledge of them passed down to later generations. That doesn't mean that every site in the Holy Land is the precise spot at which a Gospel story occurred, but often these locations may be more accurate than we imagine.

The Pool of Bethesda is one such place. According to the fifth chapter of the Gospel of John, while visiting Jerusalem, Jesus heals a paralyzed man beside a pool "which has five porticoes." It is one of my favorite stories in the Gospels, primarily because of the reversal of the man's extreme situation: he has been paralyzed for thirty-eight years. Moreover, as the man tells Jesus in a heartbreaking line, he has "no one" to help him. But Jesus, friend to the friendless, heals him.

Until the nineteenth century, however, many scholars believed that the pool did not exist. Either it was, as some believed, an "allegorical" pool, or the entire story was fabricated and added to the Gospel later. Some believed that the idea of the "five porticoes" was an allegorical representation of the five books of Moses or was simply a "construct of the imagination."[2]

But at the turn of the twentieth century, excavations in Jerusalem revealed not simply a pool but, as the archaeologists gradually cut into the rock, the foundations for colonnaded walkways or porticoes—exactly as John had described it. In another confirmation of the ancient tradition, Bethesda was said to be the birthplace of Mary. And what did the excavators see just a few yards away from the newly unearthed Pool of Bethesda? The Crusader-era Church of St. Anne, dedicated to Mary's mother.

GEORGE AND I STUMBLED upon the Pool of Bethesda by accident. Rushing headlong through Jerusalem on our second day, anxious to see all that we could, we were headed to the Garden of Gethsemane, threading our way through the Old City. In my haste, I spotted a sign pointing to an archway that said, "Church of St. Anne." That sounded dull—certainly nothing related directly to Jesus's public ministry. But on our little map I saw a minuscule notation, "Pool of Bethesda."

I stopped so fast I almost tripped over my feet. "The Pool of Bethesda!" I said to George. Earlier that month I had read the story of the rediscovery of this place and knew I wanted to see this, a physical confirmation of a Gospel story.

George trailed me as we walked under a limestone archway and stopped at a ticket booth. The quiet courtyard was paved with broad white stones and dotted with tall pine trees. A handful of pilgrims ambled around. I breezed past the Church of St. Anne, a simple but imposing structure in Jerusalem stone, with clean lines and little ornamentation, and made a beeline for the Pool of Bethesda.

The excavations revealed the general outlines of the pools, the bases of the colonnades and, yes, the porticoes mentioned in John's Gospel. The complex was surprisingly large; many people in antiquity would have come to bathe and seek healing here. The pool may have had its origins first as an ancient reservoir and later as part of a Roman *asklepion,* a temple dedicated to Asklepios, the god of healing. Today you can peer down over a metal railing into the complicated series of pools and cisterns.

At first, it was difficult to get a sense of what was where—is that the pool over there or some sort of patio? But it didn't matter. Jesus had been here. That's all that mattered to me.

Unlike the other spots we had seen in Jerusalem the Pool of Bethesda was untouched by accretions. There was no church, basilica, shrine, or gift shop nearby. Certainly there was the imposing Church of St. Anne next door, but the pool itself was almost naked, with few indications that this was a holy site. As George snapped some photos, I descended into the ruins. Several metal staircases took you lower and lower into the excavations. Afterward, seated on a bench, surrounded by aromatic trees and bushes, I prayed for all those who needed healing.

One person I prayed for was my six-year-old nephew. My sister had been worried about his rather obsessive tendencies to frequent hand washing, sometimes several times in one hour, despite her reassuring him, "Matthew, your hands are clean." She hoped it wasn't reflective of any psychological problems. My cousin was also undergoing breast cancer surgery that week, and I was glad to pray for her as well at this holy place.

Closing my eyes, I imagined Jesus healing both of them right here. Afterward, I texted my sister and my cousin, to let them know of my prayers, and attached a photo of the Pool of Bethesda. My cousin's surgery was successful, as was her later treatment, which lasted several months.

Matthew's healing was *euthus*. After I returned from the Holy Land, my sister told me, with astonishment, that a few *hours* after I texted her, Matthew said, "You know, Mommy, you're right. I don't need to wash my hands all the time. They're already clean."

Over the next few days I returned to this spot every time I could. I loved being where I knew with near certainty Jesus had been, a place that was a graceful response to those who thought that all the Gospel stories were just stories.

The second time I dropped by a surprise awaited me: a White Father I had known in Kenya. A little background: The Missionaries of Africa are a Catholic religious order that has been active in East Africa since the nineteenth century. The order has cared for the Church of St. Anne since 1878. Members of the order are popularly known as the White Fathers, not because of the color of their skin, but of their habits. As one African-born member of the community told me in Nairobi, "You can be a black brother and still be a White Father!" Père Michel had heard that I had dropped by earlier (I had asked if any of the White Fathers were around) and greeted me with a big grin.

He gave me an extensive tour of the Church of St. Anne. Murphy-O'Connor has high praise for the edifice, located in the Muslim Quarter: "Crusader Jerusalem is seen at its best in the simple strength of St. Anne's (A.D. 1138), certainly the loveliest church in the city."[3] From as early as the fifth century, a church commemorating Jesus's miracle stood by the pools, and that church survived the destruction visited on some other churches by Islamic rulers in 1009. Later, a community of Benedictine nuns erected a small chapel in the middle of the large Byzantine church; still later, that structure was replaced by the current church. Finally, it was enlarged by builders who extended the façade by seven meters. The architectural additions are evident; you can see clear differences in size and height among the supporting piers inside. Although the church survived, the famous pools were gradually covered up, first thought to be "lost" and then "legendary."

The chatty White Father led me through the cool interior of the austere church. Père Michel described how St. Anne's was intentionally designed to be "imperfect and asymmetrical" to remind us of our human imperfections. He also related the story of a group of architecture students who made a careful study of St. Anne's under the tutelage of their professor. As the professor intended, the students pored over their architectural renderings and mathematical calculations and reached the conclusion that the almost thousand-year-old lopsided structure should not be standing!

The building's acoustics are justly famous; the little pamphlet from the ticket counter celebrated its "special echo." To demonstrate, Père Michel ushered me to the front of the aisle, and said, "What shall we sing?" Without waiting for a response, he began to sing a Swahili hymn called "Simama" at the top of his lungs. I laughed—it was one of my favorite hymns, with an easy, joyful melody. *Simama* means "stand firm," in this case for God. I marveled at the universality of the church. There we were, a White Father from Canada and a Jesuit from the United States singing a Swahili hymn from Kenya in a church built by European Crusaders in Jerusalem. Our song echoed perfectly throughout the church.

Afterward Père Michel led me down into the pools of Bethesda. He pointed out two huge piers that supported the fifth-century church and the healing baths. Then we descended a rickety metal staircase into a darkened cavern. At the very bottom of the well, water was trickling into the pools as it had since the eighth century BC, when a dam was built to capture runoff rainwater. Here I felt connected to Jesus through the living water, as I had at the Sea of Galilee.[4]

IRONICALLY, WITH ALL THIS emphasis on historicity, the event at the pool is a double-edged historical sword, for it occurs during one of Jesus's visits to Jerusalem, a topic on which the Synoptic Gospels disagree with the Gospel of John. In Matthew, Mark, and Luke, Jesus makes a single journey to the holy city, a momentous trip that includes his Passion, death, and resurrection. In John's retelling, Jesus, an observant Jew, travels there at least three times for the annual Jewish festivals. (This also means that John counts Jesus's ministry as lasting for at least three years.)

The fifth chapter tells us that Jesus is in Jerusalem "for the festival of the Jews," which might be Passover or any number of festivals. He comes upon a pool near the Sheep Gate in Jerusalem. At the pool are gathered the "many invalids—blind, lame, and paralyzed." The place is called "Bethesda" or "Beth-zatha" (in Hebrew and Aramaic, either "House of Mercy" or "House of Shame," perhaps a double meaning given the presence of the sick).⁵ Later explanatory additions to the Gospel, included in most modern versions, add that the sick waited for the "stirring of the water," when it was believed that an angel caused the movement, making it the best time to seek healing. A natural explanation for the "stirring" is the flow of water from the subterranean current.

Beside the pool is a man who has been ill for thirty-eight years. Jesus somehow knows that the man has been ill for many years, and asks him, "Do you want to be made well?" It's a strange question that may make the reader wonder, "Why would he ask that? Of course a paralyzed man sitting by a healing pool wants to be healed."

The man, unaware of Jesus's identity, tells the Galilean pilgrim a poignant story. "Sir, I have no one to put me into the pool when the water is stirred up; and while I am making my way, someone else steps down ahead of me."

Whenever I read the man's words, I hear two things, both mirroring the experiences of many who are sick. First I hear the voices of those who desperately hope for healing but have met only failure: "I've seen so many doctors, and none of them seem to know what to do." "They told me about some experimental surgery, but I didn't qualify." "I tried that medicine, but it only made it worse."

Second, and more poignant, I hear a terrible loneliness. The man has "no one" in his life (*Kyrie, anthrōpon ouk echō:* "Lord, a person I have not"). He is alone. Why else would no one have helped him in thirty-eight years? It's almost unbearably sad to think of the friendless man calling out daily to complete strangers and hurried passersby for help. Or perhaps he has stopped trying—his long illness may have led him to the brink of despair. Worse, when he is able to make a tentative move toward the pool, probably by slowly and painfully dragging himself along the ground, another person steps in front of him.

This may explain why Jesus is drawn to him. The disciples or perhaps those around the pool might have pointed him out as the one who had been suffering the longest. This may be how Jesus knows of his long illness. Or perhaps Jesus instinctively knew who was the loneliest. Barclay writes, "He had no one to help him in, and Jesus was always the friend of the friendless, and the helper of the person who has no earthly help."[6]

After the man shares his plight, Jesus says to him, "Stand up, take your mat and walk." The man is instantly healed—the Greek *hygiēs* means "made healthy" or "made whole." Jesus's word alone is sufficient to do this. Now healed, the man does what he is told. He takes up his mat—his *krabattos,* the same kind of pallet or stretcher that the four friends used to lower the paralyzed man through the roof in Capernaum—and walks.

The man's response is one of unquestioning obedience after his healing. "At once (*eutheōs*) the man was made well, and he took up his mat and began to walk." He has moved from confusion over Jesus's identity to a prompt response to his word. There is no record of the response of the crowd surrounding the pool, many of whom would have known the man, who was by his own admission a frequent visitor. We can presume them to be, as so many others are described in the Gospels in the face of miracles, astonished.

But there is a dark note sounded by the Gospel. "Now that day was a sabbath."

At this point "the Jews" enter the picture. We must be extremely careful not to assume that this means "all Jews," and even more we must avoid a condemnation of the Jewish people, then or now. John's Gospel often tries to distance the story of Jesus from "the Jews," because the Christian community was beginning to pull away from its Jewish roots around the time the Gospel was being written, around AD 100. Because of antagonism between the Jewish community and the early Christians, John is sometimes divisive; and some of his words have led to centuries of Christian persecution of the Jewish people. At the beginning of this story, he notes that Jesus is not only going up to Jerusalem for a festival, but for "a festival of the Jews." It's a superfluous addition here, probably meant to underscore the division between the early Christians and "the Jews." Raymond Brown, in commenting on this passage, speaks of John's "lethal antipathy" toward the Jews.[7]

Here "the Jews" can be taken to refer to a particular group of Jews who, given their respect for the Sabbath, object to what the man is doing for legitimate reasons. Presumably they see him walking through the streets carrying his pallet. They accuse him of working on the Sabbath, which is forbidden. The man responds that he is simply following Jesus's orders. "The man who made me well said to me, 'Take up your mat and walk.'" Still the man does not know Jesus's identity.

Jesus then takes the initiative of finding the man in the Temple, where presumably the man is praying, and says to him, "See, you have been made well! Do not sin any more, so that nothing worse happens to you."

Is Jesus telling the man that his illness stemmed from his sin? This is unlikely, because later in the same Gospel, Jesus rejects that explanation when confronted with a blind man. More likely, Jesus is saying that sin can lead to something worse than physical illness. After this the man does not follow Jesus, but simply "went away." He goes off to tell "the Jews" of his healing. Some see in this a kind of betrayal of Jesus, because he reveals how Jesus healed him on the Sabbath.[8] I prefer to see him as unable to contain his joy, insistent on telling his good news—it's been thirty-eight years!

The man's departure is a reminder that not all were called to follow Jesus in the same way. This man has met Jesus and continues on with his life, made whole, transformed to be sure, perhaps returned to hope from despair, perhaps returning to a family who had given up on his ever being healed. Perhaps his healing was the sign that enabled his family to believe. There are many ways to follow Jesus.

John tells us that the miracle led to persecution by "the Jews," since Jesus had done work on the Sabbath. Amy-Jill Levine and Mark Zvi Brettler, in *The Jewish Annotated New Testament,* note that although curing a life-threatening illness was permitted, even encouraged, a chronic illness, such as this man's condition, was not deemed sufficient to break the Sabbath restriction on work—it could presumably be healed after the Sabbath.[9] Jesus responds directly to the prohibition on work by saying, "My Father is still working, and I also am working," and so he transgresses the law: by working on the Sabbath and by implicitly equating himself with God. The work of God, says Jesus, and my work are the same.

All these things, says John, increased the hatred of "the Jews" and led them "to seek all the more to kill him," because he had done these things on the Sabbath.

IT'S NOT SURPRISING THAT some of "the Jews" would be disturbed by an apparent rebuke to monotheism and an apparent profanation of the Sabbath (though, needless to say, that some were plotting to kill him is less excusable). My love for this story lies more in the figure of the paralyzed man who has lain beside the pool for thirty-eight years.

I'm writing these lines in the middle of a particularly painful bout with carpal-tunnel syndrome, something that I've had for the past twenty years. Without going into much detail I'll just say that the onset came suddenly during theology studies, when I was typing far too much. Within the space of a few days, I developed stabbing pains in my hands and arms and for the next two months could barely turn a doorknob or hold a pencil without feeling like someone was plunging a knife into my wrists.

At the beginning of this very minor medical saga, doctors (orthopedists, neurologists, even "hand specialists," a branch of medicine I had heretofore never imagined) found the condition a diagnostic challenge. After a year of visiting a variety of hospitals, clinics, and physical therapists, it was determined that I had either "repetitive strain injury," "carpal tunnel syndrome," or an "autonomic nerve disorder." "Or some combo," said one doctor, as if he were describing a special at a seafood restaurant. Surgery wouldn't work, and the symptoms probably wouldn't subside, the hand specialist finally said with a shrug.

The pain threw me into a state of confusion. After all, I was in the midst of graduate school and was expected to type papers every week. And I was just beginning to think that if theology studies went well, I might ask to pursue a doctorate in Scripture. My first course in the New Testament had proved so inspiring that I had begun to consider making an academic career of it. But after much discernment, I saw that particular hope extinguished. How could I write a dissertation if I couldn't even type a sentence?

Instead, I would be grateful just to finish theology studies, which I was able to do by asking my professors if I could take exams orally and turn in handwritten papers. Fortunately, all of them were open to that proposal, and I was able to finish my studies and enjoy them. (My friends also lent me their class notes when I couldn't use a pen.)

These days I deal with this persistent problem, as do many who live with far more serious chronic illnesses—by managing it. A combination of stretching, massage, and swimming helps. But from time to time, when I spend too much time typing, it flares up and I use voice-activated software to help me write.

Why am I bringing this up? Certainly this condition is not debilitating, much less life-threatening. It's nothing like the sickness that kept the paralyzed man on his mat for thirty-eight years by the Pool of Bethesda. And it's nothing like the serious illnesses so many people—maybe you—struggle with.

But this decades-long struggle is an entrée to the world of sadness, discouragement, and even the despair that attends illness.

Over the years, I have come to know many people living with chronic illnesses, painful ailments, and terminal diseases. And I've seen not only the grace of acceptance, but the overpowering, intensified, bottomless, passionate, almost infinite longing for healing. What can compare to a person's desperate desire to be healed from a serious illness? What can compare to a person's longing to be "made whole" physically? What can compare to the unquenchable thirst for the end of physical pain? This is true not only in cases of physical ailments and debilitation, but in emotional and spiritual ones. Some of my friends and acquaintances have been plagued by psychological problems, and their desire for release is just as intense as that of someone with a long-term physical illness. We all want to be "made whole," like the man on the mat.

Over the past decade, I've also been privileged to accompany pilgrims to the shrine of Lourdes, which I described earlier. Like the paralyzed man who sat by the pool of Bethesda, millions of pilgrims come annually to bathe in the waters at Lourdes, driven by the same thirst for healing.

Only sixty-seven cures at Lourdes have been authenticated. That is, there are copious reports from physicians attesting to serious illnesses that were once there, but are now, following a visit to Lourdes, gone. But other kinds of cures happen by those waters: emotional healings that come from being among others who suffer, spiritual healings that come from a consoling conversation, and smaller physical healings that are not documented, but that I have seen. The people who journey there on pilgrimage are hopeful. They live from a place of hope and faith.

During my very first visit to Lourdes, as I waited to enter the baths and later as I plunged myself in the icy spring waters, I prayed for healing from my carpal-tunnel problems. Then I made another prayer in the grotto where St. Bernadette Soubirous saw her visions. I prayed as hard as I could and promised that if I were healed, I would ever after write only what would glorify God. The next day I woke up, stretched out my hands, and with a sigh realized that I had not been healed.

Lately, two people very close to me have suffered bouts with cancer. Both were required to undergo surgery; both were treated with chemotherapy and radiation. Both also shared their experiences of God with me. Both reported, around roughly the same time in their illness—at the beginning of the treatment—a palpable sense of God's presence in their lives, which manifested as a sudden onset of calm. Often we are more open to God's presence in our lives when we are more vulnerable, and with our defenses down God can more easily break into our lives.

But in the past few years I've come to believe that, just as Jesus did with the paralyzed man at the pool, perhaps God *seeks out* those in special need of care. A few years ago I might have said that God is equally present to each of us. But it seems that God somehow moves closer to those who need help, as Jesus did with the man who had no one to help him. So maybe it's not surprising that some people report God's special presence during difficult times, when we are more open and God seems to move closer.

One friend undergoing cancer treatments told me that after an experience of God's peace, she found it helpful to return to that "place" in herself where God had given her calm and try to "live from there." Rather than move toward discouragement over her illness, she would return to the calm that she felt was a gift from God. Though she didn't always feel the same sense of God's presence, she could return to the memory of grace.

There is, however, another place for the sick person. There are times when the suffering person feels that nothing can change, that all is hopeless, that the pain will never end, that a "normal way of life" is no longer possible. Even though I have not suffered from a terminal illness or a life-threatening condition, I do know that place. I have spent time there, and I sometimes find myself returning to the place of discouragement and, sometimes, despair.

The paralyzed man may have lived in this dark place for many years. Perhaps this is the main reason why Jesus asked him, "Do you want to be made well?" Likewise, the man may have defined himself primarily through his illness. Jesus might also be saying to him, "Are you ready to let go of your identity as 'the paralyzed man'?"

The longer I meditate on this poignant story, the more I believe that William Barclay's explanation is apt. Barclay says that Jesus's question is not as foolish as it may sound. The paralytic lying by the pool might have been living in a "passive and dull despair." Who knows if he had been chronically depressed or had given up hope altogether? "He wanted to be healed, though he did not see how he ever could be since he had no one to help him," says Barclay. "The first essential [step] toward receiving the power of Jesus is to have intense desire for it. Jesus says: 'Do you really want to be changed?' If in our inmost hearts we are well content to stay as we are, there can be no change for us."[10]

Jesus is asking the man, "Have you given up hope?" Jesus is asking the man if he still has faith.

God asks the same question to those of us who enjoy perfect physical health, but who may have given up in other areas. A broken marriage, a miserable work environment, and overwhelming financial difficulties can lead us to despair. We can experience a spiritual paralysis that needs to be healed. But buried deep down under the despair is hope.

Hope is like the Pool of Bethesda. For years that place was thought to be lost, then just a myth. For years it was covered by dirt and gravel and trash. Perhaps it existed once, people thought, but no more. But it was always there, waiting to be uncovered, waiting to be restored, waiting to be seen again. It took work, but it was found.

This is how God comes to us—asking if we still want healing, if we still believe, if we still have faith.

Even while we dwell in despair, God excavates our hope and asks us, "Do you want to be made whole?"

THE HEALING AT THE POOL OF BETHESDA
John 5:1–18

After this there was a festival of the Jews, and Jesus went up to Jerusalem.

Now in Jerusalem by the Sheep Gate there is a pool, called in Hebrew Beth-zatha, which has five porticoes. In these lay many invalids—blind, lame, and paralyzed. One man was there who had been ill for thirty-eight years. When Jesus saw him lying there and knew that he had been there a long time, he said to him, "Do you want to be made well?" The sick man answered him, "Sir, I have no one to put me into the pool when the water is stirred up; and while I am making my way, someone else steps down ahead of me." Jesus said to him, "Stand up, take your mat and walk." At once the man was made well, and he took up his mat and began to walk.

Now that day was a sabbath. So the Jews said to the man who had been cured, "It is the sabbath; it is not lawful for you to carry your mat." But he answered them, "The man who made me well said to me, 'Take up your mat and walk.'" They asked him, "Who is the man who said to you, 'Take it up and walk'?" Now the man who had been healed did not know who it was, for Jesus had disappeared into the crowd that was there. Later Jesus found him in the temple and said to him, "See, you have been made well! Do not sin any more, so that nothing worse happens to you." The man went away and told the Jews that it was Jesus who had made him well. Therefore the Jews started persecuting Jesus, because he was doing such things on the sabbath. But Jesus answered them, "My Father is still working, and I also am working." For this reason the Jews were seeking all the more to kill him, because he was not only breaking the sabbath, but was also calling God his own Father, thereby making himself equal to God.

CHAPTER 17

Jericho

"He was trying to see who Jesus was."

As I MENTIONED A few chapters ago, during our time in Bethlehem we met up with a friendly cabdriver named Aziz. After we had spent a half hour in Shepherds' Field, George and I plopped back into the car. Aziz asked if there were any churches we might like to see before we went to our ultimate destination, the Church of the Nativity.

"Well," I ventured, "how far is Jericho?"

George looked at me quizzically.

"I want to see Zacchaeus's tree," I explained.

On a retreat a few years before I had read the story of Zacchaeus, the diminutive man who climbs a sycamore tree to see Jesus as he passed through Jericho. After I mentioned this passage in Luke's Gospel to my retreat director, he gave me a photo of the "Zacchaeus tree," by tradition the plant in question, which pilgrims still visited in Jericho. Though I wondered if the tree could possibly be two thousand years old, the photo helped me to picture the story more easily.

"Oh, Jericho is *very* near!" said Aziz. "On the way we will take a trip to Herodium." George and I looked at each other blankly.

"Herodium!" Aziz said. "King Herod's palace-fortress. Oh, people come from many countries to see it. It is beautiful. You will see! And it is a very short ride."

George and I shrugged and nodded. After all, how many palace-fortresses do you get to see in life? And now for a big detour—the "very short ride" turned out to be a two-hour journey through the desert.

Let me tell you something about the Judean desert: it's hot. When I used to read stories about Jesus's time in the desert, I imagined it like the deserts I had once seen in New Mexico: filled with attractive sagebrush and vibrantly colored flowers, with the odd green iguana scampering across the picturesque landscape. Or the terrain in northern Kenya, where the hard red earth is still hospitable for green acacia bushes and thorn trees. The Judean desert is, by contrast, empty: chalky white, completely dry, stubbled with small rocks that cover miles of undulating hills. Aziz sped on. Occasionally we passed clusters of people huddled under tents or corrugated sheets of tin. "Bedouin," said Aziz as he zipped over the smooth roads.

The highway followed the path of the "Old Roman Road," which is the imagined setting of Jesus's Parable of the Good Samaritan, in which a traveler comes to the aid of a stranger who has been attacked by robbers on the way "down from Jerusalem to Jericho." Jesus's listeners would probably have nodded as he told the story, easily picturing the vulnerability of a solitary traveler on this winding road.[1]

After a half hour I asked, "How far is Herodium?"

"Oh," said Aziz, "very near!"

Presently we saw in the distance a rounded hilltop, the shape of an overturned soup bowl. "There," he said. We slowly drove up the side of a mountain. Aziz parked.

"You go there," he said, pointing to a narrow metal staircase that led up the hill.

When George and I got out of the car a sledgehammer of heat hit us. We started to climb the staircase.

Panting and sweating, we reached the top of the palace-fortress.

Herod the Great (73 BC to AD 4), ruler of Judea around the time of Jesus's birth, is mainly known to New Testament readers as the king that sent the Magi (the Wise Men) to discover Jesus so that he could "go and pay him homage." After finding Jesus, however, the

Magi were warned in a dream not to return to Herod—who would later order the death of all the male children under age two in the area of Bethlehem as a way of eliminating the potential future rival. Joseph, Mary's husband, was warned in a dream to flee to Egypt to avoid Herod's murderous plots.[2]

Herod (whose appellation "the Great" is not used by everyone) also expanded the Second Temple in Jerusalem; the stones of the Western Wall, seen by pilgrims today, mark his construction. Indeed, whatever his many sins, Herod was a great builder. Among his largest projects was the city of Caesarea Maritima, on the Mediterranean coast; Herod was the first to use underwater cement to construct a breakwater, which created an immense harbor. (His son Herod Antipas, who succeeded him, was the Herod who questioned Jesus before his execution.)

Even with all that history, I hadn't planned to see Herodium. But when we reached the top of the citadel, I was glad we did. From the rim of the mountain one could peer down into the ruins, which looked suitably Roman (Herod, although Jewish, was a client king controlled by Rome). A courtyard, a cistern, and various baths, including a *caldarium,* a "hot room," all could be discerned in the colossal stones.

"Oh, good," said George, "just what we need today. A hot room."

After walking through the huge, empty underground cisterns and running into a group of boisterous Norwegian students, we set out for Jericho, which, I suspected from scanning the desolate landscape, was nowhere near where we were.

"On the way to Jericho," said Aziz, back in the comfort of our air-conditioned car, "we shall visit St. George's Monastery." I flipped through the guidebook.

"What's that?" whispered George.

"It is very beautiful. You will see!" said Aziz. "People come from everywhere to see it. There are still monks there."

As we drove across the chalky landscape, I opened my guidebook to the description of the Monastery of St. George of Koziba: "Clinging to the steep cliff of the Wadi Qilt above a small garden with olive trees and cypresses, this perfect example of a MONASTERY IN THE JUDAEAN DESERT has always been famous for its hospitality, which, from the C6 [sixth century], has also been extended to women."[3]

"Anything named St. George can't be that bad," said George. "What else does it say?"

Interesting legends attach to the locale. It was the place where Elijah stayed on his way to Sinai (the place, not the monastery obviously) and was tended to by ravens. It was the place where St. Joachim, the father of Mary, was supposed to have wept over his wife's barrenness. (I didn't need Jerome Murphy-O'Connor to pronounce on that legend.)

Then an alarming warning: "Hikers (who do not suffer from vertigo) can reach the monastery by a good path which follows an Herodian aqueduct." Vertigo? Also: "It is not advisable to leave cars unattended." Two things I wasn't excited about: vertigo and danger.

Aziz cheerfully remarked, "It is located in the Valley of the Shadow of Death!"

George laughed. "Oh, then I *definitely* want to go."

Later research would reveal that the location was indeed the traditional Valley of the Shadow of Death mentioned in Psalm 23. I looked out the window at the punishing landscape and could see why. I wondered how anyone in Jesus's day (or ours) could even think about traversing this terrain.

Aziz pulled off the road and parked on a small rise. We emerged, once again into the stunning heat. Climbing to the edge of a rocky lookout, we met three Bedouin men, who stood beside their mangy camel. George and I peered across a deep, dry ravine and saw a minuscule cluster of sand-colored buildings with bright-blue roofs on the opposite side.

"There," said Aziz, "St. George!"

The Bedouin men asked if we wanted to hire the camel for transport. We declined, foolishly.

We clambered down the steep rocky path and began our walk into the Wadi Qilt. Our very long, very hot walk. A camel laden with tourists passed us, its bells jingling. A man wearing shorts and climbing the other way, uphill, passed us wordlessly, panting loudly. After a few minutes of walking, George and I were bathed in sweat and took long drinks from our rapidly dwindling water bottles. The walls of the ravine were incised with small crosses.

After half an hour, we reached a ramshackle bridge that crossed the ravine. Above us, clinging to the hill like a swallow's nest was St. George of Koziba Monastery, its sandy towers topped with powder-blue domes, in the Greek style. The monastery was destroyed in the seventh century by Persians, restored in the twelfth century by Crusaders, and gradually fell into ruin. The current structure was restored in the late nineteenth century.

After the punishing walk, I expected a hidden gem, an architectural jewel, a gorgeous monastery that would be an aesthetic reward for our pilgrimage. The Greek Orthodox church in Capernaum was such a place: a small space crammed with mosaics, bursting with color and light. But St. George's monastery is a modest one, its chapel small and its artwork simple. After praying in the chapel for a few minutes, peering at some icons and lighting a few candles, we departed.

The trek back was even more grueling, as it was almost all uphill; we stopped several times just to catch our breath. It was the hottest I've ever been in my entire life, and that includes two years in East Africa. At one point I thought George was going to have a heart attack. At another point that I would faint. Between concerns about heart attacks and fainting, I thought of Jesus in the desert, and also how difficult it must have been for him and the disciples to walk from town to town. But later, when we recounted our overheated tale back at the PBI, someone pointed out that Jesus and the disciples probably traveled at night.

At one point George turned around, his face streaming with sweat. "Death . . . march," he said between breaths.

I wondered aloud if we would go straight to heaven if we died on a pilgrimage to the Holy Land.

"We . . . *better*," said George.

Back in the car, Aziz said, "Was it not beautiful?"

We nodded between breaths.

After another half hour, we pulled into Jericho, located in the West Bank. Dating back to circa 8000 BC, it is the oldest continuously inhabited city in the world.

"This better be worth it," said George.

AFTER REACHING THE ENTRANCE to the city, I realized how I had underestimated what it meant for Jesus and his disciples to travel. When the Gospel of Luke describes Jesus journeying from Galilee to Jerusalem and passing through Jericho, the text offers bland comments like, "As he approached Jericho," or "He entered Jericho and was passing through it." Not, "Jesus and his disciples walked in the blistering desert heat, over miles of dusty earth, without water. And James and John, the sons of Zebedee, almost fainted." Then again, maybe they did travel at night, and maybe they were smart enough not to travel in the heat.

Jesus is passing through Jericho—in Judea—because he is on his way to Jerusalem. It is his last trip to Jerusalem. His ministry is now drawing to a close. The town is some twenty miles northeast of Jerusalem, in the Jordan Valley. In Jericho, en route to his crucifixion, he will meet two men. One is poor and one is rich; both seek a kind of healing from Jesus. Matthew, Mark, and Luke all recount the story of the poor, blind man called Bartimaeus, but only Luke tells us the story of the wealthy man, Zacchaeus. The two stories are bright ones, preceding the darkness that awaits Jesus.

Let's begin with Bartimaeus, one of my favorite stories in the

New Testament. It was also one of the first Gospel stories I had thought about deeply.

As PART OF MY training as a Jesuit novice, I worked in a hospital for the seriously ill in Cambridge, Massachusetts. Many of the patients—with brain injuries, long-term illnesses, and serious disabilities—had been there for years. My job with the pastoral-care team, which I began only a few weeks after entering the Jesuit novitiate, was to help visit and counsel the patients. Much of the time was spent learning from the other experienced hospital chaplains. It was my first experience in real-life ministry, and I hadn't a clue what to do.

The most enjoyable part of the week was a Bible study class. Every Friday the patients, most in wheelchairs, gathered in a small conference room to talk about a particular Scripture passage. It was the first time I had ever been to anything remotely like that—I had never studied the Bible before—and I found it riveting. One week a former Catholic sister, named Julie, with a wicked thick Boston accent, introduced the week's reading. "Today weah going to read about *Bah*-timaeus," she said. "From the Aramaic word *Bah*, meaning 'son of,' and *Timaeus. Bah*-timaeus."

Julie asked a question: "What would it be like to be like Bartimaeus?" I couldn't imagine what she meant. I'm not blind, I remember thinking. Then she started to "open up" the story. Within a few minutes I felt an almost electric shock of recognition.

Matthew and Mark say that Jesus met the blind man on his way out of Jericho. Well, not quite. Matthew has Jesus meet *two* blind men, who go unnamed; in Mark Jesus meets a blind man named Bartimaeus. Luke says he meets *one* man on the way *in*. Either way, all three Synoptics have Jesus encountering a blind man (or men) sitting by the side of the road, begging. Mark introduces him as "Bartimaeus, son of Timaeus," a clue that Mark is explaining the original Aramaic name to his Greek-speaking audience.

Beggars were a common sight in Jesus's day. What was uncommon was what Bartimaeus says. When he hears that Jesus of Nazareth is passing by, he cries out, "Jesus, Son of David, have mercy on me!" Bartimaeus is not asking for money, but something deeper. The blind man also uses Jesus's royal title, which means that he can fully see what few others do. Once again in Mark, the Messianic Secret of Jesus's identity is known to those who "see" better than everyone else, including those who have been with Jesus all along.

Many in the crowd, however, tell the man to be quiet. For me, this part of the story represents all of those who try to keep us from changing, who with their hopelessness and despair and even contempt tell us not to try. It is also the voice of all those who seek to keep the "important people" from hearing the voice of the masses.

But Bartimaeus shouts out even louder (in Greek, *pollō mallon*, "much more"). "Son of David, have mercy on me!" You can feel his desperation, or perhaps his hope.

"Son of David" is a rare title, appearing in no other miracle story in Mark. (And remember there is no infancy narrative in Mark that identifies Jesus as part of David's lineage.) But it makes sense that if the people of the day knew about Jesus's miraculous deeds and heard stories of Jesus's lineage, Bartimaeus would use this appellation. It's also the first time in the Gospel of Mark that Jesus does not rebuke someone not possessed by a demon for revealing his identity.

Then Jesus stops, or in some translations, stands still (Greek: *stas*). He recognizes the poor man sitting by the road. Jesus pauses to notice.

Paula Fitzgerald, a campus minister at John Carroll University in Ohio and a friend from graduate theology studies, once told me how moving she finds the words "Jesus stood still." The Christian life is often so busy, said Paula, with its emphasis on doing and acting, that it's important to see Jesus being still. Jesus is not so busy that he cannot notice, or be attentive to, Bartimaeus, who has something important to say. Paula likened it to two friends walking side by side when one of them suddenly says something important. The listener may stop so that she can be more attentive. It's important to be active, but sometimes it's essential to be still.

Then Jesus says, "Call him here." Now the same people who were shushing Bartimaeus say, "Take heart; get up, he is calling you." There may be some intentional humor here in the portrayal of the fickle crowd: "Sit down!" "Stand up!" Perhaps they were responding to Jesus. His actions invite them to really *see* the man. Or perhaps they were protecting Jesus from being "disturbed." But now, seeing that Jesus himself wants to see Bartimaeus, they change.

In response to Jesus's call, Bartimaeus throws off his cloak, leaps up, and stands before Jesus. What confidence it must have taken for the blind man to do this! Bartimaeus may have stumbled as he walked to Jesus; perhaps one of the disciples took his hand and guided him.

Jesus asks him, "What do you want me to do for you?"

Bartimaeus says, "My teacher [Mark preserves the Aramaic *Rabbouni*], let me see again."

Two millennia after the story, Bartimaeus's enthusiasm still leaps off the page. The man shouts out Jesus's royal title, when no one else seems to know. He refuses to let the crowd prevent him from getting close to Jesus. Impetuously, he throws off his cloak and jumps to his feet.

"Go," says Jesus, "your faith has made you well." Immediately his sight is restored and he follows Jesus on "the way."

No physical touch is required for the healing; Jesus's word is sufficient. Now healed, the man becomes a disciple and follows him on "the way," an ancient way of talking about discipleship. The one who was sitting by the road now joins Jesus along the way. Bartimaeus's immediate response is gratitude and the desire to follow.

Bartimaeus is often seen as a typical disciple of Jesus, or at least a follower—one called by Jesus who then follows him on "the way," implying that Bartimaeus would now share in the itinerant life of Jesus and the Twelve. But Gerhard Lohfink reminds us that there were many ways of following Jesus and points to people like Martha and Mary (whom we will meet in the next chapter) who remained at home and most likely provided hospitality for Jesus. Lohfink calls these stay-at-home disciples "resident adherents."[4] Also important were "occasional helpers," people such as Joseph of Arimathea, who crucially helps Jesus and his followers in the wake of the Crucifixion, by begging Pontius Pilate for the body.[5] There are many ways of "following."

Mark offers the story of Bartimaeus before the Crucifixion as if to illustrate the meaning of discipleship. The story also follows two separate predictions of Jesus's Passion. In Mark's ninth chapter, Jesus predicts his death, but the disciples "did not understand what he was saying." And immediately before meeting Bartimaeus, Jesus speaks of his coming suffering, and once again two of his disciples, James and John, miss the point. (They ask Jesus instead who is going to sit alongside him "in your glory.") For Mark, discipleship means coming to see who Jesus is and learning how to follow him. The disciples are blind for the most part. The blind man, however, sees.[6]

It was also clearly a story of immense importance to the followers of Jesus, for Bartimaeus is the only direct recipient of a miracle—other than the apostles—to be named in any of the Synoptic Gospels.[7] Bartimaeus believes in Jesus's power, he refuses to let the crowd stifle his enthusiasm, and he professes Jesus as his teacher. "Get up!" Mark says to *us*, as a rallying cry. "He is calling you."[8] The story's placement also underscores the idea that discipleship means following Jesus into places of suffering.

John Meier looks at a variety of elements of this compelling narrative—the preservation of Aramaic names and words (Bartimaeus and *Rabbouni*), the unique use of the man's name, the unusual appellation "Son of David," the tying of an individual to a specific site (Jericho) at a specific time of the year (before Passover) and a specific period in Jesus's ministry (before Jerusalem)—and declares its presentation in Mark as one of the "strongest candidates for the report of a specific miracle going back to the historical Jesus."⁹ It is not surprising, says Meier, given the dramatic miracle and the fact that Jesus met Bartimaeus on the way to Jerusalem in the presence of so many of his followers, that his disciples would have remembered the persistent and faith-filled man from Jericho.

THE STORY OF BARTIMAEUS is not just a story about something most of us will never experience—a miraculous healing—it is also a story about something common to our experience: desire and conversion.

Desire often gets a bad rap in religious circles because of two common misinterpretations. First, we think of desire only in terms of surface wants. ("I want a new car!") Second, we think of it only as sexual desire or lust. ("I must have you!") But without healthy desires we would cease to exist in any real way. We wouldn't want to study or learn. We wouldn't want to earn a living to support our families. We wouldn't want to help lessen suffering. And without sexual desire, we wouldn't even be here.

Jesus sees something liberating in identifying and naming our desires. Once we scrape off any surface selfishness, our deepest longings and holy desires are uncovered: the desire for friendship, the desire for love, the desire for meaningful work, and often the desire for healing. Ultimately, of course, our deepest longing is for God. And it is God who places these desires within us. This is one way God calls us to himself. We desire God because God desires us.

People often need to be encouraged to recognize these deep longings, which can help guide their lives, especially if they have been told to ignore or eradicate their desires. Once they do so, they discover a fundamental truth: desire is one of the engines of a person's vocation. On the most basic level, two people are drawn together in marriage out of desire—physical, emotional, spiritual. Desire plays an important role in vocations in the working world. How else does the future scientist, for example, grasp her vocation to study biology other than by finding her high school biology classes interesting?

Notice that Jesus does not say, "Bartimaeus, just accept the way things are." That's what the crowd is saying: "Be quiet!" Jesus encourages him to name his desire. He asks him directly, "What do you want me to do for you?"

Bartimaeus's encounter with Jesus also highlights the importance of being honest in our relationship with God. It would be difficult for the blind man *not* to ask Jesus to heal him from something that had troubled him all his life, especially if he knew Jesus's reputation as a healer. In a similar way, when we stand before God in prayer, we should feel comfortable expressing our longings. If you say only what you think you "should" say in prayer, while denying your deep desires—if you obey the crowd's order to "be quiet"—your relationship with God might grow cold. God invites us to be honest about what we desire, even though this can be a challenge when those desires are not fulfilled. But even in those difficult times God invites us to remain in the conversation. And this includes the transparent sharing of our deep desires. God craves our honesty.

Jesus says to Bartimaeus: "What do you want me to do for you?" But more: "What does your heart tell you? What are your desires? When you listen to your heart, what does it say?" Jesus listens to Bartimaeus, who listens to his heart.

Naming our desires is also a sign of humility. Bartimaeus knows that he cannot heal himself. Neither can we. We stand before God aware of our limitations. In the simplest analysis, we need help. Why not admit it?

Finally, we sometimes need to ignore the crowd, especially when they tell us to shut up. "Don't desire something better for yourself," they say to Bartimaeus and to us. "Give up those ridiculous hopes of change. Stop hoping for something new." By contrast, Jesus doesn't shout, "Be quiet!" Jesus's voice is different than the crowd's. Gently, he asks, "What do you want me to do for you?"

The encounter with Bartimaeus is also a story of conversion, characterized by the blind man's casting off of his cloak. It was probably among his most valued possessions, an outer garment that could be used as a coat and, at night, as a blanket or even a bed. It would have been almost unthinkable for a poor man to throw aside his cloak. Thus his cloak is a beautiful symbol of conversion. "So throwing off his cloak, he sprang up (*anapēdēsas*) and came to Jesus," says Mark. Like the nets that Peter must let go of, Bartimaeus leaves behind some of his past in order to see his future.

FINALLY, THIS IS A story about ministry. My friend Paula noted that the lessons of this Gospel passage extend beyond Jesus "standing still." If you look at the narrative carefully, she suggested, Jesus's distinctive form of ministry becomes clearer.

First, Jesus enters Jericho with "his disciples and a large crowd."[10] Ministry is relational and is often carried out in groups. Being a minister also involves the idea of a journey, whether that means journeying with an individual spiritually or traveling physically to a particular place to be with someone. Jesus is happy to minister with others, not just for others. He calls people together to minister together.

Second, Mark's explicit naming of Bartimaeus shows the importance of knowing the person we're trying to help. On the road outside of Jericho, Jesus does not minister to a "blind man," a "beggar," or a "poor man"—to a member of a faceless socioeconomic group or to an anonymous person with a generic illness, but to an individual with a name and a history: Bartimaeus, son of Timaeus. This was one of the most important lessons I learned in my first year as a Jesuit. In the hospital ministry as a novice, I had initially thought I would be working with "the sick." That was true. But truer still was that I was working with individuals, people who had their own stories and dreams. I wasn't working with "the sick" as much as I was working with Rita, Gene, and Frank.

The preservation of Bartimaeus's name is a strong indication that after his healing Bartimaeus became a well-known individual in the early Christian community. It is a reminder of the importance of not simply meeting a person's needs in ministry, but treating a person as an individual.

Third, Jesus asks Bartimaeus, "What do you want me to do for you?" Jesus, said Paula, does not presume to know what the blind man would ask of him. As a minister it is tempting to believe that you already know what the other person needs.

During my hospital chaplaincy in Boston, I met an elderly woman with a long-term illness, named Rita. In my eagerness to be a good hospital chaplain, I spoke with her only about the things I thought a chaplain should speak about: God, prayer, and suffering. But Rita wanted to talk only about her two brothers, who were both Jesuits. Every time she began to talk about them, I tried to steer her to more "important" topics. One day the director of pastoral care suggested that I talk to Rita about her interests, rather than mine. I did, and we eventually became friends. In time, we did end up speaking about God, prayer, and suffering. But first I needed to give Rita the dignity of listening to her. If Jesus is willing to let the other person take the initiative, so should we.

After Jesus heals Bartimaeus he says, "Go; your faith has made you well." (In Mark and Luke the Greek is *sesōken,* saved you.) Ministry affirms people and then offers them the opportunity to grow and change. Ministry also offers them the opportunity to follow Jesus themselves and perform the works of charity. And that's not limited to professional or organized ministry—we all have opportunities to minister to, or care for, one another.

It's not clear how Bartimaeus followed Jesus, whether for a day or a lifetime. But the preservation of his story indicates that Bartimaeus became a faithful disciple in his own way.

SOMEONE ELSE WAS WAITING for Jesus in Jericho. As Luke tells it, after he heals the blind man, Jesus, accompanied by a great crowd, spies something strange. The chief tax collector in the town, a man named Zacchaeus, is perched high in a sycamore tree, straining to see Jesus.[11] "He was trying to see who Jesus was, but on account of the crowd he could not, because he was short in stature," says Luke.

For the people of Jericho, the sight of the diminutive tax collector sitting in the tree probably made them laugh derisively. Most people likely despised the chief tax collector, who worked for the Roman overlords. In Jesus's time, Jericho was a wealthy town, ideally located for commerce in the Jordan Valley, and so it served as a major center for taxation for the Romans. Zacchaeus, as chief tax collector (having responsibility over other tax collectors), would have been an integral part of a corrupt system and thus seen as one of the "chief sinners" of the area. To be chief tax collector would have brought both wealth and contempt. Any laughter over his undignified behavior would have been magnified by the people's detestation of him.

Maybe they also laughed because he was unusually short. And how would he have reached the branches of the sycamore tree? Maybe by climbing a nearby wall and jumping onto a branch, or asking someone to hoist him up—further actions to attract derision. And given the loose-fitting clothing of the time, perhaps a great deal of Zacchaeus would have been visible to the crowd below.

None of this deters Zacchaeus. He is, quite literally, going out on a limb for Jesus, risking his dignity to see the Master. Luke says, "He was trying to see who Jesus was." What a wonderful line! Weren't the disciples? Aren't we all? Zacchaeus may have thought, *Who is this Jesus, about whom everyone is so excited? Could he possibly help someone like me?*

Before hearing a word from the tax collector, Jesus calls up into the sycamore tree. "Zacchaeus," he says, "hurry and come down; for I must stay at your house today!" I can imagine Jesus laughing as he looks up into the branches.

How did Jesus know his name? He probably asked, and the people around him may have said, "Oh him? That's the chief tax collector, Zacchaeus." Jesus seems delighted by Zacchaeus's willingness to do something out of the ordinary to find salvation. *The tax collector? How wonderful!* Once again Jesus approaches someone seen as undesirable. His offer to dine with the man demonstrates an example of "table fellowship," Jesus's practice of sharing meals with all kinds of persons and a public statement of welcome and worthiness.[12] In effect, Jesus is showing God's hospitality to sinners by letting the sinners show him hospitality.

How did Zacchaeus know about Jesus of Nazareth? Luke's description makes it plausible that Zacchaeus knew something about Jesus beforehand. Reminiscent of the fishermen dropping everything to follow Jesus at the Sea of Galilee, his immediate response makes more sense when we presume prior knowledge of Jesus. Maybe Zacchaeus had heard tales about Jesus—news of Bartimaeus's healing probably traveled fast in Jericho. Perhaps he had simply been waiting for a second chance—a way out of being one of the most hated men in town. Or maybe he was looking for a way out of whatever sins he had committed.

Zacchaeus clambers down and welcomes Jesus with rejoicing (*chairōn*). Joy is a natural response to the presence of God. But the crowd doesn't approve. Why would Jesus want to dine at the house of a person who, in the view of some in the crowd, was the "chief of sinners"?[13] Plus, Jesus doesn't wait to be invited, and he doesn't wait for Zacchaeus to apologize or make an act of restitution—he makes the first move with the sinner. Luke tells us that "everyone"—this would include the disciples—grumbles.

Their resentment does not dampen the joy of the one who has met Jesus. Zacchaeus "stood there" or "stood his ground" (*statheis*), implying that Jesus and Zacchaeus had already begun walking to the house.

Then Zacchaeus says to Jesus, "Look, half of my possessions,

Lord, I will give to the poor; and if I have defrauded anyone of any-thing, I will pay back four times as much." There is some debate over whether the Greek is saying that he *will* do that or that he is *already* doing that. Either way, he is willing to give half of his earnings to the poor, and if he discovers that he has cheated anyone, he makes restitution. Zacchaeus is observing the requirements of the Jewish law at the time, even going beyond them.[14] It is as if he is trying to say to Jesus and the crowd: "You may hate me, but you don't know me. I'm trying my best to follow the Law by caring for others." It is also an unmistakable act of humility, a public confession of sin in front of people who probably despise him.

Notice that Zacchaeus already knows what he needs to do. Jesus doesn't have to tell him. Oftentimes, so do we. While we often wish that God would somehow show up in the flesh and tell us exactly what we should do, if we're honest with ourselves, we already know the right thing to do. As Mark Twain said, "It ain't those parts of the Bible that I can't understand that bother me; it is the parts that I do understand."

Some context is helpful here. The story of Zacchaeus in Luke's Gospel follows the story about the person traditionally called the Rich Young Man, in which a rich "ruler" asks Jesus what he must do to gain eternal life. After the man says that he follows the Com-mandments, Jesus tells him to do one more thing. "Sell all that you own and distribute the money to the poor." But the man, good as he is, cannot do this. So he "became sad."[15]

By contrast, Zacchaeus is already performing an act of charity. The man known to be good cannot follow Jesus because he is tied to his possessions. The man known to be bad is already following Jesus by acting generously to the poor. As Luke Timothy Johnson notes, the one who frees himself from ties to possessions can follow Jesus; the one who clings to wealth is closed to the call of Jesus, even when he is standing in front of him. "Disposition of the heart is symbol-ized by the disposition of possessions."[16]

Amy-Jill Levine suggested to me that Jesus may have given Zacchaeus another gift. The people may not know that Zacchaeus is already giving money to the poor. Jesus allows Zacchaeus to tell the crowd what he has already been doing. Contrary to what the crowd might think, he is not, at least regarding the poor, the "chief sinner" after all. The story also shows that someone as unlikely as an agent of the occupation government may work toward the betterment of the people and that we should not judge people by their reputations, or their day jobs. Appearances can be deceiving.

After speaking to the Rich Young Man, Jesus turns to his disciples and says that it is easier for a camel to enter the eye of a needle than for a rich person to enter heaven. The disciples—for whom wealth was sometimes seen as a sign of God's favor—are dumbfounded. "Then who can be saved?" they ask. Jesus says, "What is impossible for mortals is possible for God."

Is Jesus saying that you cannot have any possessions and be his follower? Not as I see it. Jesus constantly calls us to simplicity of life and asks us to have an overriding concern for the poor—how we treat the poor is one of Jesus's litmus tests for entrance into heaven—but everyone needs a certain amount of goods to live.[17] And notice that Zacchaeus has not said that he will give *all* his money to the poor. He may still be wealthy. But, as usual, Jesus puts his finger on what prevents that specific person from being free. This is why he asks the Rich Young Man to divest himself. Jesus invites people to be free of anything that keeps them from God, whether that's money or status or our inflated self-importance. Zacchaeus was free as soon as he climbed the tree. So while the Rich Young Man goes away sad, Zacchaeus is filled with joy.

So to the disciples' question, "Who can be saved?" Jesus answers, in effect, "Take a look at Zacchaeus."

Then Jesus publicly pronounces a blessing on Zacchaeus and his house, which apparently he has now entered. He too refuses to be cowed by the crowd. "Today salvation has come to this house," he says, addressing the crowd, "because he too is a son of Abraham. For the Son of Man came to seek out and to save the lost."

The story began with the image of Zacchaeus seeking Jesus, but ends by saying that Jesus was seeking Zacchaeus. To find God is to be found by God, who has been looking for us all along.

ZACCHAEUS'S TALE IS ABOUT more than material goods standing in your way of God. It also has to do with not letting others stand in your way to God, for Zacchaeus literally cannot see "on account of the crowd." As with Bartimaeus, the crowd tries to prevent the man from moving closer to God. In Bartimaeus's case, they shush him. In Zacchaeus's case, the crowd physically prevents him from even seeing Jesus and then grumbles when Jesus asks for his friendship.

How can "the crowd" prevent us from seeing God? Sometimes people overwhelm us with demands. We all need time away from the crowd, simply to refresh ourselves with solitude and prayer. Jesus himself needed to withdraw from the crowd for intimate moments with the Father.

But the crowd prevents us in other ways.

The crowd can pressure us to go along with received wisdom. Following the crowd can mean bowing to popular opinion and also refusing to think that things could be different. The herd mentality often inclines toward the status quo. Sometimes we Jesuits ruefully say about a patently foolish way of doing things: "Why do we do it this way?" "Because we've *always* done it this way." The crowd can prevent us from seeing a new way God has in store for us.

The crowd can make us fearful of rejection. Even without overt threats, such fear can hinder us from change. We may wonder, *What will everyone think if I do or say this?* Even if the crowd is not paying any attention, we may fear their rejection. We don't want to draw attention to ourselves, so we do nothing.

Finally, the crowd may actively oppose our moving closer to God.

You might be openly attacked for being charitable to an outsider. Or your desires for a holier life might be mocked. Once over a dinner I shared a spiritual experience I had enjoyed on retreat. "Yeah, *right*," someone said. He turned back to his food, and everyone chuckled. It was discouraging, but not surprising. The crowd, whether in your hometown or in your home, may prevent you from moving nearer to the Lord.

For me, then, the most touching part of the story is not Jesus's surprising blessing. It is Zacchaeus's confidence. He expresses it first by climbing the tree. Then he expresses it again by standing his ground. Try to imagine this: The man is filled with joy at what is about to happen to him, filled with hope and enthusiasm—and the crowd is furious. Everyone wants to extinguish his hope. They want to return him to despair. But he will not let them.

Zacchaeus does not let their fury dissuade him. His enthusiasm is undimmed. He does not let the crowd rule him. He does not need the approval of everyone, including presumably the disciples, any more than Bartimaeus did. He sees, he chooses, he acts. For this Jesus pronounces him saved.

Sometimes I am part of the crowd. I am the one who thinks the other person cannot possibly change. Like "everyone," I sometimes harden my heart to the possibility of conversion for others. So I have to remind myself never to close my heart to anyone. If you or I run across a "chief sinner," who are we to condemn him if God wants to welcome him?

So now the obvious question: Are you ready to be a "fool for Christ," as St. Paul would term it, as Zacchaeus was, or does the crowd keep you back?

Many of us live in fear of being seen as uncool, foolish, gullible, unsophisticated, and consequently rejected. But why not be foolish for Christ? You could be foolish about forgiveness and offer reconciliation to someone against whom you've held a grudge—even though others tell you to write him off. You could be foolish about charity and refuse to bad-mouth someone at work—even though others delight in making fun of her. You could be foolish about humility and refuse to seek acclaim—in a culture that prizes it. You could be foolish by living simply—in a world of materialism. You could be foolish about your relationship to God and set aside time for prayer—in a society that prizes nothing more than activity. You could do all this even though people disdain you.

The crowd may condemn you for wanting to get close to God, because they know that if you do, then they may have to do so as well; that is, they may be invited to change, and that frightens them. So they do the easier thing: they mock you.

Zacchaeus shows us choices. You can be like those in the crowd, keeping people down, laughing at those who want to change their lives, praying that people are punished, not forgiven. Or you can be like those in the crowd who want to do the Christian thing, who want to be compassionate, but are kept back for fear of looking foolish or being rejected.

Or you could be like Zacchaeus, the little man who doesn't care what people think, who only wants to see "who Jesus was." Because he knows that that's the most important thing in life—to know who Jesus is.

So which will it be? Are you ready to go out on a limb for Christ? If you do, then, as it did for Zacchaeus, salvation will come to your house.

AZIZ MANEUVERED HIS CAR into the center of Jericho, and soon George and I spied the Zacchaeus tree. Enclosed by a circular iron fence, the sycamore tree stood in the middle of a busy traffic circle, with small cars zooming around it. Tall and leafy, it stretched its long pale branches over the blacktopped roads. More than a few experts say that the tree could in fact be two thousand years old. But who knows? I liked looking at it, though. And I took many photos of the tree and imagined Zacchaeus sitting high in the branches, straining to see his future.

"So," said George, after I climbed back into the car. "Was it worth it?"

It always is. Just ask Bartimaeus and Zacchaeus.

THE HEALING OF BARTIMAEUS
Mark 10:46–52
(See also Matthew 20:29–34; Luke 18:35–43)

They came to Jericho. As he and his disciples and a large crowd were leaving Jericho, Bartimaeus son of Timaeus, a blind beggar, was sitting by the roadside. When he heard that it was Jesus of Nazareth, he began to shout out and say, "Jesus, Son of David, have mercy on me!" Many sternly ordered him to be quiet, but he cried out even more loudly, "Son of David, have mercy on me!" Jesus stood still and said, "Call him here." And they called the blind man, saying to him, "Take heart; get up, he is calling you." So throwing off his cloak, he sprang up and came to Jesus. Then Jesus said to him, "What do you want me to do for you?" The blind man said to him, "My teacher, let me see again." Jesus said to him, "Go; your faith has made you well." Immediately he regained his sight and followed him on the way.

JESUS MEETS ZACCHAEUS
Luke 19:1–10

He entered Jericho and was passing through it. A man was there named Zacchaeus; he was a chief tax collector and was rich. He was trying to see who Jesus was, but on account of the crowd he could not, because he was short in stature. So he ran ahead and climbed a sycamore tree to see him, because he was going to pass that way. When Jesus came to the place, he looked up and said to him, "Zacchaeus, hurry and come down; for I must stay at your house today." So he hurried down and was happy to welcome him. All who saw it began to grumble and said, "He has gone to be the guest of one who is a sinner." Zacchaeus stood there and said to the Lord, "Look, half of my possessions, Lord, I will give to the poor; and if I have defrauded anyone of anything, I will pay back four times as much." Then Jesus said to him, "Today salvation has come to this house, because he too is a son of Abraham. For the Son of Man came to seek out and to save the lost."

CHAPTER 18

Bethany

"Take away the stone."

THE SMALL TOWN OF Bethany, which is mentioned frequently in the Gospels, used to be reachable via a long path that led from Jerusalem through the Garden of Gethsemane and up and over the steep Mount of Olives. But the path that Jesus often used is used no more. The wall installed by the Israeli government dividing off Palestinian territories makes direct access impossible. Now pilgrims have to take a bus from the Damascus Gate at the Old City walls to the town. It's a long drive for such a short distance, but had I not seen the town, I would have felt that my pilgrimage was incomplete. It was a place that I had long prayed about—the town where Lazarus was raised from the dead.

A German Jesuit named Stefan was staying at the PBI, and one morning he was scheduled to celebrate Mass at the Church of the Holy Sepulchre. So at seven o'clock, Stefan and I, along with a visiting Portuguese diocesan priest named Domingo, celebrated Mass there. Afterward we rushed to catch the bus to the town called by the locals *El-Azariyeh,* after the name of Lazarus. The decrepit minibus, similar to the one George and I took to Bethlehem, was crammed with Palestinians returning home: women in hijabs, men in keffiyehs, all chatting away as the rattletrap bus bumped noisily over the streets.

Stefan wanted to exit the bus at an early stop so as to see more of

Bethany, which turned out to be quite poor, as poor as some of the worst slums in the United States. Perhaps because it was still early in the morning, only a few shops were open along the trash-filled streets. The combination of closed shops, men wandering through the streets aimlessly, and uncollected garbage reminded me of some of the slums in Nairobi. A surprising number of small children ran around carrying small toy guns, playfully pointing the black plastic replicas at one another. At first, I wondered if this was a reflection of the larger culture of violence in which they lived, but then I reminded myself that I had played with similar toys when I was a boy. Still, it was disconcerting to have a six-year-old point a realistic pistol at you, say "Bang!" and laugh.

Stefan, Domingo, and I made our way through the streets and trudged up the hill that led to the Church of St. Lazarus. (George was visiting the Holocaust History Museum that day.) It was just a few meters away from the Wall. In a few minutes we reached a white stone staircase that led to a sign, "Tomb of Lazarus," in front of a metal door. Father Doan at the PBI told us to ask for the keys to the tomb from a Muslim man. I smiled when I saw that the man's main job was not caretaker of the shrine of Jesus's greatest miracle, but owner of a shop across the street, which sold sodas, candy, and souvenirs.

Stefan and Domingo had seen the tomb a few days earlier, so the man carefully opened the cheap metal door for me alone. "You have to turn on the light," he said, and I flipped on a switch. It illumined a long, narrow staircase, which led to a place where, by tradition, Martha and Mary, the friends of Jesus, had laid their brother Lazarus.

Was this the place of Jesus's great miracle? Murphy-O'Connor writes of the town: "There is no problem about its identification. A village on the main Jericho road fits the distance from Jerusalem given in John 11:18, and its Arabic name, el-Azariyeh, preserves the Greek *Lazarion,* 'the place of Lazarus,' by which it was known to Eusebius (330) and all subsequent Byzantine and medieval pilgrims."[1] In Jesus's time the area functioned as a cemetery. The sole difference now is that the entrance to the tomb is slightly altered; the current opening was cut into the rock by Franciscans in the sixteenth century.

As I looked down the flight of uneven stairs, which led into darkness, I wondered what I would find.

HERE'S A FACT ABOUT Jesus that is sometimes overlooked: he had friends. Most of us know that Jesus had apostles, Jesus had disciples, and Jesus had followers. Jesus is often called "Rabbi" or "Teacher" in the Gospels, and his relationship to those around him was often in those roles. The Greek word for disciple (*mathētēs*) means "one who learns."

But as a fully human person with a fully human desire for companionship Jesus also needed, and had, friends. Like any other loving person, he likely had friends from his youth, people he knew from his boyhood and adolescence in Nazareth. As a young adult, he doubtless befriended fellow carpenters and local laborers. And during his public ministry, he enjoyed the friendship of those with whom he could relax, unwind, and perhaps talk about the challenges of his unique call.

Among his close friends during his public ministry were Mary, Martha, and Lazarus. The Gospels describe Jesus going at least twice to their house in Bethany, two miles east of Jerusalem. On one occasion, Martha and Mary host a dinner for Jesus, prompting Jesus's encouragement to the ever-busy Martha to relax and simply enjoy his company.[2] The second occasion for his visit to their house is far sadder. He goes to Bethany to comfort his friends after the death of their brother. It's a natural thing for a friend to do, but it would have consequences that even Jesus's closest friends could not have predicted. It will also be one of his last miracles, for after his time in Bethany Jesus will set his sights on Jerusalem for a final visit.

THE GOSPEL OF JOHN is traditionally divided into two parts, which Raymond Brown calls the Book of Signs (Chapters 1–12) and the Book of Glory (Chapters 13–21).[3] The Book of Glory includes the Last Supper; a series of long discourses in which Jesus speaks at length to the disciples; the arrest, trial, and Crucifixion; the death of Jesus; and the Resurrection. The Book of Signs focuses on Jesus's public ministry and the signs (*sēmeia*) he performs—his miracles. The last and greatest of these signs is the Raising of Lazarus.

John begins his story by saying that a "certain man" of Bethany, named Lazarus, is ailing. He is identified not only as the brother of Martha and of Mary, who had anointed Jesus's feet with perfume,[4] but with another lovely term. "He whom you love (*hon phileis*)" is ill, says the message from the man's sisters. It's a small but touching indication that Jesus and Lazarus must have been extremely close.

Strangely, after receiving word of his friend's illness, Jesus does not leave immediately for Bethany, but remains where he is for two more days. He tells the disciples that this sickness will not end in death, but "for God's glory."

The disciples must have been flummoxed by their master's response. Why would Jesus, who healed strangers, not rush (*euthus*) to the bedside of a good friend? Why would he actually *delay* going? It may have seemed heartless. Some commentators suggest that he wanted to ensure that Lazarus was truly dead in order to authenticate what he was about to do, what would be the greatest of his signs in John's Gospel.[5] Others say that Jesus may have wanted to demonstrate his freedom—he will go to the tomb when he wishes to. God acts when God acts. But as elsewhere in the Gospels, and especially in John, Jesus makes decisions that seem mysterious by human standards and that make sense only afterward, when the disciples reflect on his actions.

It also points out Jesus's existential aloneness. He is not without friends or without the comfort of his Father in prayer, but Jesus must make decisions on his own, choices that probably seem confusing, and, in this case, offensive to those around him. This is often true of all of us when we make truly free decisions.

Jesus is supremely free. But with this freedom comes loneliness. His struggles are compounded by the fact that he probably knows he is moving closer to the great test in Jerusalem. Perhaps he was wondering about this as he thought about his friend's death.

Two days later, he tells his disciples that he will return to Judea, where Bethany is located. "Our friend Lazarus," he tells them, "has fallen asleep, but I am going there to awaken him." As they often do, the disciples take him literally. If he's asleep, they say, he should be fine. "No," Jesus says plainly, "Lazarus is dead."

By the time Jesus arrives, Lazarus has been dead for four days, and many people have come to be with Mary and Martha in their time of mourning. The sisters' grief was doubtless compounded by the fact that, despite their entreaties, Jesus did not show up. The man they hoped would cure their brother didn't even bother to come.

When Martha hears that Jesus has finally come, she leaves her sister behind and rushes to meet him.

What was going through Martha's head as she ran? She was probably overjoyed at his arrival, after spending days longing for his consolation. If we remember how the crowds longed to spend time with Jesus, we already have a sense of his charisma. People wanted to be near him and wanted him near them. How much more would Martha have longed for him during her grief. All of us want friends near us in dark times.

But Martha may also have been confused, or angry. Elsewhere she is portrayed as the more practical sister, the active one who served the food for the earlier visit from Jesus, while her sister Mary was sitting at the master's feet. With a sharp tongue she asked Jesus to order her sister to help her serve. Now that Lazarus was dead, Martha's anger and confusion would not have been unwarranted over Jesus's seemingly inexcusable delay.

"Lord," she says upon meeting him, "if you had been here, my brother would not have died." Is she rebuking him or showing her faith? Perhaps both. Martha mirrors many of us in times of pain; we toggle between anger and hope, confusion and belief. In the depths of sadness it's sometimes hard to believe, much as we know we would like to, or should. Martha shows the entirely human struggle between fear and faith.

Then Martha softens. "But even now," she says, "I know that God will give you whatever you ask of him." Does she foresee what Jesus is about to do? Had she heard of his other miracles—the raising of the son of the widow of Nain or the raising of Jairus's daughter, both examples of restoration of life?[26] Either way, in the midst of her strong emotions, she gives voice to what people know about Jesus: he is a wonder-worker who can cure the sick.

Then Jesus offers her comfort. He tells her that her brother will rise again. Yes, says Martha, she knows that he will rise on the "last day," voicing a commonly held Jewish belief about the resurrection. But Jesus goes further, making an important statement in the midst of an emotion-filled day. "I am the resurrection and the life," he says. "Those who believe in me, even though they die, will live, and everyone who lives and believes in me will never die." Martha professes her faith in this and calls him the Son of God.

Martha is a fascinating figure in the Gospels. As I had mentioned, when Jesus dines at her house and her sister Mary sits at his feet, "listening to him speak," Martha complains bitterly. "Lord," she says, and you can imagine her bent over a stove saying this, "do you not care that my sister has left me by myself to do the serving?"[7] In that setting, as here, beside her brother's tomb, she is blunt. Martha can be seen, in a sense, as a kind of female counterpart to Peter: a strong, impetuous, and outspoken friend of Jesus, who believes even as she feels free to question. The memories of her retained in the Gospels are so vivid that she likely was a formidable figure in the early church. Martha's fierce honesty also reminds us that Jesus included strong women among his circle of friends.

At this point, Martha returns (we can imagine her rushing) to Mary, the quiet one, who sits in the house, and reports that Jesus has finally come. John's Gospel offers us two Greek words that bring to life their brief conversation. First, we are told that Martha spoke to Mary *lathra*—quietly or secretly.

When Martha returns home, she finds Mary surrounded by mourners. Often in the days surrounding a death—either beforehand at a hospital bed or afterward in a funeral parlor—one is enveloped by friends and family. In first-century Palestine, Martha and Mary's house would have been crowded with people; the rites surrounding Jewish burials were extensive and detailed and required help from the community. Expensive ointments and spices were often used to anoint the body; if the body were still in the house, eating meat and drinking wine were forbidden; and for the seven days following the death it was forbidden to engage in any kind of work. Attending to all the various funeral rites and consoling the survivors was a solemn duty of all friends and neighbors.

During those crowded moments, in the midst of the funeral preparations, it can be difficult to find quiet time with those closest to us. Important bits of news or small words of consolation are often relayed quietly, in the corners of rooms, outside hospital rooms, in backyards away from company. It is much the same for Lazarus's sisters. Martha speaks with her sister, quietly. It is a deeply human piece of storytelling in the Gospel and underlines the intimate relationship between the two sisters.

The word Martha uses to describe Jesus is also significant: *didaskalos,* or teacher. "The Teacher is here and is calling for you," she tells her sister. Earlier, when Martha encountered Jesus at the tomb, she referred to him as *kyrie,* Lord. Both titles show the esteem in which the sisters hold their dear friend.

Mary now rushes to meet Jesus. The contemplative one becomes active. She is joined by her friends, who by tradition would have taken every opportunity to mourn with her, as a sign of solidarity and affection. Unlike her sister, Mary is portrayed in somewhat more positive tones throughout this story. She kneels at Jesus's feet and echoes her sister's words, wishing that he had arrived earlier.

Jesus asks where the body is. Mary answers: "Lord, come and see." The next line in Greek is only three words: *Edakrusen ho Iēsous,* Jesus wept.

Some have surmised that this brief sentence means not that Jesus is weeping for Lazarus, but is upset because Mary has joined with her friends in mourning the loss of her brother and is thus showing her association with those who do not believe in him. He weeps, in the words of one scholar, because his message "will never be understood or accepted."[8]

That interpretation is supported by the fact that Mary's friends say, "Could not he who opened the eyes of the blind man have kept this man from dying?" Her friends are therefore—so goes this interpretation—presented unflatteringly, and Mary's affiliation with them viewed as undesirable. Bolstering this interpretation is the fact that immediately before he weeps, Jesus is described as "greatly disturbed in spirit." The Greek word is a strong one: *ebrimaomai* can mean frustrated or even angry and is sometimes used to describe a horse snorting.

I see things differently—and not simply because that is a negative way of portraying the Jewish faith of Martha and Mary. It seems more likely that Jesus weeps because he is sad. How could he not be? His tears are an unmistakable sign of his humanity and show his compassion for his friends. Were Jesus a stony-faced divinity untouched by emotions, he would have been unmoved, embodying the classic Greek understanding of a God characterized by *apatheia*. But Jesus is not untouched by suffering. He is not so detached that nothing moves him. The crowd notices. "See how he loved him!" they say.

Yes, see how he loved him. Once again, we should not underestimate the importance of friendship in Jesus's life. Not simply in his public ministry—in which he offers friendship to those on the margins and participates in "table fellowship," sharing food, with a wide variety of people—but in his private life as well. A careful reading of the Gospels shows that Jesus treasured people's company and enjoyed celebrating with them. It's easy to imagine Jesus spending time with Martha, Mary, and Lazarus at their home in Bethany, taking time off from the rigors of the road, perhaps sharing with them some of the loneliness of his ministry, and of course, since he was fully human and so were they, laughing.

But now, by the tomb, he weeps. Many of us know the pain of losing a close friend. Remember that Lazarus is called by the sisters *hon phileis,* he whom you love. Their friendship must have been deep. He may be weeping both for the loss of Lazarus and for the pain that his death has caused Mary and Martha.

On one retreat, I imagined Jesus breaking into tears after asking, "Where have you laid him?" and hearing the response, "Come and see." When you finally realize that someone has died, just a word is enough to push you over the edge, perhaps "coffin" or "body." In my prayer Jesus felt Mary's words to be unbearably poignant—"Come and see"—because he remembered how he first used them with his disciples, inviting them to taste new life. So he weeps.

John's Gospel invites us into an intimate moment with Jesus. His humanity is on full display. So is his divinity. He weeps, but he also publicly declares that he is "the resurrection and the life," and Mary affirms his divinity. The man who is proclaimed as divine shows compassion. God weeps for Lazarus.

When Jesus is brought to the tomb, he orders the stone to be taken away. At the time some of the tombs in the region consisted of a cave whose opening was covered by a stone that fit into a groove dug in the ground, so the stone could be rolled away. So the idea of "taking away the stone" fits with archaeological evidence; this kind of burial was widespread in first-century Palestine.[9] Many of the dead were buried in either a natural cave or a hole carved into the rocks, where there would be several shelves for bodies, each wrapped in linen, with the head and hands wrapped separately.

The practical Martha, however, protests. "Lord, already there is a stench because he has been dead four days." Why would Jesus want to open the tomb anyway? Martha might have thought that Jesus wanted one last look at Lazarus, "our friend."[10]

Martha's protests are entirely reasonable—she is concerned that if the tomb is opened, there will be a smell. Neither she nor the Gospel of John sugarcoats death. But notice something else: her inability (entirely understandable) to imagine something new, to look toward the future. Rather than anticipating something life-changing, she is concentrating on something small—the smell.

But let's not be too hard on Martha. She could not have known what Jesus was going to do. How could she? She had never seen anyone raised from the dead! By the same token, when Jesus asks that the stone be rolled away, Martha does not trust, but remonstrates with him. Her faith in God does not seem full. How often do we find ourselves focusing on the small problems (it will stink) or rehearsing past grievances (you're late) rather than trusting that God may bring about something new? She concentrates on the negative, on the privation, on the loss. Again, this is natural and human, but it prevents her from seeing the possibility of the new.

Undisturbed by Martha's protests, Jesus prays. "Father, I thank you for having heard me." Then he says in a loud voice, "Lazarus, come out!"

The dead man emerges from the tomb, wrapped head to toe in his burial clothes, before the dumbfounded and frightened onlookers. *Lusate auton,* says Jesus, *kai aphete auton hupagein.* "Unbind him, and let him go."

IT'S HARD FOR ME not to be overwhelmed by emotion even when writing about this passage. This is Jesus's supreme miracle, demonstrating the power of God over even death. Interestingly, John's Gospel says nothing about the reaction of the crowd. In other stories they are "amazed" or "astonished." Perhaps this is taken for granted.

How could they be anything *but* amazed and astonished? It is a stunning example of the life-giving word. Jesus's words literally give life to Lazarus.

As astonishing as this narrative is, it may be easy for us to identify with elements of the story. When Jesus decided to stay behind with the disciples rather than visit his sick friend, it must have seemed confusing to both the disciples and later to Martha and Mary. "What is he doing?" Who hasn't felt that God wasn't doing what God *should* be doing in a painful situation? When Mary falls at Jesus's feet and tells him that he should have come earlier and prevented so much suffering, it's easy to agree with her.

It's also hard not to think about the movies. No matter how many times I pray with this Gospel passage, I always think of my two favorite film depictions of this miracle.

In the 1977 miniseries *Jesus of Nazareth,* the director Franco Zeffirelli provides an almost word-for-word reproduction of the scene. Mary's lament about Jesus's absence is slow, heartfelt, gentle. "Lord . . . if you had been with us, our brother would not have died." Martha on the other hand, remonstrates with him about the stench. "His body must already be decaying," she says. Jesus leads the crowd down a sandy outcropping to the place of the tomb.

Then comes a close-up of Robert Powell, the British-born actor who plays Jesus, kneeling down before the tomb as he prays. He stands, lifts his arms, and shouts, "Lazarus, come *forth!*" The camera pans back and we see Jesus standing before the inky black opening of the tomb. Suddenly we see a small white figure emerge into the daylight to swelling music and hear the sounds of disbelief from the crowd. It's all terribly moving.

In *The Greatest Story Ever Told,* released in 1965, the director George Stevens handles the scene differently, particularly Jesus's words. The director gives us the widest shot possible, with the crowd peopling a hillside far below a tiny tomb hewn from the rock. Then we are in the tomb, as if we too are the dead, and we see the stone slowly being rolled away. Max von Sydow faces us and whispers,

"Lazarus." The camera pulls back, revealing more of the crowd, and we hear him say, more forcefully, "Lazarus." Then he shouts, "Come *forth!*" The music swells, and an even tinier figure in white suddenly appears at the entrance of the tomb. The dumbfounded disciples literally fall back in astonishment.

Why does Jesus shout? It is not a cinematic flourish; both films hew closely to what is described in the Gospels. John's Gospel says that Jesus spoke in a *phonē megalē,* a "great voice."[11] But why? Lazarus is dead and cannot hear. For a long time I wondered about that. Then something occurred to me about Jesus's voice.

EARLY IN MY JESUIT life, I often thought about the person I wanted to become, the person I hoped to be one day. Most of us have an image, even if it is an unconscious one, of the person we are meant to be: our true self, our best self. For some time I had thought about that person: independent, confident, loving, charitable, and not concerned about people's approval—in a word, free.

During my annual retreat one year, I mentioned all this to my retreat director, who recommended that I pray with the story of the Raising of Lazarus.

That evening, I had a revealing dream. I met my best self, whom I recognized instantly, in a dream that was so vivid, so beautiful, and so obvious that it woke me up. Now, I don't put stock in every dream, but sometimes, as in Scripture, dreams can be a privileged place where our consciousness relaxes and God is able to show us something in a fresh way. In my dream, my best self, oddly, looked like me, but wasn't me. My double seemed looser, easier, more relaxed; he even dressed in a more relaxed way!

I knew the direction I needed to travel to become a better person. But I was afraid of letting things go—a need to be liked, a propensity to focus on the negative, a desire to control things. It is precisely those kinds of unhealthy patterns, unendurable yet seemingly ineradicable, that need to die, that need to be left in the tomb.

From time to time, we need to ask, "What part of me needs to die?" For me, Lazarus's tomb became the place to leave behind whatever I no longer needed, whatever kept me from new life. For another person, what needs to die may be entirely different—an attitude of pride, a constant desire to be right, an inability to forgive, an overly cynical attitude toward life, a hatred of a particular person, anything that keeps that person from a full life.

As I prayed about Lazarus's tomb, I also imagined hearing Jesus's voice calling to *other* parts of me as well, those parts that desired new life, parts still open to the possibility of greater freedom. Some parts of us must die; other parts need to be revived. Some aspects of our lives are like dormant seeds, awaiting the sunshine of God's life-giving word. Maybe I've closed myself off to new relationships. Or I've decided not to look for love in my family. Or I've given up on finding a church that will nourish me. Sometimes the dead parts of ourselves are not meant to be dead.

But in order to experience new life, we have to listen for God— just as Lazarus did.

Often it seems that those dead parts are completely beyond the reach of God. That's probably how it seemed to Martha and Mary. Lazarus was dead. You can't get any deader than being in a tomb for four days and beginning to stink.[12] Many Jews of the time believed that the soul hovered around the body for three days, so Lazarus is meant to be seen in John's Gospel as dead in every conceivable way.[13]

But God's word can awaken anything.

On that retreat, I found it easy to imagine myself in the tomb—as Lazarus. Jesus placed his hand on the cold, dark, damp opening of the tomb and spoke to me in a whisper, the softest imaginable. It was a gentle sound, an inviting voice calling to the parts of me that wanted to live. In such tender ways does God speak to us.

Sometimes, however, God needs to speak more loudly. That's one way to look at Jesus's speaking in a "loud voice" in the story. God may need to get our attention—in a very blunt comment from a friend that prevents us from doing something sinful, in an intense prayer experience that floods us with peace, in a Bible passage that hits us like a thunderclap, or in a homily that seems tailor-made for us—so that the dead parts of us can *hear.*

Obviously, we don't hear God physically speaking to us as Jesus did to Lazarus. A few of the saints reported hearing a physical voice in prayer—it's called a "locution"—but this is exceedingly rare. Yet God calls to us in other ways and offers change in a variety of modes. Perhaps in your prayer you feel drawn to leading a more selfless life; perhaps when hearing a Bible passage read aloud you feel moved to be more generous; perhaps a conversation with a friend suddenly encourages you to think about forgiveness. God calls to us in whatever ways are needed to help us come forth from our tombs.

The family and friends of Lazarus seem so dumbfounded that Jesus has to tell them what to do: "Unbind him, and let him go." They don't know what to do with the newly alive Lazarus, just as our friends and family may not know what to do with us after we have responded to God's voice.

Jesus's final words in this story may hold another meaning too. "Unbind him, and let him go" is an invitation to all of us who are freed from old patterns and unhealthy behaviors. Untie him and let him be who he is *meant to be.* When I finished praying over the story years ago, that's how I felt: free to go wherever Jesus would take me.

BEFORE I COULD DO that, I had to confront my "stuckness." Let's consider some possible reasons that Martha is focused on the stench.

Mary and Martha may be focused on the past, on the impossibility of anything changing, and so are not as open to seeing what might lie before them. Remember, they had presumably heard (if not actually seen) Jesus do incredible things. There are several stories of Jesus raising people from the dead in the Gospels—like the raising of Jairus's daughter, recounted in all three of the Synoptic Gospels.[14] Of all people, Martha and Mary would have known these stories.

But they seemed focused on the status quo. "Look, Jesus," they seem to be saying, "this is simply the way of the world."

Offered the opportunity to change, we often focus on the possible pitfalls. Offered possibility, we often focus on the impossibility. Martha is worried, as she was before when she complained about Mary not helping her, about something other than God.

Or we may simply be afraid of the change. During that retreat I wondered, *If I let go of some of these old habits, what will people think? Will they see me as trying to be something I'm not? Will I be able to live in a new way?*

Then I realized how foolish those fears were. Why focus on these things—people's opinions, worries about the future, concerns about change? Suddenly I wanted to say to Martha, "You're worried about the smell? Just look beside you: it's Jesus! Surrender yourself to what he is about to do, and stop focusing on the smell."

But that may be unfair to Martha. I would have probably said the same thing, smelling the old and fearful of the new. Moreover, when Jesus asks Martha a direct question about her belief—"I am the resurrection and the life. Those who believe in me, even though they die, will live, and everyone who lives and believes in me will never die. Do you believe this?"—Martha responds, clearly, "Yes, Lord, I believe that you are the Messiah, the Son of God, the one coming into the world." Like most of us, Martha grapples with both faith ("Yes, I believe") and doubt, or at least confusion ("There is a stench").

Jesus, however, fears nothing. So the stone is rolled away and something else astonishing happens, accompanying the miracle of Lazarus's return from the dead. God sweeps away Martha's worries and most likely her friends' anxieties and replaces their despair with hope.

"UNBIND HIM, AND LET him go," says Jesus. It's not only a spiritual message, but also a practical one, addressed to Martha and Mary, who were probably paralyzed with shock: "Take off his bandages." Jesus is gently telling them how to help Lazarus.

The image of Jesus inviting the removal of bandages had great resonance with me. During that retreat I was worried about leaving behind what Thomas Merton called the "false self," the image that we want to present to the world, not the person who we are before God. The false self is the person we want others to see—on top of the situation, in control, cool. Merton uses the very image of bandages when talking about the false self in his book *New Seeds of Contemplation:*

> Thus I use up my life in the desire for pleasures and the thirst for experiences, for power, honor, knowledge and love, to clothe this false self and construct its nothingness into something objectively real. And I wind experiences around myself and cover myself with pleasures and glory like bandages in order to make myself perceptible to myself and to the world, as if I were an invisible body that could only become visible when something visible covered its surface.[15]

Once I realized how centered on the past I had been and how needlessly worried I was about stepping out of the tomb, I was ready to embrace new life. I wanted to leave the bandages of the false self in the tomb and step into the light.

THAT DAY IN BETHANY, I peered into the dimly lit tomb and tentatively started my climb down the stairs. When I imagined this pilgrimage, I had expected that the Tomb of Lazarus, the site of Jesus's greatest miracle, would be one of the most crowded of sites. But I was alone.

Even lit, the narrow stone stairwell was dim. As I descended, my footsteps echoed against the damp walls. In a few seconds I was in a small chamber, where there was barely enough room to stand. Perhaps, I thought, this was the tomb. But on one side of the room, cut into the wall was a small opening near the ground, perhaps three feet wide by four feet high. This opening led into another chamber: the tomb. To enter I had to get down on my hands and knees and crawl through the tight space.

Standing up in the small, dark, grayish-green stone tomb, I wondered what it was like for Lazarus to hear Jesus's voice. What must it have meant to decide to "come out"? Lazarus could have stayed behind. And who could blame him? How frightening it must have been to die (after his illness, knowing he would leave behind two unmarried sisters, crushed that his good friend Jesus had not visited). And frightening to live again. Change of any kind can be frightening.

I knelt down again in the tomb and prayed out loud. No need to be embarrassed now. Who would hear me except God? I asked God to take away everything that kept me from becoming the person God wanted me to be. And I asked God for new life.

My voice echoed in the dim stone chamber.

Then I left the tomb.

THE RAISING OF LAZARUS
John 11:1–44

Now a certain man was ill, Lazarus of Bethany, the village of Mary and her sister Martha. Mary was the one who anointed the Lord with perfume and wiped his feet with her hair; her brother Lazarus was ill. So the sisters sent a message to Jesus, "Lord, he whom you love is ill." But when Jesus heard it, he said, "This illness does not lead to death; rather it is for God's glory, so that the Son of God may be glorified through it." Accordingly, though Jesus loved Martha and her sister and Lazarus, after having heard that Lazarus was ill, he stayed two days longer in the place where he was.

Then after this he said to the disciples, "Let us go to Judea again." The disciples said to him, "Rabbi, the Jews were just now trying to stone you, and are you going there again?" Jesus answered, "Are there not twelve hours of daylight? Those who walk during the day do not stumble, because they see the light of this world. But those who walk at night stumble, because the light is not in them." After saying this, he told them, "Our friend Lazarus has fallen asleep, but I am going there to awaken him." The disciples said to him, "Lord, if he has fallen asleep, he will be all right." Jesus, however, had been speaking about his death, but they thought that he was referring merely to sleep. Then Jesus told them plainly, "Lazarus is dead. For your sake I am glad I was not there, so that you may believe. But let us go to him." Thomas, who was called the Twin, said to his fellow disciples, "Let us also go, that we may die with him."

When Jesus arrived, he found that Lazarus had already been in the tomb four days. Now Bethany was near Jerusalem, some two miles away, and many of the Jews had come to Martha and Mary to console them about their brother. When Martha heard that Jesus was coming, she went and met him, while Mary stayed at home. Martha said to Jesus, "Lord, if you had been here, my brother would not have died. But even now I know that God will give you whatever you ask of him." Jesus said to her, "Your brother will rise again." Martha said to him, "I know that he will rise again in the resurrection on the last day." Jesus said to her, "I am the resurrection and the life. Those who believe in me, even though they die, will live, and everyone who lives and believes in me will never die. Do you believe this?" She said to him, "Yes, Lord, I believe that you are the Messiah, the Son of God, the one coming into the world."

When she had said this, she went back and called her sister

Mary, and told her privately, "The Teacher is here and is calling for you." And when she heard it, she got up quickly and went to him. Now Jesus had not yet come to the village, but was still at the place where Martha had met him. The Jews who were with her in the house, consoling her, saw Mary get up quickly and go out. They followed her because they thought that she was going to the tomb to weep there. When Mary came where Jesus was and saw him, she knelt at his feet and said to him, "Lord, if you had been here, my brother would not have died." When Jesus saw her weeping, and the Jews who came with her also weeping, he was greatly disturbed in spirit and deeply moved. He said, "Where have you laid him?" They said to him, "Lord, come and see." Jesus began to weep. So the Jews said, "See how he loved him!" But some of them said, "Could not he who opened the eyes of the blind man have kept this man from dying?"

Then Jesus, again greatly disturbed, came to the tomb. It was a cave, and a stone was lying against it. Jesus said, "Take away the stone." Martha, the sister of the dead man, said to him, "Lord, already there is a stench because he has been dead four days." Jesus said to her, "Did I not tell you that if you believed, you would see the glory of God?" So they took away the stone. And Jesus looked upwards and said, "Father, I thank you for having heard me. I knew that you always hear me, but I have said this for the sake of the crowd standing here, so that they may believe that you sent me." When he had said this, he cried with a loud voice, "Lazarus, come out!" The dead man came out, his hands and feet bound with strips of cloth, and his face wrapped in a cloth. Jesus said to them, "Unbind him, and let him go."

CHAPTER 19

Jerusalem

*"Then he poured water into a basin and began
to wash the disciples' feet."*

BEGINNING OUR PILGRIMAGE IN Jerusalem meant that the trip
would start where Jesus's earthly life ended. Before leaving the States
I briefly considered avoiding the sites associated with Jesus's Passion,
death, and resurrection until after we visited Bethlehem, Nazareth,
and all the sites in Galilee. In this way George and I might trace Jesus's life in sequence. But as soon as Father Doan told me that the
Church of the Holy Sepulchre was just a few minutes away from our
residence, there was no question of waiting. I could no more resist its
pull than iron filings can resist a magnet.

So around four o'clock on the first afternoon, George and I left
our digs at the Pontifical Biblical Institute, swung open the iron gate
that enclosed the Jesuit residence, turned left, and walked a mile
downhill. After passing through the grounds of a tony apartment
complex, we spied the magnificent cream-colored ramparts of the
Old City.

After dodging cars on a busy street, we strode up the steep hill
to the imposing Jaffa Gate, one of the Old City's eight entrances,
which is flanked by two crenellated towers. As we climbed I understood why pilgrims were said to "go up" to Jerusalem. One of my favorite psalms came back to me:

I was glad when they said to me,
   "Let us go to the house of the Lord!" . . .
Jerusalem—built as a city
   that is bound firmly together.
To it the tribes go up,
   the tribes of the Lord.[1]

And I remembered a favorite line from Thomas Merton's *The Sign of Jonas,* the journal of his first years in a Trappist monastery. After Merton complained about having to chant the psalms several times daily, his abbot offered the new monk some advice. "He said," writes Merton, "I should think of Jesus going up to Jerusalem with all the pilgrims roaring psalms out of their dusty throats."[2]

Stepping onto the worn, almost glassy, paving stones of the Old City meant entering a jumble of places relating to the trial, crucifixion, and resurrection of Jesus. In these next three chapters, we'll look at the story of Jesus's "Passion" (the term comes from the Greek *paschō,* to suffer or to experience) through the lens of a visit to several sites in the Old City, some of them separated by only a few steps.

Before meditating on the last days in Jesus's life, let me offer the briefest of overviews of the events that led to his crucifixion, starting the day before Palm Sunday and ending with Good Friday. At this point it won't surprise the reader that the Gospels don't always agree on all the events of Holy Week. But, overall, the accounts of Jesus's last week follow the same general sequence.

On Saturday, around the time of Passover, after Jesus had raised Lazarus from the dead, he spends time with Mary, Martha, and Lazarus at their home in Bethany, just over the Mount of Olives from Jerusalem. That night Mary breaks open a jar of costly ointment and anoints Jesus as a sign of his impending death. The Gospels of Matthew and Mark place this scene in the home of "Simon the leper."[3] If that is accurate, it means that even as he neared death, Jesus was spending time with those on the margins.

On Sunday, Jesus rides in triumph into Jerusalem, on a small colt that he has apparently instructed his disciples to reserve for him. Enthusiastic crowds blanket the streets of the holy city with their cloaks and with palm branches, the latter a traditional sign of celebration in Jewish circles and triumph in Roman ones. The colt is a sign as well, alluding to a passage from Zechariah, in which the "king" enters the city on just such an animal.[4] At this time, the city would have been thronged with pilgrims for the holidays.

The next day Jesus enters the Temple precinct and overturns the tables of the merchants, appalled by their doing business in "my Father's House." The Cleansing of the Temple, along with the Raising of Lazarus, is most likely a precipitating factor in his death.

According to some Gospel narratives, on Tuesday Jesus preaches in Jerusalem. At this point in various Gospels, we find Jesus preaching the parables of the Rejected Stone, the Wedding Feast, the Talents, and the Sheep and the Goats; Jesus also answers questions about his ultimate authority. On the same day Judas Iscariot, one of the apostles, bargains with some Jewish authorities to betray Jesus. Wednesday seems to have been a time of rest for Jesus in Bethany and perhaps an opportunity to plan for the momentous days to come.

On Thursday, after Jesus washes the feet of the disciples in a large room in Jerusalem, the location of which he has apparently prearranged, he celebrates a Passover meal with them, the Last Supper. During the meal, after Judas leaves to carry out his betrayal, Jesus offers a long discourse, or passage of preaching (at least in John's Gospel). Jesus and the disciples visit the Garden of Gethsemane, located just outside the city walls, where he prays for guidance, is confronted by Judas, and is captured by the Roman authorities. This sets in motion his execution.

Friday's complex timetable is the source of some scholarly debate and the basis for the most serious of questions: Who was responsible for Jesus's death? The most straightforward answer comes from Father Harrington: "Pontius Pilate, with some cooperation from some Jewish leaders in Jerusalem."⁵ The day will include (again, depending on the Gospel) Jewish trials—before Annas, Caiaphas (two "high priests"), and the Sanhedrin (the Jewish assembly or council)—and Roman trials—before Pontius Pilate, Herod, and Pilate again. After his condemnation and torture at the hands of Roman soldiers, Jesus starts his long walk to the hill known as Golgotha (Aramaic for "Place of the Skull"; in Latin, *Calvaria*), where he is crucified and hangs agonizingly on the cross, uttering a few final sentences. Jesus of Nazareth dies around three o'clock in the afternoon. Later his body is removed from the cross and laid in a tomb provided by a friend.

After spending so much time with Jesus in his ministry in Galilee, such a shorthand description of his painful death may seem shocking to readers. Cold, even heartless. I felt the same way after I returned from four days in Galilee, after tracing the path of the energetic Jesus in his public ministry—preaching, walking, healing, dining, sailing, exorcising—and walking into the chapel at the Pontifical Biblical Institute. Kneeling down on the chapel's terrazzo floor, I closed my eyes to pray for a few seconds, then looked up and saw Jesus on the wall, crucified.

On a large wooden crucifix outlined in gold, Jesus hung, peering down at his mother, Mary, who stood by him, mourning. Jesus inclined his head toward her with a look of infinite sadness. Here was the lively, active, joyful person I had spent so much time with, nailed to a cross, dying. It was shocking.

THE SHOCK OF THE disciples was infinitely greater. For in the space of less than a week Jesus's friends move from elation over his triumphant entrance into the city, when they may have anticipated his being acclaimed as king, to despair over his shameful death. And although Jesus seems to have known, even predicted, his end, the disciples, as they have before, seem not to have understood what was awaiting them in Jerusalem.

There were predictions throughout the Gospels. As early as the eighth chapter of Mark's Gospel, shortly after the Feeding of the Four Thousand, while the disciples are on their way to Jerusalem, Jesus asks them, "Who do people say that I am?"[6] A surprising question for the disciples—and the one that began this book.

It seems to catch them off guard. They offer their answers: John the Baptist, Elijah, or "one of the prophets."[7] The responses are not unexpected. Jesus had been baptized by John and most likely brought some of John's followers under his wing, so the identification with the Baptist is natural. And the Book of Malachi refers to the coming of Elijah as the forerunner of the "great and terrible day of the Lord."[8]

Then Peter, either divinely inspired or simply intuiting who it must be who has fed four thousand people, says, "You are the Messiah." Mark has Peter refer to Jesus as *Christos,* in Greek, "the anointed one" (*Mashiach* in Hebrew), likening him to the priests, prophets, and kings of the Old Testament who were anointed with oil as a symbol of their divinely ordained roles. During this period, one prominent form of messianism placed its hopes in a "Davidic king who would restore justice and the good fortunes of God's people."[9] Such a messiah would therefore pose a threat to the Roman rulers. In light of what Jesus said and did, it was, as Donahue and Harrington explain, "likely that some people did identify Jesus as such a messiah."[10] In other words, if Peter believes in Jesus's messiahship, others probably do as well. Thus, Mark's readers are not surprised when Jesus tells the disciples not to share this revelation with anyone; it would have been dangerous to do so.

But Mark's early readers may have been as surprised as the disciples by what Jesus offers next—a prediction of suffering: "The Son of Man must undergo great suffering, and be rejected by the elders, the chief priests, and the scribes, and be killed, and after three days rise again." Mark notes, "He said all this quite openly."[11] Peter takes him aside and privately "rebukes him," a harsh phrase indicating Peter's strong emotional rejection of this prediction.

Why does Peter rebuke Jesus? Perhaps Peter holds out hope that the Davidic king will fulfill Jewish expectations by not only restoring Israel's fortunes and ushering in an era of peace, but also kicking out the Roman overlords. Or perhaps Peter simply doesn't want his good friend to suffer. In contemporary parlance, Peter may be saying, "God forbid!"

Whatever the reasons, Jesus will have none of it. Looking at his disciples he says, publicly, so as to teach the group: "Get behind me, Satan! For you are setting your mind not on divine things but on human things."[12]

Jesus is not saying that Peter is Satan. Rather, he recognizes that Peter is giving voice to the temptation to reject reality. Jesus recognizes this voice. It is an echo of the voice that he heard once in the desert: an appeal to self-interest and pride. Again, God forbid you should suffer!

While Jesus's words here offer some rich theological insights about the inevitable role of suffering in the Christian life, let's focus on a related question: Did Jesus accurately predict his execution? Mark is writing roughly forty years (around AD 70) after the death of Jesus, and so he may have added some details. But even if one wonders whether Jesus had perfect foreknowledge, it is easy to understand how he could have predicted his own violent end. For one thing, he knew the fate of the prophets who preceded him. For another, he faced opposition from some religious leaders throughout his days of preaching and healing, from as early as the Rejection in Nazareth.

Moreover, Jesus understood that his actions—which included breaking or at least setting aside ritual laws (like working on the Sabbath), excoriating religious authorities for hypocrisy, and gathering around him those who believed that he was the Messiah—would set him up on a collision course whose end would most likely be in Jerusalem. This may be one reason why he didn't headquarter his ministry there. Galilee may have bought him time for preaching and healing.

Others seem to have intuited his impending death as well. A few days before Passover, a woman (identified as Mary of Bethany in John's Gospel) breaks open an "alabaster jar of very costly ointment of nard," used for many occasions but also for anointing the dead.[13] She anoints his feet (in Mark, his head) and dries them with her hair in a gesture that is at once lavish, compassionate, and tender. It is also a gesture that scandalizes Judas, who complains that the money could have been put to better use for the poor.

Was she anointing him as king or as a person who was about to die? Perhaps both.

Surely by the time Jesus begins this last series of public acts in Jerusalem—entering the city in triumph (with what the theologian Gerald O'Collins calls its "perceived messianic significance") and cleansing the temple, he knows that he's bound to provoke a confrontation. O'Collins says that Jesus understood that the action in the Temple would be "dangerously provocative and could precipitate his death."[14]

The night before his assassination, the Reverend Dr. Martin Luther King, Jr., told his supporters:

> We've got some difficult days ahead. But it doesn't really matter with me now. Because I've been to the mountaintop. I don't mind. Like anybody, I would like to live—a long life; longevity has its place. But I'm not concerned about that now. I just want to do God's will. And He's allowed me to go up to the mountain. And I've looked over. And I've seen the Promised Land. I may not get there with you. But I want you to know tonight, that we, as a people, will get to the Promised Land.[15]

"I may not get there with you." Rev. King understood that his ministry had brought him opposition.

Jesus also knew how to read the signs of the times. So when I think of him allowing Mary to anoint him, entering Jerusalem on Palm Sunday, and then moving through the actions of what Christians call Holy Week, I imagine him doing so with an awareness of his impending death. But among all of the important events of the final week of Jesus's life, let me focus on one that has always captivated me, one that occurs in a place called the Cenacle.

WHEN I WAS A Jesuit novice, a Catholic sister called the novitiate to leave a message for one of the priests. I wrote down the particulars as best I could. Later in the day, David, the assistant novice director, came to me, chuckling. "What does this say?" he asked, holding up my note.

"It's the name of that sister who called you."

"And where was she from?" he said, smiling.

"Senegal," I said. "Is she visiting from Africa?"

"Not Senegal," David said, laughing. "She's a *Cenacle* Sister."

"Oh," I said. "What's that?" Not having grown up in a religious milieu, I had many such conversations during my first year as a Jesuit, in which I was forced to confess ignorance of one or another aspect of Catholicism—such as the names of the various (and many) religious orders.

"It's a women's religious order named after the Cenacle," said David.

"Uh huh," I said. That didn't help. "What's the Cenacle?"

David explained that the Cenacle (from the Latin *cenaculum,* which derives from *cena,* or dinner) is where the Last Supper was held. Sometimes called the Upper Room, it was the locus of several other events in the New Testament, including some of the Resurrection appearances and perhaps the descent of the Holy Spirit upon the disciples at Pentecost, which followed the Resurrection.[16] The room was also where the apostles later lodged while in Jerusalem, as described in the Acts of the Apostles; it was a natural gathering place considering the remarkable events that had occurred there.

The tradition of the Upper Room begins in the Gospels, when Jesus tells the disciples to prepare for a Passover meal and indicates the person with whom he has made arrangements: "He will show you a large room upstairs, already furnished. Make preparations for us there."[17] (The Greek *anagaion mega* is a large, above-ground room.) Until recently I assumed that the passages in which Jesus tells the disciples to meet a particular man who will show them a room or to procure for him a "colt that has never been ridden" were signs of his foreknowledge—that is, he was somehow predicting these things. That is certainly possible. Also possible is that Jesus arranged these preparations himself and was asking the disciples to carry out his plans.

Before our pilgrimage, I imagined the Upper Room as an ancient, decrepit, poorly lit space, where the disciples cowered behind closed doors after the Crucifixion. The actual appearance proved different. Today the Cenacle is located in a nondescript structure that is part of a complex of interlocking buildings on Mount Zion, in the southern part of the Old City. It is near Dormition Abbey, a Benedictine monastery built on the site where Mary "fell asleep," that is, exited this world peacefully.[18] Abutting the Cenacle is the Tomb of David. You ascend a metal staircase to reach the Cenacle, a large, airy room with a plain stone floor, whose high vaulted ceiling is supported by several handsome Gothic pillars. It seemed more like a chapel than a dining room. Open windows allow the strong, clear Jerusalem light to stream into the room, lending a pleasant feel.

The room, or its antecedent, finds its origins in the earliest days of the church, when the space may have served as a synagogue for Jewish Christians. In the fourth century, the emperor Theodosius built a modest church there, which was enlarged in the next century. That building was destroyed by waves of invaders over the next few centuries, and in the Middle Ages Crusaders erected another church on the site. The current room dates from roughly the fourteenth century, which explains the Gothic-era columns. At one point the room served as a mosque.[19] Jerome Murphy-O'Connor believes that a better tradition may locate the events of Pentecost within this room, but concludes that the tradition that relates it to the Last Supper is "unreliable."[20]

An odd tableau greeted George and me in the Upper Room. Near the entrance a dozen Korean tourists were softly singing a haunting hymn. On the far end of the room an Italian priest was speaking loudly, shouting really, and gesticulating as two pilgrims listened. Reading from an Italian Bible, he declaimed the story of the Last Supper. Finally, on one of a series of benches sat a man and a woman with their heads bowed, apparently trying to pray. The more the Korean pilgrims sang, the louder the Italian priest shouted, *"Questo è il mio corpo! Il quale è data per voi! Fate questo in memoria di me!"* The more he bellowed, the more the two in the pews buried their heads in their hands. The man trying to pray covered his ears. George rolled his eyes eloquently.

After the Korean pilgrims finished singing and the Italian priest finished his shouting, everyone filed out.

When we sat down to pray, I wondered, as I often did, if what was supposed to have happened here did happen here. "Unreliable," said Murphy-O'Connor about the Cenacle, but it's likely that the room that Jesus asked his disciples to locate was somewhere nearby.

The Italian priest had been shouting the words that Jesus used at the Last Supper as he sat among his disciples: "This is my body, which is given for you. Do this in remembrance of me." (Though I doubt Jesus said it so loudly.) It is this action that many pilgrims recall when they visit the Cenacle. And a few months before this pilgrimage my understanding of these words had changed, during a Mass I celebrated at a Jesuit church in New York.

PREVIOUSLY I HAD THOUGHT of those words mainly in a theological sense. "Transubstantiation," which refers to the Catholic belief that the bread and wine become the body and blood of Christ during the celebration of the Mass, is a mystery, something to be pondered rather than solved. The concept is difficult even for longtime Catholics to understand. And while I wholeheartedly believe it, I could not adequately explain it here.[21]

A Jesuit friend told me that his parish's director of religious education once expressed concerns about a boy who was about to make his First Holy Communion. She didn't think that he should participate in the sacrament. "Why not?" asked my friend.

"He's not the brightest boy in the class, and I don't think he fully understands the mystery of the Eucharist," she said.

"Do *you* fully understand the mystery of the Eucharist?" my friend asked her. Point taken. The boy made his First Communion with his classmates.

Until recently I thought of the Eucharist in primarily two ways. First, it is the culmination of all of Jesus's feeding miracles, like the Multiplication of the Loaves and Fishes and the Wedding Feast at Cana, where Jesus turned water into wine.[22] No longer does Jesus give food or drink—he gives himself. I've always liked that progression: from water and wine, to loaves and fishes, to himself.

Second, I often recall the image of the Body of Christ. In one of the most beautiful metaphors for the church, St. Paul referred to the followers of Christ as a body in which each "member" is valuable.[23] Just as the hand and eye and arm play their parts, everyone contributes to the body that is the church. Paul's image reminds us not only that we are part of a body, but that everyone's gifts contribute uniquely to the whole. The church, then, is often called the Mystical Body of Christ. In the Eucharist Jesus offers his body to the body that is the church. He desires to be with us so intimately that he gives himself as simple food. Whenever I receive the Eucharist or distribute it during a Mass, I always remember what St. Augustine, the fourth-century theologian, wrote about the Eucharist: "Behold what you are; become what you receive."

A few hours before my seven-year-old nephew Matthew received his First Communion, I asked him, "So, Matthew, what do you know about the Eucharist?"

He said, "Um, Jesus loved us so much that he turned himself into bread. And he wanted to be so close to us that he goes inside of us so we can know that he's always with us." Not bad.

Not everyone reading this book is Catholic, so this might not be a part of your faith. But I usually think of the Eucharist in such overtly theological terms: This bread is now become Christ's body; this wine is now become his blood. Take and eat, Jesus says, as a way of participating in me. Let me nourish you with myself. As I said, theological.

One Sunday, though, as I held up the host and said the words, "Take this and eat of it, this is my body," I had an insight. Jesus offered his body for us not simply at the Last Supper, and not simply in the Eucharist, but in a more ordinary way. In a very human, less mysterious, but no less profound way.

At that Mass I remembered how Jesus had taken his body all over Galilee and Judea for us. God entered our world as a human being, in the body of an infant who was hungry and thirsty, who was at times sick and feverish, and who felt pain and discomfort. When Jesus was growing up, his body underwent all the physical changes that any adolescent body does. And especially during Jesus's public ministry, his offering of his body was made visible: the Gospels speak frequently of his walking, climbing, sailing.

Think of all the places Jesus took his body. Even confining ourselves to the sites mentioned in the Gospels, we know that he walked from Nazareth to Capernaum. He visited places around the Sea of Galilee: Bethsaida, Gerasa, Tabgha. He traveled to Bethany and Jericho and Cana. He went to the region of Tyre and Sidon and to Caesarea Philippi. In all likelihood he went to places not mentioned in the Gospels (Sepphoris, for example). During his time of preparation he took his body into the harsh Judean desert. This took its toll. We know Jesus grew tired because he falls dead asleep in the boat during a howling storm. At times he no doubt went without sleep: "The Son of Man has nowhere to lay his head," he said.[24]

When I lifted the host, I realized that Jesus *took* his body to so many places; he *gave* his body to people, physically. He *brought* himself to people—saying, in essence, "This is my body. Here I am." It helped me think of the familiar words "This is my body" in a new light.

Jesus also offered himself to and for God the Father—as well as for imperfect disciples and followers who, during his Passion, denied and betrayed their friend. You cannot get more imperfect than that. Jesus's generosity did not depend on people's appreciation. These two ways of offering himself—by going where people needed him and by offering his actions for imperfect followers—were united at the Crucifixion, when he offered his entire body for an imperfect humanity.

We are called to give of ourselves as Jesus did. To bring our bodies—ourselves—to places where we are needed: at home in a delicate family situation, in a hospital beside the bed of a dying friend, at work listening to a troubled coworker. But it can be difficult. Selflessness costs because we are always giving for an imperfect person or group; the gift may not be appreciated or even acknowledged. A few years ago I read about a young gay man who was studying theology in preparation for work in the Catholic church. At times he felt unwelcome in the church (for a variety of reasons), but he compared his situation to a family you love even though you occasionally disagree with them and even though they occasionally don't understand you. He gave of himself generously anyway.

Think of parents bringing up children who afford them little respect, disobey them, or are overtly rude. Think of men and women striving to love husbands or wives who are sullen, uncommunicative, or mean. Think of children caring for aging parents who have turned truculent. A friend told me that shortly after his father had developed Alzheimer's disease, he became astonishingly callous. "Shut up!" he would say to the son who was caring for him. "I *hate* you!" It's hard to give yourself, to say in all these situations, "This is my body (energy, emotion, strength), given for you."

Two things that strengthened Jesus can strengthen us. First, Jesus did this for God the Father. God sees our hidden sacrifices and knows their cost, even when others don't. Second, with this kind of radical self-gift can come new life. We give not because Christianity is a masochistic religion, but because it is a way of love and a path to life. Jesus's death on the Cross led to an outpouring of love and an explosion of new life.

So Jesus says, "Do this in memory of me," not simply to the priest who celebrates Mass, but to all who would give their own lives out of love.

As I SAT ON the bench in the Cenacle I thought of something else Jesus did during the Last Supper, and something that happened to me earlier. The day before, while scouting around for the Cenacle, I chanced upon a room on the floor below. A sign on the wall read "The Room of the Washing of the Feet."

When I poked my head into the cramped, dark room, an elderly man greeted me and told me that Jesus washed the disciples' feet here, directly below the Cenacle. I didn't want to offend him by saying that (a) I had never heard of such a place and (b) neither had any of my guidebooks. After parting with a few shekels, I was shown a cistern in the floor. He yanked up a bucket of water on a rope from what looked like a considerable depth. "Wash," he said. So I plunged my hands into the cold water. "That," he said triumphantly, "is the water that Jesus used during the Last Supper!"

After I returned to the States I found no mention of this holy site in any guidebook. So I e-mailed my Jesuit friend David, back in Jerusalem, for an answer. He promised to reconnoiter. A few days later he wrote back, "I found the place, just at the entrance, on the right-hand side as you go into the compound of David's Tomb. The man smiled when I asked about the washing of the feet (I think he had heard it before) and said that it was nonsense. The place, he said, is a ritual washing place for Jews who want to pray at David's Tomb." A *mikvah,* then. Whoever was there that day had told me the opposite. I suppose he could tell a tourist from a local.

But that fake site led to some real emotions. When I plunged my hands into the cold water, I thought of a friend who during theology studies wrote his master's thesis on Jesus's washing the feet of the disciples. At the time I thought, *The Washing of the Feet? What an odd topic. What about the Last Supper, the institution of the Eucharist, which is more important?* But the longer I live the more I wonder how different the church would be if we spent as much time thinking about the Washing of the Feet as we do about Transubstantiation.

THE STORY APPEARS ONLY in the Gospel of John, where it serves as the beginning of the Passion narrative. We haven't spent as much time with the Gospel of John as we have with the Synoptic Gospels. John wrote his story of Jesus later than the Synoptic authors— around AD 100—for a group of Jewish Christians in the process of distancing themselves from Jewish synagogues. As we've seen, John sometimes sets up a dichotomy between the followers of Christ and, to use a shorthand, "the Jews."

If you read the Synoptics first and then come upon John's Gospel, you're in for a surprise: Jesus seems quite different. In the Synoptics Jesus is an earthy and sometimes excitable preacher and healer; in John he often seems a calm and imperturbable sage, the oracle. Some of the long discourses, particularly those after the Last Supper, which in even a small-print Bible can run for several pages, contrast with the fast-paced stories in the Synoptics, where everything seems to happen "immediately." In John, one is privileged to see more easily the divine side of Jesus, which is revealed even in his choice of words. Here, for example, is a brief passage from one of the farewell discourses at the Last Supper:

> Father, the hour has come; glorify your Son so that the Son may glorify you, since you have given him authority over all people, to give eternal life to all whom you have given him. And this is eternal life, that they may know you, the only true God, and Jesus Christ whom you have sent. I glorified you on earth by finishing the work that you gave me to do. So now, Father, glorify me in your own presence with the glory that I had in your presence before the world existed.[25]

That doesn't sound much like the carpenter from Nazareth.

Such high-flown theological disquisitions may distance a few people from the Gospel of John. On the other hand, many Christians prefer John, even love John. But the question remains: Why does Jesus sound so different in this Gospel? Mainly because John is writing after the Synoptic authors, for a different audience, is thus emphasizing a different aspect of Jesus, and often draws on different oral traditions. Most likely Jesus did not give an hour-long oration to his followers at the Last Supper. John is probably compressing several talks and perhaps fleshing things out. But then again, who knows? Maybe at his last meal Jesus did sum up things at length for fearful disciples desperate for some comfort.

For me, John is slower than the fast-paced Synoptics. I prefer texts written closer to the actual events, so I prefer the Synoptics, especially Mark. As many believers do, I sometimes find myself comparing the Synoptic Jesus with the "Johannine" Jesus.

But many parts of John I treasure, and as central as the Synoptics' account of the bread and the wine is to my spirituality, I find myself returning in prayer to John's version of the Last Supper, for he begins the second half of his Gospel with a startling portrait of humble service.

JOHN SITUATES THE STORY slightly earlier than the Synoptics do: "Now before the festival of the Passover," he begins. At the Last

Supper, he tells us, Jesus "knew that his hour had come." At this point Judas has already decided to betray Jesus. Again, John portrays Jesus in command, possessing full knowledge of what is about to happen. The supper in John is not, strictly speaking, a Passover meal: it lacks the paschal lamb. In John there is also no focus on the familiar bread and wine.[26] And in John's account, before the meal, Jesus does something striking.

He takes off or "lays aside" his outer robe, ties a towel around himself, pours water into a basin, washes the disciples' feet, and wipes them with the towel. At the time, foot washing was seen as a mark of hospitality, but also a menial task often performed by slaves to welcome a dignitary hosted by the slave's master.[27] To the disciples it would have been an unmistakable demonstration of humility, something an inferior would do for a superior. Raymond Brown calls it a "loving act of abasement."[28]

Jesus's odd gesture offers the disciples a symbol of service and self-gift, prefiguring the total act of service and self-gift that comes with his death. Indeed, the Greek used for Jesus's "laying aside" (*tithēsin*) his outer robe is the same used—several times—when Jesus earlier speaks of himself as the Good Shepherd who "lays down" his life for his flock.[29] Jesus lays *everything* down for others in service to God—his outer garment and, then, his inner garment: his body.

You don't need to know any Greek to anticipate the disciples' shock: their master is acting like a servant, a slave. According to Gerhard Lohfink, it was also the opposite of the custom of students of the day. Rabbinic traditions list forty-eight ways through which knowledge of the Torah is acquired; one is "serving the wise," which Lohfink calls "a very beautiful and moving tradition" of providing personal service for the rabbis. Among these duties are serving at table, cleaning house, and washing the feet.[30] Thus, the normal expectations are upended once again by Jesus.

When he approaches Peter to wash his feet, Peter expresses confusion. "Lord, are you going to wash my feet?" he asks. Jesus says that though Peter may not understand what he is doing now, it will become clear later. Still, Peter protests: "You will never wash my feet!" That response has always seemed to me infinitely sad; knowing that Jesus may die, Peter is consumed with sorrow, perhaps thinking, *Lord, how much will you abase yourself? At least avoid this degradation.* Peter's comment is not a command as much as a loving plea. It's similar to watching a friend doing something that seems humiliating. To give it a contemporary spin, imagine going to a wedding and seeing the bride and groom having to clean up an overturned trash can at their wedding reception, because no one else will. We would say, like Peter, "Don't *do* that!"

Perhaps it's even more radical than that. In her book *Written That You May Believe,* Sandra Schneiders, IHM, a New Testament scholar, suggests another possible meaning. She believes that in John's Gospel the Foot Washing is more about the mutual service of friendship, a mutual sharing of gifts that in no way implies any sort of domination. The message is not so much that the master has become the slave, but that all are on the *same level.* After Jesus has washed the disciples' feet, he challenges them to do the same for each other and to see that all are equal friends in the kingdom; nobody is above or below in any way.

Schneiders objects to an overemphasis on "humble service" in the Foot Washing, because of the power dynamics this interpretation may suggest. There is no domination by anyone, but rather an invitation to equality. This may help to explain Peter's strong reaction; he sees that this requires, as Schneiders says, "a radical reinterpretation of his own life-world, a genuine conversion of some kind which he was not prepared to undergo."[31]

Peter's response may also betoken an overall lack of openness to the unusual ways of God. Most of the time, not surprisingly, we are resistant to negative change. "This is not the way it's supposed to *be,*" we say. Even in our spiritual lives, we can be resistant to the actions of God. We tend to box God in, saying, "This *cannot* be the action of God." We may want to create a God in our image, when God wants to create us in God's. Peter may be similarly inclined, "I don't want a God who serves." Or "I don't want to be asked by God to serve in this way."[32]

A darker reason for Peter's hesitancy came to me one time in prayer. Perhaps Peter already knew that he wouldn't be able to accompany Jesus until the end, and that recognition made him feel doubly unworthy.

Jesus gives Peter an opaque answer: "Unless I wash you, you have no share with me." Scripture scholars suggest that this comment may relate to baptism, a practice that had already taken hold in the community for whom John wrote. If you are not cleansed from your sins, then you cannot be disciples.[33] More to the point, Jesus seems to be telling Peter that service is a way his disciples can take part in him, in his ministry of total self-giving. Or perhaps it is a way of saying that to love other people you must first accept love—in whatever form it comes. And notice that Jesus calmly continues his symbolic action in the midst of confusion and doubt among the disciples. It does not trouble him that people don't understand his gift. They will.

Peter—confused, anguished, impetuous—leaps to the challenge. As it often is, it's all or nothing for the fisherman from Galilee. "Lord, not my feet only but also my hands and my head!" he says. Jesus may have smiled inwardly, touched by Peter's enthusiasm: Anything for you, Lord! But Jesus gently tells him that this is not necessary: "One who has bathed does not need to wash, except for the feet, but is entirely clean." The word used for "who has bathed" is *ho leloumenos* and implies a total immersion, perhaps another nod to baptism.

There is a magnificent rendition of this precise moment by the English Pre-Raphaelite artist Ford Madox Brown, who painted "Jesus Washing Peter's Feet" (1852–56). Jesus kneels on the floor, clad in a grasshopper-green robe, a dun-colored towel tightly gathered around his waist. He firmly grasps the right foot of Peter, who is seated higher than Jesus, head sunk onto his chest, looking intently at his master. Peter's left foot dangles in a basin of water. The look on Peter's face perfectly illustrates the Gospel: at once embarrassed, downcast, and uncomfortable. Behind them, at table, sit the disciples: one loosens the thongs of his sandals, readying for his washing; another peers over Peter to see what is going on; another holds his anguished face in his hands. Some disciples are easily seen; others recede into the gloom of the space. Brown painted several of his friends into the scene, adding to the tenderness of the moment.

What captivates me about this image is the force with which Jesus holds onto Peter's foot. This is not a merely *symbolic* washing; he takes a firm grip, vigorously wiping off the fisherman's dirty foot. Peter is clearly appalled by what Jesus is doing.

A preliminary version painted by Brown, still seen in an extant watercolor, depicts Jesus only partially clad, with a bare torso, wearing a loincloth, and with the towel tied around his waist. The display of the painting caused an outcry, and Brown later clothed his Jesus. Besides the usual Victorian proprieties, the idea of an utterly human Jesus washing feet still may have been too much for viewers to accept.

Once finished with the ablutions, Jesus clothes himself and resumes his place with the disciples. And now he explains things to them, in case there is any doubt. Rather than summarizing let me share what he says in John's Gospel in full:

> Do you know what I have done to you? You call me Teacher and Lord—and you are right, for that is what I am. So if I, your Lord and Teacher, have washed your feet, you also ought to wash one another's feet. For I have set you an example, that you also should do as I have done to you. Very truly, I tell you, servants are not greater than their master, nor are messengers greater than the one who sent them. If you know these things, you are blessed if you do them. (*Ei tauta oidate, makarioi este, ean poiēte auta.*)

May I ask you to read that last sentence again? Jesus asks them to move from knowledge to action. It takes the form of a command; Jesus is speaking as Teacher and Lord, from a position of authority. So the disciples are expected to heed his message: It's not enough to have knowledge of Christ, you must let it inform your life's decisions. Blessedness comes not only from words and thoughts, but also from deeds. Or as St. Ignatius Loyola wrote, "Love shows itself more in actions than in words."

Whenever I hear this reading proclaimed on Holy Thursday, I never fail to think how different Christian churches would be if, in addition to our weekly celebrations of the Eucharist, we celebrated the Foot Washing. It may sound crazy, and it would be terribly complicated to arrange every Sunday—all those basins of water and towels and shoes and socks! But imagine the symbolism if every week the presider laid aside his vestments and got down on his hands and knees to scrub the feet of his parishioners. What a reminder it would be to all of us—priests included—that this is what Christ asked us to do in addition to the celebration of the Eucharist. After all, what he says about the Eucharist, "Do this in memory of me" at the Last Supper in the Synoptics, he also says about the Foot Washing in John: "If you know these things, you are blessed if you do them."

Seen every Sunday, over and over, the washing of the feet might help us see how power is more intimately linked to service.

How different would our churches be if we modeled a ministry of humble service on Sundays—or at critical moments when forgiveness is demanded? At the beginning of the sexual-abuse crisis that rocked the Catholic Church, someone suggested to me that in addition to removing priests from ministry, holding bishops accountable, making restitution to victims, and implementing programs to prevent abuse from happening, a foot washing of victims might be a powerful symbol of humility. Several bishops did this, in fact, but more would have been better.

Early in Pope Francis's pontificate, when it was announced that he would spend Holy Thursday not in the great St. Peter's Basilica or the grand Basilica of St. John Lateran, as was the custom, but at a juvenile detention center, people responded with surprise and admiration. How striking it seemed that this pope, the first to take the name of Francis, the apostle of humility, was getting down on his hands and knees to minister to poor and troubled youth.

How striking yet how appropriate. A chord was struck in many people's hearts because they knew instinctively that it represented what Jesus meant when he asked us to do precisely these things—in memory of him.

JESUS WASHES THE DISCIPLES' FEET
John 13:1–17

Now before the festival of the Passover, Jesus knew that his hour had come to depart from this world and go to the Father. Having loved his own who were in the world, he loved them to the end. The devil had already put it into the heart of Judas son of Simon Iscariot to betray him. And during supper Jesus, knowing that the Father had given all things into his hands, and that he had come from God and was going to God, got up from the table, took off his outer robe, and tied a towel around himself. Then he poured water into a basin and began to wash the disciples' feet and to wipe them with the towel that was tied around him. He came to Simon Peter, who said to him, "Lord, are you going to wash my feet?" Jesus answered, "You do not know now what I am doing, but later you will understand." Peter said to him, "You will never wash my feet." Jesus answered, "Unless I wash you, you have no share with me." Simon Peter said to him, "Lord, not my feet only but also my hands and my head!" Jesus said to him,

"One who has bathed does not need to wash, except for the feet, but is entirely clean. And you are clean, though not all of you." For he knew who was to betray him; for this reason he said, "Not all of you are clean."

After he had washed their feet, had put on his robe, and had returned to the table, he said to them, "Do you know what I have done to you? You call me Teacher and Lord—and you are right, for that is what I am. So if I, your Lord and Teacher, have washed your feet, you also ought to wash one another's feet. For I have set you an example, that you also should do as I have done to you. Very truly, I tell you, servants are not greater than their master, nor are messengers greater than the one who sent them. If you know these things, you are blessed if you do them."

CHAPTER 20

Gethsemane

"He threw himself on the ground and prayed."

AFTER THE FOOT WASHING, says the Gospel of John, Jesus spoke at length to his disciples in what is usually called the Last Discourse. It is a passage of preaching that runs for several pages in most Bibles. The discourse runs so long that I often wonder if John is recording something that he heard firsthand (some scholars identify John as the "Beloved Disciple" who appears in the Gospel), if he is reporting the talk as it was passed down in oral tradition, or if he pulled together various talks given by Jesus for his purposes here. (The Synoptics do not include this material.)[1]

The discourse begins after Jesus acknowledges Judas as his betrayer, by dipping a piece of bread in wine and offering it to Judas. Judas departs, and as the Gospel says, "It was night."[2] Suddenly we are closer to death.

Jesus tells the probably terrified and alarmed disciples that he will soon be "glorified" (on the cross, as a symbol of his obedience, and at his resurrection) and offers them a new commandment: "Love one another as I have loved you." Over the next two chapters, he will refer to himself as the vine, with the disciples as the branches, and he will try to comfort them over his coming departure. How will they survive without him? First, the Father will send the "Advocate," the Holy Spirit, to guide them. Second, they are to keep the commandments as he has taught them and thus follow his way. Finally, Jesus offers a prayer for all of them and all who believe in him.

Then it is time to move. John's Gospel has the disciples walk to the Kidron Valley, just outside Jerusalem, to "a garden." Luke has them at the Mount of Olives, overlooking the Kidron Valley, and then at a place "a stone's throw" away. But Matthew and Mark are more specific. Jesus and his friends go to the Mount of Olives, then to "the place called Gethsemane."

SINCE THE TIME OF Jesus, the location of the Garden of Gethsemane has been more or less fixed. In an aside, the Gospel of John tells us that a garden near the city was known to Judas, "because Jesus often met there with his disciples." It may have been owned by a friend who permitted Jesus and his companions to meet there often.

Here was one advantage of visiting the Holy Land: seeing the landscape made it easy to read the Gospels and say, "That makes sense." Gethsemane lies in the valley between Jerusalem and the very steep Mount of Olives. (*Gethsemane* means "oil press" in Hebrew and Aramaic, a natural function for a place on a hillside covered with olive trees.) On the other side of the Mount of Olives is Bethany, the home of Mary, Martha, and Lazarus. During times of pilgrimage the population of Jerusalem tripled, so the cost of lodging would likely have been steep. Jesus and his disciples may have spent time in Bethany to be with their friends, but also out of economic necessity. So Gethsemane would have been a natural place for Jesus to rest and reflect.

One morning early in our stay, George and I set out on what he later called our "Death March," which referred not to the fact that we walked the Via Dolorosa, the traditional path that Jesus used en route to his crucifixion, but that it was about ten million degrees outside, and our route took us up and down the hills of Jerusalem.

Walking out of the Lion's Gate at the eastern part of the Old City, we saw spread before us the vista that so many pilgrims have

beheld over the centuries: the Mount of Olives, which stands between Jerusalem and Bethany. At the bottom of the hill was the
Garden of Gethsemane, a green patch of land amid the dry landscape, marked by a large basilica with a multiple-domed roof. Slightly
to the right was the Church of Dominus Flevit ("The Lord Wept"),
where Christ is said to have paused and grieved over Jerusalem for its
hard-heartedness.[3]

Farther to the right, in the Kidron Valley, are the Jewish cem-
eteries, which were in use during Jesus's time. Their location was determined by the Jewish belief that this is where God's judgment of
the world would begin, based on passages in the prophets Joel and
Zechariah.[4] Every time Jesus passed this way, he would have been
reminded of death. As he made his way out of the room of the Last
Supper, he would have seen these tombs shining in the moonlight.

We tramped down a road and then climbed the sharp incline to
the Basilica of Gethsemane. It's an ungainly building, constructed in
1924 by the Franciscans, who funded its construction with donations
from around the world. Thus the official name, the Church of All
Nations. The architect was Antonio Barluzzi, who also designed the
Church of the Beatitudes by the Sea of Galilee. The long stone structure at Gethsemane is capped with twelve gray domes. Over the
doorway is a colorful mosaic of Christ in the Garden, surrounded by
lamenting men and women.

Inside is the Holy Stone on which Christ is said to have sweated
"drops of blood," though we were not allowed to touch it since there
was a Mass in progress. Over the stone is a mosaic of Christ slumped
in prayer atop the stone, under a deep blue background, the primary
color used for the ceilings of the church: "It was night."

The Church of All Nations (also known as the Church of the
Agony or the Basilica of Gethsemane, depending on which map you
consult) is the third church on this site. The first dated from the
fourth century, commemorating the place where the early Christian
community gathered to remember Christ at prayer in the Garden.

During the twelfth century the Crusaders erected a "new" church on top of the original. A portion of the Byzantine floor is visible, and remnants of the Crusader church were incorporated into the current structure.

Thus the site seems authentic. Murphy-O'Connor, with his usual resistance to award a seal of 100 percent certainty, notes, "No one can be sure of the exact spot at which he prayed, but this limited area was certainly close to the natural route leading from the Temple to the summit of the Mount of Olives and the ridge leading to Bethany."[5] So, once again: if not here, then nearby.

But the church wasn't as much of a draw for me (or the other pilgrims) as something else: the *Hortus Gethsemani,* as the sign on the gate read, the Garden of Gethsemane.

Perhaps from seeing too many movies I expected the Garden to be an expansive place, a veritable forest filled with trees and flowers, where one could wander freely. But today it is compact, with just a dozen or so olive trees. They are, however, impressively old. Perhaps not two thousand years old, but old. Bearing small, thin, greenish-gray leaves, the gnarled olive trees stood silently as the tourists peered over the fence that separated us from the ancient garden.

Before visiting the Holy Land, I never could have imagined how close the Garden was to Jerusalem, only a short walk away. As he rested in Gethsemane, Jesus must have stared at the holy city and the nearby graves for a long time, reflecting on his future. What would he do? Just a few minutes' walk in the other direction would bring him into the open desert, an easy escape from his enemies.

Why didn't he take that route? More to the point, how was he able to decide on his path?

THE ONLY GOSPEL THAT does not include Jesus praying in Gethsemane is John, who again chooses to emphasize Jesus's command over events as a manifestation of his divinity. Perhaps any mention of his doubt or anguish would have seemed discordant. In John's account Jesus and the disciples go to "a place where there was a garden," a spot Judas knew, as Jesus had brought his friends there frequently. But no praying occurs, only the betrayal.

Not so for the Synoptics. Let's turn to Mark, which is almost identical to Matthew, and also includes a bit more explanation than Luke.

Mark moves directly into Jesus's prayer in the Garden: "They went to a place called Gethsemane; and he said to his disciples, 'Sit here while I pray.'" Matthew begins differently, saying, "Jesus went with them to a place called Gethsemane." As Harrington notes, by naming Jesus first Matthew highlights that Jesus is directing the events of the Passion. But both point to an almost instantaneous change in his emotions. Jesus takes with him three people from his innermost circle—Peter, James, and John, three of the earliest disciples—and he "began to be distressed (*ekthambeisthai*) and agitated (*adēmonein*)."

Those two words indicate extreme emotions, and translations vary from "sore amazed . . . and very afraid" to "grieved and agitated." Raymond Brown, in his book *The Death of the Messiah,* perhaps the most comprehensive study of the Passion narratives, expounds on those two powerful words:

> *Ekthambeisthai,* "to be greatly distraught" . . . indicates a profound disarray, expressed physically before a terrifying event: a shuddering horror. *Adēmonein,* "to be troubled," has a root connotation of being separated from others, a situation that results in anguish.[6]

Only when Jesus is alone with three close friends do his emotions surface. Often when we are straining to withhold our emotions, it is not until we are with those closest to us that we can "let go." At the wake before my father's funeral, I remained relatively unemotional, until one of my closest friends entered the room, smiled, and hugged me. A surge of sadness overtook me, and I wept. Somehow the presence of my friend enabled me to be myself and to honestly express how I felt. Here Jesus, shielded from the larger group of disciples, is able to share himself. His emotions well up as soon as he is alone with his friends. They must have been very close to him, and he to them.

Episodes such as this and the story of Jesus's weeping at Lazarus's tomb reveal that Jesus is not a cool, distant sage, but a flesh-and-blood human being. The time in the Garden gives us an extraordinary window into his heart.

Then he confides in his three friends: "My soul is sorrowful unto death (*Perilupos estin hē psychē mou heōs thanatou*)."[7] Jesus may be echoing the words of Psalm 42: "My soul is cast down within me." Or perhaps he is thinking of a passage from Sirach that expresses the feelings of a person betrayed: "Is it not a sorrow like that for death itself when a dear friend turns into an enemy?"[8] Brown suggests that if Jesus had intuited his friends' coming betrayal and their scattering after his death, it must have weighed on him terribly. Thus not only his arrest, but their coming betrayal may have caused him intense sorrow. The very thought of this, writes Brown, may have felt as if it were enough to kill him.[9] Overall, the meaning seems to be: My sadness is so intense that it feels as if it may kill me.

The disciples were probably terrified to hear his words, and they may have found themselves "deeply grieved" as well. Imagine what it must have been like for them to see Jesus visibly upset. The calm teacher upon whom they depended to help them in every situation—a terrifying demoniac, a frightening storm at sea, an immense crowd asking for food, two sisters grieving over their brother's death—now admits to being "greatly distressed." Seeing the one in control lose control is always destabilizing.

At this point, perhaps knowing that the disciples would be too distraught to think clearly (Jesus had seen their responses in times of peril before) or simply craving their company in his difficult time, he asks them to stay with him, and to stay awake.

Then something perhaps more striking is described. Matthew and Mark say Jesus "threw himself on the ground and prayed." Some scholars describe this as the normal way to begin prayer: prostrating oneself in reverence before God was attested to in the Old Testament. But others see a kind of collapse as a result of the intense stress Jesus was experiencing. Michael Casey, a Cistercian monk and spiritual writer, calls it "an astonishingly graphic moment."[10] It would not be surprising if Jesus, crushed by grief, collapsed in the Garden, overwhelmed with emotion. Luke uses the vivid word *agōnia,* which occurs nowhere else in the New Testament.[11]

Now Jesus begins to pray. It's important to remember that the Gospels depict Jesus as praying frequently—both privately, when he withdraws from the disciples, and publicly, as when he teaches his disciples how to pray and when he prays outside the tomb of Lazarus. He does not turn to God simply in times of distress. Luke's Gospel, sometimes called the Gospel of Prayer, shows Jesus praying at the most important moments of his public ministry—in the desert of course, but also after his first miraculous healings, before choosing the twelve apostles, before Peter's confession of Jesus as the Messiah, and now after the Last Supper. As Harrington notes, "If you want to know what Luke regarded as the most important moments in Jesus's life, look at his mentions of Jesus at prayer."[12]

In this grave hour, he utters a simple prayer: "*Abba,* Father, for you all things are possible; remove this cup from me; yet, not what I want, but what you want."

In the Garden Jesus shows both his utter humanity and his complete divinity. He begins his prayer with an affectionate address of God as *Abba,* a word often used by a child for his or her father. One day while I was walking through Jerusalem, outside the Damascus Gate, a young girl ran across my path in pursuit of her father. "Abba! Abba!" she called out in her young voice. It was both startling and moving to hear the exact expression Jesus used.

Thus Jesus's prayer begins on a note of intimacy. Remember that when we are presented with an Aramaic word preserved in the Greek text it is almost certain to have come from the lips of Jesus. (That is, Mark does not use the Greek *patēr,* but the original Aramaic.) The word *Abba* was Jesus's highly personal way of speaking to the Father.

And as Michael Casey notes, even in this awful moment, when we could forgive him for being distracted or confused or angry, Jesus grounds his relationship with the Father. It is the starting point for all that Jesus does, even now. "By these words Jesus reaffirms the relationship of intimacy that exists between him and God." Such intimacy enables him not to ignore the impending danger but, as Casey says in a beautiful image, "fix his gaze on the One on whom his selfhood depends."[13]

But Jesus is human, and so he prays that what now seems inevitable will not come to pass. "Father, if you are willing, remove this cup from me," he says bluntly. In the Old Testament the "cup" was sometimes used by the prophets to refer to suffering.[14] Jesus's very human words here invite us to consider (at least) three important things.

First, *Jesus was not courting death.* In the previous sentence, Mark tells us that after falling on the ground, Jesus prays that "if it were possible, the hour might pass from him." Both of his statements—"if it were possible" and "remove this cup"—are not so much expressions of doubt, as a hope that God's mind be changed somehow. Jesus does not wish death for its own sake; much less does he seek out physical suffering for its own sake. His question is artfully summed up by Raymond Brown: "Could not the Father bring about the kingdom in some other way that did not involve the horrendous suffering of the Son delivered into the hands of sinners?"[15]

Or, more simply, "Do you really want this, God?" How many of us have asked the same, when confronted with a terrible inevitability. "Please, God, not this."

Second, *not only is he not courting death, it seems that Jesus at this point also does not want to die.* In Luke, he asks for the cup to be "removed." (The Greek *parenenke* is "to cause to pass, divert, take away."[16]) At roughly thirty-three years old, after gathering together so many followers, after seeing the results of his ministry—people healed, reconciled, even raised from the dead—perhaps Jesus still holds out hope for a few more years of ministry. Yes, he could foresee that last week's events would trigger a Roman reaction and earn him the enmity of some Jewish leaders, but now, in Gethsemane, he does not want to die. This makes his ultimate acceptance of death even more meaningful.

Third, *Jesus's blunt prayer shows that God desires our honesty.* In any intimate relationship, if a person says only what he or she thinks he or she should say, the relationship will grow cold, distant, or false. In the Garden, Jesus follows the tradition of many of the psalms: he laments. He says what he desires: he does not want to suffer, if that is at all possible. And he expresses, in a sense, his confusion. Barclay says bluntly, "He did not fully understand why this had to be."[17] An intimate relationship with the Father means transparency at all times, especially in times of distress.

But that is not the end of his prayer. Jesus does not simply ask for the removal of suffering or for God to change God's mind. He says something more important than what has gone before: "Yet, not what I want, but what you want."

One cannot separate Jesus's actions into human and divine; the two "natures" of Jesus are always united. But this passage may offer us a privileged glimpse of both natures. "Remove this cup" is an utterly human request. "Yet, not my will, but yours be done" is an indication of Jesus's complete union with the Father. Anything one can say about Jesus's humanity and divinity will fail to explain this great mystery. But here, even in the midst of unimaginable psychological torment, which almost drives Jesus to the ground, one might say he expresses human emotions while being fully united with the Father's will. The human person is united with the divine will, and the divine one expresses human emotions.

In his hour of decision Jesus turns to the Father. It would have been easy for him to rise, dust himself off, and walk away. None of his disciples would have condemned him for saying, "I don't want this cup," or for escaping into the nearby Judean wilderness with the explanation, "Let's leave and fight another day."

Given Peter's remonstration when Jesus predicted his suffering, if Jesus had chosen to flee, they would have probably *praised* him for his canny assessment and followed him. After all, Jesus had done the same before. In Nazareth, when an angry crowd was about to hurl him off a cliff after he declared that the messianic benefits would not come to people in his hometown, he passes "through the midst of them." This is not the only time he escapes when threatened. In the Gospel of John after Jesus declares, "Before Abraham was, I am" (in other words, "I am God"), the crowd makes ready to stone him. "But Jesus hid himself," says John, "and went out of the temple."[18]

Why doesn't he hide himself now? Why doesn't he pass through their midst? Why doesn't he do what the disciples must have wanted? Because at this moment, he was able to see that, as far as he could tell, this was what the Father had in mind. This was the future that God had in store, and it was to this that he now surrendered. Once he was able to discern this, he decisively chose to remain on that path. Lohfink writes, perceptively: "The 'will of God' is not that Jesus should be killed in Jerusalem, but that Israel everywhere, including in the capital city, should be confronted with the Gospel of the reign of God."[19] And if this means death, Jesus accepts it.

That answers only the question of how he was able to discern the Father's will. How was he able to *carry out* that decision? That's the more difficult question. Sometimes we see the right thing to do, the generous thing, the charitable thing, but feel unable to do it, unequal to the task, unwilling to pay the price. We feel that we cannot make the sacrifice and say yes to what God seems to be asking.

For Jesus, however, it was more than a matter of sacrifice. And it was more than a matter of obedience to the Father's will. It was a matter of trust. Jesus had an intimate relationship with *Abba,* and so he trusted him. He trusted that, if he did what the Father was asking, no matter how mysterious, confusing, or terrifying, he would not go wrong. So with his Father's help, he was able to do it.[20]

In the end, Jesus's actions flow from his relationship with the Father. In other words, they flow from love.

IN GETHSEMANE WE LEARN more about Jesus of Nazareth—and about ourselves. Who among us hasn't found ourselves in a situation where the inevitable seems impossible? Where the unavoidable seems unimaginable? Who hasn't said to God, in so many words, "Remove this cup"?

The most difficult thing in such a situation may be the crushing inevitability. You want to escape from your life, which suddenly feels like an oncoming train about to run you down. It is the shock you feel when you receive a frightening diagnosis from your physician. When you are laid off from a job. When a friend or family member dies. When a relationship ends. You say to yourself, *This cannot be happening.*

What's worse, these situations throw us into a panic, which makes finding God's "will" more difficult. At the very moment you want to feel most tethered in God, you feel unmoored. Sometimes panic and fear feel like the only rational responses.

When my father was first diagnosed with the cancer that would take his life, and when I heard that the treatments would only lengthen his life by a few months, I couldn't believe it. *No, no, no,* I thought, *this is not the way it is supposed to be.* Everyone, if they live long enough, will one day know this feeling. Recently when a friend discovered that his father had an inoperable cancer and had only one year to live, he said he felt lost. "I don't even know where to begin," he told me.

Even when confronted with situations that are not life-threatening, we still may say, "Remove this cup." Long-term suffering can be just as confusing as a catastrophic illness, and it can likewise test our faith. Perhaps you are stuck in a miserable job with no prospects of relief. Or you are caring for someone living with a chronic illness, and you wonder how much longer you can go on. Or you receive a diagnosis of a minor medical problem that will mean a change in the way you live. In each of these cases you want to say, "Remove this cup." And, again, exacerbating the situation is a fear that can sap your ability to make good decisions. Panic can so master you that you can barely think, let alone pray.

How can we continue? One way is to look at Jesus in the Garden. He does not avoid the hard truth of his situation. He does not ignore his pain or the pain of his friends. If you are ever tempted to hide your struggles from friends or conceal from your loved ones your deepest pain, listen to what Jesus said to his own friends, "I am deeply grieved, even to death." These are not the words of a person who is hiding his feelings.

Expressing your feelings honestly in troubled times is not a sign of weakness, but of humanity and humility. It is also a way to invite into your life friends and relatives who love you. We remember that at the Jordan River, Jesus chose to stand in line, waiting with the rest of humanity to be baptized. In Gethsemane, still in line, he experiences the full range of human emotions, and he shares them with others in a fully human way. For us, expressing sadness and fear allows us to set aside our desire to be in control. It is also an invitation to let others love us.

Jesus feels the need to pray three times in Gethsemane before he reaches a sense of peace. Too often we feel obliged to move immediately into "Yet your will, not mine" before we have lingered with our feelings and expressed them to God. Or we feel guilty for asking for what we want or what we wish to be relieved of, as if such prayers were merely complaints. But the honest expression of painful emotions is a process that even Jesus went through.

But Jesus does not end his prayer by acknowledging his feelings. He ends by trusting in God, by conforming his will to the Father's, even in a dark time. The answer to the question of "How can I go on?" is by being in relationship with *Abba*.

The invitation to surrender, to accept our cup, to acknowledge the inevitability of suffering, and to step onto the path of sacrifice comes in the context of a relationship with God. We trust that God will be with us in all that we do and all that we suffer. We do not simply grit our teeth, clench our fists, and push on, alone and unaided. Someone is with us, helping us. To use another image from the Gospels, there is someone else in the boat pulling on the oars—even if we do not feel it.

Suffering is always difficult to understand. It may have been difficult for Jesus to grasp. It was certainly difficult for the disciples to understand. But they will understand it completely in three days.

PERHAPS JESUS ALSO SAW his impending suffering not only as God's will, but the inevitable result of having come into the world. The life span of someone purely good in a world rife with sin was bound to be short. A few years ago when I was praying with this passage on a retreat in Los Angeles, I saw a peregrine falcon attack, capture, and eat a small bird. The falcon perched in a tree on the novitiate grounds and devoured its bloodied prey. It was gruesome. And surprising. I don't live near much nature. But this incident was a powerful symbol of the way of the world, in which the powerful mercilessly crush the weak.

Jesus understood this violent and bloody world, not only in nature but in his life in first-century Galilee and Judea. He may have sensed this as death was approaching.

AFTER HIS PRAYER JESUS returns to find the disciples—whether just three or all of them is unclear—sleeping. In many film versions of this event Jesus displays a more confident attitude after his prayer. This seems to fit the text. Jesus is no longer the man collapsed in barely restrained grief on the ground; he is in command. "Through prayer the situation has changed," writes Casey. "Beforehand Jesus was unmanned, in a state of deep anguish and confusion. Now after prayer has done its work, he appears almost a new man. He stands upright and takes charge of the situation."[21]

How does that "work"? It is impossible to know what Jesus's prayer life was like, but for the rest of us prayer can spark insights into our situation, provide consoling memories, and offer us feelings of comfort. Moreover, it can gently call us back into our personal relationship with God. In this way we are changed indeed, because not only does God work through us, but in our suffering we remember that we are not alone.

At this point, Jesus, once again in command of the situation, speaks to the disciples. First he addresses Peter, significantly using his old name, perhaps indicating that his friend has failed to live up to his calling. "Simon," he says, "are you asleep? Could you not keep awake one hour?" (An alternate translation, closer to the Greek, is more of a rebuke: "Were you not strong enough to stay awake for one hour?")

Then Jesus warns the tired disciples, "Keep awake and pray that you may not come into the time of trial; the spirit is indeed willing but the flesh is weak." The word used for "trial" (*peirasmon*) is the same word that Matthew uses in the Our Father, in the verse that is usually translated "Lead us not into temptation."[22] Jesus is urging them to steel themselves for the testing, which they are now failing. The contrast between Jesus, undergoing intense torment and praying to the Father, and the disciples, who cannot even stay awake, is acute. They are ruled not by the "spirit" but the "flesh," a shorthand way of delineating the battle between good and evil within us.

Jesus withdraws again and returns. Again he finds them sleeping. They are so addled that they "did not know what to say to him." Thus they are not only tired but confused—the picture Mark paints of the disciples grows darker. Jesus withdraws to pray a third time and once again—prefiguring Peter's triple denial at the Crucifixion—he finds them asleep on his return. This time he plainly tells them to face reality.

"Enough!" he says. "The hour has come; the Son of Man is betrayed into the hands of sinners. Get up, let us be going. See, my be-trayer is at hand." Judas has entered the familiar Garden. He will kiss Jesus and thus identify him for the authorities.

Jesus's time in Gethsemane is now finished, and his hour has come. He knows what he must do.

JESUS IN GETHSEMANE
Mark 14:32–42
(See also Matthew 26:36–46; Luke 22:40–46; John 18:1–2)

They went to a place called Gethsemane and he said to the disciples, "Sit here while I pray." He took with him Peter and James and John, and began to be distressed and agitated. And he said to them, "I am deeply grieved, even to death; remain here, and keep awake." And going a little farther, he threw himself on the ground and prayed that, if it were possible, the hour might pass from him. He said, "Abba, Father, for you all things are possible; remove this cup from me; yet, not what I want, but what you want." He came and found them sleeping; and he said to Peter, "Simon, are you asleep? Could you not keep awake one hour? Keep awake and pray that you may not come into the time of trial; the spirit indeed is willing, but the flesh is weak." And again he went away and prayed, saying the same words. And once more he came and found them sleeping, for their eyes were very heavy; and they did not know what to say to him. He came a third time and said to them, "Are you still sleeping and taking your rest? Enough! The hour has come; the Son of Man is betrayed into the hands of sinners. Get up, let us be going. See, my betrayer is at hand."

CHAPTER 21

Golgotha

*"Then Jesus gave a loud cry
and breathed his last."*

THE CHURCH OF THE Holy Sepulchre was the first holy site George
and I visited in the Holy Land. As I mentioned earlier, we made our
way through the Old City to find the church just a few hours after
arriving in Jerusalem.

The next day, I set out to find it on my own. It was unexpectedly difficult to locate, as one of Christendom's greatest shrines is
not as highly visible as many of the great medieval cathedrals—such
as Notre Dame, plunked on its own little island in the heart of Paris;
or the cathedral of Chartres, rising gracefully over the wheat fields
of France; and certainly not like St. Peter's Basilica, whose massive
dome is a prominent fixture of the Roman skyline. By contrast, the
Church of the Holy Sepulchre is buried within a jumble of buildings in the Old City—and it could be easily mistaken for just another
large church. To add to the confusion, chapels, buildings, and other
structures cling to it, as Jerome Murphy-O'Connor says in *The Holy
Land,* "like barnacles."[1]

On the plane ride to Tel Aviv, I was thrilled by Murphy-
O'Connor's lengthy entry on the church. By now accustomed to his
scholarly reluctance to pronounce a site authentic unless it had the
most impressive bona fides, I was astonished to read: "Is this the
place where Christ died and was buried? Yes, very probably."

Murphy-O'Connor then provides evidence for his conclusion. At the beginning of the first century, the area was an unused quarry. Tombs cut into one wall of the quarry—and similar to the tomb around which the church is built—can be dated to the time of Jesus. The church was also constructed around a rocky mount very similar to the one described in the Gospels as Golgotha, the hill on which Jesus was crucified. Also, the tomb of Jesus is, as the Gospels say, "nearby" the place of his crucifixion, and the great church encompasses both Golgotha and the tomb. "The site," says Murphy-O'Connor, "is compatible with the topographical data supplied by the Gospels."

But what convinces the New Testament scholar and archaeologist is not the persuasive topographical data, but something else: "The most important argument for the authenticity of the site is the consistent and uncontested tradition of the Jerusalem community, which held liturgical celebrations at the site until AD 66." That's *until* AD 66, as early a date as you can imagine for a site in the Holy Land.

Around AD 40, the site was encircled by the city walls, and the emperor Hadrian filled in the quarry to erect a Roman temple. In the third century, after Christianity was declared the official religion of the empire, the bishop of Jerusalem petitioned Emperor Constantine to demolish the temple in order to unearth the tomb of Christ, whose location was, not surprisingly, still known by Christians in Jerusalem.[2] The location of that important spot could not have been forgotten by the Christian community.

As excavations were carried out in the fourth century, an eyewitness, Eusebius of Caesarea, the church historian, recounts what happened during the digging: "As layer after layer of the subsoil came into view, the venerable and most holy memorial of the Saviour's resurrection, beyond all our hopes, came into view."[3] As with the tomb of Peter in Rome, graffiti most likely identified the tomb of Jesus. Work started almost immediately on the new church, and it remained a popular site for pilgrimage until the eleventh century, even after the transfer of Jerusalem to Muslim control in 638.

In 1009, however, Caliph Hakim set about to demolish the church, and nearly did so, with his men attacking the tomb with picks and hammers. In the wake of this destruction pilgrims' donations fueled restorations that began soon afterward. The Crusaders gradually built a new place for worship, thus starting an extended period of construction when apses, chapels, and finally a bell tower were added. Since Crusader times the church has been in constant use, though a fire in 1808 and an earthquake in 1927 caused major damage. In 1959 the three major groups responsible for the maintenance of the church—Latins, Greeks, and Armenians—agreed on an organized program of repair.

That seems to be one of the few things that they agreed on. Today the Church of the Holy Sepulchre is a place of occasional infighting among the groups managing the site. It was disheartening to learn that the six groups—Roman Catholics, Greek Orthodox, Armenians, Syrians, Copts, and Ethiopians—each with its own particular territories within the church, eye each other for any encroachment on their space or infringement of what they consider their rights. In general, relations are friendly. But Jesus's desire expressed at the Last Supper that "they may all be one" sometimes seems frustratingly elusive here.[4] During one visit to the church I told a friendly Franciscan friar that I'd heard that recently there had been a fistfight. "Oh no," he said, "just some shoving, that's all."

"Really?" said George when I reported his comment. "Is there a scheduled time for that?"

On the other hand, it's edifying that the six disparate groups manage to run the place at all. Rivers of tourists flow in and out; Masses are celebrated; pilgrims pray. Occasionally gaining access to certain chapels is a complicated process, and the ease of entrance depends on which religious group has oversight and which schedule is in place, but at least you can enter without showing any identification. The church welcomes prayer.

From the modest plaza one cannot gauge the size of the church.

On the morning of my first visit on my own, I stood outside and looked at the great door, which itself is an emblem of the contentiousness within the church. Every night at eight o'clock the door is locked by a Muslim guardian (apparently to prevent any of the Christian groups from squabbling) whose family has been entrusted with this job for thirteen hundred years. The door is opened every morning at four in an elaborate ritual in which religious representatives hand the guardian, who stands outside, a ladder through a small square opening in the massive wooden door. The door is unlocked with a foot-long iron key and great fanfare.

When I walked in, I heard singing. From somewhere before me came the unmistakable harmonies of chanting. To the side, in a small Catholic chapel, a group of Franciscan monks said their morning prayers. Immediately in front of me was a long marble slab that a man knelt to kiss. This was the Anointing Stone, on which Jesus is supposed to have been anointed before his burial. Murphy-O'Connor dates it to the twelfth century. I kissed it anyway.

Overwhelmed and overjoyed, I wandered around the complicated edifice, trying in vain to identify all that I was seeing. Within a few minutes I located the Tomb of Christ, positioned under the rotunda and housed in what can only be described as another small church—a small Romanesque structure, called the Aedicule (a small shrine) topped off with a dome. In front of the holy site, the place where Jesus's lifeless body was brought, dozens of hanging lanterns burned brightly. On the exterior walls of the shrine were shelves that held lit candles. Behind the Tomb were the Coptic monks whose chanting I had heard. That morning a long line of people—perhaps a hundred in all—waited to enter the Tomb. Entering looked impossible, so I knelt down a few feet away, beside a column under the rotunda on the cold marble floor.

The area surrounding the Tomb was the perfect place to pray, and was in fact my favorite place in the Holy Land for prayer next to that balcony overlooking the Sea of Galilee. And how different the two were. On the balcony all was fresh air and sunshine and breezes, and I was by myself. Inside the Holy Sepulchre, it was dark and claustrophobic and musty, and I was surrounded by scores of pilgrims. But I could pray nonetheless. I took out my New Testament and read the story of the Passion from each of the Gospels.

THE STORY OF JESUS's death is complex, and one that I will not examine line by line. Taken together, the four Gospels provide an extensive account of his last hours—even if they don't agree on each detail. But they align on most of the basic points. Harrington sums up those as follows: "Jesus was arrested, underwent two hearings or trials, was sentenced to death by crucifixion, and died on a cross."[5]

Immediately after Jesus's agonizing prayer in the Garden of Gethsemane at night, the Gospel of Mark describes a "crowd" sent from the "chief priests, the scribes, and the elders" who arrest Jesus. He is identified by Judas with a kiss; all three Synoptic Gospels include Judas's distinctive act of betrayal. It is likely that the authorities' arrest of Jesus at night shows his renown with the crowd: they did not dare to act against him publicly during daylight—at least for the time being.

Jesus's "trials" included three inquests before Jewish authorities—one each before the Jewish leaders Annas and Caiaphas and one before the Sanhedrin, the Jewish governing body. They would find him guilty of blasphemy—for admitting, as he does in Mark, that he is the "Messiah, the Son of God, the Blessed One."[6] The Jewish penalty for blasphemy was stoning. Depending on the Gospels, two or three inquests conducted before the secular authorities (first Pontius Pilate; then Herod Antipas, the local Jewish client-ruler under the Romans; then Pilate again) led to his condemnation for sedition (rebellion or treason). The number of trials or hearings and the individuals involved vary in the Gospels.

The Gospels portray Herod Antipas (in Luke only), the Sanhedrin (in the Synoptics only), Annas, the father-in-law of the high priest (in John only), and the Roman procurator Pontius Pilate as maneuvering to force someone else to take responsibility for the elimination of Jesus. At times, the Gospels can lead one to conclude that both Jewish and Roman sides held equal sway (or that "the Jews" were the driving force). Ultimately, though, Pilate was responsible for the death, since the only person with authority to condemn a person to die in Roman lands was the Roman procurator. It is also important to recall that when the Gospels talk about "the Jews," we should consider this as a particular group of Jewish leaders in a particular place at a particular time—not all the Jews. After all, Jesus's followers were Jewish.[7] So was Jesus.

So who was responsible for Jesus's death? Again, Harrington's explanation is to the point: Jesus was executed under the orders of Pontius Pilate, with the cooperation of some of the Jewish leaders in Jerusalem.[8]

Before his crucifixion, Jesus was beaten, which was the custom, and whipped. (Jewish practice also prevented anyone from being whipped more than forty times.)[9] The Gospels describe soldiers mocking Jesus by adorning him with symbols of royal power and authority (a purple cloak, a crown of thorns, and a reed). The irony is not lost on readers: he truly is a king even if the soldiers are unaware.

Forced to carry his crossbeam to Golgotha, the place of his crucifixion, Jesus was marched through the streets of the city he had triumphantly entered the week before. Golgotha was an abandoned stone quarry just outside Jerusalem. It is named for its shape, a rounded knoll. The Synoptics describe the Romans pressing into service Simon of Cyrene to help Jesus carry his heavy burden. John omits this (perhaps to emphasize Jesus's command of the situation). In Luke Jesus speaks to a group of women on the way to the cross.

Jesus was nailed probably to a T-shaped cross, not far off the ground, and guarded by soldiers, who were posted to prevent anyone from taking him off the cross. Over the cross was placed a sign reading either "Jesus of Nazareth, King of the Jews" or "This is the King of the Jews," a title evidently ordered by Pilate. The Gospels describe Jesus uttering several remarks from the Cross—traditionally called the Seven Last Words.

Witnessing the Crucifixion were, in the Synoptics, several women. The Gospel of Mark, for example, lists Mary Magdalene, Mary the mother of James and Joses, and Salome. In John's Gospel, Jesus's mother stays by her son, along with three other women, and "the disciple whom he loved."

Some victims of crucifixion died quickly, due to a loss of blood, but others survived for several days, the nails pulling horribly on the hands, before succumbing to either dehydration or more likely asphyxiation, as the weight of the body made expanding the lungs difficult. To prolong the agony, the victim's feet would be nailed or tied to the beam, so he could push himself up in a desperate struggle to breathe. In order to expedite the death, the soldiers could, if they desired, break the legs of a victim. By any measure, it was an appalling way to die.

The Gospels report that Jesus died after several hours. (According to Mark, Jesus was crucified at nine in the morning, the sky darkened at noon, and he died at three o'clock in the afternoon.) He was placed in a tomb secured for him by Joseph of Arimathea, a wealthy man who had asked Pilate for permission to care for the body. The burial was done quickly, because it was a Friday afternoon and the Sabbath was about to begin. The body was placed in a tomb and anointed with a mixture of spices, according to the Jewish tradition.[10]

THE FIRST THING I noticed in the Church of the Holy Sepulchre was a stairway under a stone arch to the right of the main door. I wondered why there would be a second floor in the church. Then it dawned on me that the steps led up to the summit of Golgotha, around which the church is built. As I walked up the stairs I realized that I was ascending the same or nearly the same hill that Jesus had climbed, and I was moved to tears.

This was another spot in the Holy Land where I felt intimately connected to Jesus. Sometimes one can surmise where Jesus "might have" walked, say, along the Sea of Galilee, or "might have" stood, say, at the Pool of Bethesda, or what he "might have" seen, say, in Nazareth. But each of the Gospels records his being crucified on the very hill I was now ascending. I felt embarrassed, unworthy to participate in this act in such a physical way.

At the top of the stairs two small but ornate chapels commemorated the Crucifixion. They are built directly on top of Golgotha. Once again, I was unprepared. Before coming here I had assumed that the church would be built in a general way around the supposed spots where the Crucifixion "might have" happened. But the building conformed precisely to the terrain. Murphy-O'Connor describes the location of the two chapels with none of the "probablys" or "maybes" that pepper his book: "The floor above is on a level with the top of the rocky outcrop on which Christ was crucified."[11]

Under an elaborate altar festooned with icons and illuminated by lamps, pilgrims lined up, and knelt. What were they venerating? Perhaps an icon or a fragment of the "True Cross." But they seemed to be reaching down into a cavity.

"What are they touching?" I whispered to another pilgrim.

"Golgotha," he said quickly.

As I moved closer, I noticed, to my amazement, a hole cut in the marble floor. When my turn came, I crouched under the altar, with several pilgrims jostling me, and I gingerly stretched out my hand through the opening, wondering how far I would have to reach. My hand touched the cold rock. Immediately I withdrew it out of shock.

FOR THE DISCIPLES, JESUS'S public ministry probably seemed to end with terrifying speed. Let's look mainly at the Gospel of Mark, with some help from the Gospel of John, to understand better Jesus's final few hours.

The Gospel narratives describe those final hours—Jesus's journey to Golgotha, his crucifixion, and his death—simply. Mark, Matthew, and Luke paint his death in swift strokes.[12] John even omits the traditions of the Via Dolorosa, or Way of the Cross, the saga of Jesus's path from his condemnation by Pilate to Golgotha. The story of Simon of Cyrene also is absent from John. So is Jesus meeting the women of Jerusalem, from Luke, in which Jesus, bent under the weight of the cross, says, "Daughters of Jerusalem, do not weep for me, but weep for yourselves and for your children."[13] These absences are sometimes a surprise for Catholics accustomed to praying with what are known as the Stations of the Cross.

In fact, the Via Dolorosa is a late addition when compared to many other traditions in the Holy Land. Scattered around the Old City, affixed to the sides of buildings, are gray metal disks that mark the Stations of the Cross with simple Roman numerals. Usually a knot of pilgrims is stationed before them, along with a guide telling the story of Jesus's suffering at this particular point or leading a prayer or a hymn.

While I had expected the Stations of the Cross to be one of the highlights of our pilgrimage, for some reason I found myself largely unmoved. Oddly enough, I experienced more powerful reactions when praying with the stations in local parishes, either alone or in a group, usually during Lent. Catholic tradition includes fourteen stations, from "Jesus Is Condemned to Death" to "Jesus Falls for the First Time" to "Jesus Is Nailed to the Cross," and the walls of nearly every Catholic church include these artistic vignettes from the Passion, though some are not included in any Gospel.

But here in the Holy Land the stations held little appeal for me. Maybe it was the touristy setting. Underneath the station marked "Veronica Wipes the Face of Jesus" was a metal rack stuffed with postcards. My response was also influenced by having read that the devotion had started, at the earliest, in the fifth century and that a few centuries later there were actually two routes followed by pilgrims. So though clearly Jesus made his way through Jerusalem, the specific sites were not well attested. Bargil Pixner writes, "Jesus's bitter path probably did not pass along today's Via Dolorosa."[14]

In the fifteenth century, Christians in Europe began to promote the practice of praying with the stations in their home parishes (because few people could make the trip to Jerusalem). They arrived at the standard fourteen stations. But this posed a problem: in Jerusalem there were only *eight* stations. Over time the fourteen European stations took hold even in Jerusalem. The general route that Holy Land pilgrims know today wasn't fixed until the eighteenth century, and some stations did not have their final locations set until the nineteenth century. All of this made it harder for me to appreciate the Way of the Cross in Jerusalem.

Other people, however, have told me that the Stations of the Cross were among their most powerful spiritual experiences in the Holy Land. Walking where Jesus walked—even if it wasn't the precise historical path—moved some of my friends to tears. Different places evoke different feelings from different people. While I had intense experiences at the Pool of Bethesda, others told me the site left them cold. Why did I once experience strong emotional reactions to the stations on a chilly mountainside in Lourdes, France, instead of in the city where Jesus had actually walked? Grace is mysterious. So is pilgrimage.

MARK BEGINS THIS LAST stage of Jesus's earthly life by telling us about Simon of Cyrene, whom the Romans pressed into service. Roman soldiers had the right to require any civilian to help carry out a task for them. Simon is described as the "father of Alexander and Rufus," so presumably Mark's readers would have known him.[15] (A Rufus is mentioned in Paul's Letter to the Romans.[16]) Although it's possible that the Romans asked Simon's assistance out of compassion for their prisoner, it's more likely that Jesus, weakened severely after his torture, was unable to carry the crossbeam on his own.

John's Gospel affords the Way of the Cross scant attention. His account begins simply: "So they took Jesus; and carrying the cross by himself, he went out to what is called The Place of the Skull, which in Hebrew is called Golgotha." The site of execution would have been visible to all, perhaps set by the road deliberately to deter other criminals or insurrectionists. This, after all, was a public execution. As George often told the inmates on death row at San Quentin, Jesus is the most famous victim of capital punishment.

The descriptions of the actual crucifixion in the Gospels are stripped down, as if the evangelists could barely bring themselves to describe anything but the naked facts. This is sometimes baffling to those who have seen films or read books that focus on the horrible act itself. But there might be another reason for the unadorned description: the early Christians knew well what crucifixion was.[17] Victims were first affixed to the kind of crossbeam that Jesus carried by ropes or by nails driven through the wrists or forearms. In earlier times that part of the cross (which the Romans called the *patibulum*) was a piece of wood used to bar a door. The crossbeam was set into a vertical wooden beam that stood perhaps six feet high. The victim was placed in a small seat and perhaps a footrest—not out of any attempt to comfort, but to prolong his agony.[18]

To breathe, victims were forced to prop themselves up momentarily on the footrest in order to draw air into their lungs, but the pain in their nailed feet and cramped legs would have gradually made it impossible to support themselves, and they would have slumped down violently, pulling on the nails in their wrists, tearing the skin and ripping the tendons, causing searing pain. It would have been nearly impossible for any human being (with a body involuntarily trying to avoid physical pain) not to experience panic. The awful process would have been repeated over and over. Victims of crucifixion died from either loss of blood or asphyxiation.

There was little need to explain this to the first readers of the Gospels.

Kai estaurōsan auton, writes Mark simply. "And they crucified him."

Jesus may have been stripped of his garments and left naked, completing the shaming intended by crucifixion, but this is unclear. Roman practice was to crucify the victim naked, but there might have been a nod to Jewish sensibilities. All four Gospels, however, describe the soldiers' gambling for Jesus's outer garment, which John reports was a well-made cloak, "seamless." But the most that Jesus would have been wearing was a loincloth.

Pilate's inscription—*Ho Basileus tōn Ioudaiōn*—which Mark calls the "accusation" or "charge," was affixed to the cross as a savage warning to insurrectionists or anyone with messianic designs. Beside Jesus were crucified two "thieves" though the word (*lēstas*) may also imply a kind of Robin Hood figure—"social bandits," as Donahue and Harrington suggest.[19] Jesus died as he lived, in solidarity with outcasts, in this case criminals.

We can imagine, then, a public scene calculated not only to warn, but also to magnify the shame for the victim, who suffered an agonizing death. All were invited to watch and comment. The Gospel of Mark describes passersby blaspheming. They "shake their heads," and Mark recounts a common word—*oua*—that begins their taunts, "Aha!" or "Well, well." They scorn him: "Aha! You who would destroy the Temple and build it in three days, save yourself, and come down from the cross." Next the chief priests and scribes come to deliver their own imprecations: "Let the Messiah, the King of Israel, come down from the cross now, so that we may see and believe."

In Luke "the leaders" (*archontes,* most likely, some of the Jewish leaders) scoff: "He saved others; let him save himself if he is the Messiah of God, his chosen one!" The soldiers join in, saying: "If you are the King of the Jews, save yourself." Their taunts of "save yourself" mirror what he heard when he was tested in the desert.

Jesus does not answer. Most likely he could barely breathe.

All three Synoptics describe a darkness coming "over the whole land." In Mark's Gospel the darkness lasts from noon to three. Then Jesus shouts out, *"Elōi, Elōi, lama sabachthani!"*

Many translations say that he "cried out in a loud voice," but "scream" may be more accurate. The Greek *eboēsen* is indicative of "intense physical suffering."[20]

Mark's narrative preserves the words of Jesus from the cross in Aramaic, a sign of their authenticity.[21] Jesus's screaming these words from the cross must have so imprinted itself on witnesses as to be unforgettable: "My God, my God, why have you forsaken me?"

Why does Jesus scream these words?

Though we have almost no access into the mind of Jesus, especially at this moment, there are several ways to think about what he says. The first possibility is that Jesus's words are not an expression of abandonment, but of hope in God. He is quoting Psalm 22, which would have been recognizable to any Jew who had received religious training. And although the beginning of the psalm expresses the frustration of a speaker who feels God has abandoned him, the second part is a hymn of thanksgiving to God, who has heard his prayer: "He did not hide his face from me, but heard when I cried to him."

In this interpretation, Jesus is invoking the psalm in its totality, as the prayer of one who cried out to God and was heard. An example based on a more well known psalm might be someone who says, "The Lord is my shepherd," trusting that his hearers are familiar with the rest of the psalm ("Even though I walk through the darkest valley") and its overall thrust. That is, "The Lord is my shepherd" is taken not simply as an affirmation of God as shepherd but as shorthand for the entire psalm. This is a frequent tack taken in theological explanations of Jesus's cry.

But there is another possibility: Jesus felt abandoned. This is not to say that he despaired. I don't believe that someone with such an intimate relationship with the Father could have lost all *belief* in the presence of God in this dark moment. But it is not unreasonable to imagine his *feeling* as if the Father were absent. It is important to distinguish between a person's believing that God is absent and feeling it.

Of all people, Jesus—having faced the betrayal of his closest friends (Mark says earlier that the disciples had fled by this point, whether out of terror or confusion or shame), subject to an exhausting series of late-night inquests, brutalized by Roman guards, marched through the streets under a crushing weight, and now, nailed to a cross and suffering excruciating pain—could be forgiven for feeling abandoned. He who has abandoned himself to God's will in the Garden now wonders, *Where are you?*

In a lengthy treatment of this passage entitled "Jesus's Death Cry," Raymond Brown suggests this was in fact what Jesus was experiencing.[22] Many Christians, he suggests, might want to reject the literal interpretation that would imply feelings of abandonment. "They could not attribute to Jesus such anguish in the face of death."[23] Yet, as Brown says, if we accept that Jesus in the Garden could still call God *Abba,* then we should accept this "screamed protest against abandonment wrenched from an utterly forlorn Jesus who now is so isolated and estranged that he no longer uses 'Father' language but speaks as the humblest servant." The shift from the familiar *Abba* to the more formal *Elōi* is heartbreaking. Jesus's feeling of distance reveals itself not only in the scream, not only in the line of the psalm that he screams, but also in the word *Elōi.*

How could Jesus feel abandoned? How could the person who enjoyed such an intimate relationship with God express such an emotion? It may help to look at a similar situation closer to our own time.

In the early years of her life, as I mentioned earlier, Mother Teresa, the founder of the Missionaries of Charity, enjoyed several mystical experiences of closeness with God and then—nothing. For the last fifty or so years of her life, she felt a sense of great emptiness in her prayer. When her journals and letters were published posthumously, many readers were shocked by these sentiments, finding it difficult to understand how she could continue as a believer and indeed flourish as a religious leader. But Mother Teresa was honestly giving vent to her feelings of abandonment and speaking of what spiritual writers call the "dark night." This state of emotion moves close to, but does not accept, despair. She wrote to her confessor, "In my soul I feel just that terrible pain of loss—of God not wanting me—of God not being God—of God not really existing."[24]

In time, Mother Teresa's questions about God's existence faded, and she began to see this searing experience as an invitation to unite herself with Jesus, in his abandonment on the cross, and with the poor, who also feel abandoned. Her feelings did not mean that she had abandoned God or that God had truly abandoned her. Hers was a radical act of fidelity based on a relationship that she still believed in—even if she could not sense God's presence.

Jesus, it seems to me, does not despair. Yeshua is still in relationship with *Abba*—calling on him from the cross. Yet in the midst of horrific physical pain, abandoned by all but a few of his friends and disciples, and facing death, when it would be almost impossible for anyone to think lucidly, he might have felt abandoned. To me this makes more sense than the proposition that the psalm he quoted was meant to refer to God's salvation.

In the Gospel of John, however, there is no scream. Even from the cross, Jesus is in full command of the situation and thereby maintains what Gerald O'Collins terms his "divine composure."[25] Jesus asks the Beloved Disciple to care for his mother, who stands under the cross with three other women: his mother's sister, Mary the wife of Clopas, and Mary Magdalene. "Woman, here is your son," he says to his mother. And to the disciple, "Here is your mother."

Hearing the scream from the cross, the passersby in Mark suddenly seem to take pity on Jesus. But they are confused by his calling on *Elōi,* mistakenly thinking (for a variety of possible reasons, for example, Jesus's Aramaic or his Galilean accent) that he is calling to Elijah. Then "someone" (whether out of pity is unclear) gives him some "sour wine," of the type that soldiers would have used. Is the "someone," who uses a sponge and a stick to reach Jesus's lips, a soldier?

Is this vinegary wine (*oxos*), which also appears in Matthew, supposed to help him quench his thirst, revive him with its sharp smell, or mock him? It is hard to say. "Let us see whether Elijah will come to take him down," says the someone. Is this a taunt or the hope of an onlooker moved by Jesus's calling on Elijah? Again, it is hard to say. In John the wine is given after Jesus says, "I am thirsty," and can be viewed as a compassionate act. But in Mark the motives are unclear.

What is clear is that this marks the end of Jesus's earthly ministry. *Ho de Iēsous apheis phōnen megalēn exepneusen,* And Jesus, letting out a loud cry, expired.

The word *exepneusen* means "gave up one's breath." Its root is the word for "spirit," *pneuma.* We do not know what Jesus cried. Donahue and Harrington say, "It may simply have been the last shout of someone in great physical pain."[26]

The Gospel of John reports that Jesus utters, "It is finished," and "gave up his spirit."

Then the veil in the Temple of the sanctuary is torn (*eschisthē*) in two. The only other use of this word in Mark is when the sky is torn in two at Jesus's baptism at the Jordan River.[27] So at the beginning and the end of his public ministry there is a dramatic opening of the heavens, a dissolution of the boundaries between above and below.

At the same time, the centurion standing beside the cross, struck by the man's death, says, "Truly this man was God's Son!" The Messianic Secret is no longer secret. One of Mark's ironies here is that the person who finally and fully proclaims Jesus's identity is the Roman soldier who has presumably presided over his execution. Unless this is a sarcastic remark, the formerly doubtful onlooker either has been convinced by the tearing of the sanctuary veil (though it is nearly impossible for him to have known this) or more likely has been moved by Jesus's calling on God in his final moments. What has moved the man—Jesus's divinity or his humanity?

To conclude the terrible story, Mark lists the women who have been present all along "from a distance." These are Mary Magdalene, Mary the mother of "James the younger" (one of the apostles) and Joses, and a woman named Salome. When describing the women,

Mark uses the word for discipleship (*akolouthein*), and so it is accurate to say they were considered disciples, who "followed him and provided for him."

The women and the Beloved Disciple do for Jesus what many of us can do out of love when we are faced with suffering. When my father was dying, my family gathered around him in his hospital bed and simply stayed. We wanted to be there and to help him—if at all possible—and not leave him alone. Even if we are unable to do anything that will alleviate a person's physical pain, we can remain.

Mark also notes that there were also "many other women," something that the evangelist explicitly highlights for the first time—that is, the existence of a larger group of women who followed him on the way to Jerusalem. These women will prove to be of great importance in the next few days.

MANY MEDITATIONS ON THE Cross tend to focus on Jesus's physical suffering. And this is appropriate: the carpenter from Nazareth suffered terrible physical pain. It would have begun from the moment of his arrest, with the guards treating him roughly and, according to John, binding him, most likely by the hands. After his trial he is whipped by the Roman soldiers. The Gospels treat this gruesome event sparingly. In Matthew and Mark the information comes in the middle of another sentence: "So Pilate, wishing to satisfy the crowd, released Barabbas for them, and after flogging Jesus, he handed him over to be crucified." John is similarly laconic: "Then Pilate took Jesus and had him flogged." (The modest Church of the Flagellation in the Old City commemorates this.) Afterward the soldiers weave a crown of thorns and press it onto his head.

Jesus must have been sleepless throughout this night, which means that any reserves of physical strength are already depleted as he faces the physical pain. After this ordeal he has to shoulder a rough and heavy wooden beam. Finally he is nailed to the cross.

Yet physical pain is not the only kind of suffering we endure—or that Jesus suffered. And so this is not the only kind of pain he understands. Consider the other kinds of suffering.

There is the suffering of *abandonment*. In an aside, describing the events after Gethsemane, Mark writes, "All of them deserted him and fled." The disciples, who had always vacillated between understanding and confusion and thus between following and leaving, now make their break. The one who invited them to "Follow me" now witnesses their final answer. They will not follow him here. This—his sudden shaming, his unwillingness to defend himself, his mission's apparent failure, and his acceptance of physical pain—is a place they cannot go to. It's easy to imagine the disciples not only terrified, but also ashamed as they fled, compounding their misery.

Thus, when he needs their support the most, Jesus is abandoned by his closest friends. Even though his disciples proved a fractious group, he always had the benefit of their company. Early on, he could have chosen to carry out his ministry alone or with just one person, say Peter. But Jesus chose a group—a large one, twelve apostles—to be with him almost all the time, and they also traveled with the larger circle of disciples. He must have been a naturally social person. As someone who craved company, Jesus relied on them not only for help in his ministry, but for simple friendship. Now that friendship is gone.

With the disciples unable or unwilling to participate, Jesus also suffers from *loneliness*. Throughout the Gospels we have seen Jesus's desire to be alone—he will withdraw from the disciples in order to pray by himself. Or he will remove himself from the crowds. But for the most part in his public ministry he is surrounded by other people.

Nonetheless, Jesus's life was one of existential aloneness. Shortly before Jesus's final entry into Jerusalem, the Gospel of Mark describes him walking with the disciples toward the holy city: "Jesus walked ahead of them; they were amazed, and those who followed were afraid." The image of Jesus walking alone, trailed by his fearful disciples, is a striking portrait of the solitary nature of his vocation.[28]

When I once spoke to a spiritual director about loneliness, he asked if I had ever thought about Jesus in that light. When the followers of Jesus look around, he asked me, whom do they see? They see their peers, perhaps hundreds of people with whom they can share their experiences. When the disciples look around, whom do they see? Dozens of people with whom they have much in common. When the apostles look around, whom do they see? They see eleven other men, whom they know well, and with whom they can share their concerns, joys, and hopes, their griefs and anxieties. Even assuming Jesus shared with Mary, Martha, and Lazarus, there were parts of him that remained difficult for them to understand.

When Jesus looks around, whom does he see? My spiritual director held up his index finger. "There is only Jesus," he said. He relies on the Father, but in many ways he is alone. This loneliness is complete—and brutal—in the Crucifixion.

As if that weren't enough, he suffers the terrible feeling of outright *betrayal* by one of his closest friends: Judas Iscariot.

A FEW YEARS AGO I served as a "theological adviser" to an Off-Broadway play that put Judas on trial for Jesus's death.[29] We spent many hours sifting through the possible reasons for history's most famous betrayal. The Gospel of Mark gives no motivation for Judas's sudden betrayal. Confusing things further, Matthew has Jesus telling Judas at the Last Supper, "Do what you are here to do," which seems to imply some acquiescence or at least foreknowledge on Jesus's part. Matthew attempts to clarify things in his account by introducing the motive of greed: "What will you give me if I betray him to you?" Judas asks the Jewish chief priests.

The Gospel of John echoes this theme. Before the Last Supper, Judas is depicted by the evangelist as the greedy keeper of the common purse. When Jesus is anointed in Bethany, shortly before his crucifixion, Judas complains, asking why the money was not given to the poor. In an aside, John writes, "He [Judas] said this not because he cared about the poor, but because he was a thief; he kept the common purse and used to steal what was put into it." Thus John paints Judas as greedy, and dishonest as well. Finally, Luke's Gospel tells us that at the Last Supper "Satan had entered into Judas." Father Harrington told me that this phrase from Luke explained "either everything or nothing."

There is another hypothesis that sometimes remains unstated by commentators: the evangelists concocted the entire story of Judas's betrayal for dramatic purposes. Some have posited that the one who betrayed Jesus could have come from outside the Twelve and that Judas was simply a convenient fall guy. Similarly, Judas may have been invented as a generic "Jewish" character in order to lay the blame for the Crucifixion on the Jewish people. The name "Judas" (the Hebrew would be Judah) lends credence to this idea. So might Paul, who suggests that Jesus was "handed over" not by Judas or anyone else, but by God.[30]

But a wholesale invention is unlikely. Mark wrote his Gospel around AD 70, only a few decades after the death of Jesus. Luke and Matthew wrote some ten to fifteen years later. The Christian community of that time still would have counted among its members those who were friends of Jesus, who were eyewitnesses to the Passion, or who knew the sequence of events from conversations with the previous generation. They most likely would have criticized any wild liberties taken with the story. Rather, as Father Harrington told me, "Judas's betrayal of Jesus was a known and most embarrassing fact." The ignominy of having Jesus betrayed by one of his closest friends is something the Gospel writers would have wanted to avoid, not invent.

Overall, none of the Gospels provides a convincing reason for why one of the twelve apostles would betray the teacher he esteemed so highly. Greed fails as an explanation—why would someone who had traveled with the penniless rabbi for three years suddenly be consumed with greed? (Unless he was indeed stealing from the common purse.)

William Barclay conjectures that the most compelling explanation is that by handing Jesus over to the Romans, Judas was trying to force Jesus's hand, to get him to act in a decisive way. Perhaps Judas expected the arrest to prompt Jesus to reveal himself as the long-awaited Messiah by not only ushering in an era of peace, but over-throwing the Roman occupiers. Barclay notes that none of the other traditional explanations (greed, disillusionment, jealousy) explain why Judas would have been so shattered after the Crucifixion that, according to the Gospel of Matthew, he committed suicide; only if Judas had expected a measure of good to come from his actions would suicide make any sense. "That is in fact the view which best suits all the facts," Barclay concludes.[31]

Finally, there is an explanation at once simple and complex: sin. Why do we do what we know is wrong? It is an inexplicable mystery. Perhaps Judas's reasons for betrayal were obscure even to himself.

Whatever the reason, Jesus is betrayed by one of his closest friends. Here is further sorrow for him as he hangs on the cross.

Jesus also undergoes the suffering of *humiliation and contempt*. His humility has been on display throughout the Gospels, most recently in the Foot Washing. We witness it in his reluctance to be named king, and in his withdrawal from the crowds after a miracle. Perhaps his withdrawal is both a sign of fatigue or tiredness and a further sign of his humility—shunning adulation after performing his great deeds.

But being struck and mocked by soldiers and taunted by crowds must have been—for even the humblest man—a difficult thing to bear. A few years ago I saw a woman being arrested in a parking lot, apparently for stealing something from a convenience store. The police had bound her hands behind her with plastic handcuffs. When her eyes met mine, she immediately turned her face away in shame. I wish I could have apologized for looking. Jesus was no criminal, and he had nothing to be ashamed of, but the taunts must have stung him nonetheless.

Contempt is a hard thing to bear, and Jesus received contempt from the beginning of his ministry. In the synagogue at Nazareth, the people in his hometown can barely stand to hear him—they grow so wrathful that they drive him out of the town. In the challenges from some of the scribes and Pharisees you can hear not simply questions about his authority, but outright contempt. "It is blasphemy! Who can forgive sins but God alone?"[32]

There is also the suffering of *seeing others suffer because of your suffering.* The last thing that a child wants is for his mother or father to see him suffer. Jesus knows how difficult this must be for his mother.

Recently a friend told me how painful it was to watch her eight-year-old son cry during a basketball game. She could hardly bear it. And the more we age, the more we realize this truth about our parents. After I passed my fiftieth birthday and started to experience the normal aches and pains of growing older, and whenever a physician told me that these aches and pains would mean minor surgery, physical therapy, or simply a change in lifestyle, I decided not to tell my mother. She didn't need to hear about my suffering, no matter how minor. Like every good mother, she suffered when her child suffered.

So imagine Jesus's sadness at seeing his mother suffer. If anything could have tempted him to walk away from the cross, it may have been this. I can imagine him asking the Father, "I will drink this cup, but must she drink it too?"

FINALLY, THERE IS THE suffering of *seeing his great work ended.*

Just outside the Old City walls, down the slope of Mount Zion, is the Church of Peter in Gallicantu, which marks the spot where Peter denied Jesus. Gallicantu, which means "cock crow," refers to

Peter's fulfillment of Jesus's prediction that Peter would deny him "before the cock crows twice."[33] A golden rooster perches delicately atop the church's great dome, mid-crow. While the structure is relatively new (1932), since ancient times the site has been venerated as the location of Caiaphas's house and therefore where Jesus was held after his arrest.[34]

The main cavern is called the Sacred Pit or Christ's Prison. It is a haunting place, which was empty on the day George and I visited. One descends a narrow stone staircase into a darkened cavern illuminated with a few wall sconces. At the bottom of the pit a bookstand holds a loose-leaf notebook bearing the text, in many different languages, of Psalm 88, which reads in part:

> *I am counted among those who go down to the Pit;*
>   *I am like those who have no help. . . .*
> *You have caused my companions to shun me;*
>   *you have made me a thing of horror to them.*
> *I am shut in so that I cannot escape.*

Who knows if Jesus was taken to this site, or if he was confined to this pit. But as a deeply religious Jew, wherever he was held, he probably recalled this psalm. As I stood in the Sacred Pit, alone in the half darkness, and read those words, I thought of Jesus saying good-bye to his great project.

Think about the months and perhaps years that Jesus poured into his ministry. Think of the effort that had gone into selecting the apostles and teaching them, as well as all the energy expended in traveling, healing, and preaching—all work undertaken to help people understand what it means to be invited into the reign of God. Accepting the end of the project into which he had poured himself, body and soul, must have been overwhelmingly difficult.

Jesus also may have wondered whether his project could continue after his death. After all, he knew that the disciples often quailed before difficulties; he watched them scatter in the Garden. *So,* he may have thought, *it is finished.* (Arguing against this possibility is Jesus's clear establishment of a church in Matthew with Peter as its head.[35])

In a meditation on retreat years ago I suddenly imagined the imprisoned man crying, out of sadness. Jesus wept for his friend Lazarus and for the future of Jerusalem; how could he not have wept for the seeming end of all he had worked for? Jesus trusts in the Father. He trusts that his obedience will in some way bring new life. He intimates that he expects his resurrection: "Destroy this temple that is made with human hands, and in three days I will raise it up."[36] But it would have been impossible for him not to be sorrowful "to death," as he admits in the Garden.

THESE SUFFERINGS ARE AN essential entry for us into the life of Jesus. For those who think of Jesus as far removed from the suffering we face, the Gospels show us not simply physical sufferings, but emotional ones as well. We do not, as St. Paul said, have a God who does not understand our suffering, but who participated in it.[37] This is an entry for us into Jesus's life and an entry for him into ours.

Yet even in the midst of this suffering—physical pain, abandonment, betrayal, seeing others suffer, and then seeing one's great project collapse—Jesus did not waver. It must have been an enormous temptation to vacillate in the face of this mountain of suffering. But out of obedience to what the Father is asking he does not.

Jesus has done as much as he could. It is finished. Now, into his Father's hands he commends his spirit. He commends his body. He commends everything.

After all the temptations to turn away from the path that the Father was asking him to follow, and even in the face of his intense physical, emotional, and spiritual suffering, Jesus is resolute. Like his mother at the Annunciation, he says—perhaps not knowing fully what it will mean—yes.

THE CRUCIFIXION

Mark 15:22–41

(See also Matthew 27:33–56; Luke 23:33–49; John 19:16–30)

Then they brought Jesus to the place called Golgotha (which means the place of a skull). And they offered him wine mixed with myrrh; but he did not take it. And they crucified him, and divided his clothes among them, casting lots to decide what each should take.

It was nine o' clock in the morning when they crucified him. The inscription of the charge against him read, "The King of the Jews." And with him they crucified two bandits, one on his right and one on his left. Those who passed by derided him, shaking their heads and saying, "Aha! You who would destroy the temple and build it in three days, save yourself, and come down from the cross!" In the same way the chief priests, along with the scribes, were also mocking him among themselves and saying, "He saved others; he cannot save himself. Let the Messiah, the King of Israel, come down from the cross now, so that we may see and believe." Those who were crucified with him also taunted him.

When it was noon, darkness came over the whole land until three in the afternoon. At three o'clock Jesus cried out with a loud voice, "Eloi, Eloi, lema sabachthani?" which means, "My God, my God, why have you forsaken me?" When some of the bystanders heard it, they said, "Listen, he is calling for Elijah." And someone ran, filled a sponge with sour wine, put it on a stick, and gave it to him to drink, saying, "Wait, let us see whether Elijah will come to take him down." Then Jesus gave a loud cry and breathed his last. And the curtain of the temple was torn in two, from top to bottom. Now when the centurion, who stood facing him, saw that in this way he breathed his last, he said, "Truly this man was God's Son!"

There were also women looking on from a distance; among them were Mary Magdalene, and Mary the mother of James the younger and of Joses, and Salome. These used to follow him and provided for him when he was in Galilee; and there were many other women who had come up with him to Jerusalem.

CHAPTER 22

Risen

"Jesus said to her, 'Mariam!'"

THE MOST POWERFUL SPIRITUAL experience of my entire pilgrimage came inside the Church of the Holy Sepulchre. On my second visit I decided to wait in the long snaking line to enter the Tomb of Christ, housed in the Aedicule, the church-within-the-church. Almost impossibly ornate, the entrance to the tomb is flanked by tall candles, with a small wooden door set into a façade of rose marble. The people in line were orderly, but fidgety. The man in front of me kept checking his smartphone. Probably ignoring some code of pilgrim's etiquette, I peeked over his shoulder to see what could be so important and half-expected him to be typing, "Can't talk. In church where Jesus died. Call you in 5." Instead, he was playing a video game.

The line inched closer to the tomb—the church guards were permitting only three or four people to enter at a time. The holiest site in Christendom was packed, with rivers of tourists flowing in and out. Franciscan friars and Orthodox monks and Ethiopian priests crossed the marble floor, carefully avoiding one another. Chanting came from somewhere nearby.

After thirty minutes I reached the door. Along with a handful of other pilgrims I was waved into a small anteroom where we awaited entrance to the tomb. Over the doorway the marble was carved to resemble folds of cloth, as if a curtain were overhanging the entrance. A guard offered instructions: we could kiss the stone if we wished or reverence it in some way, but we were not to spend too much time inside. Looking over someone's shoulder, I could tell why they had only allowed a few in; it was a tiny space. When finished, we would exit the same way we entered.

The appointed time came. As at the entrance to the Church of the Nativity, you must crouch to enter. Bending slightly, I walked in with a man and woman. Before me was a pinkish gray stone, about waist high. On ledges around the stone, which also served as an altar, dozens of tapers burned brightly. Already I knew that besides reverencing this holy site, I wanted to ask God for something, an intention. Accustomed to asking the saints for their prayers, I figured that here at this holy site, I would bypass asking the saints to pray for me to Jesus and go directly to Jesus himself. My mother was thinking of moving into a retirement community, and I prayed for that process to go well. "Make this happen, Lord," I said. It was one of those times in prayer that I felt that I had really expressed myself, that I had been as clear as I could about this single intention.

I knelt on the floor and bent my forehead to the cool stone, touching it with my hands as well. The moment I did this, I had an instant, powerful, vivid image of Jesus lying on the stone and then sitting up. I could see him, feel him, rising up. The image filled my mind. Emotions overwhelmed me, and I started to cry.

Stumbling out of the tomb, I stopped by the columns outside of the Aedicule and knelt down. Why had I not understood that this was not simply the Church of the Holy Sepulchre, the church of his tomb? It was also the *Church of the Resurrection*. George appeared from around the corner, and I asked him for time to pray.

"Give me an hour or so," I said.

I spent two hours by the pillars meditating on the Resurrection. *He rose from here,* I thought. I thought of how he did it for everyone—past, present, and future. I thought of all the pilgrims who had come to this spot—past, present, and future. And how it changed everything.

Around me the church almost seemed to dissolve. The marble was replaced by earth, the pillars by trees, and the pilgrims by, well, no one. It was easy to imagine the site on Easter Sunday morning. Was it a garden? In my mind's eye it was. But what did it really look like? What happened on that first morning of Jesus's new life?

THE GOSPEL WRITERS MAKE it clear that Jesus was dead. As in the story of Lazarus, the evangelists note how long Jesus was in the tomb: three days (Friday, Saturday, Sunday).[1] Jewish belief was that the soul would linger around the body for only three days.

All three Synoptics describe the discovery of the empty tomb as the work of women. Mark mentions "Mary Magdalene, and Mary the mother of James, and Salome." Matthew has "Mary Magdalene and the other Mary." Luke first talks about "women who had come with him from Galilee"[2] and then later identifies them as "Mary Magdalene, Joanna, Mary the mother of James, and the other women with them."

The story unfolds in the Synoptics in different ways, but with the same outcome. The women, ready to anoint the body or to see the tomb, arrive there. In Matthew "a great earthquake" comes and an "angel of the Lord" rolls back the stone and sits upon it. His appearance is "like lightning" and he wears clothing "white as snow." The soldiers, still guarding the tomb, "shook and became like dead men." In Mark the women reach the tomb and, wondering who would roll away the stone for them to enter, find that it has already been moved. And a "young man, dressed in a white robe," sits inside the tomb. In Luke, the women find the stone rolled away and enter the tomb. As they are trying to make sense of things, "two men" in "dazzling clothes" suddenly stand beside them. In Mark and Luke, the women are "alarmed" or "terrified and bowed their faces to the ground."

In each of the Synoptics the "angel of the Lord," the "young man," or the "two men" bear the same message. It is the message that will change the women's lives; the lives of the apostles, disciples, and followers; the lives of all who knew Jesus; the rest of world history; and my own life. Luke's may be the most beautiful retelling.

"Why do you look for the living among the dead?" the young men say. "He is not here," they say, "but has risen."

Jesus has risen!

In all the Synoptics the women then receive another crucial message. They are to proclaim to his disciples this great news. In Matthew and Mark they are also to tell them that Jesus will meet them in Galilee. In Mark they depart in "terror and amazement" and tell no one, so frightened are they. The earliest versions of Mark's Gospel end at this point. Some of Mark's text could have been lost, but the evangelist may have purposely concluded his story here, as if to draw readers in, allowing them to imagine themselves in the place of those who would hear what the women would tell.

Matthew, who wrote his account after more time had passed and when fewer people were living who had direct experience with the Risen Christ, may have wanted to be less literary and more concrete about what the women experienced. In his version the women leave "with fear and great joy," and on the way they are surprised to encounter Jesus himself. When they worship Jesus, he tells them to tell the "brothers" to go to Galilee, where he will meet them. In Luke, the women remembered Jesus's words and tell everything to "the eleven and to all the rest." But "these words seemed to them an idle tale, and they did not believe them." Peter rushes to the tomb, stoops down and sees the linen clothes, and goes home, "amazed at what had happened."

The Gospel writers use vivid words to convey the intensity of the women's emotional reactions. In Mark the appearance of the angels causes them to be *ekthambeisthai,* shocked or amazed, a word conveying deep feeling, which was also used for Jesus's prayer in Gethsemane. "Distraught" comes close. When they leave they are described as *tromos kai ekstasis,* trembling and astonished, the last word meaning "standing outside themselves." They say nothing to anyone because of their fear. Matthew and Luke depict similarly overpowering emotions. Seeing the angels leads the women in Luke to bend "their faces to the ground" in fear. In Matthew the women, having met the Risen Christ himself, race to the disciples with *phobou kai charas megalēs,* fear and great joy. In contrast to their silence in Mark, joy impels them to rush off and proclaim the good news.

John's Gospel, though, shares a different story, and it is his narrative on which I'd like to dwell. And it is largely the story of two friends—Jesus and Mary Magdalene.

AS IN THE SYNOPTICS, Mary Magdalene plays a central part in John's account of the Resurrection. The role of women in reporting the stories of Jesus's resurrection is all the more remarkable, because at the time women were often considered unreliable witnesses. Indeed, one of the arguments against the notion that the Resurrection accounts were somehow "made up" is that if the evangelists wanted to concoct a story designed to convince doubters, they would not have chosen women as the main witnesses. We can see residues of this first-century stereotype of women as unreliable in Luke's comment that the disciples find the women's story an "idle tale." The Greek word used is *lēros,* nonsense. Luke Timothy Johnson notes, "There is a definite air of male superiority in this response."[3]

But careful readers of the Gospels (and this book, I hope) will have seen women at every stage of Jesus's ministry, from the very beginning. Remember that at the Annunciation Mary does not feel required to ask a man—either her father or her betrothed—for permission to accept God's invitation to bear a son. It is Mary who gently prods Jesus to perform his first miracle, at the Wedding Feast at Cana, even when her son protests that it is not yet the right time. During his public ministry, many of Jesus's miracles are performed to heal women and those for whom women plead—he cures a woman with a hemorrhage; he raises the son of a widow in the town of Nain; he heals a woman with scoliosis or curvature of the spine.

As a man who sees them as more than simply objects of pity, Jesus spends time with women. In Mark's Gospel, the earliest we have, Jesus is taught by a woman from Syrophoenicia who, in response to Jesus's harsh words that he will not heal her daughter because she is not Jewish, challenges him. Jesus changes his mind and heals her daughter. Mary and Martha are clearly Jesus's cherished friends, close enough to him to feel free to scold him, "Lord, if you had been here, my brother would not have died."

As his death approaches, more women emerge in the Gospel stories. Mary and Martha are prominently featured in the story of the raising of Lazarus; a woman anoints Jesus's feet (or head) with precious oil; he speaks to the women of Jerusalem on the way to the cross; and it is the women who remain with him at his death, with Mary his mother joining women whom Jesus met later in his ministry, a kind of alpha and omega of his life.

The inclusion of women was a central part of Jesus's ministry. Gerhard Lohfink, looking at the Near Eastern context of the time, calls it "remarkable." It would appear, writes Lohfink, "that here Jesus deliberately violated social standards of behavior."[4] For her part, Amy-Jill Levine believes the idea of any social transgression is overstated: "A look at the women in the Old Testament should immediately signal this," she told me. "The Pharisees had women patrons. No one in the Gospels, by the way, finds this kind of friendship surprising."

The question of whether the inclusion of women in Jesus's ministry broke social boundaries may be disputed. What is not disputed is that throughout Christian history women's contributions have often been downplayed, ignored, or mislabeled. Mary Magdalene, to take one prominent example, often has been identified as a prostitute— though there is no evidence in the New Testament that she was one. The historic mislabeling apparently stemmed from the fact that

Jesus was said to have driven "seven demons" from her.[5] Mary was thus thought to have led a sinful early life. Also, at one point in the Gospels she is mentioned *near* the story of a prostitute.[6] Taken together, this led some early church fathers (church leaders after the time of the disciples), especially St. Gregory the Great in an influential homily, to label her as one. But whatever Mary's "demons" were or had been, it is clear that she was a key member of the disciples. So one of the first witnesses of the Resurrection—in some accounts *the* first witness—was classified as a prostitute.

But although maligned is not the norm for women disciples, ignored may be. One of the most helpful books on the topic is Elisabeth Schüssler Fiorenza's *In Memory of Her,* a study of how women's place in the early church has been misunderstood. A professor at Harvard Divinity School, Schüssler Fiorenza begins her book by reminding readers that the woman who anointed Jesus's head before his Passion goes unnamed in two of the Gospels.[7] As she points out, in Luke's Gospel, which moves the story to earlier in Jesus's ministry, the woman is identified mainly as "a sinner."

The author suggests that Luke, a man of his times, may have modified this story to fit the expectations of a male-dominated culture. No longer the one who foretells Jesus's death and understands his role as the one who must suffer (more than do the male disciples), the woman who anoints Jesus is portrayed as a sinner. How odd this is when we consider what she did, and how disconcerting when we consider who else is afforded the privilege of a name—like Judas. Schüssler Fiorenza suggests, "The name of the betrayer is remembered, but the name of the faithful disciple is forgotten because she was a woman."[8]

The notion of the women finally coming into the light at the end of the Gospels is also noticed by Schüssler Fiorenza:

Whereas according to Mark the leading male disciples do not understand this suffering messiahship of Jesus, reject it, and finally abandon him, the women disciples who have followed him from Galilee to Jerusalem suddenly emerge as the true disciples in the passion narrative. They are Jesus's true followers (*akolouthein*) who have understood that his ministry was not rule and kingly glory but *diakonia,* "service" (Mark 15:41). Thus the women emerge as the true Christian ministers and witnesses. The unnamed woman who names Jesus with a prophetic sign-action in Mark's Gospel is the paradigm for the true disciple. While Peter had confessed, without truly understanding it, "you are the anointed one," the woman anointing Jesus recognizes clearly that Jesus's messiahship means suffering and death.[9]

I'm not sure if I would agree that Peter doesn't understand that Jesus needs to suffer. Perhaps he does, but cannot accept it. Schüssler Fiorenza's larger point is that the women are depicted as more faithful to Jesus as his death approaches. It is the difference between saying and doing. So it may not be surprising that Jesus appears first to the women.

They are also the first to believe. "The Apostles and disciples find it harder to believe in the Risen Christ," said Pope Francis early in his pontificate, "not the women, however!"[10] Pope Francis grasped this, but it may have been an uncomfortable truth in the largely patriarchal culture of the early church. But the role of Mary Magdalene in Christian history is undeniable.

The day that George and I visited Magdala, only a few minutes' drive from Capernaum on the shore of the Sea of Galilee, we were surprised by how modest the site was. The location of the town, whose name comes from the Aramaic *Migdal Nunia* (Fish Tower), has been in dispute, but until 1948 there had been a village called al-Majdal (Tower), which preserved the ancient name. Not long ago archaeologists unearthed remnants of a settlement from the time of Jesus, which included an ancient synagogue and, from a later date, a Byzantine monastery. Today in Jerusalem stands a great Russian Orthodox church dedicated to Magdala's most famous daughter. But in Galilee today, where a large modern church is dedicated to Peter, all Mary can claim is a dusty archaeological site. That may change in the future, but it is notable that, at least in Galilee, the one who is more honored is not the one who immediately believed in the Resurrection, but the one who didn't.

ACCORDING TO THE GOSPEL of John, early on the first day of the week Mary Magdalene comes to the tomb, alone, and sees that the stone has been removed.[11] She races to see Peter and "the other disciple, the one whom Jesus loved." (Again, many believe that this is the evangelist himself, who does not mention his name out of humility, or that the writer of the Gospel was a follower of John, who didn't want his name in the story.)

Confused, Mary tells Peter that the body is gone. Peter and the other disciple race to the tomb. The other disciple arrives first, peers in, but does not enter. Peter arrives and, perhaps exercising his role as leader, enters the tomb and sees the burial cloths. Then the other disciple enters and "saw and believed." (This account may reflect a subtle competition between two early Christian communities, one who followed Peter, the other John. Here John is depicted as the more believing disciple.) Then the disciples, oddly, return to their homes.

What about Mary? The Gospel of John tells us that she lingers outside the tomb, weeping. Some have pointed to this as a sign of her unwillingness to believe—as the Beloved Disciple had believed— but it may also betoken her great love for Jesus. John initially mentions her weeping twice: *klaiousa* (weeping), *eklaien* (as she wept). I am always reminded of Jesus's weeping at Lazarus's tomb. It is as if John wants to say, "See how much she loved him."

As Mary weeps, she stoops into the tomb and sees two figures in white. Notice again that the angels have not appeared to Peter or the other disciple, who were just near the tomb, but to a woman. One angel asks her, "Woman, why are you weeping (*klaieis*)?" She answers, "They have taken away my Lord, and I do not know where they have laid him."

Then Mary turns around. We can imagine her peering out of the darkness of the tomb into the dawn. She sees Jesus, but fails to recognize him. "Woman," he says, "why are you weeping? For whom are you looking?" The Risen One understands her grief and seeks to help her, gently. Then comes a mysterious line: "Supposing him to be the gardener," she says, "Sir (*kyrie,* Lord), if you have carried him away, tell me where you have laid him, and I will take him away."

How can Mary Magdalene not recognize the man she had followed for so long? Was she so blinded by grief that she could not think clearly? Perhaps. Were her eyes filled with tears? Perhaps. After all, we are told three times that she was weeping. Or perhaps the position of her body provides a simpler explanation. Mary has stooped inside the tomb and, at the sound of Jesus's voice, peers out. So perhaps she is staring into the bright light of dawn, and Jesus's body is silhouetted against the light, making him hard to recognize.

Or is there a more theological explanation? The "glorified body," never seen by human eyes before now, may be hard to comprehend, and even harder for the Gospels to describe. As Stanley Marrow, SJ, a New Testament scholar, aptly notes, "All the resurrection narratives necessarily share this strangeness, for what they recount is, strictly speaking, not of this world."[12] (More about that strangeness in the next chapter.) Whatever the explanation, Mary believes him to be the gardener.

Mary's confusion has given rise to an artistic tradition of portraying Mary addressing a Jesus who is dressed like a gardener, or at least carrying gardening tools. There is also a line of preaching that traces its roots to the early centuries of the church in which theologians and preachers speak of Jesus as the "gardener of the soul." Jesus weeds out all that is evil and harmful from our lives and instead plants, as St. Gregory the Great says, "the flourishing seeds of virtue."[13] It is, to turn a phrase, a fruitful metaphor. How might we allow Jesus to till the soil of our soul and plant within us his life-giving words?

Mary's inability to recognize Jesus may stem from any of the reasons mentioned—grief, disbelief, or the more theological reason that his glorified body did not have the same appearance as did his earthly body. Or maybe she is just stunned by a dead man suddenly alive. Imagine one of your favorite relatives simply showing up at the grave. We can imagine her standing there motionless, waiting for an answer.

Then comes one of the tenderest passages in the whole Gospel: "Jesus said to her, '*Mariam.*' She turned and said to him in Hebrew, '*Rabbouni!*'"

The two words are preserved in Aramaic, transliterated into Greek.[14] Jesus calls her by name—*Mariam*. She responds with the Aramaic word for rabbi—*Rabbouni*. Aramaic words, you'll remember, likely reach back to the lips of Jesus, and in this case, of Mary. Imagine her hearing that familiar voice speak her name. The experience would have been unforgettable, and she would have been sure to repeat those very words when she recounted the story, at first to the disciples, perhaps to the evangelist, and to anyone who would listen, probably until the day she died. Her own friends and circle of admirers would have treasured and preserved this Aramaic call and response: *Mariam . . . Rabbouni*.

Not until Jesus speaks her name does Mary know him. At first, Mary couldn't recognize him, but she knew that distinctive voice with the Nazarean accent—the voice that called her into wholeness when it expelled whatever demons troubled her, the voice that welcomed her into his circle of friends, the voice that told her she was valued in the eyes of God, the voice that answered her questions, the voice that laughed over a meal, the voice that counseled her near the end of his earthly life, the voice that cried out in pain from the cross. Mary knew that voice because it was a voice that had spoken to her in love. Then she recognized who it was. Because sometimes seeing is not believing. Loving is.

We learn to recognize the voice of God in our lives, but often only gradually. St. Ignatius Loyola said that the voice of God can be recognized because it is uplifting, consoling, encouraging. In time we learn to listen for that voice in our hearts; it becomes easier to identify, and when we hear it clearly, it is easier to answer. It is the voice that calls us to be who we are meant to be. It is the voice that called Peter from the shores of the Sea of Galilee, Matthew from his tax collector's booth, Bartimaeus from the side of the road, Zacchaeus from the sycamore tree, and Mary Magdalene from whatever had kept her unfree. As Jesus says in the Gospel of John, he calls his sheep by name and they know his voice.[15]

Mary apparently reaches out to embrace Jesus, for he says, "Do not hold on to me, because I have not yet ascended to the Father. But go to my brothers and say to them, 'I am ascending to my Father and your Father, to my God and your God.'"

That strange utterance must have further baffled an already baffled Mary. Jesus is referring to the Ascension, when he will "ascend" to the Father in full view of the disciples. Somehow Jesus is not in a state where he can be touched—something that changes when Jesus later appears to the disciples. Later Jesus will demonstrate that he is corporeal by eating a fish before his friends and by saying to them, "Touch me and see; for a ghost does not have flesh and bones as you see that I have."[16] Jesus will even invite Thomas to probe the nail marks on his hands and his feet and the wound in his side, where a centurion thrust his lance during the Crucifixion. But not now.

"Do not hold on to me" may have another meaning. Jesus reminds the woman who loves him so much and who now wants only to embrace him that the more urgent task is to spread the Good News. As much as we want to cling, in a sense, to profound spiritual experiences, they are often given to us so that we might share them.

But Mary asks nothing about the Ascension. She has something else to do first. Jesus gives her a mission, and she immediately carries it out. She races to the disciples to proclaim, "I have seen the Lord" (*Eōraka ton kyrion*), and recounts all that she has seen. Thus my favorite title for Mary is not "prostitute" or "sinner" or even "female disciple," but "Apostle to the Apostles." She is the one sent to those who are sent. She announces the Good News to those who are to announce it.

Mary Magdalene reminds us that the most powerful tool for spreading the Good News is not knowledge, but experience. There is place for both in the Christian life, and scholarship and learning have provided inestimable riches for the faith. But the true disciple does not say simply, "I have studied Jesus," but as Mary Magdalene did, "I have seen the Lord."

THE RESURRECTION APPEARANCES SHOW that the Risen Christ understood what each of the disciples needed in order to believe. Mary needed to hear her name. A few lines after Mary's story, the Gospel of John recounts the story of the Apostle Thomas, who was not present when Mary announced Jesus's resurrection to the other disciples.[17] Thomas does not believe their reports and demands more tangible proof. "Unless I see the mark of the nails in his hands, and put my finger in the mark of the nails and my hand in his side, I will not believe."

For this statement, he is saddled with the unfortunate moniker Doubting Thomas, which seems unfair. Consider that his fellow disciple Peter not only doubted, but denied Jesus at a crucial juncture. Despite this lapse, he is called Prince of the Apostles and has a great basilica named after him in Rome. And Thomas had good reason to doubt. "Jesus come back from the dead? Are you kidding? Preposterous." Thomas may have thought his friends labored under some mass delusion.

Sometimes I wonder if Jesus chose Thomas as an apostle specifically for his probing mind or his inability to be deceived, both important attributes for a disciple. Thomas may simply have been more demanding when it came to proof—moreover, he is asking for nothing more than what Jesus offered the others when he appeared to them in the Upper Room in John's Gospel.[18] On the other hand, perhaps Thomas should have believed what so many of his close friends, so many reliable witnesses, had told him.

Or conceivably Thomas was sad that he missed his chance to see Jesus. During a meditation on this passage, I once imagined Thomas not only feeling crushed after the Crucifixion, but also devastated that he wasn't there to see the Risen Christ with the others. He missed out. Thomas may have felt hurt, wondering if Jesus considered him to be unworthy to witness an appearance.

We have to wonder if Thomas grew tired of hearing the story of his famous doubt. There is a tradition that Thomas eventually traveled to India, where he preached the Gospel. Maybe it was to get away from all those stories.

But if tradition is hard on Thomas, Jesus was not. When he appears to the group a week after Mary's announcement, Thomas is present. But Jesus doesn't castigate his friend, or say, "Get behind me, Satan," as he had in the face of Peter's misunderstanding. Jesus begins by saying to the assembled crowd, "Peace be with you."

What does Jesus do then? Scold Thomas or condemn him? Cast him out of the community? No, he gives Thomas what he needs: physical proof. "Put your finger here and see my hands."[19] Then he reminds others about the value of faith. Without even putting his hands into Jesus's wounds, Thomas exclaims: "My Lord and my God!" He is overcome with the person before him, and perhaps embarrassed.

The Risen Christ is gentle with doubters, with those who need reconciliation, and with those who are so confused that they cannot see him. This is especially important today when many Christians handle doubt and confusion with threats and expulsion. See how the Risen Christ responds to doubt. He calls someone's name. He shows. He explains. He welcomes. He forgives. In such quiet ways are people invited to know the Risen One.

The Risen One shows us that God meets us where we are. God understands the variety of ways in which disciples live out their faith. So the Gospels tell us not simply about God, but also about ourselves. Are you confused, or do you sometimes even deny God, as Peter does? Do you need God to speak to you in a personal way, as Mary does? Are you like Thomas, who needs concrete evidence of God's activity in your life? Or are you like the Beloved Disciple, who is so united with Jesus that, without evidence, he simply believes? However you come to your belief, God understands, just as the Risen One understood the disciples.

THE APPEARANCE STORIES ARE also a reminder that the Risen Christ is identifiable with Jesus of Nazareth; the Christ of faith is identifiable with the Jesus of history. The idea that Jesus of Nazareth died and a new person was created is a misunderstanding of the miracle of the Resurrection. The Jesus who is risen from the tomb knows what the disciples need because he knew them. And they know him now because they knew him during his public ministry. Mary recognizes his voice because she had heard it before. The appearances beautifully link Jesus of Nazareth with the Risen Christ.

Stanley Marrow has a marvelous summation of this idea:

The risen Lord had to be recognizably and identifiably the Jesus of Nazareth, the man whom the disciples knew and followed, whom they saw and heard, with whom they ate and because of whom they now cowered behind closed doors for "fear of the Jews." For him to have risen as any other than the Jesus of Nazareth that they knew would void the resurrection of all its meaning. The one they had confessed as their risen Lord is the same Jesus of Nazareth that they had known and followed. Showing them "his hands and his side," which bore the marks of the crucifixion and the pierce by the lance, was not a theatrical gesture, but the necessary credentials of the identity of the risen Lord, who stood before them, with the crucified Jesus of Nazareth whom they knew.[20]

The Risen One carries within himself the experiences of his humanity. Jesus Christ is fully human and fully divine.

THE RESURRECTION IS THE center of my faith. Other Christians may focus more on, say, the Incarnation—how God became human, how God understands us in the most intimate way possible. Or they may center their discipleship on the Beatitudes—as a template for the Christian life and a guideline for their actions. These are important aspects of the life of Christ. But the Resurrection is my own spiritual center. Every day I return to that theme—or more broadly, the story of the death and resurrection of Jesus.

What does the Resurrection have to do with us? After all, in all likelihood, we are not going to be crucified, though Christians are still persecuted around the world. And here's another question we haven't yet explored—because we couldn't answer it without considering the Resurrection: What does Jesus mean when he says, in the Synoptics, "Take up your cross daily"? After that seemingly masochistic invitation, he says, "For those who want to save their life will lose it, and those who lose their life for my sake will find it."[21] What does it all mean?

Here are a few thoughts on those questions.

First, *you don't need to look for your crosses.* Life gives them to you. Some young people tell me, sincerely, that they feel that they don't have enough suffering in their lives. It's tempting to say darkly, "Just wait." Whether it's a catastrophic illness, an accident, a death in the family, a fractured relationship, financial worries, long-term loneliness, trouble in school, or struggles on the job, problems will come. And the real cross is the one that you don't want—because otherwise it's hardly a cross. Remember that Jesus did not court death, nor did he beg for the Cross in the Garden of Gethsemane. The Cross eventually came to him. And, of course, the Cross is not the result of sin. It's true that some suffering is the result of bad or immoral decisions. But most suffering is not. Even the sinless one suffered.

Second, *we are invited by God, as Jesus was, to accept our crosses.* This does not mean that we accept things unthinkingly, like a dumb animal laboring under a burden. Nor do bromides like "Offer it up" solve the problem of suffering. The idea of offering one's pain to God is helpful in some situations, but not in others. For many years, my mother visited my grandmother in her nursing home. Residing in that home was an elderly Catholic sister, confined to a wheelchair because of debilitating pain. One day her religious superior came to visit. When the sister spoke of the pain she was enduring, her superior replied, "Think of Jesus on the Cross." The elderly sister said, "He was only on the Cross for three hours." Some advice does more harm than good.

What does it mean, then, to accept our crosses?

To begin with, it means understanding that suffering is part of everyone's life. Accepting our cross means that at some point—after the shock, frustration, sadness, and even rage—we must accept that some things cannot be changed. That's why acceptance is not a masochistic stance, but a realistic one. Here is where Christianity parts ways with Buddhism, which says that suffering is an illusion. No, says Jesus from the Cross, suffering is part of the human reality. The disciples had a difficult time understanding this—they wanted a leader who would deliver them from pain, not one who would endure it himself. We often have a difficult time with this too. But acceptance is what Jesus invites us to on the Cross.

Acceptance also means not passing along any bitterness that you feel about your suffering. That doesn't mean you shouldn't talk about it, complain about it, or even cry about it with friends or family. And of course we are invited to be honest in prayer about our suffering. Even Jesus poured out his heart to *Abba* in the Garden of Gethsemane.

But if you're angry about your boss, or school, or your family, you don't pass along that anger to others and magnify their suffering. Having a lousy boss is no reason to be mean to your family. Struggling through a rotten family situation is no excuse for being insensitive to your coworkers. Problems at school do not mean that you can be cruel to your parents. Christ did not lash out at people when he was suffering, even when he was lashed by the whip.

As I said, this does not mean that you do not share your suffering with others. Pain and suffering resulting, to take one example, from abuse or trauma often need to be shared with others (whether with friends or professional counselors) as part of the healing process. Also, people living with long-term challenges like, say, raising a child with special needs or caring for an elderly parent often find comfort and support by speaking with others in similar circumstances. Like Jesus, you can allow others to help you carry the cross. Jesus was not too proud to let Simon of Cyrene come to his aid. If your friends offer to help, let them.

Thus, there is a difference between having a fight with your teenage son and then being insensitive at work, and sharing the challenges (and joys) of a special-needs child in a support group. It is the difference between passing on suffering and sharing it.

In short, your cross shouldn't become someone else's.

Third, *when Jesus speaks about those who "lose their life," he is not talking only about physical death.* Christians believe that they are promised eternal life if they believe in Jesus and follow his way. But there are other deaths that come before the final one. We are called to let some parts of our lives die, so that other parts may live. Is a desire for money preventing you from being more compassionate on the job?

Perhaps your need for wealth needs to die. Are you so yoked to your own comfort that you don't allow other people's needs to impinge on yours? Maybe your selfishness needs to die so that you can experience a rebirth of generosity. Is pride keeping you from listening to other people's constructive criticism and therefore stunting your spiritual growth? Maybe all these things need to die too.

In Christian spiritual circles this is called "dying to self." What keeps you from being more loving, more free, more mature, more open to following God's will? Can you let those things die? If you do, you will surely "find" your life, because dying to self means living for God. This is in part what Jesus means about those who desperately try to save their lives. That kind of "saving" holds on to the parts of ourselves that keep us enslaved to the old ways of doing things. Trying to keep those things alive can lead to death. Letting them die allows us to truly live.

Fourth, *wait for the resurrection.* In every cross, there is an invitation to new life in some way, and often in a mysterious way. To me it seems unclear whether Jesus understood *precisely* what would happen after he entrusted himself to *Abba* in the Garden. Clearly he gave himself over entirely to the Father. But did he know where that would lead? There are indications of his foreknowledge, such as Jesus's challenge to the Jewish leaders, "Destroy this temple, and in three days I will raise it up"; John explicitly labels this a foretelling of the Resurrection.[22] But Jesus's agony in the Garden and his cry of abandonment on the Cross seems to indicate that even he didn't know what kind of new life the Father had in store. Perhaps even Jesus was surprised on Easter. For me this makes his self-gift even more astonishing.

This is why Christians speak of meeting God in the Cross. By ignoring or failing to embrace the Cross we miss opportunities to know God in a deeper way. The Cross is often where we meet God because our vulnerability can make us more open to God's grace. Many recovering alcoholics point to the acceptance of their disease as the moment when they began to find new life. This is why Thomas Merton could write, "In tribulation, God teaches us. The most unfortunate people in the world are those who know no tribulations."[23]

Fifth, *God's gift is often not what we expect.* Mary Magdalene discovered that on Easter Sunday. And—as with Mary—sometimes it takes time to grasp that what we are experiencing is a resurrection. Later on, as we will see, the other disciples will have a hard time recognizing Jesus. As the apostles discovered on Easter, resurrection also does not come *when* you expect it. It may take years for it to come at all. And, it's usually difficult to describe, because it's *your* resurrection. It may not make sense to other people.

When I was a Jesuit novice, as I mentioned, I worked in a hospital for the seriously ill in Cambridge, Massachusetts. Every Friday the hospital chaplaincy team ran a discussion group. One woman, named Doris, who was confined to a wheelchair, told us something that completely surprised me. She used to think of her chair as a cross, which would have been my reaction. But lately, she had started to see it as her resurrection. "My wheelchair helps me get around," she said. "Without it, I wouldn't be able to do anything. Life would be so dull without it."

Her comment has stayed with me for twenty-five years. It was so unexpected. And so personal. And so hard for me to understand. Doris's cross led to her highly personal resurrection. It was a reminder that where the world sees only the cross, the Christian sees the possibility of something else.

Finally, *nothing is impossible with God.* That's the message I return to most often. On the first day of the week, the Gospel of John tells us that most of the disciples were cowering behind closed doors, out of fear. After Good Friday, the disciples were terrified. Earlier, on Holy Thursday, we are told by Matthew and Mark that all of them fled from the Garden, in fear. That evening Peter denied knowing Jesus. If they were afraid before Jesus was sentenced to death, imagine their reactions after seeing him marched through the streets of

Jerusalem, nailed to a cross, and hung there until dead. Their leader was executed as an enemy of the state.

Locked behind closed doors after the death of the person in whom they had placed all their hopes—is there a more vivid image of fear?

The disciples fail to realize—again—that they are dealing with the Living God, the same one whose message to Mary at the Annunciation was "Nothing will be impossible with God." They could not see beyond the walls of that closed room. They were unwilling to accept that God was greater than their imaginations.

Perhaps they can be forgiven—Jesus was dead, after all. And who could have predicted the Resurrection? Then again, maybe we shouldn't let the disciples off so easily. Jesus had *always* confounded their expectations—healing the sick, stilling a storm, raising the dead—so perhaps they should have expected the unexpected. But they did not.

Often we find ourselves incapable of believing that God might have new life in store for us. "Nothing can change," we say. "There is no hope." This is when we end up mired in despair, which can sometimes be a reflection of pride. That is, we think that we know better than God. It is a way of saying, "God does not have the power to change this situation." What a dark and dangerous path is despair, far darker than death.

How many of us believe parts of our lives are dead? How many believe that parts of our family, our country, our world, our church cannot come to life? How many of us feel bereft of the hope of change?

This is when I turn to the Resurrection. Often I return to the image of the terrified disciples cowering behind closed doors. We are not called to live in that room. We are called to emerge from our hiding places and to accompany Mary, weeping sometimes, searching always, and ultimately blinded by the dawn of Jesus's new life—surprised—delighted and moved to joy. We are called to believe what she has seen: he is risen.

THE RESURRECTION IS A message of unparalleled hope—and unparalleled joy. A seriously underappreciated part of the Christian life, joy undergirds Jesus's preaching, is the fruit of most of his miracles, and is the most natural response to the Resurrection. Consider how often the word is mentioned in some form in the Gospels:

> "Jesus *rejoiced* in the Holy Spirit and said, 'I thank you, Father . . .'"
>
> "The entire crowd was *rejoicing* at all the wonderful things that he was doing."
>
> "You have pain now; but I will see you again, and your hearts will *rejoice,* and no one will take your *joy* from you."
>
> "Ask and you will receive, so that your *joy* may be complete."
>
> "While in their *joy* they were disbelieving . . ."
>
> "The disciples *rejoiced* when they saw the Lord."[24]

The most joyful day in the disciples' lives was Easter Sunday. We'll look at two more Easter appearances in the next two chapters, which are characterized first by confusion, but then joy. So, with joy in mind, let me end this chapter with one of the more amusing things that happened during the pilgrimage. It happened in the Church of the Holy Sepulchre, also known as the Church of the Resurrection.

ALTHOUGH THE CHURCH OF the Holy Sepulchre is closed from eight at night to four in the morning, on some evenings pilgrims can be "locked in" to spend the night in prayer. Father Doan had casually mentioned that to George and me early in our stay at the PBI. George's ears perked up. "Oh, I definitely want to do that," he said over dinner one night.

Did I? Not really. I worried that, like the apostles, I wouldn't be able to stay awake. Also, I was concerned that the experience might be too intense. Even standing before the Tomb of Christ for a few minutes overwhelmed me—imagine being there for an entire night! So I declined. George looked disappointed.

The big day came near the end of our pilgrimage. That evening we dined at the Jesuit community with Peter, an American Jesuit who taught religious studies at Bethlehem University. Like all the Jesuits I had met there, Peter was highly knowledgeable about the region's politics, and he also knew the city well. Even though we had been in the Holy Land for almost two weeks, it was still amusing to hear the holy sites referred to in casual conversation: "The traffic from Bethlehem was a *nightmare* today!"

Around seven o'clock, George excused himself so that he could make it to the Holy Sepulchre in time for the closing. Peter said, "Oh that's a wonderful thing to do. You won't be sorry." Instantly I was filled with regret. What a bad Jesuit I was, missing out on an evening vigil before the Tomb of Christ. But by the time my regret registered, it was too late. George had cleaned his plate, left the table, and departed for what promised to be a night of mystical prayer.

The next morning I rose early. There was, I had been reliably informed, a Mass at the Holy Sepulchre celebrated by the Franciscan priests at seven thirty. If I couldn't spend the entire night in rapt prayer at the holiest spot in Christendom, at least I could begin the day with a Mass there. On my way to breakfast I noticed George's door was closed. Apparently, he was still asleep, which was to be expected given that he must have returned home at four in the morning. I wolfed down a breakfast of toast and juice and arrived at the church with time to spare.

But there was no Mass. The friendly Franciscan friar, an American whom I had come to know, said that no liturgy had been scheduled for that time. "By the way," he said, "your friend left early last night."

"Really?" I said. "What time?"

"Around midnight," he said. I thought it strange, so asked why.

"Beats me," he said.

While I puzzled over that news, I noticed that the line to enter the Tomb was the shortest I had yet seen, only two or three people. "Shhh!" said someone beside me. "Mass is starting." I hung around the entrance to the Tomb, and a priest approached us, wearing his Mass vestments and holding a chalice and paten. He had a vaguely Gallic air, so I asked in French if I could join him. "*Ja,*" he said and started speaking German to a sister standing behind me. We entered the Tomb.

In that cramped space, perhaps three by five feet, he began the Mass on the stone slab that I had kissed. Next to the German sister was another sister who introduced herself; she was from Burma. After Mass had begun, another woman pushed her way into the chamber. I had noticed her over the past few days praying her Rosary near the Tomb. She was either very holy, like Anna, the woman who spent "night and day" in the Temple and who greeted Mary and Joseph and Jesus, or very crazy.[25] Or both. Maybe because I was squeezed in next to the crazy/holy woman who kept poking me in the ribs, my first and only Mass in the Tomb of Christ wasn't especially moving. Again I regretted not going to the vigil with George.

After Mass I popped by some favorite sites in the Old City and spent an hour in prayer at the Pool of Bethesda. For good measure, I purchased small souvenirs in the market. For my nephews, ages twelve and five, I bought a variety of headgear—*yarmulke*s (or *kippa*s) worn by the majority of the Jewish men in Jerusalem; *taquiya*s, the colorfully embroidered round caps worn by many Muslim men, and even a bright red fez, which I knew my older nephew would like. For a Jewish friend's son, age ten, I bought a handful of rubber wristbands stenciled with a Hebrew saying that the shopkeeper promised was the *Shema* prayer ("Hear O Israel, the Lord is One"), but which turned out to be the name of the shop.

When I checked my watch it was lunchtime. On my way to the PBI dining room I ran into George. I looked forward to hearing about his night of prayer, and started to regret my decision all over again.

"So how was your night?"

"*Not* what I expected!" he said.

"What happened? Weren't you alone?"

"Well, I *thought* I was going to be alone," he said. "So I got there around eight, just in time for the big closing of the door, and the caretaker let me in. But just as the guy was closing the door, a group of about twenty tourists from God knows where scooted in. And they were incredibly noisy. I thought, *Well it's a big church. I'm sure there will be a quiet place to pray.* So I went over to the tomb. Anyway, they followed me, and then started to take out their cameras and rustle their bags of food, and talk some more, and eat, and take pictures and talk, and walk around, and eat some more, and they would just not *shut up.*"

"What were they talking about?"

"I don't know!" he said. "But they sure had a *lot* to say!"

After an hour of vainly hoping the tourists would move on, George decided to withdraw to a more secluded spot. So he walked downstairs to the Chapel of the Finding of the True Cross, a lovely space where St. Helena, the mother of the emperor Constantine supposedly discovered the remnants of the cross. (The chapel is most likely not from the time of Constantine, but was built on the remains of a quarry dug three centuries later.) I knew the chapel, an ideal place to pray, away from most tourists, dark, quiet, secluded. George sat on a small wooden chair near the altar.

"Then some priest comes out of nowhere and says, 'Hey! You can't pray there.' I guess you can't sit in those chairs."

George searched for another spot. He chose one of the most unusual altars, positioned in front of a window affording a view of the side of the hill of Golgotha. Here the architects had removed a portion of a wall to expose the side of the hill on which Jesus was crucified. A window was placed there, so that the faithful can see the chalky white hill. George figured that the tourists were busy chatting, the priest wouldn't be bothered, and so this would be his place to pray for the entire evening. He settled in and closed his eyes.

"So just as I was getting into my prayer, these eight nuns carrying plastic buckets came up next to me, dropped their buckets on the marble floor with a bang, took out some window cleaner, sprayed the windows, took out a squeegee, and started cleaning the windows! It was incredibly loud! Squeeeak! Squeeeak! Squeeeak! I couldn't *believe* it!"

George rolled his eyes and shrugged his shoulders.

"So I left at midnight and came back here. It's a good thing you didn't go."

I felt sorry for George, who had high hopes for his vigil. It was another reminder that spiritual experiences often don't happen when you expect them and do when you don't. God is always a God of surprises.

Afterward George laughed about his silent night in the Holy Sepulchre. "I'll have to find somewhere a little quieter to pray today," he said over lunch. "Like a construction site."

The Resurrection
John 20:1–18
(See also Matthew 28:1–10; Mark 16:1–8; Luke 24:1–12)

Early on the first day of the week, while it was still dark, Mary Magdalene came to the tomb and saw that the stone had been removed from the tomb. So she ran and went to Simon Peter and the other disciple, the one whom Jesus loved, and said to them, "They have taken the Lord out of the tomb, and we do not know where they have laid him." Then Peter and the other disciple set out and went toward the tomb. The two were running together, but the other disciple outran Peter and reached the tomb first. He bent down to look in and saw the linen wrappings lying there, but he did not go in. Then Simon Peter came, following him, and went into the tomb. He saw the linen wrappings lying there, and the cloth that had been on Jesus's head, not lying with the linen wrappings but rolled up in a place by itself. Then the other disciple, who reached the tomb first, also went in, and he saw and believed; for as yet they did not understand the scripture, that he must rise from the dead. Then the disciples returned to their homes.

But Mary stood weeping outside the tomb. As she wept, she bent over to look into the tomb; and she saw two angels in white, sitting where the body of Jesus had been lying, one at the head and the other at the feet. They said to her, "Woman, why are you weeping?" She said to them, "They have taken away my Lord, and I do not know where they have laid him." When she had said this, she turned round and saw Jesus standing there, but she did not know that it was Jesus. Jesus said to her, "Woman, why are you weeping? For whom are you looking?" Supposing him to be the gardener, she said to him, "Sir, if you have carried him away, tell me where you have laid him, and I will take him away." Jesus said to her, "Mary!" She turned and said to him in Hebrew, "Rabbouni!" (which means Teacher). Jesus said to her, "Do not hold on to me, because I have not yet ascended to the Father. But go to my brothers and say to them, 'I am ascending to my Father and your Father, to my God and your God.'" Mary Magdalene went and announced to the disciples, "I have seen the Lord," and she told them that he had said these things to her.

CHAPTER 23

Emmaus

"Their eyes were kept from recognizing him."

WE GOT LOST ON the road to Emmaus. On our way back from Galilee to Jerusalem, after visiting the River Jordan, George and I decided to visit the site of one of the most beloved Gospel stories.

Losing our way wasn't surprising. Jerome Murphy-O'Connor's guidebook adduces as many as *four* places that claim to be Emmaus, where Jesus appeared to two of the disciples after the Resurrection. Much of the confusion stems from two ways of translating the distance mentioned in the Gospel of Luke. Some ancient copies of Luke say that Emmaus was 160 stadia (31 kilometers) from Jerusalem; others say 60.

The oldest tradition situates it at Emmaus-Nicopolis, a town mentioned by St. Jerome in the third century, which today is near the Trappist monastery of Latrun. The other three claimants are: Abu Ghosh, which boasts a twelfth-century Crusader church; Qubeiba, a town venerated since the sixteenth century; and, finally, an even more ancient town called Emmaus, nearer to Jerusalem, whose name was supplanted after the emperor Vespasian sent Roman troops in AD 70 to establish a colony, which eventually subsumed the old city. That last location might be the most accurate, but after the town was "lost" its absence gave rise to other claimants, which now have a longer history of veneration by pilgrims.[1]

Confused? So were we. In the end, I remembered Drew, my

editor at *America* magazine, waxing eloquent about the beauty of one site. "Don't miss Abu Ghosh," he said several times.

An hour outside of Jerusalem, the town of Abu Ghosh was easy to find. Inside the city limits, we spied a gleaming white statue of Mary atop a Benedictine monastery that crowns the highest point in the hilly city. Our guidebook described a Crusader-era church and historic mosaics and, to further whet our pilgrim appetites, noted that the town had for twenty years allegedly been the resting place of the Ark of the Covenant. Indiana Jones sprang to mind.

In a few minutes we spotted a blue sign reading "Crusader Church" with a helpful arrow. This would be easy. George drove up the hill, in the direction of the arrow until we reached a drab, cinder-block school, which had nothing to do with the monastery.

"Where are we?" asked George.

Carefully we traced our way back to the sign and started over. Fifteen minutes later we were at a dead end, though we could still see the statue of Mary, looking down at us, somewhat mournfully I thought.

"Uh!" said George. "Who puts up signs that don't *work*?"

On the third try, we nearly got trapped in a roundabout and almost collided with a small white van. Its passengers shook their fists at us.

Finally George said, "Let's go to the *next* Emmaus."

The Emmaus near the monastery of Latrun held more appeal for George, because of its identification with the Good Thief crucified alongside of Jesus. In his ministry to prisoners, George often uses this Gospel character as an entrée to the compassion of Jesus. While Jesus hangs on the cross between two thieves, one says, "Are you not the Messiah? Save yourself and us!" The other thief (known as Dismas from later manuscripts) rebukes the impenitent thief, saying that though the two of them had sinned, Jesus had done nothing wrong.

"Jesus, remember me when you come into your kingdom," says

the Good Thief. Jesus replies, "Truly I tell you, today you will be with me in Paradise."[2]

Latrun was sometimes said to be the birthplace of the Good Thief, and George had read about a chapel in the monastery dedicated to the patron saint of prisoners, which he much hoped to see. The word *Latrun* comes from either the words *Castellum boni Latronis* ("Fortress of the Good Thief") or the Crusader-era *Le Toron des Chevaliers* ("Castle of the Knights"). Over time these two names supposedly evolved into Latrun. Yes, I know, more confusion.

We spied the towers of the Abbaye Notre Dame de Latroun from the highway. After our frustrating experience at Abu Ghosh, Latrun was easy to find. As we pulled into the driveway, I had consoling thoughts of a cool, quiet, spacious chapel where we could pray for an hour or two. There were many notable sites in Latrun, said our guidebook, and I cheerfully ticked them off for George: a Crusader-era church, a Byzantine monastery, a modern-day Trappist monastery, and even some Roman baths. I couldn't wait. We pulled up to the monastery gates.

To find them closed.

"Closed from 11:00 to 3:30," George read from the sign posted.

"They're closed for *four and a half hours*?" I said. "What are they *doing*?"

"Praying?" said George.

I protested that the Trappist monasteries in the States at least allowed you to enter their chapels while the monks were going about their monastic business.

We pounded on the immense wooden doors and rang the bells, fruitlessly.

On the lush grass outside the monastery walls were small rectangular stones marked with crosses. I was confused. Not only couldn't we figure out which Emmaus was real, but the ones we were able to locate didn't pan out. We couldn't see what we wanted to see. George was disappointed that we wouldn't see the chapel of St. Dismas.

"Well, if we can't see the place, at least we can read the story," he said, and we opened up my New Testament to the Gospel of Luke. It too is a story about confusion and about seeing.

ON THE DAY OF the first Easter, a disciple named Cleopas and his friend[3] are discussing the events surrounding the Crucifixion, as they journey to whatever Emmaus was the real Emmaus. They are walking west, into the sunset, at the close of day, which adds an element of melancholy to the tale that Luke tells.

As they walk along the road, they are joined by a mysterious stranger, whom they do not recognize. Luke, however, tells the reader plainly who it is: the Risen Christ. Strangely, though, the disciples' "eyes were kept from recognizing him."

When Christ asks the two what they are talking about, at first they simply stand there, silently, "looking sad." (The Greek word, *estathēsan,* implies coming to a complete stop on the road.[4]) Then Cleopas says, somewhat sharply, "Are you the only stranger in Jerusalem who does not know the things that have taken place there in these days?" They recount for him in detail the story of Jesus of Nazareth, who was "mighty in deed and word."

They then sadly describe the events of the Crucifixion and share with him their crushed hopes: "We had hoped that he was the one to redeem Israel." You can hear their dejection as they explain what they wanted to happen, instead of what did happen. But they also share the confusing news reported from "women of our group" of Jesus's empty tomb and even "that he was alive." Some have returned to the tomb and found it just as the women had described.

"We had hoped" may be the saddest words in the New Testament. All of us have known the sorrow of having high expectations dashed. We fall in love, hoping this might be the right person for us, but then a messy breakup comes, and we are left alone. We start a new job filled with excitement and then can barely believe how miserable the work becomes. Recently one of my friends told me that his child had received a terrible evaluation from a psychologist, crushing many of his loving desires for his child. "We had hoped."

Among the saddest of lost hopes is a miscarriage—where dreams for a child give way to sorrow. You thrill to the exciting news of a friend's pregnancy, and you listen with anticipation over the next few months as she and her husband tell you about visiting the doctor, buying furniture for the baby's room, purchasing baby clothes, celebrating at the baby shower, and arranging the details for the delivery. And then you hear the awful news. All that planning and hoping and dreaming have ended. It is an unspeakable sadness. "We had hoped." These are the words of the disciples; they are crushed and lost.

Far from not knowing "the things that have taken place," the stranger explains why Jesus had to suffer, according to the Scriptures. He even scolds them for not understanding how these things had been foretold. "Oh, how foolish you are, and how slow of heart to believe all that the prophets have declared!" Jesus then interprets for them the passages in Scripture that refer to himself. For the confused disciples, Jesus makes sense of things.

Here is an irony we have seen often in the Gospel stories: Those who supposedly don't know anything in fact know everything—like a demon-possessed man who identifies Jesus early in the Gospel of Mark. And the ones who should know—like the learned scribes and Pharisees, or the disciples, particularly as portrayed in the Gospel of Mark—continue to misunderstand him. The secret knowledge here in Luke's Gospel is similar to the Messianic Secret in the Gospel of Mark, but with a twist. Here the Messianic Secret is revealed by the Messiah himself, though his identity escapes the notice of the two disciples, who were given repeated signs of who Jesus was.

All this may seem obvious to those of us who read the story today. Of course it must be Jesus! Who else would it be? How could the disciples not have expected something wonderful to happen?

But we are looking backward, at the past from the present, when the disciples are leading their lives forward—as we do today.

After the two disciples press the stranger to stay with them in an inn or in their house, he agrees. The resurrected Jesus does not force himself on the people he meets; he waits for an invitation.

Then, over dinner, he distributes the bread in a striking way. "He took bread, blessed and broke it, and gave it to them." It is the familiar pattern: *take, bless, break, give,* which occurs in the Multiplication of the Loaves and Fishes and the Last Supper. Perhaps Cleopas and the other disciple were present at both of those events. Just then "their eyes were opened," and they suddenly recognize who he is.

A beautiful painting by Caravaggio, "The Supper at Emmaus," completed in 1601, depicts this precise moment. Jesus sits at a rough-hewn table between the two disciples. Poised over the tabletop, Jesus extends his right hand, having pronounced the blessing. The disciple on the right, on whose garment is pinned a scallop shell—the symbol of the pilgrim—is stunned by the sudden revelation of the stranger's identity. He flings his arms wide as he stares at Jesus. And, in my favorite depiction of surprise in the history of art, the other disciple grips tightly the arms of his chair. He seems ready to spring from his seat entirely, unable to control himself, or perhaps he is hanging on for dear life.

As Luke tells the story, as soon as the two recognize him at table, Jesus "vanished from their sight." Not surprisingly, the disciples castigate themselves for their inability to realize who was in front of them. "Were not our hearts burning within us while he was talking to us on the road, while he was opening the scriptures to us?" Scripture and daily life are both places in which to recognize Jesus.

After Cleopas and his friend race home to Jerusalem—seven miles!—they are told that Jesus has already appeared to Peter. "The Lord has risen indeed!" they say, "and he has appeared to Simon!"[5] Then the two recount to the disciples how Jesus became known to them "in the breaking of the bread." Notice that after Jesus vanishes, he leaves behind the bread, the Eucharist, as a sign of his presence in the community.

The Road to Emmaus is a story packed with deeply human emotions, familiar to anyone who has suffered loss and seeks hope: the sorrow that Cleopas and the other disciple express about their dashed hopes, their petulance about the stranger's seeming indifference toward the news of the day, their shock over the baffling report of the empty tomb, their frustration that they had missed seeing Jesus when he was in front of them, and the enthusiasm of hearts that "burned within them."[6] The story also demonstrates how the disciples came to understand the Resurrection not only through direct experience of the Risen Lord, but by reflecting on it *together*, as a community.

THE ROAD TO EMMAUS is also a story suffused with mystery. To begin with, the identity of the disciples is confusing. One, of course, goes unnamed. And the one named Cleopas is mentioned nowhere else in the Gospels, unless he is the "Clopas" in John.[7] Further adding to the mystery is, as George and I discovered, the controverted location of the town itself.

But the main mystery is this: Why couldn't the two disciples recognize Jesus, of all people? Luke has already attempted an explanation: "Their eyes were kept from recognizing him." In Greek, their eyes were "held" from recognizing him.

What could this mean? It strains credulity to imagine that Cleopas and his friend, who are obviously distraught about the death of Jesus, wouldn't notice the person who was the subject of their conversation. Presumably they had spent months following their master, watching him perform miracles, and listening carefully to his words, probably concentrating on his face as he spoke. Obviously they knew what he looked like.

Two explanations suggest themselves. The first is a "natural" explanation, the second a more "supernatural" one.

The natural explanation is that Jesus might have purposely hidden his face with a hood or similar covering. Perhaps he wanted to conceal himself to avoid frightening them. After all, Jesus is supposed to be dead, and it would terrify people if he suddenly emerged in the dusky evening.

But it's hard to believe a disguise would work. When the stranger started explaining Scripture to Cleopas and his friend, they probably stared at him in disbelief, as if to say, "Who *is* this guy?" And while at table, it's even less likely that his face could be concealed. An even less plausible (but common) explanation is that because the disciples were traveling into the sunset, the dazzling sun prevented them from seeing him. But that hoary explanation fails as soon as they enter the inn.

So we have to move onto a more supernatural explanation, which has to do with what the Risen Christ looked like.

To the question of what Jesus looked like after his resurrection we may have to respond in the way that my New Testament professor did when asked about the precise contours of Jesus's inner life. "What was going on in Jesus's mind at this point?" asked a student. "We have no idea," said our professor. Likewise, we have no idea what Jesus looked like after the Resurrection.

But he must have looked like *something*. As I've noted, in some theological circles it is common to suggest that the post-Resurrection experiences of the disciples were not so much about actual appearances as about "shared memory." That is, the real "resurrection" came after the disciples remembered and discussed what Jesus meant to them—as well as his powerful words and deeds during his earthly ministry. Revivified with the power of this communal remembrance, the disciples were then emboldened to preach the word. In this way Jesus's spirit was, in a sense, "resurrected" among them. He didn't need to rise physically from the dead; he lives anew in their shared memory and commitment to continue his work.

This may be similar to what happens in the wake of the murder of a beloved political or spiritual leader, like Martin Luther King, Jr.,

or Archbishop Oscar Romero, the slain Salvadoran leader, or Dorothy Stang, the American sister who worked with the landless poor in
Brazil before her martyrdom in 2005. In reflecting together on the
words and deeds of the charismatic leader, their followers are filled
with a renewed sense of purpose and are empowered to carry on his
or her mission. Thus, in a sense, the person "lives."

This theological approach to the Risen Christ may be an attempt to make the incredible events of the Resurrection more credible to a modern audience, who would presumably have less trouble
accepting this explanation than the notion that someone physically
rose from the dead, as the Gospels report. And indeed, in the story
of the Road to Emmaus the disciples gather at the end of the story
to share their experiences of the Risen Lord. So "shared memory" is
important for the community of believers.

But particularly when we look at the disciples, the idea of a
shared memory doesn't seem a credible explanation of the Resurrection at all. Remember that the Gospel of John notes that the disciples
were so frightened that they barricaded themselves behind locked
doors, "for fear of the Jews." They had good reason to be fearful. *If
the Romans and Jewish authorities dealt that way with the man whom the
crowd wanted to make king,* they must have thought, *what will they do to
us?* Even *before* the Crucifixion Peter shrank in fear from being identified as one of Jesus's followers. Imagine how their fears would have
intensified after witnessing the Romans' brutal execution of their
master.

With only one exception, all of Jesus's male followers were
so fearful that they shrank from standing at the foot of the cross,
unable to accompany Jesus during his final hours. Some of their reluctance might have stemmed from an inability to watch the agonizing death of their friend, but more likely it was out of fear of being
identified as a follower of a condemned criminal, an enemy of Rome.
(The women showed no such fear, though the situation may have
posed less danger for them.)

The disciples, then, were terrified. Does it seem credible that something as simple as sitting around and remembering Jesus would snap them out of this fear? Not to me. Something incontrovertible, something dramatic, something undeniable, something visible, something tangible was needed to transform them from fearful to fearless. To me, this is one of the strongest "proofs" for the Resurrection. The appearance of the Risen Christ was so dramatic, so unmistakable, so obvious—in a word, so *real*—that it transformed the formerly terrified disciples into courageous proclaimers of the message of Jesus. In John's Gospel, the disciples move from cowering behind locked doors to boldly preaching the Resurrection even in the face of their own death. To my mind, only a physical experience of the Risen Christ, something they could actually see and hear (and in the case of Thomas, touch) can possibly account for such a dramatic conversion.

Doubtful fishermen and quarreling disciples simply talking about Jesus and sharing their memories, no matter how vivid, would not effect that kind of dramatic change. Certainly the idea of shared memory, whereby the disciples recalled together what Jesus had said and done, would have aided their faith, but it wouldn't have convinced them of the unmistakable reality of the Resurrection. The men and women of first-century Palestine needed to experience something—see something—they would never forget: something that would sustain them through years of ministry, suffering, and in some cases martyrdom.

And what they saw was Jesus, raised from the dead.

BUT WHAT HE LOOKED like is hard to pin down. Some of the Gospel stories are confusing on this point, seemingly at odds with one another. In some post-Resurrection stories, Jesus seems distinctly *physical*. In one instance, he asks for something to eat.[8] In another, as we have seen, he shows Thomas his wounds: "Put your finger here and see my hands," he says.⁹ Therefore can we conclude that the Risen Christ had a body, and so it was easy for the disciples to recognize him?

Not exactly—because in other Gospel passages the disciples have a hard time identifying him at all. As we just saw, on Easter morning Mary Magdalene mistakes him for the gardener, until he says her name. Then suddenly, like the disciples en route to Emmaus, she recognizes him and says, "*Rabbouni!*" In another appearance the disciples are fishing on the Sea of Galilee and even when Jesus calls to them from the shore, they seem not to know him (or recognize his voice), until they draw closer to the shore. Then suddenly the Beloved Disciple grasps who this is and says to Peter, "It is the Lord!"¹⁰ In these cases, it seems that Jesus has a body, but not a recognizable one.

But in still other stories Jesus seems distinctly *unphysical*. He suddenly appears in a locked room (i.e., he walks through walls) or, as in the story of Emmaus, he simply vanishes in front of their eyes. What's going on?

Here we tread on mysterious territory. As we've seen, many parts of the Gospel story are familiar to us and can be more or less understood two thousand years after they occurred. Even though none of us lives in first-century Galilee, we know what it feels like to be sick, what a farmer does, and what a lily looks like. Most of us have seen a sheep, been on a boat, and had a sick relative. Many of us have been fishing. We've all seen violent storms, maybe even over a lake. Many parts of the Gospels are part of our experience.

But the story of Road to Emmaus poses an unanswerable question: What does someone look like after rising from the dead? None of us can say. We are walking on unknown ground, and what we say about his appearance is mere speculation.

Only those who saw the Risen Christ could say what he looked like, and their descriptions, passed along through the Gospels, indicate that, above all, it was hard to describe. Theologians sometimes refer to Jesus's appearance in his "glorified body," a state that is both physical (he still has a body) and wonderfully transformed (his new body is unlike other bodies and is difficult to recognize). It's a helpful way of thinking about it: there is a body, but it is glorified, created anew by God. And remember that Jesus wasn't simply "revived," as if he had been unconscious: this new body will never die.

For me, the seemingly contradictory descriptions (physical/spiritual, recognizable/unrecognizable, natural/supernatural) indicate two things: the difficulty of describing the most profound of all spiritual experiences and the unprecedented and non-repeatable quality of what the disciples witnessed.[11]

In the first case, you need only speak with someone who has gone through a life-altering experience to grasp the difficulty in describing what happened. Imagine speaking with a woman who has just given birth. "What was it like?" you might say. "Well, it was wonderful!" she says. So it was joyful. "But also frightening," she might say. So was it joyful or frightening? "Well . . . both." Just as I was writing this chapter a friend wrote to say that her niece had sent her an e-mail after the birth of her first child. It read: "Full of unexplainable love. And exhausted to the bone."

Some things are difficult to describe, even for the most articulate, and sometimes the descriptions seem contradictory. It's hard to put big experiences into words.

How much harder it must have been for those who were the first ones—the only ones—to experience the Resurrection firsthand to describe the greatest event in history. At least in the case of giving birth, there is some precedent. Other mothers can say, "Yes, I know just what you mean," even if their own experiences differ. But to whom could the disciples appeal when describing Jesus's appearance?

Their experience of the Risen Christ was unique. So it's not surprising that the descriptions seem at once convincing and confusing.

Here, at least for me, is another sign of the authenticity of the Gospels. Had the evangelists been concerned with providing airtight evidence, rather than trying to report what the disciples saw, they would have paid more attention to ensuring that their stories matched. But the evangelists, as I see it, were more concerned with preserving the authentic experiences of those who saw the Risen Christ, confusing as they might sound to us.

LET'S STEP BACK ON the road to Emmaus. Maybe now it's easier to understand how the disciples could not know Jesus in his "glorified body." They could not recognize him until "the breaking of the bread," when his identity became manifest.

There are many reasons for own our inability to recognize God. Like the two disciples on the road to Emmaus, we might be too focused on the past. Perhaps the disciples didn't recognize Jesus (apart from the strangeness of his glorified body), because they were stuck on the events of a few days before. Rather than paying attention to what the stranger was telling them, or looking at what was in front of them, or listening to the Living Word, they were focused on death. They may have been stuck in the past.

When I hear stories about people who are unable to forgive, I often think of the Road to Emmaus. A friend of mine once described another person who was unwilling to forgive someone as "unable to climb out of the hole he is in." It's easy to feel consumed with past hurts; but when we're mired in it, we may not recognize the new things that God has in store for us. Ironically, it is at such times when we are most in need of God's help.

The disciples' inability to recognize Jesus is understandable. Cleopas and the other disciple accompanied Jesus during his ministry and saw how the crowds responded to his preaching. They might have started to think, almost despite their better judgment, "Could this be the one?" Perhaps when they saw Jesus perform his first miracle, they allowed themselves to think, first tentatively, then with growing confidence, that this was indeed the Messiah. Their expectations rose as they spent time with him, witnessed more of his miracles, and noticed his growing fame. Finally, when Jesus entered

Jerusalem, they probably thought that surely this was the final stage in the coming of the Messiah.

But then disaster strikes. Jesus is executed like a common criminal. Shame. Confusion. Terror. Everything stops. How hard it must have been for them to talk with the stranger about all the good things Jesus had done, now that it was all for nothing.

"We had hoped" are words of total dejection. Not only have things gone badly, but the months they spent with Jesus now seem a waste of time. The two disciples might be leaving Jerusalem because things turned out so disastrously. Barclay says, "They are the words of people whose hopes are dead and buried."[12]

So the sadness of Cleopas and his friend is natural. Yet a certain hopelessness may be preventing them from seeing Christ. And the fact that Jesus has not met their expectations leads them to conclude that his mission has failed. Their sadness and their sense of what should have happened may prevent them from seeing who walked beside them and from fully accepting the story of the women who reported his resurrection. They are stuck.

The disciples understand what it means to feel loss. But here is something we often forget: the Risen Christ understands it too. It is quite possible that, as he died on the Cross, he thought, *But Father, I had hoped that my ministry would be a success. I had hoped.* After the Resurrection, Jesus does not forget his human experiences; he carries them with him. And he is still human.

And so the Risen Christ tells the two disciples that hope is never dead and nothing is impossible with God. Then he shows them this by revealing himself fully. Seeing this, they are filled with joy. Hope has been rekindled and so their hearts burn. Their first impulse, as always in the Gospels and with us, is to announce the Good News.

The Resurrection shows us that there is always hope. Whether or not we can see it, it is there. Or, more precisely, he is there.

YEARS AGO ON A retreat, my spiritual director asked me to pray about
this passage. The past few months had marked a difficult time in my
Jesuit life, and I felt beset by problems in my ministry. It was easy to
imagine myself as Cleopas's companion, dejected and forlorn.

In my prayer, the road to Emmaus was sandy, bordered by a high,
grassy embankment on our left side. Cleopas and I tramped along
silently. Presently Jesus approached us. He wore a dark hood; his
face was down, obscured as he greeted us. When he asked what we
were talking about, I gave the answer from Luke, "Are you the only
stranger in Jerusalem who does not know the things that have taken
place there in these days?"

But when he asked, "What things?" I was surprised to find
myself sharing the pain that I was facing in my ministry and how
focused I had been on my worries. I could feel some of Cleopas's
anger when he responded to Jesus. He may have even vented some
anger: "Are you the only stranger in Jerusalem who does not know
the things that have taken place?" In other words, "How could you
not *know* this, God? Where have you been?"

"I had hoped," I told Jesus sadly, "that this ministry would be
more life-giving."

In my prayer, Jesus sat down by the roadside. As he placed his
hands on his knees, his sleeves slipped back, and I suddenly saw the
wounds from the Crucifixion. As he drew back his hood, I saw that he
was still wearing a crown of thorns. The man walking beside us still
carried the signs of his suffering. I felt an urge to remove the thorns,
but realized that this would hurt him. So I simply sat with him.

Then I noticed his hands, dry and dust-covered. His thin wrists
stuck out of the frayed cuffs of his tunic. "Why is it like this?" I asked
him. His look seemed to answer me: trying to do good often leads to
suffering—in my case, a little bit of suffering, in Jesus's case far more.

Later on, Jesus joined us for dinner. The inn was crowded; Cleopas and I were seated in front of a fireplace, surrounded by other
diners, who seemed not to notice us.[13] When Jesus broke the bread, I

imagined him vanishing before our eyes. And I was conscious of my desire for him to stay behind. My eye was drawn to the bread, the Eucharist, which remained. But I was also conscious of a desire to look for God even amid the sadnesses of life. With a start, I realized that I had not been doing as much as I could: I had not been seeking him actively. My problems in ministry had been so distracting that I failed to look for Jesus elsewhere.

It was a somber prayer. Typically, when praying with this favorite passage, I am reminded of places in which I have overlooked the presence of God—in friendships, in my family, in my community, in nature, in prayer, in the world around me—and I am filled with a sense of gratitude. Thus, it is usually a passage that leads to happiness. This time, however, I was reminded not only that suffering is part of everyone's life, but also that I hadn't been seeking God as attentively as I could have been. I wasn't paying attention.

Experiences in prayer aren't always joyful. Often they can point out an area that needs some attention. On that particular retreat, it seemed that Jesus was asking me to turn my gaze to other parts of my life.

But I also had to ask myself: Why don't we find God more in the midst of our daily life?

SOMETIMES WE DON'T FIND God because we are miserable. Life is often filled with suffering. We should not minimize the desolation of the two disciples, who seem on the brink of walking away (they are literally walking away from Jerusalem) from all that they have experienced with Jesus. Yet God has not given up on them. God appears to them, in the midst of their desolation, and helps to reconcile them to what has happened.

If we are patient, sometimes we are afforded a glimpse of a new way of looking at suffering; over time we can find meaning in its midst. But we must work hard at it. One of the Greek words used in this story provides a clue about how to do this. Cleopas and his friend are described by Luke as "talking and discussing." The Greek word for discussing is *syzetein,* which can also mean "inquiring" or "examining." Luke Timothy Johnson says, "We are to picture the two disciples trying to figure out the meaning of the events."[14] All of us are invited to inquire and examine during times of suffering, though our eyes may be kept from seeing God, if only for a time.

So perhaps I'm being too hard on Cleopas and his companion. Perhaps in their "talking with each other about all these things that had happened," they tried to make sense of things, even as they dealt with the evaporation of their hope. Though they feel distant from God, they are still struggling to be in relationship with God. Maybe we need to be more generous with them—and with all who struggle or question or doubt in the Gospels.

The disciples' eyes are fully open to seeing Jesus only after they offer him hospitality. "Stay with us," they say. Remember, they still believe that they are offering hospitality to a stranger. Freed from their focus on self, the two begin to listen to the stranger, to turn outward, and then invite him to dine with them. The attentive reader sees that Cleopas and his friend, even in their grief, imitate Jesus through hospitality and table fellowship. Notice also that Jesus waits to be invited; just as God often awaits an invitation to accompany us.

Cleopas and his friend move from their own sadness to a willingness to care for someone else. And in doing so they recognize God.[15]

ANOTHER REASON WE OVERLOOK God's presence is that we don't bother to look. Finding God is often a matter of paying attention, but sometimes we're spiritually lazy.

In the Jesuit novitiate, we were taught a simple daily prayer called the examination of conscience, also known as the examen. Popularized by St. Ignatius Loyola, it consists of five steps. First, you recall things for which you're grateful and give thanks for them; second, you review the day, looking for signs of God's presence; third, you call to mind things for which you are sorry; fourth, you ask for forgiveness from God (or decide to reconcile with the person you have harmed or seek forgiveness in the sacrament of reconciliation); fifth, you ask for the grace to see God in the following day.

In this prayer we are invited to work against natural laziness. Noticing takes work. If you think about your relationship with God in terms of a close friendship, it is an invitation to pay attention to your friend when he or she is talking to you about an important matter. Noticing also helps you find God in times of difficulty, when you might be tempted to focus only on the painful parts of life. Either way, it is an invitation to do what Cleopas and his companion finally realized that they had to do: pay attention.

These need not be dramatic events. On the road to Emmaus Christ does not appear in a burst of flame or dazzled in sunlight. He is simply another person on the path.

A few years ago, my two nephews came to visit me with their parents—my sister and brother-in-law. My sister had taken them to a museum in New York City, and before we met their father for dinner, they stopped by my Jesuit community.

It's always a joy when toddlers or small children drop by our Jesuit community, because everything seems new to them. "Oooh," said my five-year-old nephew when I showed him our house chapel. "It's a little tiny church!" Later on, my nephews decided that what they most wanted to do was what they always most want to do: watch TV. We huddled around my television and watched cartoons. Matthew climbed up into the chair next to me, and I was surprised at how much love I felt for him. At that moment I thought of what an amazing gift my nephews were. My sister had tried for years to have children, and finally, and with God's grace, she gave birth to two wonderful boys, and they are one of the best parts of my life.

All at once, watching cartoons, I noticed God. I was happy to notice this sign of God's presence in the most ordinary circumstance. The ability to notice God is what the two disciples undoubtedly learned in the wake of their much more dramatic encounter.

ON THAT SAME RETREAT my spiritual director gave me a copy of a painting of the Road to Emmaus that I had never seen, by the Spanish painter Diego Velázquez. It's an atypical depiction of the familiar scene, in which Velázquez concentrates on a servant girl who stands in the foreground. She is bent over a table, cleaning up after the meal. Behind her in the next room, at table with Cleopas and his friend, is Jesus, just revealed in his true identity.

The young woman notices what is going on behind her. In her hand, she is half holding a ceramic pitcher, as if she were losing her grip. The other items on the tabletop look ready to topple, a metal bowl is slanted; porcelain ones are overturned. Things are not the same, the world has changed, and she knows this, even if the disciples don't.

Because she is paying attention.

GEORGE AND I NEVER found Emmaus. At least we don't think we did. Perhaps we stood on the exact spot where Jesus met the disciples in Latrun, outside the gates of the Trappist monastery. Or maybe we were exactly where the inn once stood when we stopped in front of that school in Abu Ghosh. Who knows? In the end, we simply continued our trip back to Jerusalem, and we were happy to return to our lodgings at the Pontifical Biblical Institute.

Late that afternoon, in the slanting sunlight, I took a long walk through the Old City and got completely lost in the maze of streets and alleys. This time, though, I didn't mind being lost, because I knew that even in our confusion God is with us.

THE ROAD TO EMMAUS
Luke 24:13–35

Now on that same day two of them were going to a village called Emmaus, about seven miles from Jerusalem, and talking with each other about all these things that had happened. While they were talking and discussing, Jesus himself came near and went with them, but their eyes were kept from recognizing him. And he said to them, "What are you discussing with each other while you walk along?" They stood still, looking sad. Then one of them, whose name was Cleopas, answered him, "Are you the only stranger in Jerusalem who does not know the things that have taken place there in these days?" He asked them, "What things?" They replied, "The things about Jesus of Nazareth, who was a prophet mighty in deed and word before God and all the people, and how our chief priests and leaders handed him over to be condemned to death and crucified him. But we had hoped that he was the one to redeem Israel. Yes, and besides all this, it is now the third day since these things took place. Moreover, some women of our group astounded us. They were at the tomb early this morning, and when they did not find his body there, they came back and told us that they had indeed seen a vision of angels who said that he was alive. Some of those who were with us went to the tomb and found it just as the women had said; but they did not see him." Then he said to them, "Oh, how foolish you are, and how slow of heart to believe all that the prophets have declared! Was it not necessary that the Messiah should suffer these things and then enter into his glory?" Then beginning with Moses and all the prophets, he interpreted to them the things about himself in all the scriptures.

As they came near the village to which they were going, he walked ahead as if he were going on. But they urged him strongly, saying, "Stay with us, because it is almost evening and the day is now nearly over." So he went in to stay with them. When he was at the table with them, he took bread, blessed and broke it, and gave it to them. Then their eyes were opened, and they recognized him; and he vanished from their sight. They said to each other, "Were not our hearts burning within us while he was talking to us on the road, while he was opening the scriptures to us?" That same hour they got up and returned to Jerusalem; and they found the eleven and their companions gathered together. They were saying, "The Lord has risen indeed, and he has appeared to Simon!" Then they told what had happened on the road, and how he had been made known to them in the breaking of the bread.

CHAPTER 24

Tiberias

"Do you love me?"

ONE OF THE FIRST places that George and I visited in Galilee was the scene of one of the last places mentioned in the Gospels. The morning after checking into the Franciscan hostel, we drove directly to Capernaum, and afterward we drove south for roughly a mile, to the Church of the Primacy of Peter. Here tradition has it that the Risen Christ stood on the shoreline of the Sea of Tiberias (aka the Sea of Galilee), called out to the disciples who were fishing, and prepared a breakfast of fish for them over a charcoal fire.

The modest gray stone chapel, built by the Franciscans in 1933, stands close to the shore. Its interior is dominated by a low, undulating, cream-colored rock, the size of a kitchen table, elevated just a foot off the floor. *Mensa Christi* reads a sign marked with a cross, "The Table of Christ." Touching the cold stone was unexpectedly moving. Was this the rock on which Jesus prepared his meal? Hard to say, though the stone has been venerated by pilgrims since the early Byzantine period; indeed, incorporated into the current structure are the walls of a structure built in the fourth century.

As with many places in the Holy Land, it was easy to imagine the Risen Christ standing on this spot. Here—or near here—he watched his friends fish as he stood on the sandy beach. It's not hard to think that Jesus was joyful at seeing his friends. And joyful because he was preparing a gift for them.

THE STORY BEGINS PROSAICALLY. Peter is by the Sea of Tiberias with six disciples: Thomas, Nathanael, James and John, and "two others of his disciples." It is either late in the evening or just before the dawn. Already assuming the role of a leader, Peter says bluntly, "I am going fishing." The others tell Peter they will join him.

To many New Testament scholars, the story seems to be in the wrong place. Though John describes it as the third appearance of the Risen Christ, it sounds more like an *initial* appearance.[1] Not only are the seven disciples surprised by Jesus's appearance and not only do they fail to recognize him, but they have returned to their previous occupations. As the New Testament scholar Francis J. Moloney, SDB, asks, how could they "so easily give themselves to this prosaic return to their everyday activity?"[2] Perhaps the post-Easter appearances have disoriented them, and they are confused about what to do next. Maybe they simply needed to earn money. Or perhaps this is, in fact, an earlier appearance, and some of them have not yet seen the Risen Christ.[3]

If it is an early or even the first appearance, it is not surprising that some of the disciples had returned to the sea. Though they had accompanied Jesus through his ministry and seen his wondrous deeds, they were crushed by his public execution. Conceivably, they have resigned themselves to returning to Galilee and have climbed back into their fishing boats. How often this happens to us. Even after a profound experience of God, we often revert to our old ways of doing things—with predictable results. The same could be said about the disciples: They have caught nothing. They cannot accomplish anything without Jesus.

Just as commonly, we doubt that the profound experience even happened. "It was all in my mind," people often say after an experience of God's presence. I doubt that after seeing so many miracles the disciples thought that their experience of Jesus was "in their heads," but they may have succumbed to doubt about the future.

At dawn, "just after daybreak," Jesus appears on the shore near where they are fishing. He calls to them: "Children," he says, using a form of address (*paidia*) found nowhere else in the Gospel of John, indicating parental concern. Moloney believes the word conveys an "intimate authority."[4] "Children, you have no fish, have you?" The question in Greek is phrased in the negative and might also be rendered, "You haven't caught any fish, have you?" Jesus sounds like a parent sad over a child's failure to accomplish something.

The man on the beach asks them to cast their nets to the right side of the boat. This must have startled the disciples, particularly Peter, whose initial call from Jesus happened just in this way. Maybe they strained to see who was calling to them. *Who is that? Could it be?* Sometimes when we are the most dejected and we feel that God has abandoned us, God simply turns up.

When they follow his orders, their nets are filled to the bursting point. Is this a miracle or simply Jesus's perceptive eye? William Barclay suggests that it's often easier for a person on shore than for those in a boat to see a shoal of fish. Perhaps. Distance gives perspective. Still, it's hard to imagine Peter not knowing where to fish. Either way, the identity of the man on the shore dawns on the Beloved Disciple.

"It is the Lord," he says. As at the tomb, the Beloved Disciple is always eager to believe.

But it is Peter who joyfully and impetuously leaps into the water. The marvelous Greek word *ebalen* is the same word Jesus used for the action of the men throwing the net: "cast." Peter casts himself into the water. Peter doesn't have to say that he believes—his actions are a physical profession of faith. Perhaps he bitterly regretted the last time he was asked to profess belief in Jesus with words—during his Passion. Better to *act*.

Maybe this is as much a profession of desire as it is of faith. Peter simply may want to be with Jesus. Peter probably missed Jesus's *company* and mourned the loss of simply being around him. The word *company* is rich in meaning for Jesuits: the original phrase used for our order is the *Compañia de Jesus* and connects not only to the company (as an organization) of Jesus, but also to the company (as in companionship) of Jesus. Peter wanted to be in Jesus's company.

The disciples follow Peter, dragging ashore the heavy net filled with fish—153 of them. Why that odd number? Over the centuries, various explanations have been set forth. That was the number of species of fish thought to exist in the known world, so it represents all of creation. Or the number had a mystical significance.[5]

Or maybe someone actually counted the fish. Remember John's counting of the porticoes at the Pool of Bethesda—five—which turned out to be accurate. Perhaps John's Gospel contains more historical detail than we imagine.

Readers today can just say that there were *a lot* of fish, so many that the net should have been torn, but remained unbroken. Their catch is a symbol of the missionary success the disciples will have—working together—with Jesus's guidance. It is as if Jesus is telling the disciples, "I will give you a net so big that it can catch the world."

Reaching the shore, they discover that Jesus has prepared a simple breakfast of fish cooked over a charcoal fire (hearkening back to the charcoal fire beside which Peter had betrayed Jesus before the Crucifixion) and some bread.[6] He will feed them as he did at the Last Supper and at the Multiplication of the Loaves and Fishes. Once again Jesus uses everyday foods—bread, fish, wine—to invite the disciples to encounter God. As they sit on the beach, the Gospel tells us that none of the disciples "dared" to ask him who he is. They know.

We may be so familiar with this scene that we miss something important. Peter has, not that long ago, denied that he even knew Jesus. What strange behavior he displays. If you were told that the person you had betrayed was waiting for you, would you rush to him joyfully? Many of us would slink away or approach him shamefacedly. Yet Peter grasps that he has already been forgiven—because he knows Jesus. Peter understands that forgiveness is part of who

Jesus *is*. So instead of shrinking before his sins, Peter jumps at the opportunity for forgiveness. It is, quite literally, a leap of faith.

Notice how Peter has changed over the course of Jesus's ministry. At the Miraculous Catch of Fish, recognizing his own sinfulness, he shrinks before Jesus. He cannot bear his own limitations. At the Breakfast by the Sea, he does not fail to rush to Jesus, even knowing his sinfulness. It is a transformation that has come from spending time with Jesus.

JESUS IS NOT FINISHED with Peter. He knows that his friend needs something else—a public opportunity to be forgiven. So after the meal, beside the fire, he asks Peter a question.

"Simon son of John, do you love me more than these?" he says, pointedly using his friend's original name. "These" may refer to the other disciples. (Do you love me more than you love your friends? Or, likewise, do you love me more than your friends love me?) Or it may refer to his livelihood, as he points to the fish flopping around in the net. (Do you love me more than these fish, more than your old life?) Whatever the case, Peter seems surprised.

"Yes, Lord," he says, "you know that I love you." Perhaps his vehemence is not only for Jesus's benefit, but for that of his friends. Peter may have flushed under Jesus's apparent scrutiny, like a boy being scolded in class before his classmates.

But Jesus isn't trying to embarrass Peter. With great compassion he brings up what Gerard O'Collins calls Peter's "buried past," to help heal old memories.7

"Feed my lambs," says Jesus. Then he asks a second time, "Simon son of John, do you love me?"

"Yes, Lord; you know that I love you," says Peter again.

"Tend my sheep," says Jesus.

Jesus asks the same question again. At this third mention Peter "felt hurt." Maybe he wondered: *Doesn't Jesus believe me? Is he trying to make me look like a fool? I know I did a terrible thing in denying him. Why is he rubbing it in?* Or does it dawn on Peter that Jesus is offering him a chance to redeem himself three times, to counterbalance the three denials before the Crucifixion?

Perhaps Peter is hurt because he realizes the depth of his sin. As at the Miraculous Catch of Fish in the Gospel of Luke, Peter comes face-to-face with his own humanity.[8] This is an important step in the spiritual life.

"Lord," Peter says, as if embracing his human frailty and expelling his pride, "you know everything; you know that I love you."

"Feed my sheep," Jesus says again.

Jesus tells Peter that in his youth Peter went where he wanted to go. "But when you grow old," Jesus says, "you will stretch out your hands, and someone else will fasten a belt around you and take you where you do not wish to go." John adds that this was a prediction of Peter's ultimate crucifixion, which occurred around AD 64, some forty years before John wrote his Gospel.

Finally, Jesus says, "Follow me."

At the beginning of his ministry, Jesus performs a miracle on the Sea of Galilee, in Peter's backyard, as it were, with familiar things: fish. Peter saw the miracle and was ashamed; Jesus nonetheless asked him to follow. Now the pattern is repeated. It is as if Jesus is saying, "I asked you to follow at the beginning, when you didn't know me and you hadn't done anything wrong. Now at the end, when you know me well and you have sinned against me and need forgiveness, I ask you to follow me. Again."

In the original Greek text Jesus uses two different words when he poses the question of love. The first two times he says, *"Agapas me?"* The word *agape* means a universal love or selfless love of all human beings. Peter says yes both times. But in the last instance Jesus uses *philein,* a brotherly love or the love between friends. *"Phileis me?"* Most scholars believe that the Gospel writer is simply varying the words, and in any event, Jesus and Peter were not speaking in Greek, but

Aramaic.⁹ (If I were writing about visiting Capernaum I wouldn't use "amazing" three times on one page, even if it was amazing.)

But it's possible that Jesus tailored his question to the needs of his friend. He probably knew that Peter, limited as he was, couldn't *agape* him. For Peter responds to Jesus's *agapas* with *philō*. Okay, says Jesus, can you *phileis* me? Can you love me like a brother? Even in his questioning Jesus may be showing his compassion for his friend.

Or as a Jesuit friend once said in a homily, given the spirit of reconciliation in this passage, it cannot be that Jesus ever intended to hurt Peter's feelings. Then why did Jesus repeatedly question Peter? Like a person hearing someone profess affection for the first time, perhaps Peter's first confession of love was such music to Jesus's ears on the beach that day, that he simply delighted in hearing it a second time, and then a third.¹⁰

JESUS GIVES PETER THE opportunity to set things right without asking for an apology. He doesn't say, "Are you sorry?" much less, "Grovel before me." Christian reconciliation is motivated by love and shuns revenge. Moreover, Jesus calls on Peter to validate his affirmation of love by feeding his sheep, the community at large. Peter is "cast" by Christ into the sea of ministry and into the role of shepherd, a role linked to service and a willingness to lay down his life.

Notice that Jesus knows exactly who he is asking to lead his community: a sinner. As all Christian leaders have been, are, and will be, Peter is imperfect. And as all good Christian leaders are, Peter is well aware of his imperfections. The disciples too know who they are getting as their leader. They will not need—or be tempted—to elevate Peter into some semi-divine figure; they have seen him at his worst.

Jesus forgives Peter because he loves him, because he knows that his friend needs forgiveness to be free, and because he knows that the leader of his church will need to forgive others many times. And Jesus forgives totally, going beyond what would be expected—going so far as to establish Peter as head of the church.[11] It would have made more earthly sense for Jesus to appoint another, non-betraying apostle to head his church. Why give the one who denied him this important leadership role? Why elevate the manifestly sinful one over the rest? One reason may be to show the others what forgiveness is.

In this way Jesus embodies the Father in the Parable of the Prodigal Son, who not only forgives the son, but also, to use a fishing metaphor, goes overboard. Jesus goes beyond forgiving and setting things right. A contemporary equivalent would be a tenured professor stealing money from a university, apologizing, being forgiven by the board of trustees, and then being hired as the school's president. People would find this extraordinary—and it is.

In response, Peter will ultimately offer his willingness to lay down his life for Christ. But on the shore of the Sea of Galilee, he can't know the future. He can't understand fully what he is agreeing to. *Feed your sheep? Which sheep? The Twelve? The disciples? The whole world?* This is often the case for us too. Even if we accept the call we can be confused about where God is leading us. When reporters used to ask the former Jesuit superior general Pedro Arrupe where the Jesuit Order was going, he would say, "I don't know!" Father Arrupe was willing to follow, even if he didn't know precisely what God had in mind. Peter says yes to the unknowable, because the question comes from Jesus.

Both Christ's forgiveness and Peter's response show us love. God's love is limitless, unconditional, radical. And when we have experienced that love, we can share it.

The ability to forgive and to accept forgiveness is an absolute requirement of the Christian life. Conversely, the refusal to forgive leads ineluctably to spiritual death. You may know families in which vindictiveness acts like a cancer, slowly eating away at love. You may know people whose marriages have been destroyed by a refusal to forgive. One of my friends described a couple he knew as "two scorpions in a jar," both eagerly waiting to sting the other with barbs and hateful comments. We see the communal version of this in countries torn by sectarian violence, where a climate of mutual recrimination and mistrust leads only to increasing levels of pain.

The Breakfast by the Sea shows that Jesus lived the forgiveness he preached. Jesus knew that forgiveness is a life-giving force that reconciles, unites, and empowers. The Gospel by the Sea is a gospel of forgiveness, one of the central Christian virtues. It is the radical stance of Jesus, who, when faced with the one who denied him, forgave him and appointed him head of the church, and the man who, in agony on the Cross, forgave his executioners. Forgiveness is a gift to the one who forgives, because it frees from resentment; and to the one who needs forgiveness, because it frees from guilt.

Forgiveness is the liberating force that allowed Peter to cast himself into the water at the sound of Jesus's voice, and it is the energy that gave him a voice with which to testify to his belief in Christ.

Forgiveness enables us to renew ourselves as disciples and respond when we hear Jesus say to us, as he said to the disciples by the Sea of Galilee, "Follow me."

WHAT DID THE RISEN CHRIST do during the remainder of his time on earth?

The Gospels are tight-lipped about this period. While they describe at length the Passion and death of Jesus, they list relatively few Resurrection appearances beyond the four I have mentioned (to Mary Magdalene, to Thomas, to the disciples on the road to Emmaus, and at the Breakfast by the Sea.) In Mark, he also appears to "the eleven"; in Matthew he appears to the disciples in Galilee, as he told Mary Magdalene and the other women; and in Luke, after Emmaus, he appears to the disciples and reassures them that it is truly him by eating some fish in their presence. In the Gospel of John, he also appears to the disciples, who were locked behind closed doors. But all in all, there are not very many Resurrection appearances, which is often a surprise for newcomers to the Gospels. And it's always been something of a frustration for me, because my spirituality is so closely tied with the Resurrection.

Almost as maddening is a line from John saying that Jesus did "many other signs in the presence of the disciples."[12] I want to ask, "Does that include after the Resurrection? If so, like what?" But perhaps this literary diffidence reflects the inability to describe experiences that were essentially indescribable. Rather than lament the appearances we do not have, it is better to be grateful for the few we do.

This brings us to how Jesus closed his time on earth, a story commemorated in both the Gospel of Luke and the Acts of the Apostles, in a spot that has been venerated by countless pilgrims and at least one saint.

ON OUR FIRST EXCURSION to the Mount of Olives, George and I had hiked to the top of the hill in order to see the Chapel of the Ascension, which commemorates the end of Jesus's time on earth, when the Gospels of Mark and Luke (and the Acts of the Apostles) report that he was "taken up" from the disciples into heaven.[13] Luke reports that Jesus led them to Bethany, blessed them, withdrew from them, and then "was carried up into heaven." This seems to happen almost immediately following the Resurrection.

The Acts of the Apostles, also written by Luke, provides further details—but Acts places the Ascension forty days after the Resurrection, somewhere on the Mount of Olives. Jesus ascends into a cloud. As the disciples stare into the sky, "two men in white robes" suddenly stand beside them and ask, "Men of Galilee, why do you stand looking up toward heaven? This Jesus, who has been taken up from you into heaven, will come in the same way as you saw him go into heaven."[14] In other words, "Why are you standing around? Get to work!"

The attraction of the Chapel of the Ascension for George and me was not only that it marked the traditional place where Jesus ascended into heaven, but that it held an important place in the life of St. Ignatius Loyola. In 1523, early after his conversion from a hotheaded soldier to a devout believer, Ignatius set out on a pilgrimage to the Holy Land. For a number of reasons, Ignatius felt drawn to visit the Holy Land; mainly he was determined to visit the "holy places" and remain to "help souls" there. One of the places Ignatius longed to see was this spot, particularly to venerate the stone on which Jesus was standing before the Ascension—and where, legend had it, he left behind two footprints.

I didn't need Jerome Murphy-O'Connor to tell me that the historicity of the stone, let alone the footprints, was highly unlikely, but one thing was historically certain: St. Ignatius had visited that location. That was good enough for George and me. So after our visit to the Garden of Gethsemane we trudged up to the Chapel of the Ascension.

It was grueling. Not as punishing as our trek through the Valley of the Shadow of Death but grueling nonetheless, almost straight up the hillside in the heat. We paused every few minutes to catch our breath. I imagined Jesus and the disciples commuting between Bethany and Jerusalem.

"The disciples must have been very fit!" I said to George.

"I'm on the Mount of Olives," he said, "and I know I'm supposed to be thinking pious thoughts. But all I can think about is how much I'd like a martini with olives right now."

It was a near miracle that Ignatius made it up this hill. Before his conversion experience he had suffered a dreadful wound—a cannonball had fractured his leg in a battle in 1521—that left him with a lifelong limp. His entire pilgrimage to Jerusalem from Barcelona was crowded with peril. The future saint faced illness, met up with a mother and daughter who, like him, were begging for alms (they at one point were in danger of being "violated" in a rooming house until Ignatius intervened), and passed an uncomfortable night in a leaky church. And he hadn't even made it past Rome. Later in Venice, Ignatius gave away what little money he had and then he fell so ill that when he asked a local doctor if he could make it to Jerusalem, the doctor said that it was possible, "if he wanted to be buried there." He sailed via Cyprus and arrived in Jaffa, in what is now Israel, and finally reached the Holy City after several uncomfortable donkey rides.

Ignatius had planned to stay in Jerusalem to "help souls," and so he carried with him letters of recommendation for the Franciscans, who were in charge of the holy sites. To his dismay, however, the Franciscans felt that it was too dangerous a time for him to stay. Other pilgrims had been abducted and even killed. Ignatius protested, telling the Franciscan local superior that he felt this to be a call from God. The Franciscans told him that they had the authority from the pope to kick him out. Which they did.

But not before Ignatius could see the chapel commemorating the Ascension. Here, from his autobiography, is the saint's vivid description of the end of his pilgrimage to the Holy Land, which comes immediately after his narrative about the meeting with the Franciscans, in which they ordered him to leave. Ignatius refers to himself as "he."

When this [his meeting with the Franciscans] was over, returning to where he had been before, he felt a strong desire to visit Mount Olivet [the Mount of Olives] again before leaving, since it was not Our Lord's will that he remain in those holy places. On Mount Olivet there is a stone from which Our Lord rose up to heaven, and his footprints are still seen there; this was what he wanted to see again.

So without saying anything or taking a guide . . . he slipped away from the others and went to Mount Olivet. But the guards would not let him enter. He gave them a penknife that he carried, and after praying with great consolation, he felt the desire to go to Bethphage [where Jesus began his journey into Jerusalem on Palm Sunday]. While there he remembered that he had not noted on Mount Olivet what side the right foot was, or on what side the left. Returning there, I think he gave his scissors to the guards so they would let him enter.[15]

Almost five hundred years later, George and I trudged up the same hill. As I panted up the steep incline, I expected to catch sight of another grand church like the Church of All Nations, in the Garden of Gethsemane, or another church nearby, the Church of Dominus Flevit, which marks the spot where Jesus is supposed to have wept over the city of Jerusalem not only for its rejection of his message but, as the Gospel of Luke says, for coming tribulations for the city.[16]

The Ascension shrine is more modest—much more modest. Originally, a fourth-century church, the center of whose roof was open to the sky, probably stood on the site. In later years, the Crusaders built a reconstruction of that church as well as a monastery adjoining it. In the twelfth century the site passed into the hands of Muslims, who also believe in the Ascension. Today it is a simple, small stone building, shaped like an igloo, with an opening in the domed ceiling. We paid a Muslim caretaker a few shekels to enter (not having a penknife or scissors).

Inside were roughly twenty Indian pilgrims. Their priest was reading from a Bible in Malayalam, presumably about the Ascension. George and I squeezed in. Suddenly they started singing a lovely hymn, which sounded almost like a chant. It seemed to float up to the ceiling and leave through the oculus in the roof. In between the feet of our fellow pilgrims we could see a small, shiny, uneven stone in the floor, bordered by a marble square. Two indentations in the rock were clearly visible: these were the legendary footprints of Jesus. After two weeks of feeling connected to Jesus, I suddenly felt connected to Ignatius, the poor man with a limp who, knowing he was being kicked out of the Holy Land, walked painfully up the

Mount of Olives to pay his devotion to the site where he believed Christ had stood.

After Ignatius snuck into the chapel, one of the Franciscans got wind of it, entered the chapel, grabbed him by the arm, and led him away. But for Ignatius, seeing those footprints was enough. "He [Ignatius] felt great consolation from Our Lord, so it seemed to him that he saw Christ over him continually."[17]

George and I walked down the hill, following the path that Jesus had taken as he made his way down from Bethany to Jerusalem, and the path Ignatius had taken as he made his way back to his new life, a pilgrimage that would lead him to the founding of the order named after the one whose footprints he believed he had just seen.

THE BREAKFAST BY THE SEA
John 21:1–19

After these things Jesus showed himself again to the disciples by the Sea of Tiberias; and he showed himself in this way. Gathered there together were Simon Peter, Thomas called the Twin, Nathanael of Cana in Galilee, the sons of Zebedee, and two others of his disciples. Simon Peter said to them, "I am going fishing." They said to him, "We will go with you." They went out and got into the boat, but that night they caught nothing.

Just after daybreak, Jesus stood on the beach; but the disciples did not know that it was Jesus. Jesus said to them, "Children, you have no fish, have you?" They answered him, "No." He said to them, "Cast the net to the right side of the boat, and you will find some." So they cast it, and now they were not able to haul it in because there were so many fish. That disciple whom Jesus loved said to Peter, "It is the Lord!" When Simon Peter heard that it was the Lord, he put on some clothes, for he was naked, and jumped into the lake. But the other disciples came in the boat, dragging the net full of fish, for they were not far from the land, only about a hundred yards off.

When they had gone ashore, they saw a charcoal fire there, with fish on it, and bread. Jesus said to them, "Bring some of the fish that you have just caught." So Simon Peter went aboard and hauled the net ashore, full of large fish, a hundred and fifty-three of them; and though there were so many, the net was not torn. Jesus said to them, "Come and have breakfast." Now none of the disciples dared to ask him, "Who are you?" because they knew it was the Lord. Jesus came and took the bread and gave it to them, and did the same with the fish. This was now the third time that Jesus appeared to the disciples after he was raised from the dead.

When they had finished breakfast, Jesus said to Simon Peter, "Simon son of John, do you love me more than these?" He said to him, "Yes, Lord; you know that I love you." Jesus said to him, "Feed my lambs." A second time he said to him, "Simon son of John, do you love me?" He said to him, "Yes, Lord; you know that I love you." Jesus said to him, "Tend my sheep." He said to him the third time, "Simon son of John, do you love me?" Peter felt hurt because he said to him the third time, "Do you love me?" And he said to him, "Lord, you know everything; you know that I love you." Jesus said to him, "Feed my sheep. Very truly, I tell you, when you were younger, you used to fasten your own belt and to go wherever you wished. But when you grow old, you will stretch out your hands, and someone else will fasten a belt around you and take you where you do not wish to go." (He said this to indicate the kind of death by which he would glorify God.) After this he said to him, "Follow me."

CHAPTER 25

Amen

ON THE FINAL DAY of our pilgrimage, I rose early and rushed to the Church of the Holy Sepulchre. This time I made it to a Mass in the Franciscan chapel. After breakfast George and I walked to the Church of St. Peter in Gallicantu, outside the city walls.

I wanted to help George find something he had been searching for. The Church of St. Peter commemorates the place where Peter had denied Jesus three times. And early in our stay we were told that in this church was a chapel dedicated to St. Dismas, the "Good Thief." You'll remember that when we were looking for Emmaus, we stopped at the Trappist monastery in Latrun, which reputedly had a chapel to Dismas. Because the monastery was closed, we never were able to see it (if it was indeed there), and since then we had heard conflicting reports about the actual location of the chapel. Or, as George had started to call it, the *Legendary* Chapel of St. Dismas.

The last time I had visited St. Peter in Gallicantu I spent my time in the dungeon where Jesus was supposedly held captive before his crucifixion, but I failed to visit the upstairs church. Today, however, as George picked up a brochure at the entrance, I started exploring the lovely interior, which is decorated with several large mosaics. A few seconds later, I noticed it. On the left side of the church was an especially elegant mosaic. Under a lapis sky, a man looking heavenward stretched out his arms in a cruciform position. Behind him were the creamy walls of Jerusalem. Two figures knelt on either side of him in prayer. Above was a legend: *S. Dismas, Le Bon Larron*, St. Dismas, the Good Thief.

"Pssst," I said to George. He wandered over. "Look who I found."

George looked up, smiled, and said, "Finally."

I let him sit for some time, to pray and perhaps think about the inmates with whom he worked. I've always admired my friend's work with inmates, whom many people think don't even deserve to be ministered to. At one point during my theology studies in Boston I ended up working for George as part of my ministry practicum. In the Suffolk County House of Corrections I watched him treat the inmates, both men and women, with great care. And on a recent trip to San Francisco, I visited him at San Quentin and watched him work in death row, where seven hundred men were incarcerated for some of the worst crimes imaginable.

As ever, his sense of humor does not desert him on the job, nor does his eye for the amusing fail him. One Friday an inmate wished him a good weekend by saying, "Don't do anything I wouldn't do!" George said to me, "Coming from a serial killer, that leaves me a lot of latitude." Another man on death row said, "Father George, we like you so much, we wish you lived here with us!" George accepted that as a compliment.

After he finished his prayer, I asked if he wanted to walk up the hill to the Chapel of the Ascension as a way of completing our stay and paying tribute to St. Ignatius.

"Are you kidding?" he said. "I've had enough exercise for one pilgrimage."

ON THE AFTERNOON BEFORE our return to the States, George and I decided to do some faith sharing, a practice we had both begun in the Jesuit novitiate. Every Sunday evening the novices would gather with the novitiate staff to discuss how God had been active in our prayer and our daily lives over the past week. Ever since then, I have participated in faith-sharing groups with my brother Jesuits. It's a fine way of not only sharing with friends God's activity in your life, but also seeing how God is at work in theirs. Often when your spiritual life feels sluggish, it helps to see God elsewhere.

Confidentiality is key to faith sharing, so I won't include what George shared about his spiritual experiences. But I can share my own.

The trip was one of the high points of my life. So I was filled with gratitude. To begin with, I was grateful to God that all went smoothly logistically—no small feat given how little I knew about our destinations. The flight worked out; we had marvelous accommodations at the Pontifical Biblical Institute, where Father Doan and Brother Tony couldn't have been more hospitable; we were able to rent a car in Jerusalem with relative ease and not get lost on the way to Galilee (well, not *very* lost); the Franciscan hostel in Galilee was comfortable beyond our wildest pilgrim dreams; neither of us got sick; the weather was sunny (if unbelievably hot); and we were able to see nearly all of the sites we had wanted to see.

Not to mention the smaller graces: comfortable beds at the PBI, a rental car within our limited budget, air-conditioned rooms that overlooked the Sea of Galilee. And this: The day before we left for the States thirty Jesuit students poured into the PBI for a weeklong course. We were delighted to meet them, although the formerly quiet hallways became noisy indeed. We were glad that we came during a slow time at the PBI, when the silence made for a more contemplative atmosphere.

I was grateful for George's companionship too. Apart from a few minutes at the Jordan River, we got along swimmingly for two weeks, at each other's sides at almost every waking moment—no small accomplishment even for close friends. His flexibility to go wherever I asked to go, his willingness to drive, and his ever-present sense of humor—whether commenting on the Gerasene pig's bacon, making funny asides about less-than-reliable places we visited, riffing on sites that Jesus clearly never visited ("Jerome Murphy-O'Connor says that this drugstore is built over a first-century store where Jesus bought his aspirin," he said at a shop in Tiberias), or recounting his adventures in the Church of the Holy Sepulchre—made him a great travel partner.

Most of all, I was grateful for the spiritually profound moments I experienced. Seeing the Sea of Galilee for the first time and feeling almost speechless with joy. Standing on the shores and thinking, *Jesus saw this.* Being moved to tears when I spied Capernaum from my hotel room. Feeling astoundingly close to Jesus at the Pool of Bethesda. And, most of all, seeing, feeling, and experiencing Jesus rise up from the tomb at the Church of the Holy Sepulchre, which I still think should be renamed the Church of the Resurrection.

Of course it wasn't the perfect trip—we missed a few places I would have liked to have seen, got lost frequently, and nearly succumbed to heat stroke. And on the last day someone jostled me in the Old City and, apparently sensing I was a Christian, spat on the ground directly in front of me and said, contemptuously, "Jesus!"

DURING THE TRIP I knew that I would be writing a book about Jesus. "Oh," I would say to George if something funny happened, "this is definitely going in the book!" If he did something embarrassing, he would say, "That's *not* for the book!" On the other hand, if *I* did something embarrassing he would say, "Well, I'll bet you'll leave *that* one out."[1] And I made careful notes every night so as to get things right.

When I began this book a few years ago, in my hubris I planned to comment on every Gospel passage. That's right—every Gospel passage. But as soon as I started writing, I realized how absurd a goal that was. Better to focus on the passages that were more meaningful to me and that occurred in the places we visited on pilgrimage.

Looking back, I can see how many chapters focus on Jesus's miracles. I can offer a few reasons for that. First, more of the sites we visited commemorated his deeds—the Multiplication of the Loaves and Fishes, the Healing of the Paralytic at the Pool of Bethesda—than they did his words. Second, the miracle stories seem more difficult for people to accept today. As I said in the introduction, Jesus's humanity is a problem for people, but his divinity is even more so. Some accept him as a wise teacher, but not as the Son of God—the one who can still the sea, heal the sick, and raise the dead. So it made sense to give the miracles pride of place.

But mostly, my inclination to his "signs and wonders" reflects the centrality of those Gospel stories in my own life. They are stories to which I return almost every day. That is not to say that I don't find Jesus's preaching compelling! There were many times when I wanted to write about particular phrases: "My yoke is easy, and my burden is light," "I will be with you until the end of time," "Consider the lilies." But his miracles, and the great miracle of the Resurrection, captivate me.

This book has been an invitation for you to meet the Jesus I have studied, the Jesus I follow, and the Jesus I met in the Holy Land. As I was writing I realized that one can never encompass the man, never fully explain him. You cannot capture any individual even if you speak to every person who knew him or her, read all of his or her letters, read dozens of biographies, and even visit the places where he or she lived. To slightly alter a philosophical distinction, people are not a problem to be solved, but a mystery to be lived. For Jesus this saying is more apt than for anyone who ever lived. Intellectually I knew this, but not until I started writing did I realize that the book would be incapable of containing Jesus or conveying all I felt about him.

I pray that this book, limited as it is, will prompt you to explore more about Jesus. Maybe you'll read the Gospels again. Or for the first time. Maybe you'll pick up a Bible commentary or read one of the books I've mentioned along the way. Maybe you'll join a Bible study group at your church. Maybe you'll take a course in the New Testament at a nearby college or university. Maybe you'll make a retreat and have time to pray about certain passages in the Gospels. Maybe you'll even visit the Holy Land one day.

What I want most for you is to meet Jesus. You've met my Jesus. Now meet your own.

BY WAY OF CONCLUSION, here is a story about an out-of-the-way place in the Holy Land. On the afternoon of our last day, after I had finished packing and had checked my airline tickets, George and I stumbled upon a small church that I hadn't before noticed, the Church of St. Mark, the center of the Syrian Orthodox community in Jerusalem. The church stands on the site of a fourth-century church in the Armenian Quarter of the city and is a fascinating repository of traditions.

When we ducked into the entrance, we found ourselves in a small, ornate space. The altar stood before a wall decorated with gold filigree and colorful icons and lit by elaborate chandeliers. Upon our entrance an enthusiastic woman, probably in her sixties, dressed entirely in black, with a black kerchief tied firmly around her cheerful face, greeted us. "This is a Syrian Orthodox Church," she said with evident pride. "Do you want to know about this church?" We did.

She pointed to a small sign, recovered in the 1940s and dating back to the sixth century, that declares the church to have been the house of the mother of St. Mark, the writer of the first Gospel. Also, she said, there is a painting in the church of the Virgin Mary reputed to have been painted by St. Luke. We stared at the obscure image, painted on leather. Most scholars believe it comes from the later Byzantine period.

"This is also where the Last Supper took place," she said.

I thought, *You're kidding, right?*

"I know what you are thinking," she said good-naturedly. "But listen, the ground level was much lower in the first century. Twelve feet lower!" (Later research into archaeological texts proved her correct.) "So any room for the Last Supper, even if it was called the Upper Room, would be below ground today. And this is a very old tradition. They came to the place where St. Mark's mother lived."

She pointed us to the stairwell that led down to what her tradition believed was the location of the Last Supper. It was a small room, ten by twenty feet, with a stone floor, and in fact it seemed a more likely place than the Cenacle we had seen a few days before.[2]

The room typified the manifold paradoxes of the Holy Land. Some sites are clearly authentic—Capernaum, the Pool of Bethesda, Golgotha, Gethsemane, and many more. Others could have been accurate but one couldn't be sure, though they were most likely near where the event had occurred—the Mount of Beatitudes, for example. Other sites seemed probably inauthentic—the Via Dolorosa, for example, at least in terms of the specific stations. And some things were almost certainly legendary. And now the Upper Room was a Lower Room. It symbolized the mix of authentic and legendary that typified the Holy Land. But again, who knows? The Last Supper may have taken place precisely where we were standing.

When we came upstairs, she asked us how we had liked our pilgrimage to the Holy Land.

"Very much," I said.

She asked us what places we liked best. George said Kursi, where the Gerasene demoniac had been healed. I said the Sea of Galilee and the Pool of Bethesda. She nodded approvingly.

George told her that I was writing a book about Jesus, and she said, "Well, you know that Jesus spoke Aramaic, don't you?" I did.

"So now," she said, "I wish to sing for you the Our Father—in Jesus's own language. Would you like that?"

I said that I would, very much. I told her that I had always wanted to hear Aramaic and found it incredible that people still spoke the language of Jesus, but that I had never heard it spoken.

She opened her mouth and in a strong, clear voice began singing. Our new friend wasn't an opera singer, but it was probably one of the most beautiful songs I'd ever heard—because it was in Jesus's language. She sang in the lilting cadences of Aramaic, more and more strongly as she went on, and her prayer echoed throughout the ancient church that we had found by accident on our last day of our pilgrimage.

Then she turned to us, smiled, and said, "Amen."

ACKNOWLEDGMENTS

MY LOVE OF THE Gospels owes much to Daniel J. Harrington, SJ, my professor of New Testament during graduate studies at the Weston Jesuit School of Theology in Cambridge, Massachusetts (now the Boston College School of Theology and Ministry). Father Harrington's Introduction to the New Testament was one of the most popular courses in the school, primarily because Father Harrington is a man whose vast learning seemed to know no bounds. In addition to being a teacher and a prolific author on the Gospels, he is also the longtime editor of the journal *New Testament Abstracts,* which means that he read almost everything published on the topic. His approach—sensible, balanced, cautious, grounded in scholarship, yet enlivened by faith—is the one I hope to use for the rest of my life. Father Harrington has also been a friend and mentor and has, for the last fifteen years, reviewed all of my books for any errors in Scripture. This book is dedicated to a superb scholar, a great priest, and one of the holiest men I know.

As for the writing of this book, I would like to extend special thanks to a generous group of scholars and friends who agreed to read this book in manuscript form, at various stages, and offer their insights, suggestions, and corrections. Many are Scripture scholars who generously spent time poring over the manuscript with an eye to reviewing particular sections or themes. I cannot express how grateful I am that these men and women took the time to review my writing. So I am exceedingly grateful to: Daniel J. Harrington, SJ, for his overall and typically careful review of the entire manuscript; to Thomas D. Stegman, SJ, Robert F. O'Toole, SJ, and John Martens, for their overall review and especially their help in my use of New Testament Greek; to John R. Donahue, SJ, for his overall help and specifically with my discussions of the parables and Jesus's self-consciousness; to Drew Christiansen, SJ, and David Neuhaus, SJ, for their attention to the details of the Holy Land and also for helping me better explain some of the political and sociological realities of the region; to Amy-Jill Levine for her expert attention to the entire manuscript, especially to my presentation of first-century Judaism; to Michael Peppard for his overall review and for special attention to questions of texts in the first and second century; to Elizabeth Johnson, CSJ, for her attention to the topic of Jesus's two natures; to Donald Hinfey, SJ, for his attention to theological and specifically Christological questions; to William A. Barry, SJ, for his insights on my spiritual reflections as well as on other theological matters; to Paula Fitzgerald, who read the book from the vantage point of a pastoral minister (and also as a student of theology, a wife, and a mother); and finally, to Anthony SooHoo, SJ, a scholar of ancient languages, for answering some obscure questions about transliterating *koinē* Greek and settling an endless debate about the *iota* subscript.

A great deal of insight came to me during a two-week pilgrimage to the Holy Land, taken for the purpose of deepening my knowledge of the life and times of Jesus. So I would like to thank my friend George Williams, SJ, who never flagged in the broiling heat while we walked along the shores of the Sea of Galilee looking for the elusive Bay of Parables or breathlessly trekked through the Valley of the Shadow of Death. Thanks to David Neuhaus, SJ, the Latin Patriarchal Vicar in Jerusalem, for his initial advice and later welcome in Jerusalem; to Joseph Doan Công Nguyên, SJ, and Antony Sinnamuthu, SJ, of the Pontifical Biblical Institute in Jerusalem, for our comfortable home base for those days of pilgrimage; to Sister M. Télesfora Pavlou, CIM, and the Franciscan Sisters at the Mount Beatitudes hostel on the Sea of Galilee, which offered us a place to rest on the very spot of the Sermon on the Mount. Thanks also to Matthew Monnig, SJ, William Bergen, SJ, Thomas Fitzpatrick, SJ, Brendan Lally, SJ, Donald Moore, SJ, Jeremy Harrington, OFM, Garret Edmunds, OFM, Anthony Habash, and Rateb Rabie for their advice on the holy sites, and especially to Drew Christiansen, SJ, for encouraging me to make this pilgrimage.

As for the writing of the book, I am grateful to Roger Freet, my editor at HarperOne, for his encouragement, support, and good cheer; to Donald Cutler, my terrific literary agent; to Julie Baker and Kelly Hughes, my indefatigable publicists; to Suzanne Quist, Ann Moru, and Noël Chrisman for helping to get the final manuscript in shape; and to Matt Malone, SJ, the editor in chief at *America* magazine, for his support and enthusiasm. Thanks to Joseph McAuley, assistant editor at *America,* for his amazing, cheerful, and tireless help inputting all of my many edits and helping me check all of my Scripture citations. I could not have finished this book (on time or otherwise) without him. Thanks to an extraordinary copy editor who wishes to remain anonymous—a truly humble friend. Heidi Hill remains the world's greatest fact-checker, and she saved me from several howlers. And thanks to David Quigley for helping with the initial bibliography.

Most of all I want to thank the one whose book this is: Jesus.

NOTES

Introduction: *Who Is Jesus?*

1. Mk 8:27–30. I will cite New Testament passages in the standard way — book, chapter, and verse — with the standard abbreviations. So: Mt (Matthew), Mk (Mark), Lk (Luke), and Jn (John). Thus, Mk 8:27–30, where this story appears, is the Gospel of Mark, chapter 8, verses 27 to 30. Except for a few instances, I'll use the New Revised Standard Version (NRSV) translation, because it most accurately reflects the original Greek texts. Also, I'll list New Testament citations when quotes are taken from passages that are not the main focus of the individual chapters. For an explanation of the Greek transliterations, see chapter 2, note 9.

2. Technically, "Palestine" was a Roman term. Jesus likely would have spoken instead of "Galilee," "Judea," and "Samaria." I will use the term "first-century Palestine" because it's the most common way of referring to Jesus's homeland in the first century.

3. Mk 7:24–30; Mt 15:21–28.

4. Levine and Brettler, eds., *Jewish Annotated New Testament*, 75.

5. Mk 2:12.

6. Mt 8:23–27.

7. Mt 12:9–14; Mk 3:1–6; Lk 6:6–11.

8. Sanders, *Historical Figure of Jesus*, 7.

9. Mt 25:14–30.

10. Jn 11:1–44.

11. Lk 2:52: "And Jesus increased in wisdom and in years, and in divine and human favor." The other Gospels are silent about this crucial period in Jesus's life.

12. Jn 5:1–9.

13. Mt 13:1–9; Mk 4:1–9; Lk 8:4–8.

Chapter One: *Pilgrims*

1. Murphy-O'Connor died in 2013, as this book was being completed.
2. The prestigious school is, technically, the École Biblique et Archéo-logique Française de Jérusalem.
3. Ps 121–22. Also, in Mt 20:18 Jesus speaks of "going up" to the city.
4. Lk 9:3.

Chapter Two: *Yes*

1. Mt 8:28–34; Mk 5:1–20; Lk 8:26–39.
2. Lk 7:11–17.
3. Pixner, *With Jesus Through Galilee,* 15.
4. Jn 1:46.
5. Pixner, *With Jesus Through Galilee,* 14–17.
6. Lk 1:18, 24.
7. For an estimate of Mary's age at betrothal, Amy-Jill Levine, co-editor of *The Jewish Annotated New Testament,* pointed me to the Babylonian Talmud, which mentions a woman's age at marriage.
8. Levine and Brettler, eds., *Jewish Annotated New Testament,* 4. Betrothal was formalized with a marriage contract (Hebrew: *ketubah*).
9. For transliteration of the Greek, I'll use the standard letters, with a "long mark," or macron, to indicate the *eta* (ē) and *omega* (ō); *eta* is pronounced like a "long *a*" in English (as in the word "bay") and *omega* a "long *o*" ("doe"). Also, for any ancient Greek scholars reading, I won't use the *iota* subscript; omitting it is the convention for New Testament transliteration according to the Society of Biblical Literature. As we move through the book, you'll be able to sound out the transliterated words, even if you've never studied Greek. So, χαῖρε, κεχαριτωμένη, the angel's greeting to Mary, is transliterated as *Chaire, kecharitōmenē* and is pronounced more or less as *Kie-reh kay-kar-eh-toh-men-ay*.
10. Zerwick, *Grammatical Analysis of the Greek New Testament,* 171.
11. Meier, *Marginal Jew,* 1:205–8.
12. Lk 8:28.
13. Some scholars suggest this difference between Zechariah and Mary: Zechariah asks for understanding, while Mary is simply wondering how her pregnancy will happen. Or perhaps as an elder and a priest educated in the faith, Zechariah was expected to demonstrate more faith.
14. This process is elaborated in Meier's book *A Marginal Jew,* 1:41–48. The idea of the multistage development of the Gospels is supported by nearly all New Testament scholars.
15. Other ancillary figures, like Simon of Cyrene, who helped to carry

Jesus's cross, could have also provided eyewitness accounts.

16. Wright, *Jesus and the Victory of God,* 170.

17. Harrington, *Jesus,* 7. Traditionally, Mark was seen as relying heavily on Peter's testimony, Luke was associated with Paul, and John was associated with the "Beloved Disciple" mentioned in that Gospel.

18. Jn 14:6.

19. Fitzmyer, *Christological Catechism,* 8.

20. Mt 9:9; Mk 2:14; Lk 5:27.

21. Mt 13:18–23; Mk 4:13–20; Lk 8:11–15.

22. Lk 6:20; Mt 5:3.

23. Meier, *Marginal Jew,* 1:210.

24. Fitzmyer, *Gospel According to Luke, I–IX,* 335.

25. Lk 2:19.

26. Mt 14:13–21; Mk 6:30–44; Lk 9: 10–17; Jn 6:1–14. Possibly there were *more* than five thousand — Matthew adds "besides women and children."

Chapter Three: *Bethlehem*

1. Murphy-O'Connor, *Holy Land,* 477.

2. Some sources say Luke may have gotten a fact wrong: the census is supposed to have occurred in AD 6, but Quirinius began his governorship in AD 7. Other scholars conclude that Luke is accurate. In his massive book *The Birth of the Messiah,* Raymond E. Brown, SS, includes an extensive discussion on the question (547–55) and casts doubt on the historicity of a Roman census at that time.

3. According to Donahue and Harrington, "The term *prōtotokos* does not demand more than one child" (*Gospel of Luke,* 50).

4. Herod had a record for murder, having slaughtered his father-in-law, his mother-in-law, his first wife, and two of his sons; and he was about to murder a third.

5. Murphy-O'Connor, *Holy Land,* 230.

6. Jn 6:35.

7. Raymond Brown in *The Birth of the Messiah* offers a lengthy explanation of the significance of *kataluma* and the competing theories about where, precisely, Jesus was born (668–672). The word will appear again in Luke's Gospel near the close of Jesus's earthly life: the Last Supper takes place in a *kataluma* (22:11). Also, the use of the word *manger* reminds us that Jesus is destined to provide, and become, food.

8. Johnson, *Gospel of Luke,* 50.

9. Brown, *Birth of the Messiah,* 419.

10. Von Speyr, *Book of All Saints,* 27.

11. Mt 1:18–24.

12. Gn 28:10–22.

13. Gn 37:5–11; 40:1–23; 41:1–36.

14. Von Speyr, *Book of All Saints,* 27.

15. Luke's Gospel will later report a meeting between Mary and Joseph and a devout man named Simeon, who foretells Jesus's future and tells Mary, "a sword will pierce your own soul too" (Lk 2:25–35).

16. Mk 6:3.

Chapter Four: *Nazareth*

1. Murphy-O'Connor, *Holy Land,* 427.

2. Lk 2:48–49.

3. Some of the "apocryphal gospels," that is, gospels not ultimately accepted by the universal church (and in general written later than the four canonical Gospels), include stories about Jesus's childhood and adolescence, as if to satisfy believers' natural curiosity about this time in his life. The *Infancy Gospel of Thomas,* for example, written in the second century AD, focuses specifically on Jesus's childhood.

4. David Neuhaus, SJ, our Jesuit friend in Jerusalem, told me later that the walled-in property was once run by the Poor Clare sisters, but that a portion of the property had been given over to a community of a branch of the Little Brothers of Jesus and to a school for special-needs children.

5. Reed, *HarperCollins Visual Guide to the New Testament,* 57.

6. Reed, *HarperCollins Visual Guide to the New Testament,* 54.

7. Crossan and Reed, *Excavating Jesus,* 66.

8. Johnson, *Truly Our Sister,* 143.

9. Mt 13:55–56.

10. Crossan and Reed, *Excavating Jesus,* 54.

11. Magness, *Stone and Dung, Oil and Spit,* 110.

12. Magness, *Stone and Dung, Oil and Spit,* 130.

13. Crossan and Reed, *Excavating Jesus,* 54.

14. Johnson, *Truly Our Sister,* 141.

15. Amy-Jill Levine, interview.

16. Crossan and Reed, *Excavating Jesus,* 54.

17. Johnson, *Truly Our Sister,* 145.

18. There is a lively debate among scholars over how poor Jesus was. Meier argues for someone in the "lower middle class" (*Marginal Jew,* 1:282), but Johnson believes that, although his poverty may not have been, as Meier notes, the grinding, degrading poverty of the slave, it is mislead-

ing to compare him to a member of the "lower middle class." "The analogy does not work," says Johnson, "because there was no middle class. The family of [Mary and Jesus] lived on the economic underside of a two-sided system" (*Truly Our Sister,* 148). In *Excavating Jesus,* Crossan and Reed write simply, "Jesus was a Jewish peasant" (52).

19. Crossan and Reed, *Excavating Jesus,* 69.
20. John R. Donahue, SJ, a New Testament scholar, told me, "Galilee was as Jewish as other parts of Palestine, but it was not dominated by the Temple in Jerusalem." Jonathan Reed suggests that the phrase "Galilee of the Gentiles" refers to a region inhabited by Jews, but encircled by Gentiles (*HarperCollins Visual Guide to the New Testament,* 64).
21. Reed, *HarperCollins Visual Guide to the New Testament,* 55.
22. Magness, *Stone and Dung, Oil and Spit,* 16–31, 77–84, 85–96, 145–80. Some of these customs were also designed simply to promote basic cleanliness and health.
23. Jn 1:46.
24. Andrew Overman, "Who Were the First Urban Christians? Urbanization in Galilee in the First Century" (1988), quoted in Crossan, *Historical Jesus,* 19.
25. Eric M. Meyers and James F. Strange, *Archaeology, the Rabbis, and Early Christianity* (1981), quoted in Crossan, *Historical Jesus,* 16.
26. Crossan and Reed, *Excavating Jesus,* 152.
27. Sanders, *Historical Figure of Jesus,* 12.
28. Andrew Overman, "Who Were the First Urban Christians? Urbanization in Galilee in the First Century" (1988), quoted in Crossan, *The Historical Jesus,* 19.
29. Crossan, *Historical Jesus,* 19.
30. Chancey, *Greco-Roman Culture and the Galilee of Jesus,* 161.
31. Mk 5:41; Mk 7:34; Mt 5:22; Mk 15:34.
32. Mk 14:70.
33. Meier, *Marginal Jew,* 1:276. Crossan and Reed, in *Excavating Jesus,* doubt this. "The best specific work on ancient literacy in the Jewish homeland concludes about a 3 percent literacy rate." Someone from Jesus's milieu, they maintain, would probably have been unable to read or write. But: "If Jesus was an illiterate peasant . . . that does not mean that he could not think, does not mean he did not know his tradition, and does not mean he did not teach. It just means he did not read" (64–66).
34. Meier, *Marginal Jew,* 1:278.
35. Meier, *Marginal Jew,* 1:276.

36. Meier, *Marginal Jew,* 1:279. Again, Mk 6:3 speaks of Jesus as the brother—*adelphos*—of James and the others, and mentions Jesus's *adelphai,* sisters. These could easily be the children from a first marriage of Joseph. Catholics and Orthodox believe in the perpetual virginity of Mary: she had no other children after Jesus. For some other Christian denominations the idea that Mary bore children after Jesus and that he had natural brothers and sisters does not pose a theological problem.

37. Mt 13:1–9; Mk 4:1–9; Lk 8:4–8; Mt 13:31–32; Mk 4:30–32; Lk 13:18–19; Mt 13:24–30.

38. Mk 6:3; Mt 13:55–56; Lk 4:22; Jn 6:42. Not all scholars agree with the idea that a *tektōn* was seen as an undignified career by Matthew, Luke, and John. Still, it is notable that only in Mark, the earliest Gospel, is the question posed in a way that so directly identifies Jesus by his profession: "Is this not the *tektōn?*"

39. Johnson, *Truly Our Sister,* 147.

40. Meier, *Marginal Jew,* 1:281.

41. Mt 19:13–15; Mk 10:13–16; Lk 18:15–17.

42. My book *Between Heaven and Mirth* (San Francisco: HarperOne, 2011) examines other indications in the Gospels of Jesus's humor.

43. For example, Mark's Gospel calls James and John "Boanerges," or "Sons of Thunder" (Mk 3:17), a nickname that may have been given to them by Jesus. Also, Daniel Harrington told me that he suspected that the name Jesus gives to Simon (Peter, from *petrus,* "rock") not only indicates Peter as the "rock" on which Jesus builds the church, but also could be a playful comment about Peter's sharp and "angular" personality. In other words, a nickname: Rocky.

44. Mt 17:14–20.

45. Mt 12:46–50; Mk 3:31–35; Lk 8:19–21.

46. Meier, *Marginal Jew,* 1:332–45. Also, in *The Jewish Annotated New Testament* Levine and Brettler note that "rabbi," originally meaning "my master," "became at an uncertain date the term for one qualified to pronounce on matters of Jewish law and practice" (160).

47. Meier, *Marginal Jew,* 1:332.

48. Meier, *Marginal Jew,* 1:345.

49. Jn 11:3.

50. Mt 11:30.

51. Lk 15:8–9.

52. Mt 7:24–27; Lk 6:47–49.

53. Lk 9:62.

54. Mt 21:42; Mk 12:10–11; Lk 20:17.

55. Mt 9:24; Jn 10:30; Lk 2:52.

56. Mk 13:31–32.

57. Mk 7:24–30.

58. Jn 2:1–11.

59. Sheed, *To Know Christ Jesus,* 127.

60. On the other hand, John Donahue reminded me that Raymond Brown often emphasized that in the Gospel of John Jesus is "from above" and he speaks "a language from above" that we are not meant to understand. "So even some of the more 'human statements,' such as those from the Wedding Feast at Cana," Father Donahue told me, "have a meaning 'from above.'" In other words, this may not be a case of Jesus's not yet understanding his vocation, but of our not understanding Jesus.

61. Mt 8:2–3; Mk 1:40–41; Lk 5:12–13.

62. Mt 26:39; Mk 14:36; Lk 22:42.

63. Elizabeth A. Johnson, *Consider Jesus,* 42. There is more about the speculative question of Jesus's self-consciousness and his understanding of his vocation in my book *Becoming Who You Are* (Mahwah, NJ: Hidden Spring, 2006). N. T. Wright, in *Jesus and the Victory of God,* summed up his approach to Jesus's understanding of his vocation as follows: "[A]s part of his human vocation, grasped in faith, sustained in prayer, tested in confrontation, agonized over in further prayer and doubt, and implemented in action, he believed he had to do and be, for Israel and the world, that which according to scripture only YHWH himself could do and be" (653).

64. Lohfink, *Jesus of Nazareth,* 10–11.

65. Haughey, *Housing Heaven's Fire,* 85.

Chapter Five: *Jordan*

1. Jn 1:28.

2. Why was the Jordan River that sickly green color? Christiana Z. Peppard, a theology professor at Fordham University, who in her book *Just Water* explores the question of fresh water's value from theological, ecological, and historical perspectives, told me: "Fertilizer and petrochemical effluent from agricultural runoff is a large part of the putrid state of the lower Jordan River, though the problem is also exacerbated by heavy water withdrawals from surface and shallow groundwater on both sides of the river—which means that there is less un-irrigated water to mix with or dilute the effluent. In some place, the river still receives sewage."

3. Ps 51:3.

4. Mk 1:1–8; Lk 3:1–6.

5. Meier, *Marginal Jew,* 1:168. In *Jesus: A Historical Portrait,* Daniel Harrington lists embarrassment along with several other criteria used by most scholars of the historical Jesus. They are: "when a tradition appears in several different sources (Last Supper); local Palestinian coloring (Aramaic words, Palestinian farming methods); embarrassment at what might reflect badly on Jesus (his reception of John's 'baptism of repentance for the forgiveness of sins,' see Mark 1:4); what led to Jesus's death (the 'cleansing of the Temple'); and coherence (what fits with what can be established by other criteria)." These criteria cannot tell us everything we would like to know about the Jesus of history, says Harrington, but they can tell us something (8–9).

6. Though many New Testament scholars use "John the Baptizer," to avoid any confusion with modern-day Baptists (not that there's anything wrong with that), or "JBap," which sounds more like a rapper's name, I prefer the traditional "John the Baptist," mainly because the name is so widely used.

7. Mt 3:7–12.

8. Mt 3:4.

9. Mal 4:5.

10. Lohfink, *Jesus of Nazareth,* 27.

11. Jn 2:6.

12. In *The Anchor Bible Dictionary,* vol. 3, Ben Meyer offers a juxtaposition of the ministries of John the Baptist and Jesus. While representing a new kind of prophet, the Baptist nonetheless "maintained the classic biblical structure of repentance: conversion first, communion [that is, inclusion in the group] second." "The daring of Jesus's initiative," writes Meyer, "lay in its reversal of this structure: communion first, conversion second." ("Jesus Christ," 782). For example, Jesus eats with tax collectors and sinners before preaching conversion. John Donahue summed up Meyer's insight as follows in a conversation with me: "John preached that repentance and change of heart led to conversion; Jesus practiced a communion that leads to conversion."

13. Harrington, *Gospel of Matthew,* 53. Harrington believes that Jesus's seeking out of John and requesting his baptism "indicates some contact between the two in which John has the role of mentor." Indeed, John's reputation was so widespread that the early church took pains to distinguish between the Baptist's ministry and that of Jesus.

14. Lk 3:4, 16.

15. In Mark and Luke, the word *agapētos,* usually translated as "beloved," can also connote in this context "unique" or "only."

16. Moloney, *Gospel of John,* 59.

17. Interestingly, John says to his disciples, about Jesus, "I myself did not know him" (Jn 1:33). This can mean either that John did not realize that Jesus was the Messiah until it was revealed to him, or that John literally did not know him despite the fact that the two were related. F. J. Sheed speculates in *To Know Christ Jesus* that John may have not known Jesus as an adult, because John had entered a religious community and "gone to the desert" early in his life (96). Most scholars today, however, believe Jesus and John had met, and that Jesus may have been a disciple of John's for a time. So it is more likely that John (or at least the Gospel) is speaking of John not knowing Jesus as Messiah.

18. Green, *God's Fool,* 84.

19. So does St. Paul, who wrote, "For our sake he [God] made him [Jesus] to be sin who knew no sin so that in him we might become the righteousness of God" (2 Cor 5:21). Another way of looking at Jesus's baptism is that he acts as a kind of "representative" of all humankind.

20. Scirghi, *Everything Is Sacred,* 50–51.

21. Harrington, *Gospel of Matthew,* 62.

22. "Thrust forth": Marshall, *Interlinear Greek-English New Testament,* 138. "Hurled": Sheed, *To Know Christ Jesus,* 98.

23. Quoted in Crace, *Quarantine,* vii.

24. Mt 4:1–11; Lk 4:1–12.

25. Barclay, *Mind of Jesus,* 33.

26. Merton, *Seven Storey Mountain,* 449.

27. Scirghi, *Everything Is Sacred,* 41.

Chapter Six: *Rejection*

1. Crossan and Reed, *Excavating Jesus,* 64.

2. Mk 7:24; Mt 14:13; Mt 14:23; Jn 6:15; Lk 5:16. In *Jesus: A Historical Portrait,* Harrington writes, "If you want to know what Luke regarded as the most important moments in Jesus's life, look at his mentions of Jesus at prayer" (47).

3. Mt 9:20–22; Mk 5:25–34; Lk 8:43–48.

4. Luke offers an edited version of Is 58:6 and 61:1–2, revising the text for his readers. Interestingly, in Luke's account Jesus stops reading halfway through the passage from Isaiah, ending his proclamation at the words "the year of the Lord's favor." The next phrase would have been "and the day of vengeance of our God . . ."

5. Levine, *Misunderstood Jew,* 57.

6. John Meier calls the kingdom of God a "major component" of Jesus's

message (*Marginal Jew,* 2:237–39). The Scripture scholar Joachim Jeremias called the reign of God the central theme of Jesus's preaching.

7. Of course one could argue that the entire Old Testament is concerned with the idea of God as king, but the specific phrase "reign of God" seems to have originated with Jesus.

8. Sanders, *Historical Figure of Jesus,* 170–78.

9. Matthew's Gospel also uses, at times, instead of "reign of God," the phrase "reign of heaven" (*basileian tōn ouranōn*). Most scholars say that the two phrases are identical. Matthew, whose audience was more heavily Jewish than Mark's and Luke's, was probably trying to avoid the word "God," which was considered too holy to be pronounced or even written. It is unclear which term—"reign of God" or "reign of heaven"— was used by Jesus, but it is significant that the earliest Gospel, Mark, uses "reign of God."

10. Another translation that is possible, given that the same phrase appears in the Acts 20:32 in another context, is "words of salvation."

11. 1 Kgs 17:8–16; 2 Kgs 5:1–4.

12. In Greek, *amēn legō humin*: "Truly I tell you."

13. Harrington, *Jesus,* 16.

14. This is a reference to the "Jubilee Year" (or "Sabbatical Year") mentioned in the Book of Deuteronomy (15:1–7), in which every seventh year, debts were wiped away, and in Leviticus (25:8–12), which counts it as every fiftieth year. In general, it is a proclamation of a time of freedom.

15. Johnson, *Gospel of Luke,* 82.

Chapter Seven: *Galilee*

1. Trueblood, *Humor of Christ,* 18.

2. Donahue and Harrington, *Gospel of Mark,* 74.

3. Jn 1:40, 44.

4. Thanks to Thomas D. Stegman, SJ, for this insight.

5. Meier, *Marginal Jew,* 3:159.

6. In *A Marginal Jew,* Meier points to Jer 16:16, where God sends "many fishers" to catch the enemies of Israel (3:160).

7. Meier, *Marginal Jew,* 3:160.

8. Lohfink, *Jesus of Nazareth,* 73–76.

9. Meier, *Marginal Jew,* 3:160–61.

10. Mt 8:14–15; Mk 1:29–31; Lk 4:38–39.

11. "The Gospel of Luke," in Brown, Fitzmyer, and Murphy, eds., *The New Jerome Biblical Commentary,* 691. The *NJBC* estimates a population of fifteen thousand. Crossan and Reed, in *Excavating Jesus* (119), estimate a

far more modest number of inhabitants based on more recent archaeo-logical data, around a thousand.

12. Some scholars surmise that Peter may have been a widower. In the Gospel passages cited in footnote 10, after Jesus heals Peter's mother-in-law, she "got up and began to serve him" (Lk 4:30). This may be a way of highlighting her complete healing. But some say this task would have more likely fallen to Peter's wife, who is apparently not on the scene. (Notice that the evangelists do not write, "Peter's wife asked Jesus to heal her mother.") Either way—married man or widower—Peter was probably responsible for caring for his mother-in-law.

13. Horns and Martens, *Let the Little Children Come to Me*, 174–75.

14. Daniel-Rops, *Daily Life in Palestine*, 237. And of course beyond the memory of women too.

15. Pixner, *With Jesus Through Galilee*, 29.

16. Mt 13:47–50.

17. Sanders, *Historical Figure of Jesus*, 102–3. Sanders includes an excellent brief description of Galilean fishing practices in his chapter "The Set-ting and Method of Jesus's Ministry."

18. Reed, *HarperCollins Visual Guide to the New Testament*, 69.

19. Crossan and Reed, *Excavating Jesus*, 123.

20. Lk 5:10.

21. Donahue told me, "Jesus proclaims and enacts his kingdom proclama-tion not as a charismatic individual alone, but with a group whom he calls and forms, so his activity is radically social, and is the genesis of the church (*ekklēsia*: literally, 'called out')."

22. Is 9:1.

23. Jn 1:40–42.

24. Pixner suggests this scenario in *With Jesus in Galilee*, 30–32.

25. "When he returned to Capernaum after some days, it was reported that he was *at home*" (Mk 2:1, my italics).

26. In *Breathing Under Water*, the Franciscan Richard Rohr points out that Jesus often says, "Follow me," but never, "Worship me" (77). It's a needed reminder to those who would focus only on his divinity.

Chapter Eight: *Immediately*

1. The number of variations in the spelling of the town's name is mad-dening. Most English translations use Capernaum. (That's what road signs in Galilee use today—along with Hebrew and Arabic.) Other translations use Capernahum or Kapernaum. The Hebrew name is Kfar Nahum ("the village of Nahum") and the Greek name used in the New

Testament is Καφαρναουμ: *Kapharnaoum*. So perhaps the best translation would be Kapharnaum. Still, Capernaum is the most common usage today, though the English pronunciation is quite unlike the original.

2. "An oppressive heat hovers over Capernaum during the long summers," write Crossan and Reed in *Excavating Jesus* (119). I concur.

3. Murphy-O'Connor, *Holy Land*, 251. He is referring to Lk 7:1–6: "He loves our people," say the Jewish elders of Capernaum, "and it is he who built our synagogue for us." On the other hand, Amy-Jill Levine suggested to me that the town may have had more than one synagogue; the structure built by the centurion may have been one of several places of worship.

4. Mt 9:1.

5. This translation is not reflected in the New Revised Standard Version, but Mark writes, *Kai euthus tois sabbasin,* literally, "And immediately on the Sabbath."

6. Brown, Fitzmyer, and Murphy, eds., *New Jerome Biblical Commentary*, 600.

7. Donahue and Harrington, *Gospel of Mark*, 79.

8. Donahue and Harrington, *Gospel of Mark*, 80.

9. Donahue and Harrington, *Gospel of Mark*, 80.

10. It is "What have we to do with thee?" in Marshall, *Interlinear Greek New Testament*, 139.

11. Brown, *Introduction to the New Testament*, 129.

12. Meier, *Marginal Jew*, 2:630. And: "The historical fact that Jesus performed extraordinary deeds deemed by himself and others to be miracles is supported most impressively by the criterion of multiple attestation of sources and forms and the criterion of coherence. The miracle traditions about Jesus's public ministry are so widely attested in various sources and literary forms by the end of the first Christian generation that total fabrication by the early church is, practically speaking, impossible." Barclay writes in *The Mind of Jesus*: "If we remove the stories of the miracles, the whole framework of the Gospel story falls to pieces, and often even the teaching of Jesus is left without an occasion and a context" (66).

13. In Matthew (17:14–21) he is described as *selēniazetai,* or "moonstruck," from the Greek word for "moon." The boy's condition was thought to be related to the phases of the moon. (The word "lunatic" preserves the Latin word for moon, *luna*.) From the description of the boy's falls and what was believed in ancient medicine, the condition is considered by most contemporary scholars to be epilepsy (Harrington, *Gospel of Matthew*, 257). In Mark (9:14–29) and Luke (9:37–43) the boy is afflicted by "a spirit."

14. Mt 17:15–18.

15. We should also remember, as Meier points out in *A Marginal Jew,* the "description of the illness or other difficulty presented to Jesus is often vague. . . . What the precise pathology of each condition was, what its cause was, how serious or irreversible it was, and whether the cure Jesus worked was permanent are not stated" (2:647). The writers of the Gospels were not modern-day physicians or diagnosticians.
16. Bloom, ed., *C. S. Lewis,* 41.
17. Harrington, *Who Is Jesus?,* 25.
18. Mt 11:29.
19. Rom 7:19.

Chapter Nine: *Gennesaret*
1. Mk 1:16–20; Mt 4:18–22.
2. Johnson, *Gospel of Luke,* 88.
3. Prv 9:10.
4. Jer 29:11.
5. Coles, *Dorothy Day,* 51.
6. Sheed, *To Know Christ Jesus,* 148.

Chapter Ten: *Happy*
1. Harrington, *Gospel of Matthew,* 78.
2. Murphy-O'Connor, *Holy Land,* 316.
3. A Jesuit told me that he was once invited by his spiritual director to meditate on the Sermon on the Plain during a retreat. Unfamiliar with that nomenclature, he imagined Jesus on an *airplane.* "I thought it was some creative Jesuit meditation technique," he said.
4. The expression "Blessed are" was a standard Jewish formula, appearing many times in the Old Testament, particularly in the Psalms, as well as in the Jewish liturgy (Levine and Brettler, eds., *Jewish Annotated New Testament,* 10).
5. Barclay, *Gospel of Matthew,* 97.
6. Harrington, *Gospel of Matthew,* 78.
7. Lohfink, *Jesus of Nazareth,* 29. In his book *The Historical Figure of Jesus,* E. P. Sanders offers an excellent response to the question of "When?" Sanders also asks, "Where?" That is, in heaven or on earth? Sanders concludes that, while it is impossible to say precisely what Jesus intended and no one statement encompasses his teaching, "There is no difficulty in thinking that Jesus thought that the kingdom was in heaven, that people would enter it in the future, and that it was also present in some sense in his own work" (178). In other words, everywhere and at every

time. But Lohfink's emphasis on immediacy is important, particularly when considered in light of some of Jesus's parables.

8. Noted in Levine and Brettler, eds., *Jewish Annotated New Testament* (113). See also Dt 15:11 ("I therefore command you, 'Open your hand to the poor and needy neighbor in your land' "); Is 49:10; Jer 31:25; Ez 34:29.

9. Harrington, *Jesus,* 33.

10. As for the crowd's reactions, it's hard not to recall the film *Monty Python's Life of Brian,* which follows the travails of a fictional counterpart to Jesus named Brian. In the film, the real Jesus is proclaiming the Beatitudes from a mountain (or at least a hill), and the camera pans back to a group of people who can barely hear him. One man, straining to hear, reports to the crowd, "I think it was 'Blessed are the cheesemakers.'" A woman laughs and asks: "What's so special about the cheesemakers?" Then comes my favorite line, by someone who is obviously a theologian, "Well, obviously, this is not meant to be taken *literally.* It refers to any manufacturers of dairy products."

11. Barclay, *Gospel of Matthew,* 122.

12. Ps 24:3–4.

13. Harrington, *Gospel of Matthew,* 79.

14. Jesus also described *himself* using this word, as in Mt 11:29, when he says, "I am meek (*praus*) and humble in heart."

15. Barclay, *Gospel of Matthew,* 119.

16. Mt 20:16.

17. Mt 25:31–46.

18. And, particularly in Matthew, a portrait of who Jesus is.

19. Mt 19:24; Mk 10:25.

20. Mt 23:11.

21. Barclay in *Gospel of Matthew* writes, "*Makarios,* then, describes that joy which has its secret within itself, that joy which is serene and untouchable, and self-contained, that joy which is completely independent of all the chances and the changes of life" (1:103).

Chapter Eleven: *Capernaum*

1. Mt 8:20; Lk 9:58.

2. The New Revised Standard Version uses "at home." So do Marshall, *The Interlinear Greek-English New Testament,* 142; and Zerwick, *Grammatical Analysis of the New Testament,* 104.

3. As Donahue and Harrington write in *The Gospel of Mark:* "Perhaps we are to imagine that the house belongs to Peter (see 1:29–31), though some scholars suppose that it belonged to Jesus (see 2:1, 15)" (284).

4. Murphy-O'Connor, *Holy Land,* 252.

5. Crossan and Reed, *Excavating Jesus,* 130.

6. Murphy-O'Connor, *Holy Land,* 254. Mt 8:14 says that Jesus "came to" or "entered" Peter's house, when he cured Peter's mother-in-law, implying that Jesus did not live there or lived elsewhere.

7. Again, Jesus says, in Mt 8:20 and Lk 9:58, "[T]he Son of Man has nowhere to lay his head," which argues against the idea of Jesus having a permanent dwelling. On the other hand, it may simply indicate that he stayed in Capernaum for a limited time.

8. The presence of a centurion (Mt 8:5–13; Lk 7: 1–10; Jn 4:46–54) argues for a "small Herodian garrison with an official" (Reed, *HarperCollins Visual Guide to the New Testament,* 74).

9. Reed, *HarperCollins Visual Guide to the New Testament,* 75.

10. Crossan and Reed, *Excavating Jesus,* 120.

11. Crossan and Reed, *Excavating Jesus,* 119.

12. An overview of the typical house in Capernaum can be found in Crossan and Reed, *Excavating Jesus;* Korb, *Life in Year One;* and Barclay, *Gospel of Mark.*

13. Luke, writing for a more citified audience, roughly twenty years later, uses the word *klinidion,* a small bed.

14. Donahue and Harrington, *Gospel of Mark,* 94.

15. Zimmerman, *Woman Un-Bent,* 35.

16. Matthew's version (9:1–8) of the greeting is even more tender: "Take heart, son; your sins are forgiven."

17. Levine and Brettler, eds., *Jewish Annotated New Testament,* 62–63.

18. Sanders, *Historical Figure of Jesus,* 37.

19. Jn 9:2–3.

20. Barclay, *Gospel of Mark,* 55.

Chapter Twelve: *Parables*

1. Lk 5:1–3.

2. Mk 4:1–9; Mt 13:1–9.

3. Mt 13:1–9; Mk 4:1–9; Lk 8:4–8.

4. Mt 13:18–23; Mk 4:13–20; Lk 8:11–15.

5. Dodd, *Parables of the Kingdom,* 16.

6. Harrington, *Jesus,* 30.

7. Wright, *Jesus and the Victory of God,* 176.

8. There was dislike on both sides, as Amy-Jill Levine reminded me: "Samaritans disliked the Jews as much as the Jews disliked Samaritans."

9. Brueggemann, *Finally Comes the Poet,* 109.

10. Reed, *Archaeology and the Galilean Jesus*, 220.

11. Lk 16:19–31.

12. Donahue, *Gospel in Parable*, 2.

13. Lohfink, *Jesus of Nazareth*, 102.

14. Mt 18:12–14; Lk 15:3–7.

15. Johnson, *Gospel of Luke*, 235.

16. There is a longer discussion of this topic in my book *Between Heaven and Mirth*, which considers the ways in which some of Jesus's parables and images would have seemed to the original hearers not simply provocative, but funny.

17. Harrington, *Jesus*, 31.

18. Mk 4:10–12.

19. Lk 8:9–10; Mt 13:10–16.

20. Mk 3:21.

21. Mk 3:31–35; Mt 12:46–50.

22. Lohfink, *Jesus of Nazareth*, 118.

23. Mt 13:44.

24. Mt 25:14–30; Lk 19:11–27.

25. Donahue, *Gospel in Parable*, 107.

26. Donahue, *Gospel in Parable*, 108.

27. Mt 20:1–16.

28. Barbara Reid, "Unmasking Greed," *America*, Nov. 7, 2011, 47.

29. Only the Gospel of Luke (15:11–32) includes the Parable of the Prodigal Son.

30. Johnson, *Gospel of Luke*, 237.

31. Mt 14:14; Lk 7:13; 10:33.

32. Gn 45:1–15.

33. Johnson, *Gospel of Luke*, 237. Johnson also notes that for the early Christians the idea of a son who was dead and now lives would have had deep resonances.

34. Lk 15:1–2.

35. Johnson, *Gospel of Luke*, 241–42.

36. Nouwen, *Return of the Prodigal Son*, 72.

Chapter Thirteen: *Storms*

1. Don't let the fact that Mussolini liked the Holy Land dissuade you from visiting.

2. Murphy-O'Connor, *Holy Land*, 318.

3. At one point Luke describes Jesus sending out "the seventy," which may be a good indication of the number of disciples (10:1–20).

4. Ps 69.

5. Acts 27:27–32.

6. Donahue and Harrington, *Gospel of Mark,* 158. The authors draw parallels to the "unconcerned sleep" of the farmer who trusts in God's provident care of the harvest in Mk 4:27.

7. The *kibbutz,* a communal settlement, was called Ginosar, a variant of Gennesaret.

8. Pottery shards and carbon dating securely date the boat from the time of Jesus (Crossan and Reed, *Excavating Jesus,* 4).

9. Donahue and Harrington, *Gospel of Mark,* 158.

10. Gn 1:6–8. The Canaanite God Baal and the Babylonian god Tiamat were "storm gods." Thus, when God divides the waters in the Book of Genesis (between the rains in the heavens and the seas on the earth), the Hebrew people would have seen this as God implicitly subduing not only the chaos and peril that threatened them, but also the lesser gods of their enemies.

11. Ps 89:9. Also Ps 107:29: "He made the storm be still, and the waves of the sea were hushed." And Ps 65:7: "You silence the roaring of the seas, the roaring of their waves." Richard Clifford, SJ, an Old Testament scholar, reminded me of a line from the hymn "For All the Saints." One line speaks of the saints "casting down their golden crowns around the glassy sea." The glassy sea is the image from Revelation, in which God exerts his authority over all things and calms the raging seas.

12. Ps 13.

13. Mt 14:22–33; Mk 6:45–52; Jn 6:16–21.

14. *Eremos* is Greek for solitary, lonely, or desolate, specifically as in a wilderness or desert. The word "hermit" comes from the same root.

15. Ex 3:14.

Chapter Fourteen: *Gerasa*

1. John Meier, in *A Marginal Jew,* includes a fascinating discussion about the place's name (and the variants Gergesenes, Gergesines, and Gergystenes) and offers arguments about the event's historicity, which he supports (2:650–56). Bargil Pixner, in *With Jesus Through Galilee,* suggests that it may mean the "region of the expelled peoples," that is, the Girgashites driven away from Israel by Joshua's conquest of the land (Jo 3:10). "Perhaps the original text of Mark, which caused so much confusion," Pixner writes, "should have read simply 'They went across the lake to the country of the expelled people (Hebrew: Gerushim or Gerashim)'" (45). Levine and Brettler, in *The Jewish Annotated New Testament* (69), suggest that the confusion may indicate that Mark was not from northern

Galilee, or perhaps that Gerasa evokes the Hebrew *gerash,* which means "expel," not simply in the way that Pixner relates, but also as an evocation of the expelling of the demons into the pigs; so, "Place of Expulsion."

2. Brown, Fitzmyer, and Murphy, eds., *New Jerome Biblical Commentary,* 607.

3. Donahue and Harrington, *Gospel of Mark,* 163.

4. Barclay, *Gospel of Mark,* 135.

5. Mk 1:24.

6. Donahue and Harrington, *Gospel of Mark,* 165.

7. Scholars sometimes interpret this as a philosophical (or "ontological") statement: "I am who am" could mean "I am Being itself" or even "I am with you." But given the other times that this locution occurs in Scripture, it is more likely that the meaning I mentioned in the chapter is the case: it indicates the unwillingness to fully reveal the divine name. Richard Clifford, SJ, an Old Testament scholar, told me, "It's first of all wordplay on the divine name YHWH. 'I am who am' in Hebrew is ''HYH.' It thus seems to be revelatory of the divine being, yet with a further sense that one cannot control God by knowing his name. Know me, that I am God, not your best friend, but I want you to know that I am with you in this extraordinary formative moment."

8. Brown, Fitzmyer, and Murphy, eds., *New Jerome Biblical Commentary,* 607. In this interpretation, "legion" is not a name so much as a number.

9. In the Greek λεγιών (*legiōn*).

10. Donahue and Harrington, *Gospel of Mark,* 166.

11. Brown, Fitzmyer, and Murphy, eds., *New Jerome Biblical Commentary,* 607.

12. Interestingly, the mascot of the Roman legion garrisoned in the region, the Legio X Fretensis, was a boar, which was emblazoned on its standard, adding yet another layer of meaning to the story.

13. Joseph Fitzmyer remarks wryly: "The stampede of pigs from Gerasa to the lake would have made them the most energetic herd in history!" (*Gospel According to Luke, I–IX,* 736).

14. Murphy-O'Connor, *Holy Land,* 354.

15. Murphy-O'Connor, *Holy Land,* 355.

Chapter Fifteen: *Tabgha*

1. Donahue and Harrington, *Gospel of Mark,* 211.

2. Lohfink, *Jesus of Nazareth,* 132. Also, not even Jesus's opponents deny his powers of healing and wonder-working. They challenge the *source* of his power, not the power itself.

3. The theme is common in the Acts of the Apostles: "All who believed were together and had all things in common; they would sell their pos-

sessions and goods and distribute the proceeds to all, as any had need" (2:44–45).

4. Meier, whose work on the historical Jesus strives to determine which events have the greatest claim to historicity, writes, "[T]he feeding of the multitudes is supported by an unusually strong attestation of multiple sources." *A Marginal Jew*, vol. 2, 965.

5. Lohfink, *Jesus of Nazareth*, 134.

6. Harrington, *Jesus*, 38.

7. The Feeding of the Five Thousand appears in Mk 6:30–44; Mt 14:13–21; Lk 9:10–17 and Jn 6:1–15; the Feeding of the Four Thousand appears in Mk 8:1–10 and Mt 15:32–39. Donahue and Harrington write in *The Gospel of Mark*: "Innumerable theories have been offered to explain the relation of the different versions of the feeding to each other and to a postulated primitive narrative [i.e., from before the writing of the Gospels]" (208). Meier's *A Marginal Jew* describes the possible interplays between the various accounts (2:950–67). N. T. Wright's reminder of the possibility of several versions is also helpful: "My guess would be that we have two separate versions of the great supper parable [and other stories and parables that seem duplicated] not because one is adapted from the other or both from a common written source, but because these are two out of a dozen or more possible variations that, had one been in Galilee with a tape recorder, one might have 'collected,'" that is, from the various witnesses (*Jesus and the Victory of God*, 170).

8. Again, the idea of several versions is helpful. Meier writes in *A Marginal Jew*: "Their amnesia about Jesus's previous feeding miracle when faced with a very similar problem is difficult to comprehend. The most likely explanation is that Mark has incorporated two versions of the same story into his narrative" (2:957).

9. Mk 6:13.

10. Mk 6:31–32.

11. Ez 34. Elisha's feeding of the multitude in 2 Kings 4:42–44 might have also been on their minds.

12. Brown, *Introduction to the New Testament*, 136.

13. Or a "bed for leeks." Brown, Fitzmyer, and Murphy, eds., *New Jerome Biblical Commentary*, 610.

14. Donahue and Harrington, *Gospel of Mark*, 207.

15. Bergant and Karris, eds., *Collegeville Bible Commentary*, 990.

16. Meier, *Marginal Jew*, 2:963.

17. Thus the "Feeding of the Five Thousand" may have included not just

five thousand men but, additionally, women and children. As Amy-Jill Levine suggested to me, the miracle might be more accurately called the "Feeding of the Twenty-Five Thousand."

18. The barley harvest takes place around the time of Passover, so John's inclusion of the barley loaves (6:9) is another link to the Jewish festival and thus perhaps a way of drawing a parallel to the Last Supper.

19. Mt 22:1–14: "The kingdom of heaven may be compared to a king who gave a wedding banquet for his son." See also Lk 14:8–24.

20. Ex 17:1–7; Ex 16:1–36; Nm 11:4–9.

21. Jn 6:35.

22. Pope Benedict XVI writes in *Jesus of Nazareth: From the Baptism in the Jordan to the Transfiguration:* "The fundamental context in which the entire chapter [John's narrative of the miracle] belongs is centered upon the contrast between Moses and Jesus. Jesus is the definitive, greater Moses — the 'prophet' whom Moses foretold in his discourse at the border of the Holy Land and concerning whom God said, 'I will put my words in his mouth and he shall speak to them all that I command him' (Deut 18:18). It is no accident, then, that the following statement occurs between the multiplication of the loaves and the attempts to make Jesus king: 'This is indeed the prophet who is to come into the world!' [Jn 6:14]" (264).

23. Mt 8:11.

24. Lohfink, *Jesus of Nazareth,* 58.

25. Mk 10:17–31.

26. Mt 13:8; Mk 4:8; Lk 8:8.

27. Lohfink, *Jesus of Nazareth,* 109.

Chapter Sixteen: *Bethesda*

1. The story is told at length in *St. Peter's Bones* by Thomas J. Craughwell.

2. For citations see *The Gospel of John,* by Francis J. Moloney, SDB, 171–72. Also, Barclay notes as well that several elements in the story had previously appeared to be simply allegorical: the thirty-eight years, for example, as standing for the time that the Jewish people wandered in the desert, and so on, which lent credence to the idea that the entire story was an allegory (*Gospel of John,* 1:210).

3. Murphy-O'Connor, *Holy Land,* 29.

4. "Running water" and "living water" are the same expression in Hebrew, according to Amy-Jill Levine.

5. There is a dispute over how the Greek text should read — different ancient manuscripts use different names: "Bethesda," "Beth-zatha," and "Bethsaida." "Bethesda" is found in many texts and is the most common

way of referring to the place today (McKenzie, *Dictionary of the Bible*, 92). The New Revised Standard Version, however, uses "Beth-zatha." For a longer discussion of the Greek variations, see Brown, *Gospel According to John I–XII*, 206.

6. Barclay, *Gospel of John*, 1:208.

7. Brown, *Introduction to the New Testament*, 345.

8. Gerald O'Collins calls him a "first betrayer," an anticipation of Judas, in *Jesus*, 216. Thomas Stegman said that he (and scholars like Gail R. O'Day and Jeffrey L. Staley) see the man more positively. "The verb *anangellō* ('announce') is used elsewhere in John with the positive sense of announcing who Jesus is," Stegman told me. "O'Day notes that while the healed man focuses on healing, the religious leaders focus on the Sabbath violation. To me, it seems more likely that he would want to announce the good news of his healing, rather than betray Jesus."

9. Levine and Brettler, eds., *Jewish Annotated New Testament*, 168.

10. Barclay, *Gospel of John*, 1:209.

Chapter Seventeen: *Jericho*

1. Lk 10: 25–37.

2. Mt 2.

3. Murphy-O'Connor, *Holy Land*, 394.

4. Lohfink, *Jesus of Nazareth*, 93.

5. Mk 15:42–46.

6. Mk 9:30–32; 10:32–34.

7. Meier, *Marginal Jew*, 2:687.

8. An insight from Philip Van Linden, CM, "The Gospel of Mark," in Bergant and Karris, eds., *Collegeville Bible Commentary*, 925.

9. Meier, *Marginal Jew*, 2:690.

10. That is, in Mark. In Matthew he is leaving "with a large crowd," and in Luke he is entering with "a crowd."

11. "Zacchaeus" is from the Hebrew word meaning righteous, upright, or clean.

12. Also known by Scripture scholars as "open commensality," table fellowship is one of the actions that earned Jesus the enmity of many (Harrington, *Historical Dictionary of Jesus*, 154).

13. Bergant and Karris, eds., *Collegeville Bible Commentary*, 970.

14. Mays, ed., *HarperCollins Bible Commentary*, 949.

15. Lk 18:18–28. Also Mt 19:16–30 and Mk 10:17–31. He is identified as a "young man" in Matthew. Here I call him the "Rich Young Man," the most common way of referring to him today.

16. Johnson, *Gospel of Luke,* 287.

17. Mt 25:31–46.

Chapter Eighteen: *Bethany*

1. Murphy-O'Connor, *Holy Land,* 152.

2. Lk 10:38–42.

3. Brown, *Introduction to the New Testament,* 334. Technically, Brown does not include the Prologue (1:1–18) or the Epilogue (21:1–25) in this two-part schema.

4. Interestingly, we are not told yet in the Gospel of John that Mary had done this. (The anointing comes in the next chapter.) Apparently, John's audience would have known this already.

5. A "sign" in John's Gospel points beyond itself and to the coming of the reign of God. As elsewhere, Jesus's signs underline his words. In *A Marginal Jew* (2:799) Meier notes that the Raising of Lazarus will be "the greatest, most striking symbol of the divine life that Jesus offers the believer."

6. Lk 7:1–17; Mk 5:21–43; Mt 9:18–26; Lk 8:40–56.

7. Lk 10:38–42. This Gospel passage, in which Jesus tells the busy Martha that her sister has chosen the "better part" by choosing to sit with him rather than serving the meal, is sometimes used to denigrate Martha and, by extension, to elevate prayer over work. But without Martha neither Jesus nor Mary nor Lazarus would have eaten that night. As I see it, the story is more about Jesus's reminder to a busy woman that sometimes it's more important to rest and pray. It's also a reminder that there is a time for work, but also a time for prayer.

8. Moloney, *Gospel of John,* 331.

9. Barclay, *Gospel of John,* 2:310; also Moloney, *Gospel of John,* 341.

10. Barclay suggests this in *Gospel of John,* 2:115.

11. The multipart TV series *The Bible* showed Jesus entering Lazarus's tomb and weeping as he says, "I am the resurrection and the life." Jesus says Lazarus's name quietly and kisses him on the head. Lazarus's eyes immediately open, in surprise. It was an unusual portrayal, but effective and moving.

12. The King James Version is unintentionally risible: "Lord, by this time he stinketh."

13. Moloney, *Gospel of John,* 337.

14. Mt 9:18–26, Mk 5:21–43, Lk 8:40–56. Also, the raising of the son of the widow of Nain, in Lk 7:11–17.

15. Merton, *New Seeds of Contemplation,* 35.

Chapter Nineteen: *Jerusalem*

1. Ps 122.
2. Merton, *Sign of Jonas,* 116.
3. Mk 14:3; Mt 26:6.
4. "Rejoice greatly, O daughter Zion! / Shout aloud, O daughter Jerusalem! / Lo, your king comes to you; / triumphant and victorious is he, / humble and riding on a donkey, / on a colt, the foal of a donkey" (Zec 9:9). Lohfink in *Jesus of Nazareth* says of this act: "Jesus was deliberately exhibiting an unmistakable sign" (247)
5. Harrington, *Jesus,* 75.
6. Mk 8:27–30.
7. The same list of possible identities—John the Baptist, Elijah, or one of the prophets—is offered in Mk 6:14–15 after the time of death of John the Baptist. N. T. Wright in *Jesus and the Victory of God* suggests that Jesus "consciously seems to imitate Elijah" (167).
8. Mal 4:5.
9. Donahue and Harrington, *Gospel of Mark,* 261.
10. Donahue and Harrington, *Gospel of Mark,* 261.
11. Mk 8:31–32.
12. Mk 8:33.
13. Mk 14:3–9; Mt 26:6–13; Jn 12:1–8. In Mark she anoints his head, a more "royal" sign.
14. O'Collins, *Jesus,* 152.
15. "I've Been to the Mountaintop," April 3, 1968.
16. Acts 1:13; Acts 2:1 speaks of the disciples gathered in a "house."
17. Lk 22:12.
18. Catholic theology holds that she was "assumed" into heaven. Today there is a Church of the Dormition of Mary in Jerusalem and, not far from it, the Church of the Death of Mary.
19. A large semicircular niche in one of the Cenacle's walls, called a *mihrab,* still indicates the direction of Mecca, the direction faced by Muslims during prayer.
20. Murphy-O'Connor, *Holy Land,* 118.
21. Robert Barron, *Eucharist,* Catholic Spirituality for Adults series (Maryknoll, NY: Orbis Books, 2008) and John Baldovin, SJ, *Bread of Life, Cup of Salvation* (Lanham, MD: Rowman & Littlefield, 2003) are two good resources for understanding this theology.
22. Sorry, George and I didn't make it to Cana. Next time.
23. 1 Cor 12:12–14.
24. Lk 9:58.

25. Jn 17:1–5.
26. Levine and Brettler, eds., *Jewish Annotated New Testament*, 184.
27. Jodi Magness includes a lengthy discussion of ritual washing of the body and hands in a book whose title may also give a sense of the general state of feet in the day (*Stone and Dung, Oil and Spit*, 16–31, 73–74).
28. Brown, *Introduction to the New Testament*, 351.
29. Jn 10:11–18.
30. Lohfink, *Jesus of Nazareth*, 74–75.
31. Schneiders, *Written So That You May Believe*, 76–92.
32. Thomas Stegman offered a gentler interpretation of the fisherman's hesitancy: "The Foot Washing," he told me, "foreshadows Jesus's giving his life on the cross. Both are acts of love. And as an act of love the Foot Washing is not forced on others, but must be received. Peter's hesitation, like our own, reflects the difficulty and challenge of accepting God's love as it is revealed through Jesus."
33. Marrow, *Gospel of John*, 229.

Chapter Twenty: *Gethsemane*
1. The identity of the Beloved Disciple and his relationship to the Gospel of John is a complex question. But overall most scholars believe that the Beloved Disciple is the "source and inspiration for much of the unique material in the Gospel of John," as Thomas Stegman told me.
2. Jn 13:30.
3. Lk 19:41.
4. "Joel declared for a valley called Jehoshaphat (3:2, 12), whereas Zechariah opted for the Mount of Olives (14:4)," writes Murphy-O'Connor (*Holy Land*, 133). The "obvious harmonizing solution" was the location here. The Kidron Valley, near the Mount of Olives, was also known as the "Valley of Jehoshaphat" ("Jehoshaphat" means "Yahweh judges").
5. Murphy-O'Connor, *Holy Land*, 147. Murphy-O'Connor notes that the slopes of the Mount of Olives would have provided a great deal of timber for the Roman legions at the time.
6. Brown, *Death of the Messiah*, 1:153.
7. The translation of Mk 14:34 in the New Revised Standard Version, "I am deeply grieved, even to death," does not adequately capture the connection to Jesus's soul, or *psychē*.
8. Ps 42:6; Sir 37:2.
9. Brown, *Death of the Messiah*, 1:156.
10. Casey, *Fully Human, Fully Divine*, 252.
11. Luke also says that in Jesus's agony, his sweat was "like great drops of

blood." This odd phrase deserves some attention. Raymond Brown notes that at the beginning of his Gospel Luke says that he will try to provide a "reliable" account, and so "we may assume that Luke would not have included what he considered unbelievable." There are, Brown says, some modern medical explanations of capillaries bursting into the sweat gland, which causes a clotting of the blood, which is then "carried to the surface of the skin by the sweat." Or, says Brown, it may be simply that Luke did not mean literally "sweating blood." Luke writes *hōsei thromboi haimatos,* in which *hōsei* means "as if" or "like." In other words, his sweat was so profuse it was *as if* it were a flow of blood (*Death of the Messiah,* 1:184–86).

12. Harrington, *Jesus,* 47.
13. Casey, *Fully Human, Fully Divine,* 255.
14. Donahue and Harrington, *Gospel of Mark,* 408. Also see Is 51:17; Jer 25:15–16; 51:57; Ez 23:33; Ps 75:8.
15. Brown, *Death of the Messiah,* 1:177–78.
16. Zerwick, *Grammatical Analysis of the New Testament,* 272.
17. Barclay, *Gospel of Mark,* 400.
18. Jn 8:59.
19. Lohfink, *Jesus of Nazareth,* 225–26.
20. Pope Francis made this point in one of his homilies, when he spoke of the importance of conscience "even for Jesus," who listened "in his heart" to the Father's voice. But an important insight: "Jesus, in his earthly life was not, so to speak, 'remote-controlled.'" That is, he freely made decisions. "He was the Word made flesh, the Son of God made man, and at one point he made a firm decision to go up to Jerusalem for the last time—a decision taken in his conscience, but not on his own: with the Father, in full union with Him . . . in profound, intimate attunement to the Father's will. For this reason, then, the decision was steadfast: because it was taken together with the Father." (Sunday Angelus, June 30, 2013).
21. Casey, *Fully Human, Fully Divine,* 259.
22. "And do not bring us into *peirasmon*" (Mt 6:13). The word can be translated as trial, test, or temptation.

Chapter Twenty-One: *Golgotha*

1. Murphy-O'Connor, *Holy Land,* 49.
2. Murphy-O'Connor, *Holy Land,* 50–51.
3. Murphy-O'Connor, *Holy Land,* 50.
4. Jn 17:21.
5. Harrington, *Jesus,* 69.

6. Mk 14:61–62.

7. It is also worth noting the Second Vatican Council's document *Nostra Aetate,* which addressed "non-Christian religions" and opened up a new era in relations with the Jewish people. The document, which enjoys the highest level of authority in the Catholic Church, addresses those who would hold "the Jews" responsible for Jesus's death: "True, the Jewish authorities and those who followed their lead pressed for the death of Christ; still, what happened in His passion cannot be charged against all the Jews, without distinction, then alive, nor against the Jews of today. Although the Church is the new people of God, the Jews should not be presented as rejected or accursed by God, as if this followed from the Holy Scriptures. All should see to it, then, that in catechetical work or in the preaching of the word of God they do not teach anything that does not conform to the truth of the Gospel and the spirit of Christ." Thomas Stegman reminded me that the Jewish leaders are usually identified as chief priests, scribes, and elders. Stegman noted, "The Pharisees, at least as a concerted group, are not mentioned [in the Passion], which is of interest given the way they had been sometimes portrayed as Jesus's opponents during his ministry." In other words, it is not simply that not all "the Jews" were involved; not even all the "Jewish leaders," as they were often called, were involved.

8. Harrington, *Jesus,* 75.

9. Dt 25:3. Also, Brown writes in *The Death of the Messiah:* "Rods were used on freemen; sticks on military personnel; and scourges on others. These scourges were generally leather thongs fitted with pieces of bone or lead with spikes" (1:851).

10. I am indebted to Felix Just, SJ, for this summary of the overall sequence of the events of the Crucifixion.

11. Murphy-O'Connor, *Holy Land,* 54.

12. I'm reminded of one of my favorite quotes about the Gospel of Mark from an unlikely source, Nick Cave, a rock star, who wrote a moving introduction to *The Gospel of Mark* published by Grove Press in 1999: "Scenes of deep tragedy are treated with such a matter-of-factness and raw economy they become almost palpable in their unprotected sorrowfulness."

13. Lk 23:28.

14. Pixner, *With Jesus in Jerusalem,* 125. Murphy-O'Connor is more blunt: "The present Way of the Cross has little chance of corresponding to historical reality" (*Holy Land,* 38).

15. Mk 15:21.

16. Rom. 16:13.
17. As did those in first-century Palestine. Josephus, the Jewish historian, writes that after the death of Herod the Great, one Roman general, to quell the ensuing unrest, lined the roads of Galilee with two thousand crosses (*Antiquities of the Jews,* 17.10.10).
18. There is a lengthy description of the Roman practice of crucifixion in the book *The Day Christ Died,* a popular but thorough treatment by Jim Bishop. Brown's *The Death of the Messiah* also includes an exhaustive and more scholarly account.
19. Donahue and Harrington, *Gospel of Mark,* 443.
20. Donahue and Harrington, *Gospel of Mark,* 447.
21. More precisely, both Mark and Matthew transcribe Jesus's words using a curious mix of Aramaic and Hebrew. In Matthew Jesus cries out, "*Ēli, Ēli, lema sabachthani.* Mark's *Elōi* is closer to Aramaic, Matthew's *Ēli* to Hebrew; but Mark's *lama* is closer to Hebrew, Matthew's *lema* to Aramaic.
22. Brown, *Death of the Messiah,* 2:1043–58.
23. Brown, *Death of the Messiah,* 2:1051.
24. Mother Teresa, *Come Be My Light,* 192–93.
25. O'Collins, *Jesus,* 174.
26. Donahue and Harrington, *Gospel of Mark,* 448.
27. Mk 1:10, *schizomenous.*
28. Mk 10:32.
29. *A Jesuit Off-Broadway* (Chicago: Loyola Press, 2007) is a look at the development of the play "The Last Days of Judas Iscariot," by Stephen Adly Guirgis, which places Judas on trial for his betrayal of Jesus and examines the possible reasons for his actions. The book includes a lengthy examination of the possible motivations behind Judas's betrayal, some of which are included here in an abbreviated form.
30. Rom 4:24–25.
31. Barclay, *Gospel of Matthew,* 2:388.
32. Mk 2:7; Mt 9:3; Lk 5:21.
33. Mk 14:26–72; Lk 22:34–62.
34. Pixner, in *With Jesus in Jerusalem,* believes that Byzantine-era crosses roughly carved into the rock support this tradition, and the Benedictine scholar lists a series of documents dating as far back as the fourth century that put the location of Caiaphas's house where the church stands today. In the 1990s, mosaics were discovered at the site, lending further credence to the tradition. Some of the stone columns in the caves were also discovered with iron rings affixed to them, suggesting

that a prisoner could have been chained here—but again this is speculative (102–3). Others are not as sure about the authenticity of the place. Murphy-O'Connor is doubtful: "It is much more likely that the house of the high priest was at the top of the hill" (119).

35. Mt 16:13–19.
36. Jn 2:19.
37. Heb 4:15–16.

Chapter Twenty-Two: *Risen*

1. Jews in Jesus's time calculated a day beginning at sunup and ending at sundown. In this case, Friday is the first day (since Jesus died before sundown, Friday counts as one day), Saturday is the second, and Sunday (since it is already dawn) is the third.
2. Mk 16:1; Mt 28:1; Lk 24:10.
3. Johnson, *Gospel of Luke,* 388.
4. Lohfink, *Jesus of Nazareth,* 89.
5. Lk 8:2.
6. See Lk 7:36–50; 8:1–3.
7. Mt 26:7; Mk 14:3, "a woman." Also, Elizabeth Johnson reminded me that the unnamed woman in Mark anoints Jesus's head, not his feet. That is a key point in Schüssler Fiorenza's book, she said. "It is vital," Johnson told me, "because anointing the head is a prophetic act—this woman commissions Jesus to his messianic destiny—while anointing the feet is a sign of repentance or affection." Schüssler Fiorenza points out that only Mark includes the story in this form. "Later on Matthew and Luke switched to feet," said Johnson, "but head is the earlier remembrance."
8. Schüssler Fiorenza, *In Memory of Her,* xiv.
9. Schüssler Fiorenza, *In Memory of Her,* xiv.
10. Pope Francis, General Audience, April 3, 2013.
11. Sheed suggests that the stone is removed not to let Jesus out, but to let the disciples *in* (*To Know Christ Jesus,* 358).
12. Marrow, *Gospel of John,* 356.
13. Quoted in Franco Mormando, "Christ in the Garden," *America,* April 20–27, 2009, 27–28.
14. Moloney says: "The name Jesus calls Mary and her response are Greek transliterations of Aramaic, though the narrator explains that it is Hebrew. There is a level of intimacy implied by the recourse to an original language in both the naming and the response" (*Gospel of John,* 528). Earlier in the text the Greek *Maria* is used.
15. Jn 10:11–16.

16. Lk 24:39.
17. Jn 20:24–29.
18. Jn 20:20.
19. Jn 20:27.
20. Marrow, *Gospel of John,* 360.
21. Mt 16:24–28; Mk 8:34–9:1; Lk 9:23–27.
22. Jn 2:19.
23. Merton, *Run to the Mountain,* 346.
24. Lk 10:21; Lk 13:17; Jn 16:22; 16:24; Lk 24:41; Jn 20:20.
25. Lk 2:36–38.

Chapter Twenty-Three: *Emmaus*

 1. Murphy-O'Connor, *Holy Land,* 363.
 2. Lk 23:32–43.
 3. Or his wife, or his son, or his daughter. Luke says only "two of them."
 4. Johnson, *Gospel of Luke,* 393.
 5. This may be Luke's subtle way of highlighting Peter's authority.
 6. Johnson points out the emphasis on the deep emotions of the story in *Gospel of Luke,* 398–99.
 7. Jn 19:25.
 8. Lk 24:41.
 9. Jn 20:27.
10. Jn 21:1–19.
11. Not to mention some seemingly contradictory actions by the Risen Christ—for example, asking Mary not to touch him, but inviting Thomas to do just that.
12. Barclay, *Gospel of Luke,* 350.
13. Some scholars suggest that since Cleopas and his companion are traveling to "the village to which they were going," it is more likely that the story is set in one of their houses, not an inn. So here my prayer was not as scholarly as it might have been.
14. Johnson, *Gospel of Luke,* 393.
15. For the Christian community, Luke's story also tells us that Christ is always waiting to be met, and waiting for us to meet him, especially in Scripture and the Eucharist.

Chapter Twenty-Four: *Tiberias*

 1. The appearance to Mary Magdalene is apparently not "counted," perhaps because John is referring to appearances to "the disciples" as a group.
 2. Moloney, *Gospel of John,* 549.

3. Some scholars suggest that this is the same story as Lk 5:1–11 (the Miraculous Catch of Fish), and that Luke has placed what is actually a post-Resurrection story earlier in his narrative. Others surmise that John has blended two stories—an earlier call narrative and a post-Resurrection appearance.

4. Moloney, *Gospel of John,* 549.

5. Another interpretation is that the number represents the Ten Commandments plus the seven sacraments multiplied by the three persons of the Trinity twice: 153.

6. Peter denies Jesus during the Passion while warming himself by an *anthrakia* (charcoal fire) in Jn 18:18; and he is now rehabilitated by Jesus beside another *anthrakia* in Jn 21:9.

7. O'Collins, *Jesus,* 195.

8. Lk 5:1–11.

9. Marrow, *Gospel of John,* 373.

10. Thanks to James Carr, SJ, for this insight.

11. Or re-establish him. In Matthew (16:16) Peter identifies Jesus as the Messiah after the question "Who do you say that I am?" Jesus then declares, "You are Peter (*Petros*) and on this rock (*petra*) I will build my church." Jesus's interchange with Peter on the shore that day may also have been for the benefit of the other disciples, as if to say, "I still trust this man."

12. Jn 20:30. St. Paul, in his First Letter to the Corinthians, also recounts Resurrection appearances (1 Cor 15:3–11).

13. Mk 16:19; Lk 24:50–53.

14. Acts 1:9–12.

15. Ignatius, *A Pilgrim's Testament,* 63–65.

16. Lk 19:41–44.

17. Ignatius, *A Pilgrim's Testament,* 64.

Chapter Twenty-Five: *Amen*

1. And I did.

2. Acts 12:12 identifies Mark's mother as the owner of what historians call a "house church." "As soon as he realized this, he [Peter] went to the house of Mary, the mother of John whose other name was Mark, where many had gathered and were praying."

BIBLIOGRAPHY

Achtemeier, Paul, ed. *Harper's Bible Dictionary*. San Francisco: Harper & Row, 1985.

Aland, Kurt, Matthew Black, Carlo M. Martini, Bruce M. Metzger, and Allen Wikgren, eds. *The Greek New Testament*. Stuttgart: United Bible Societies, 1983.

Aron, Robert. *The Jewish Jesus*. Maryknoll, NY: Orbis Books, 1968.

Attridge, Harold W., ed. *The HarperCollins Study Bible*. Rev. ed. San Francisco: HarperSanFrancisco, 2006.

Au, Wilkie, SJ. *By Way of the Heart: Toward a Holistic Christian Spirituality*. Mahwah, NJ: Paulist, 1989.

Barclay, William. *Crucified and Crowned*. Amsterdam: SCM, 1961.

——.*The Mind of Jesus*. New York: Harper & Row, 1960.

——. *The New Daily Study Bible: The Gospel of John*. 2 vols. Louisville: Westminster John Knox, 2001.

——. *The New Daily Study Bible: The Gospel of Luke*. Louisville: Westminster John Knox, 2001.

——. *The New Daily Study Bible: The Gospel of Mark*. Louisville: Westminster John Knox, 2001.

——. *The New Daily Study Bible: The Gospel of Matthew*. 2 vols. Louisville: Westminster John Knox, 2001.

Bergant, Dianne, and Robert Karris, eds. *The Collegeville Bible Commentary*. Collegeville, MN: Order of St. Benedict, 1989.

Berry, George. *The Interlinear Literal Translation of the Greek New Testament*. Grand Rapids, MI: Zondervan, 1975.

Bishop, Jim. *The Day Christ Was Born, The Day Christ Died*. New York: Harper, 1957.

Bloom, Harold, ed. *C. S. Lewis*. New York: Chelsea House, 2006.

Bock, Darrell L., and Robert L. Webb. *Key Events in the Life of the Historical Jesus: A Collaborative Exploration of Context and Coherence*. Grand Rapids, MI: Eerdmans, 2009.

Brettler, Marc Zvi, Peter Enns, and Daniel Harrington, SJ. *The Bible and the Believer*. New York: Oxford Univ. Press, 2012.

Brown, Raymond E. *The Birth of the Messiah: A Commentary on the Infancy Narratives in the Gospels of Matthew and Luke*. New York: Doubleday, 1993.

———. *The Death of the Messiah: From Gethsemane to the Grave: A Commentary on the Passion in the Four Gospels*. 2 vols. New York: Doubleday, 1994.

———. *The Gospel According to John, I–XII*. Anchor Bible, vol. 29. New York: Doubleday, 1966.

———. *An Introduction to the New Testament*. New York: Doubleday, 1997.

Brown, Raymond E., Joseph A. Fitzmyer, and Roland E. Murphy, eds. *The New Jerome Biblical Commentary*. Englewood Cliffs, NJ: Prentice Hall, 1990.

Brueggemann, Walter. *Finally Comes the Poet: Daring Speech for Proclamation*. Minneapolis: Fortress Press, 1989.

Campbell, Brian. *The Romans and Their World: A Short Introduction*. Cornwall, UK: TJ International, 2010.

Casey, Michael. *Fully Human, Fully Divine: An Interactive Christology*. Liguori, MO: Liguori/Triumph, 2004.

Chancey, Mark A. *Greco-Roman Culture and the Galilee of Jesus*. Cambridge: Cambridge Univ. Press, 2005.

Coles, Robert. *Dorothy Day: A Radical Devotion*. Boston: Da Capo Press, 1987.

Cowan, James. *Fleeing Herod: A Journey Through Coptic Egypt with the Holy Family*. Brewster, MA: Paraclete, 2013.

Crace, Jim. *Quarantine: A Novel*. New York: St. Martin's Press, 1998.

Craughwell, Thomas J. *St. Peter's Bones: How the Relics of the First Pope Were Lost and Found . . . and Then Lost and Found Again*. New York: Image, 2014.

Crossan, John Dominic. *The Historical Jesus: The Life of a Mediterranean Jewish Peasant*. San Francisco: HarperSanFrancisco, 1991.

Crossan, John Dominic, and Jonathan L. Reed. *Excavating Jesus: Beneath the Stones, Behind the Texts*. San Francisco: HarperOne, 2001.

Cunningham, Philip A., Joseph Sievers, Mary C. Boys, Hans Hermann Henrix, and Jesper Svartvik, eds. *Christ Jesus and the Jewish People Today*. Grand Rapids, MI: Eerdmans, 2011.

Dahood, Mitchell, SJ. *Psalms II: 51–100*. Anchor Bible Series. Garden City, NY: Doubleday, 1968.

Daniel-Rops, Henri. *Daily Life in Palestine at the Time of Christ*. London: Phoenix, 2002.

Dodd, C. H. *The Founder of Christianity*. London: Collins, 1971.

———. *The Parables of the Kingdom*. New York: Scribner, 1961.

Donahue, John R., SJ. *The Gospel in Parable*. Philadelphia: Fortress, 1990.

Donahue, John R., SJ, and Daniel Harrington, SJ. *The Gospel of Mark*. Sacra Pagina series. Collegeville, MN: Liturgical Press, 2002.

Downey, Michael. *The New Dictionary of Catholic Spirituality*. Collegeville, MN: Order of St. Benedict, 1993.

Fitzmyer, Joseph A. *The Gospel According to Luke, I–IX*. Anchor Bible, vol. 28. New York: Doubleday, 1982.

———. *A Christological Catechism: New Testament Answers*. Mahwah, NJ: Paulist Press, 1991.

———. *The Gospel According to Luke, X–XXIV*. Anchor Bible, vol. 28A. New York: Doubleday, 1985.

Green, Julien. *God's Fool: The Life and Times of Francis of Assisi*. New York: Harper & Row, 1985.

Harrington, Daniel J., SJ. *The Gospel of Matthew*. Sacra Pagina series. Collegeville, MN: Liturgical Press, 2007.

———. *Historical Dictionary of Jesus*. Lanham, MD: Scarecrow, 2010.

———. *How Do Catholics Read the Bible? Come and See Series*. Lanham, MD: Sheed & Ward, 2005.

———. *Jesus: A Historical Portrait*. Cincinnati: St. Anthony Messenger Press, 2006.

———. *Who Is Jesus? Why Is He Important? An Invitation to the New Testament*. Come and See series. Franklin, WI: Sheed & Ward, 1999.

Harrington, Wilfred J., OP. *Jesus Our Brother: The Humanity of the Lord*. Mahwah, NJ: Paulist, 2010.

Haughey, John, SJ. *Housing Heaven's Fire: The Challenge of Holiness*. Chicago: Loyola Press, 2002.

Horns, Cornelia B., and John W. Martens. *Let the Little Children Come to Me: Children and Childhood in Early Christianity*. Washington, DC: Catholic Univ. of America Press, 2009.

Ignatius of Loyola. *A Pilgrim's Testament: The Memoirs of Saint Ignatius Loyola*. St. Louis: Institute of Jesuit Sources, 1995.

Johnson, Elizabeth A. *Consider Jesus: Waves of Renewal in Christology*. New York: Crossroad, 1991.

———. *Truly Our Sister: A Theology of Mary in the Communion of Saints*. New York: Continuum, 2003.

Johnson, Luke Timothy. *The Gospel of Luke*. Sacra Pagina series. Collegeville, MN: Liturgical Press, 1991.

Keith, Chris, and Larry W. Hurtado. *Jesus Among Friends and Enemies: A Historical and Literary Introduction to Jesus in the Gospels*. Grand Rapids, MI: Baker Academic, 2011.

Komonchak, Joseph A., Mary Collins, and Dermot A. Lane, eds. *The New Dictionary of Theology*. Collegeville, MN: Liturgical Press, 1987.

Korb, Scott. *Life in Year One: What the World Was Like in First-Century Palestine*. New York: Penguin, 2010.

Lassalle-Klein, Robert. *Jesus of Galilee: Contextual Christology for the 21st Century*. Maryknoll, NY: Orbis Books, 2011.

Levine, Amy-Jill. *The Misunderstood Jew: The Church and the Scandal of the Jewish Jesus*. San Francisco: HarperOne, 2006.

Levine, Amy-Jill, and Marc Zvi Brettler, eds. *The Jewish Annotated New Testament*. New York: Oxford Univ. Press, 2011.

Licona, Michael. *The Resurrection of Jesus: A New Historiographical Appraisal*. Downers Grove, IL: InterVarsity, 2010.

Lohfink, Gerhard. *Jesus of Nazareth: What He Wanted, Who He Was*. Collegeville, MN: Liturgical Press, 2012.

Magness, Jodi. *Stone and Dung, Oil and Spit: Jewish Daily Life in the Time of Jesus*. Grand Rapids, MI: Eerdmans, 2011.

Marrow, Stanley B. *The Gospel of John: A Reading*. Mahwah, NJ: Paulist, 1995.

Marshall, Alfred. *The Interlinear Greek-English New Testament*. London: Samuel Bagster, 1958.

Matthews, Christopher R., and Daniel J. Harrington, SJ, eds. *Encountering Jesus in the Scriptures*. Mahwah, NJ: Paulist, 2012.

Mays, James L., ed. *HarperCollins Bible Commentary*. San Francisco: HarperSanFrancisco, 2000.

McKenzie, John L., SJ. *Dictionary of the Bible*. New York: Touchstone, 1995.

McNamer, Elizabeth, and Bargil Pixner. *Jesus and the First Century of Christianity in Jerusalem*. Mahwah, NJ: Paulist, 1989.

Meier, John P. *A Marginal Jew: Rethinking the Historical Jesus*, vol. 1, *The Roots of the Problem and the Person*. New York: Doubleday, 1991.

——. *A Marginal Jew: Rethinking the Historical Jesus*, vol. 2, *Mentor, Message, and Miracles*. New York: Doubleday, 1994.

——. *A Marginal Jew: Rethinking the Historical Jesus*, vol. 3, *Companions and Competitors*. New York: Doubleday, 2001.

——. *A Marginal Jew: Rethinking the Historical Jesus*, vol. 4, *Law and Love*. New Haven: Yale Univ. Press, 2009.

Merton, Thomas. *New Seeds of Contemplation*. New York: New Directions, 1961.

——. *Run to the Mountain: The Story of a Vocation*. New York: HarperCollins, 1995.

——. *The Seven Storey Mountain*. New York: Harcourt, 1998.

——. *The Sign of Jonas*. New York: Harcourt, 1953.

Meyer, Ben F. "Jesus Christ." In David Noel Freedman, ed., *The Anchor Bible Dictionary*, vol. 3. New York: Doubleday, 1992.

Moloney, Francis J., SDB. *The Gospel of John*. Sacra Pagina series. Collegeville, MN: Liturgical Press, 1998.

Murphy-O'Connor, Jerome. *The Holy Land*. Oxford: Oxford Univ. Press, 2008.

Nouwen, Henri J. M. *The Return of the Prodigal Son*. New York: Doubleday, 1992.

O'Collins, Gerald, SJ. *Christology: A Biblical, Historical, and Systematic Study of Jesus*. 2nd ed. New York: Oxford Univ. Press, 1995.

——. *Following the Way: Jesus, Our Spiritual Director*. Mahwah, NJ: Paulist, 2001.

——. *Jesus: A Portrait*. Maryknoll, NY: Orbis, 2008.

Pilch, John J. *A Cultural Handbook to the Bible*. Grand Rapids, MI: Eerdmans, 2012.

Pixner, Bargil. *With Jesus in Jerusalem: His First and Last Days in Judea*. Israel: Corazin, 1996.

——. *With Jesus Through Galilee According to the Fifth Gospel*. Israel: Corazin, 1992.

Powell, Mark Allan, ed. *HarperCollins Bible Dictionary*. Rev. ed. San Francisco: HarperOne, 2011.

Pritchard, James B. *HarperCollins Atlas of Bible History*. San Francisco: HarperOne, 2008.

Ratzinger, Joseph, Pope Benedict XVI. *Jesus of Nazareth: From the Baptism in the Jordan to the Transfiguration*. New York: Doubleday, 2012.

——. *Jesus of Nazareth: Holy Week: From the Entrance into Jerusalem to the Resurrection*. Vatican City: Libreria Editrice Vaticana, 2011.

——. *Jesus of Nazareth: The Infancy Narratives*. New York: Doubleday, 2007.

Reed, Jonathan L. *Archaeology and the Galilean Jesus: A Re-examination of the Evidence*. Harrisburg, PA: Trinity International, 2000.

——. *The HarperCollins Visual Guide to the New Testament: What Archaeology Reveals About the First Christians*. San Francisco: HarperOne, 2007.

Rohr, Richard. *Breathing Under Water: Spirituality and the Twelve Steps*. Cincinnati: St. Anthony Messenger, 2011.

Sanders, E. P. *The Historical Figure of Jesus*. London: Penguin, 1995.

Schneiders, Sandra M. *Written That You May Believe: Encountering Jesus in the Fourth Gospel*. New York: Crossroad, 2003.

Schüssler Fiorenza, Elisabeth. *In Memory of Her: A Feminist Theological Reconstruction of Christian Origins*. New York: Crossroad, 1983.

Scirghi, Thomas J., SJ. *Everything Is Sacred: An Introduction to the Sacrament of Baptism*. Brewster, MA: Paraclete Press, 2012.

Senior, Donald. *Jesus: A Gospel Portrait*. Rev. ed. Mahwah, NJ: Paulist, 1992.

Sheed, F. J. *To Know Christ Jesus*. New York: Sheed & Ward, 1962.

Stegemann, Ekkehard, and Wolfgang Stegemann. *The Jesus Movement: A Social History of Its First Century*. Minneapolis: Augsburg Fortress, 1999.

Teresa, Mother. *Come Be My Light: The Private Writings of the Saint of Calcutta*. New York: Doubleday, 2007.

Throckmorton, Burton H., Jr. *Gospel Parallels: A Comparison of the Synoptic Gospels*. Nashville: Nelson, 1992.

Trueblood, Elton. *The Humor of Christ*. San Francisco: Harper & Row, 1964.

Von Speyr, Adrienne. *Book of All Saints*. San Francisco: Ignatius, 2008.

Wright, N. T. *The Challenge of Jesus*. Downers Grove, IL: InterVarsity, 1999.

———. *Jesus and the Victory of God: Rediscovering Who Jesus Was and Is*. Minneapolis: Fortress, 1989.

Zerwick, Maximilian, SJ. *A Grammatical Analysis of the Greek New Testament*. Translated by Mary Grosvenor. Rome: Editrice Pontificio Instituto Biblico, 1988.

Zimmerman, Irene. *Woman Un-Bent*. Winona, MN: St. Mary's, 1999.

FOR FURTHER EXPLORATION

To LIST ALL THE resources that have helped me understand the New Testament since I entered the Jesuits would make this book far too long. So I have limited this list to resources I used specifically in writing this book. First, let me single out several that were my constant companions and that I recommend for further exploration.

The Sacra Pagina series, edited by Daniel J. Harrington, SJ, was, after the Bible, my bible. Each book in the superlative series provides not only a line-by-line analysis of the New Testament, but also solid theological exegesis, so that you are able both to study the Jesus of history and to come to know the Christ of faith. The series is learned, wise, balanced, thoughtful, and well organized. It grounds itself on what is known and can be proven, and its use of Greek is helpful for both scholar and newcomer. The authors of the four books on the Gospels are: Daniel J. Harrington, SJ (Matthew); John R. Donahue, SJ, and Daniel J. Harrington, SJ (Mark); Luke Timothy Johnson (Luke); and Francis J. Moloney, SDB (John). I cannot recommend this series highly enough or thank the authors enough for their scholarship and industry.

Let me also recommend three other books on Jesus that I kept close at hand. *A Marginal Jew,* by the Rev. John P. Meier, a massive, multi-volume study of the historical Jesus, offers a wealth of information and the most detailed analysis of Gospel texts from a historical standpoint you will find anywhere. His first volume has an especially good chapter on the tools of historical analysis of the Gospels. *Jesus of Nazareth: What He Wanted, Who He Was,* by Gerhard Lohfink, is a superb book that beautifully combines the Jesus of history and the Christ of faith. *The Misunderstood Jew,* by Amy-Jill Levine, provides an overview of Jewish practices from the time of Christ and corrects some common errors in the "standard" ways that we look at Jesus and "the Jews."

Several relatively brief books on Jesus were also very useful. To my mind these are the best short books on Jesus for the general reader. *Jesus: A Historical Portrait,* by Daniel J. Harrington, SJ, is a concise and popular treatment of what we can know about Jesus historically. *The Historical Figure of Jesus,* by E. P. Sanders, is a somewhat longer version of the same topic, and a bit more academic. *Consider Jesus,* by Elizabeth Johnson, CSJ, looks at Christology and has an especially interesting chapter on Jesus's self-consciousness. *Fully Human, Fully Divine,* by Michael Casey, OCSO, is particularly strong on how the two "natures" of Jesus work together. Gerald O'Collins, SJ, has written a fine book, *Jesus: A Portrait,* which looks at Jesus in his various roles, for example, as "healer," "storyteller," and "Lord." The fine volume *Jesus Our Brother,* by Wilfred Harrington, OP, looks at the human Jesus, and *Jesus: A Gospel Portrait,* by Donald Senior, CP, is particularly good on Jesus in his Jewish context. And although I didn't use his book in my research for this work, Albert Nolan's *Jesus Before Christianity,* the first book I read in the Jesuit novitiate on the historical Jesus, is a fine introduction to the historical Jesus.

As more devotional titles about the Christ of faith that I've enjoyed and used in this book, let me cite two authors from the past and one from more recent times. William Barclay's *Daily Study Bible* not only offers an analysis of the Gospels, but also draws spiritual lessons from it. (Barclay's approach is methodical and creative; he offers you, for example, three insights from a particular passage and then illustrates with an example from real life. Barclay's books *The Mind of Christ* and *Crucified and Crowned* are also fine.) F. J. Sheed's *To Know Christ Jesus,* one of the first books on Jesus I read in the novitiate, retains its power more than fifty years after its publication. Though some of the historical research is outdated, it still ushers us into the life of Christ in a powerful way. More recently, *Jesus of Nazareth,* by Pope Benedict XVI, is an inspiring three-volume series, each book designed for both the scholar and the curious, with an emphasis on Christ of faith. (A longer list of the books that have inspired me to come to know the Risen One would take several pages.)

For information about the Holy Land, needless to say, I relied on Jerome Murphy-O'Connor's *The Holy Land,* which was unfailingly helpful. At times Murphy-O'Connor started to feel like the third person in our pilgrimage. *With Jesus through Galilee* and *With Jesus in Jerusalem* are both excellent guides written by Bargil Pixner, a Benedictine monk of Dormition Abbey in Jerusalem, who spent twenty-five years living in Israel, half of them in Galilee. His guidebooks (which include detailed maps of Galilee and Jerusalem) are popular in Israel but somewhat harder to locate elsewhere. Finding them is worth the effort.

Regarding what archaeology can reveal about life in the first century, the work of Jonathan L. Reed was a boon. I started with his *The HarperCollins Visual Guide to the New Testament: What Archaeology Reveals About the First Christians,* a presentation whose lavish illustration does not detract from its scholarship. Most helpful of all was his book, written with John Dominic Crossan, *Excavating Jesus,* which examines what archaeology can tell us about the area in which Jesus lived. Reed's *Archaeology and the Galilean Jesus* offers many essays on the most recent finds in and around Galilee. Father Harrington recommended Jodi Magness's delightfully named and impressively researched *Stone and Dung, Oil and Spit: Jewish Daily Life in the Time of Jesus* as well as Mark A. Chancey's *Greco-Roman Culture and the Galilee of Jesus,* which is equally scholarly and equally helpful.

Several excellent one-volume Bible commentaries I have long found helpful will serve general readers well. From the more scholarly to the more popular, they are: *The New Jerome Biblical Commentary*

(Raymond E. Brown, Joseph A. Fitzmyer, and Roland E. Murphy, eds.), *The HarperCollins Bible Commentary* (James L. Mays, ed.), and *The Collegeville Bible Commentary* (Dianne Bergant and Robert Karris, eds.). The Catholic scholar Raymond E. Brown's *Introduction to the New Testament* and his monumental books *The Birth of the Messiah* and *The Death of the Messiah* also provide excellent scholarly commentary. Also, *The Jewish Annotated New Testament,* edited by Amy-Jill Levine and Marc Zvi Brettler, provides superb commentary on specifically Jewish terms, practices, and beliefs for the relevant New Testament passages.

For textual analysis I used *The Interlinear Greek-English New Testament* (the Nestle Greek text), by Alfred Marshall, which provides a word-by-word translation of the *koinē* Greek; *The Greek New Testament,* edited by Kurt Aland, Matthew Black, Carlo M. Martini, SJ, Bruce M. Metzger, and Alan Wikgren; *A Grammatical Analysis of the Greek New Testament,* by Maximilian Zerwick, SJ, translated by Mary Grosvenor; as well as *Gospel Parallels,* by Burton Throckmorton, which provides a comparison of the sequence of the Synoptics.

INDEX

abandonment, 232, 381–83, 386
Abba, 360–61
Abu Ghosh, 422–23, 440
abundance, 271
acceptance, 411–12
Acts of the Apostles, 338, 452
addictive behavior, 242, 249–50
agricultural practices, 77
Ancient Galilee Boat, 229–30
Andrew, Apostle, 131–34, 136, 137,
    139, 140, 143, 182, 263–64
angelos (messenger), 34
Annunciation
    biblical account, 33–38, 49–50
    historicity, 45–47
    lessons of the, 36–40, 415
    Mary's faith following the,
        48–49
    site of the, 33
"Annunciation, The" (Levertov;
    poem), 40
anointing of Jesus, 332, 335, 337, 338
apostles. *See* disciples
Aramaic, 82–83, 464–65
arrest of Jesus, 333
Ascension, 406, 452–56
Aziz (taxi driver), 52–53, 65, 66–
    67, 289–92, 294

Baptism
    biblical accounts, 103–5, 113

criterion of embarrassment
    theory, 100–101
as demarcation event, 110
desert temptation following,
    103, 107–9
John the Baptist's role, 101–5
Jordan River site, 96–98
participation in humanity by
    Jesus, 105–7
baptism ritual, 99, 105–6, 110
Bartimaeus. *See* Healing of Bar-
    timaeus
Basilica of Gethsemane, 356–57
Basilica of the Annunciation,
    32–33, 70, 114
Bay of Parables, 12–13, 195–98,
    219–20
Beatitudes
    groups named in, 171–75
    "happy" translation, 179–80
    in Matthew, 167, 168–69, 180–81
    message of the, 175–80
    sermon location and audience,
        167–71
    varying Gospel accounts, 44,
        168–70
beatus (blessed), 179
Bellagamba, Anthony, 179
Bethany, 312–14, 355
Bethesda, 275–76. *See also* Healing
    at the Pool of Bethesda

Index

About the Author

JAMES MARTIN, SJ, is a Jesuit priest, editor at large at the Catholic magazine *America*, and the author of several books, including the *New York Times* bestseller *The Jesuit Guide to (Almost) Everything* as well as *Between Heaven and Mirth, A Jesuit Off-Broadway,* and *My Life with the Saints,* which were named "Best Books of the Year" by *Publishers Weekly.* Among his other books are *This Our Exile, In Good Company, Lourdes Diary, Searching for God at Ground Zero, Becoming Who You Are,* and the e-book *Together on Retreat.*

Before entering the Jesuits in 1988, Father Martin graduated from the University of Pennsylvania's Wharton School of Business and worked for six years in corporate finance. As part of his Jesuit training, he worked in a hospice for the sick and dying in Kingston, Jamaica; in a hospital for the seriously ill in Cambridge, Massachusetts; at a school for poor boys in New York City; with street gangs in Chicago; in a prison in Boston; and for two years with the Jesuit Refugee Service in Nairobi, Kenya, where he helped East African refugees start small businesses. He studied philosophy at Loyola University Chicago and received his graduate degrees in theology at the Boston College School of Theology and Ministry. He was ordained a Catholic priest in 1999 and pronounced his final vows as a Jesuit in 2009.

Father Martin has written for many religious and secular publications, both in print and online, including *The (London) Tablet, Commonweal, U.S. Catholic,* the *New York Times, The Washington Post, The*

Wall Street Journal, and *Slate*. He is a frequent commentator in the national and international media, and he has appeared on the major radio and television networks and in venues as diverse as NPR's *Fresh Air* with Terry Gross, PBS's *NewsHour* with Jim Lehrer, FOX's *The O'Reilly Factor,* and Comedy Central's *The Colbert Report*. He lives in a Jesuit community in New York City.